The Memoirs Of Cordell Hull V2, Part Two

Cordell Hull

102: Britain and Argentina

THROUGHOUT the three troublesome years of our relations with Argentina while I was in office, 1942–1944, the attitude of Great Britain toward Argentina was of great importance to us and eventually became one of the major stumbling blocks in our solution of the problem. I have waited until this point to discuss this angle of the situation so as to deal with it consecutively.

Britain's economic ties with Argentina were appreciably stronger than ours. Her annual purchases of Argentine products were almost double ours. Furthermore, British subjects had made large investments in Argentina over a period of several generations, and the British colony in Buenos Aires enjoyed considerable prominence. After the European War broke out, and especially after the German conquest of most of Western Europe, Britain's dependence upon Argentina for food and other supplies became yet more acute.

At various times in 1942 Ambassador Armour cabled us that the Argentine Government was attempting to justify its position to its people by the argument that the British Government, in contrast with the United States, was entirely reconciled to the Argentine policy of neutrality and complete relations with the Axis. In December, Armour suggested that a member of the British Government make a public statement to overcome this argument. We knew that the British Embassy in Buenos Aires had made the position of its Government clear to the Argentine Foreign Ministry, yet we could not expect the Argentine Government to make this known since it was to their interest to convey the opposite impression.

Under Secretary Welles urged Armour's suggestion on British Ambassador Halifax on December 26. He remarked that, notwithstanding the official statements made by the British Government to the Argentine Government, many of the most important commercial and financial figures in the British colony in Argentina were consistently and publicly stating that Argentina should not break relations with the Axis, and that British interests favored the Argentine position of "neutrality."

The British Foreign Office received this suggestion favorably. It issued a statement to the effect that it wished to make it clear that both Britain and America were as one in regretting that Argentina had not yet moved forward in line with almost all other South American countries.

The British stated that the Argentine Government had arrested one or two more German spies, but still procrastinated in stopping Axis communications. The British Ambassador had therefore pointed out to President Castillo that, unless his Government could find a solution which would preclude U-boats from picking up such messages, the scarcity of shipping, and particularly of refrigerator ships, would make it impossible for Britain to go on receiving Argentine products.

Early in 1943 we took up with the British through Ambassador Halifax here and through Ambassador Winant in London our desire for greater coordination of the relations of Great Britain and the United States on the one hand, with Argentina on the other. We said to Britain that we were delighted that the recent British statement, together with Chile's probable break with the Axis, was making a good impression which it was to our advantage to increase. Since Britain and Argentina were then negotiating an agreement for the purchase of Argentine meat, we suggested that the signing be delayed until we could induce Argentina to prohibit the transmission of radio code messages from that country and to take more vigorous action toward Axis espionage and subversive activities. We urged that if these questions were injected into the meat negotiations, the hands of our friends in Argentina would be greatly strengthened. But at the same time we made clear we did not wish to interfere with Britain's procurement program, since we appreciated that the interests of the United Nations might be injured if meat shipments to Britain were interrupted.

The British Foreign Office went along with us in this suggestion, and their action, plus our own, had at least the effect of persuading the Argentine Government to prohibit the use of radio code messages.

Throughout 1943, however, British relations with Argentina continued close and reasonably cordial. It seemed to me absolutely essential, if we were to swing Argentina away from her dangerous connections with the Axis countries, that a combined British-American movement should be organized. We had close relations with the other American Republics, enhanced by Lend-Lease operations, and we could join with them in bringing pressure to bear on the Argentine Government; but Britain, because of her valuable economic relations with Argentina, was in position to bring still more effective pressure.

I went into this aspect of the question on two occasions with British Ambassador Halifax at the end of 1943. On December 27 I elaborated on the statement I had made to him the previous week when I earnestly urged the British Government to see to what extent it could cooperate with us in a general embargo against Argentina. Although I had opposed the blocking of Argentine funds in the United States because I believed it would have the opposite effect of that intended, it seemed to me that a joint British-American move along economic lines would produce the desired result.

I now suggested to Halifax, for transmission to his Government: "The British Government might determine whether it could go against the Argentine Government with a battering ram, so to speak. It could strenuously insist that that Government desist from all acts helpful to Germany and refrain from giving aid to movements calculated to bring on revolutions in neighboring countries. If the British and the United States Governments should at the same time make a pressing demand that this be done, this—probably within thirty days—would greatly change the attitude of the Argentine Government."

It would be of no use, however, I added, unless the British Government were willing to approach the Argentine Government most strongly. I pointed to the evidence we had that German money, with Argentine Nazi agents cooperating, was being used in Bolivia, and that these same agents reportedly were threatening to install in three or four other South American countries hard-boiled pro-Nazi military Governments similar to that in the Argentine. Such activities, if successful in other countries, would do the Allied cause serious harm.

"In the end," I said, "the vast British investment in Argentina would greatly suffer, and hence the very real interest the British should have in the proposal I'm suggesting. The British could let the Argentines know that they can get all the meat they need from other parts of the world as soon as the fighting ends, and that for the next twelve months they can hold out without serious suffering by using such supplies as are available."

Ambassador Halifax said he felt this was worth considering, and he would get it before his Government at once.

I pursued my argument further with Halifax when he came to see me on January 5, 1944, and stated my conclusion that the Argentine Government was an important factor in bringing about the revolution in Bolivia. I also said we had indications that there was a general movement of totalitarian and pro-Axis forces centered in the Argentine to overthrow the Governments of such countries as Uruguay, Chile, Peru, and Paraguay.

"Part of the propaganda being disseminated inside and outside of the Argentine," I said, "is that Great Britain is showing no concern about this movement. It is being said, on the contrary, that Britain is secretly pleased to see the United States in this trouble, especially with Argentina, for the reason that the British expect to buy meat and other foodstuffs during the war and then will have very little competition in trade and finance in Argentina after the war."

I made clear to Halifax that I was merely trying to state the attitude of the opposition and show how it might spread until Britain would be seriously concerned. The outlook, I added, was serious, and the time had come for the United States and Great Britain to make a frank, strong statement vigorously condemning the totalitarian influences that were conducting these subversive activities.

Halifax seemed much impressed and agreed that something should be done jointly by our two Governments. He said he would present a full picture to the Foreign Office at once.

Two weeks later, however, he indicated to me that his Government apparently did not intend to give the cooperation I had suggested. I pointed out that at least it could issue a strong statement simultaneously with one we were contemplating, to expose the pro-Axis movement with its base in Argentina and to warn all the other American Republics of the increasing dangers to them. I added that we also contemplated recalling our Ambassador in Buenos Aires for consultation. I asked Halifax to check again with the Foreign Office, saying that a statement by his Government would have a splendid effect on the pro-Axis authorities in the Argentine Government.

Britain's reply to this appeal came in the form of a message from Prime Minister Churchill to President Roosevelt, a copy of which, dated January 23, Halifax handed me on that day. Mr. Churchill stated that Britain would help all she could, and above all would avoid any public divergence with us in regard to Argentina. However, he begged the President to look into the formidable consequences that would follow Britain's losing Argentina's hides, meat, and other supplies. Saying that Britain received one-third of her meat supply from the Argentine, he asked how, if this supply were cut off, the British were to feed themselves plus the American Army being marshaled in Britain for the invasion of northern France. Cessation of Argentine supplies would disrupt military operations on the scale planned for this year. Before we leaped, he said, we really had to look; we could always pay the Argentines back when our hands were clear. He said he must inject his solemn warning of the gravity of the situation that would follow if the Argentine supplies were interrupted. To recall our Ambassadors meant only that the field would be left open for the Germans. These Argentine rascals, he concluded, knew the hold they had over us for the time being, and had calculated very carefully.

After Halifax made an argument in support of the Prime Minister's position, I remarked that the British were interested primarily in one situation in Argentina—meat supplies—while the United States was interested primarily in breaking up the ever-increasing pro-Axis elements based in the Argentine and steadily moving up the continent with the idea of overthrowing other Governments and setting up pro-Axis Governments as in Bolivia. I added that this movement was spreading and becoming increasingly dangerous.

"If my Government," I said, "should hesitate or falter at this time in carrying forward its known program of penalties against the Argentine, as has been thoroughly agreed and planned, the effect on the subversive movements in South America would be terrible. Apart from its resultant injury to the prosecution of the war and the security of South American countries, the United States would be discredited in the eyes of all countries interested in the war, especially the other South American countries."

I added that my Government must, without fail, go forward with the action we intended to take the following day, January 24; namely, the publication of a statement formally linking Argentina with the overthrow of the Bolivian Government. I suggested that the British Foreign Office might call in the Argentine Ambassador and strongly protest the pro-Axis attitude of the Argentine Government and insist on a break with the Axis Powers and a general housecleaning.

As I have already stated, we did not publish the statement we had in mind because the Argentine Government of General Ramírez broke diplomatic relations with the Axis. Foreign Secretary Anthony Eden nevertheless adopted the suggestion I had made, called in the Argentine Ambassador to Great Britain and counseled the Argentine Government to continue its program of housecleaning. When Ambassador Halifax on January 28 read me extracts from Eden's conversation with the Argentine Ambassador, I expressed much appreciation for his Government's cooperation.

During the next few months we kept in close touch with the British on all aspects of the Argentine situation. It was obvious, however, that our viewpoints, much as we both wanted to keep them identical, differed.

We desired a consistently strong attitude toward the Argentine Government, including refusal to recognize the Farrell regime. The British, fearful of an interruption in their meat supply, wanted to reach an agreement with the Farrell regime and to recognize it.

As the situation came to a head, I asked Ambassador Halifax to come to my office on June 23 and said that the Argentine situation was becoming worse from the Allied point of view, that the Army men constituting the Government at Buenos Aires were tough and hard-boiled and had been aiding the Axis from time to time to a considerable extent. I then informed him that we were withdrawing Ambassador Armour for consultation, and I expressed the hope that the British Government would take similar action with respect to their Ambassador at Buenos Aires, Sir Davis Kelly.

Halifax came back to see me three days later. Evidently having received his Government's reaction to my suggestion concerning the recall of its Ambassador in Buenos Aires, he proceeded with a line of talk about amicably working out the whole matter with the Argentine Government. He suggested that Ambassador Kelly might approach the Argentine Government, bring up its failures to meet the Allied Governments in this hemisphere halfway, refer to the seriousness of the situation from everybody's point of view, especially that of Argentina, and propose some acts of a pro-Allied nature that the Argentine Government should perform as a condition previous to recognition. Halifax emphasized Britain's difficulties in withdrawing her Ambassador, particularly because his Government within another two months would have to renew its meat contract with the Argentines.

"The British," I argued, "don't have to worry about Argentina cutting off their meat supply. Argentina has a huge surplus piled up, and has to sell her meat. Britain, being in the buyer's seat, has an advantage over the seller, especially since the Argentines cannot sell that portion of their meat elsewhere. The Argentines want a four-year contract with the British at a certain price. I suggest that Britain make contracts on a thirty-day or sixty-day basis, renewing them every month or two. This will bring the Argentine Government to reason and send it running after the British."

As for an approach by Ambassador Kelly to the Argentine Government, I said that Kelly was supposed already to have been saying all the things to the Argentine regime which it was now suggested he should say. I added that my Government had also put forth every kind of proposal about pro-Allied acts that might be performed by the Argentine Government to precede further conversations looking toward a settlement, but that the Argentine officials were becoming more indifferent and, in fact, unfriendly and more disposed to maintain friendly relations with pro-Axis elements. Now, I said, they had reached a stage of practically demanding recognition as a condition precedent to their doing anything to aid the Allied cause and to cut loose from their Axis contacts.

Most of the ambassadors at Buenos Aires, I added, had already left, but the Argentine Government was strenuously giving out the impression everywhere abroad and at home that the position of the nonrecognizing countries had broken down, and that recognition was only a question of days. This crisis, I concluded, had made it necessary for us to act at once; hence the action we had taken of recalling our Ambassador.

When Ambassador Halifax called on June 29 to say goodbye before going to London on leave, I said to him that the solution in Argentina at an early date depended on the attitude of the British Government. It was not necessary, I pointed out, to get into a name-calling match or a quarrel of any sort with the Argentines. But Britain should approach them firmly and state that the Argentine regime was getting into such friendly cooperation with the Axis enemies that it was creating a thoroughly unpleasant situation for the British as well as for the other nations. The British Government, I said, should with firmness and candor let Argentina understand that this course could not be carried on without upsetting the conduct of the war by Britain and the United States and their relations toward Argentina, that the Argentines were forcing a choice, and that they would be hurt worse than any other country if they continued their efforts to play up the Axis and to antagonize and undermine the Allies in this hemisphere.

When it seemed evident to me that the British Government did not intend to go along with us in our stronger policy toward Argentina, I went to the President and asked his intervention. I had no difficulty in obtaining it, for his thoughts on the Argentine situation dovetailed with mine.

The President thereupon sent a fervent personal message to Prime Minister Churchill on June 30, appealing to him to take a common stand with us and recall the British Ambassador in Argentina. Mr. Roosevelt said he was informed that the importance which we attributed to the proposal that the British Ambassador to Argentina be called home for consultation was fully known to the Foreign Office. The announcement of the recall of Ambassador Armour had been made, he added, and nearly all the other Republics were taking parallel action. It was clear, however, that if the British Ambassador remained in Buenos Aires the collective effect of this action would be seriously weakened.

The Prime Minister very reluctantly, and almost angrily, agreed with the President. In a message to Mr. Roosevelt on July 1, he said he had discussed the matter with Eden and had reached a decision to act as the President wished. A message had been sent to the British Ambassador in Buenos Aires recalling him for consultation.

The Prime Minister said they had taken this decision in response to the President's appeal for a common stand. In the War Cabinet and the Foreign Office, he continued, there was a good deal of anxiety. He did not see what we expected to get out of the Argentines by this method, and he did not himself see where this policy was leading. He only hoped that our vital interests and our war effort would not be affected adversely.

Finally he remarked that he hoped the President would not mind his saying, as was his duty, that this American decision had placed Britain in an invidious position, having been taken without consultation, and that Britain had been faced with a fait accompli.

The President sent me this message with a request that I prepare a reply. I sent this to him on July 4. In it we stated that the Prime Minister's decision to recall Ambassador Kelly, taken in conjunction with identical action by us and others, had already produced significant, concrete results. The immediate reaction, we pointed out, had been prompt, conciliatory, and definitely in the right direction, with a complete absence of irritation or threats toward any country. If we continued to stand firm, letting the Farrell regime understand, in a tone not necessarily unfriendly, that it should not, in violation of its pledge of hemispheric unity and solidarity, support the Axis in opposition to its sister nations, there was a good chance that the entire matter could soon be cleared up. It was everywhere recognized, we pointed out, that the issue at stake in Argentina was the same as that which was involved in the war against the Axis. The President was therefore confident that there was no risk in pursuing a firm and forthright policy toward the Farrell regime.

I held a conference in my office on July 17 with Ambassador Kelly, who was returning home via Washington, with Ambassador Armour, and with British Minister Sir Ronald Campbell. Kelly said he wished to make clear that his Government and certainly he himself held the same opinion of the present Argentine Government that we held, and that, if any difference of opinion existed, it was only as to the best procedure to follow to force that Government to change its policy into one of cooperation and

support of the United Nations. He said he personally felt we should present the Farrell regime with specific conditions, strict compliance with
which might be calculated to bring recognition.

I replied that I felt that Farrell and his Government must certainly
know what was expected of them. I added, however, that, after Argentina's
desertion of the other American Republics, followed by the aid that the
Argentine Government and those around it had given to the enemy, it
would be impossible, without abandoning our principles, to go to Argentina
and say that all would be forgiven, and that we would be willing to enter
into official relations with her.

Kelly then asked whether this meant that our Government would not
be disposed to recognize the present Argentine regime under any circumstances. In that case, he said, we might have to be prepared for a long wait,
since he did not see any opposition sufficiently strong to throw out the
Farrell regime. He also wondered whether we should be able to hold the
other American Republics with us.

Successive Argentine Governments, I replied, had found no difficulty
in making clear their adherence to the Axis side, and I could not see that
they required any suggestions as to how to proceed if they now wished to
come over to our side. I said we had information that Axis subversive
activities were continuing in Argentina, and that important intelligence of
value to the enemy was still being sent from that country through clandestine radio stations.

I then repeated that I felt that the desertion by the Argentine Government of the American nations and the Allied cause in the most critical
juncture in history, and the comfort it had given and was still giving to
the enemy, called for a firm attitude on the part of all of us. I hoped, I
said, that the British Government would be prepared to take this stand.

Minister Campbell remarked that it would be useful to Churchill and
Eden to give Kelly a message as to how I felt the British Government
could best use its influence at this time.

I said I felt that both Churchill and Eden had been inclined to
minimize the serious nature of the Argentine situation, to overlook the
principles at stake and the grave underlying issues involved, and to view
the matter largely as a question only of meat and Britain's war requirements of certain Argentine supplies. This was not a question, I added, of
future—and I stressed "future"—continental unity but an immediate
threat to the whole unity of the continent and the prosecution of the war.

I said I did not ask the British to do anything that might jeopardize their sources of supply in Argentina. Furthermore, I did not believe that withholding of recognition would bring retaliation by the Argentine Government through an embargo on exports of meat to England. I recalled that for many years the United States Government had refused to recognize the Soviet Government, but this had in no way affected commerce between the two countries. In other words, the political and economic aspects could be kept separate.

In view of all we were doing and spending, I concluded, it was not too much to expect that the other Governments, including the British Government, should approach this whole question from the larger aspect rather than on a basis of whether or not the Argentine Government had complied, or would be willing to comply, with this or that point. The fact was that the line-up of the Argentine Government and the whole atmosphere in Argentina was bad and was a menace to the Allied cause, and I felt that the only way to handle it and perhaps bring that Government to reason would be for all the nations to continue in their policy of non-recognition.

At the time of my conversation with the British Ambassador, the war was being waged with increasing intensity; Allied forces were battling desperately with the Germans in northern France, and fighting ferociously to drive the Japanese from island to island in the Pacific. Argentina, I felt, could rejoin her former allies and aid us in the conflict; but, if she refused, it would be monstrous for the Allies to forgive a deserter who had not requested forgiveness but instead was continuing actively to aid the enemy.

The summer went by, however, without Britain's bringing the pressure to bear upon the Argentine Government which I seriously believed she could and should. The gesture in grudgingly recalling Ambassador Kelly was obviously as far as Mr. Churchill intended to go. The Farrell regime was fully aware of this situation, believed it held all the cards in the form of invoices for meat and could successfully defy the United States and most of the other American Republics.

We argued with Britain—and the President and the Prime Minister had an exchange of cables on the subject—that the British had a sufficient surplus of meat on hand to do without Argentine meat for a time or at least to deal with Argentina on a month-to-month basis. The British, on the other hand, wanted to accede to the Argentine Government's request that they sign a four-year contract. We sought to prove that the buyer, Britain, was in the driver's seat in a situation where Argentina, because of the blockade, could sell nowhere else the meat that would go to Britain. The British thought that the seller, Argentina, was in the driver's seat because they were obliged to get the majority of their meat from her.

In one of my last conversations with Ambassador Halifax, prior to my resignation, I read to him on September 16, 1944, extracts from economic memoranda prepared in the State Department showing clearly that the British could aid us to the extent necessary without endangering their meat situation. I remarked that President Roosevelt, at an early stage when conditions were very different from what they were now, had said something to the effect that we, of course, wanted Britain to get all the meat she desired. The President, I said, had in mind that Britain could cooperate fully with us without in the least endangering the meat situation and could exercise powerful influence as the controller of the buyers' market, which would be acquiesced in by the sellers. However, I remarked, it seemed that the British officials were far more fearful about the risk than the President, myself, and other members of this Government, and we were basing our views on the most elaborate and careful examination of all the facts and circumstances.

"Argentina," I said, "under the control of the Fascist lawless government, is the refuge and headquarters in this hemisphere of the Fascist movement. That movement, entrenched in Argentina under the protection of a Fascist Government, is dangerous. If the United States and most of the other American nations should become seriously handicapped in their efforts to resist this movement and should fail because of the British attitude, the repercussions would be very loud throughout the hemisphere. This Government would then be obliged to state the full facts as it found them, for the reason that the whole future of Pan Americanism is measurably at stake."

Such were our relations with Great Britain over Argentina at the moment of my resignation. I believe that, if Britain and the United States had brought common economic, diplomatic, and moral pressure to bear upon the Argentine Government, with the backing of most of the American Republics, we could have induced that Government to cease being an active friend of our active enemies. There was no other way to do it.

103: The Good Neighbors

IN SUMMING UP our policy toward Argentina in the years 1942 to 1944, I feel that Prime Minister Churchill and Foreign Secretary Eden, along with some others in Britain, the United States, and Latin America, failed to realize the depth and danger of the relationship between Germany and members of the Argentine Government, beginning with Castillo and continuing to Ramírez and Farrell.

These persons did not fully grasp the fact that in 1942, when Japan had overrun the Southwest Pacific, when Germany, already in possession of most of Western Europe, had pushed deep into the Caucasus, and when Nazi U-boats were sinking masses of Allied shipping in the Atlantic, many influential Argentines in and out of the Government concluded that the Axis would win. They therefore determined to be on the winning side, and, with Axis assistance, make Argentina the leading, and perhaps the ruling country in Latin America, the capital of a Latin American federation pointed at the United States. Believing, at least at first, in a German victory, they were anxious to do what they could to assist in its early arrival or at least to do nothing to endanger Argentina's relations with the probable victors.

Some persons failed to see that the danger to the Allied cause lay not only in the Nazi spying, subversive, and propaganda activities in Argentina, but also, and even more importantly, in the designs and efforts of many of the principal members of the successive Argentine Governments to overthrow other South American Governments and bring the new regimes into virtual alliance with Buenos Aires, into friendship with the Axis, and into opposition to the United States.

They did not sufficiently appreciate the fact that the Argentine Government had deserted every basic principle of Pan Americanism, the foundation of which was peace and nonintervention. That Government had, in place of Pan American principles, installed the doctrines of Nazism and Fascism; namely, internally to destroy the party system of government and make the entire nation subservient to one ruling clique, and externally to dominate all neighboring countries and achieve the headship of a continent.

The strong policy we adopted toward Argentina did not bring Argentina to the United Nations side. Only a strong policy backed equally by

Great Britain, the United States and the other American Republics could have achieved that end.

Could a weak policy—that is, one of appeasement—have succeeded where the strong policy failed? It would naturally have succeeded in reestablishing diplomatic relations between ourselves and Argentina. Had we sought a settlement with the Argentine Government we doubtless could have reached one. But it would have been an agreement which in effect condoned the Argentine Government's desertion in the past and ignored its present and future connivance with the Axis.

We could not on the one hand sacrifice hundreds of thousands of our finest youth and immense quantities of treasure in fighting to overcome Nazism in the Old World, and on the other hand pay the lip service of diplomatic recognition to a transplanting of exactly the same poisonous plant to our own garden in the New World.

But our strong policy did succeed in one all-important respect. It effectually thwarted the ambitions of the extreme Argentine nationalists to upset one Government after another in South America, beginning with the Republics adjacent to Argentina, and to replace them with Governments subservient to the pro-Nazi program embraced by these nationalists. Those ambitions had their first expression in the revolution in Bolivia— the initial page of a book of blueprints.

If at that point we had adopted a policy of appeasement; if we had indicated by our actions that we would not oppose this march up the Continent; if we had not banded together with the other American Republics to stop this movement before it was too late, we should have found ourselves confronted not with one question over Bolivia but with four or five questions over other Republics upon whom the Argentine nationalists had fixed their designs. We then should have found ourselves in serious difficulty, to say nothing of danger. We should have had to divert some of our attention from the conflict in Europe and Asia, and the prosecution of the war would have suffered.

In that respect our policy succeeded. As between a policy that would restore a friendly relationship with Argentina and a policy that would prevent the formation of a bloc of Governments in South America antagonistic to the United States and the United Nations, there was only one choice to make.

Our growing military might, our victories in the Pacific in 1942 and 1943, and our landings in North Africa, Italy, and finally in Normandy were a powerful backing for our policy. Had there been defeats instead of victories, the hands of the Argentine nationalists would have been greatly strengthened. The military successes we achieved in Europe, Africa, and the Pacific, however, tended to obscure in many minds the potential dangers we faced in Latin America through a combination of Argentine nationalists and Axis representatives. A moment's reflection brings easily into focus the dangers that would have confronted us in the southern part of South America had we been defeated in Europe and Asia, or had the war ended in a negotiated peace.

As I bring these observations on our policy toward Argentina to a close I wish to say again that I do not for an instant associate the great mass of Argentine citizens with the aid to the Axis rendered by the Castillo, Ramírez, and Farrell Governments. Large numbers of Argentine individuals did all they could to aid the United Nations cause. In my condemnations of successive Argentine Governments I constantly recognized that the majority of Argentine citizens favored the United Nations and opposed the Axis leanings of these Governments in so far as they were aware of them. Our quarrel was not with the Argentine people but with the Government at Buenos Aires.

It is a matter of real regret to me that the writing of some portions of these memoirs has had to follow the principle of relative importance of news as exemplified by headlines. Conflicts, whether personal, national, or international, crimes, disasters, and depressions naturally attract attention; whereas the daily progress and the doings and sayings of the man of peace go almost unnoticed. I find I have devoted considerable space to this discussion of the actions of Argentina, which were a crime against democracy, whereas I should greatly have preferred to give this space to an acknowledgment of the splendid relations we enjoyed throughout this period with the other American Republics and to the truly wonderful assistance they gave us in the prosecution of the war.

Despite the discouragement induced by the course of the successive Argentine Governments, I drew daily encouragement from the cooperation of the other American Republics even in the most trying days of the war. Thirteen of them declared war on the Axis, and six broke off diplomatic relations. All of them made a valid contribution to the winning of the victory. In general, the help of all kinds we received from Latin America during the Second World War was incomparably greater than that received in the First.

The assistance they gave us took many forms. Some of them, such as Brazil, Mexico, Ecuador, and Peru, gave us the use of naval or air bases.

When it is recalled that for many decades a number of the Latin American Republics feared armed intervention by the United States, their willingness to welcome armed forces of this country within their borders assumes added significance.

Without the air bases Brazil permitted us to construct on her territory victory either in Europe or in Asia could not have come so soon. These bases, jutting far out into the South Atlantic, permitted us to fly war planes across that ocean in waves to West Africa and thence to the theaters of operation in Europe or on to the Far East. Had it not been for these Brazilian bases we could not have got so much help to the British in Egypt as we did at the crucial moment of the Battle of El Alamein.

From Brazil, too, we received valuable diplomatic assistance in our negotiations with her mother country, Portugal. That farsighted statesman, Oswaldo Aranha, Brazil's Foreign Minister, never wavered from the cause of the Allies, and neglected no opportunity to give us his backing. In this he had the full support of President Getulio Vargas. Even in the dark days of the first half of 1942 they were willing to assume all the risks that aid to the United Nations comported.

Brazil sent an expeditionary force to Europe. Her small navy played its share in patrolling the Atlantic. She lost an appreciable portion of her merchant marine in the effort to transport supplies to the United States. She assisted us in keeping an eye on Dutch and French Guiana.

Mexico offered another outstanding example of helpful cooperation. Even before Pearl Harbor, Mexico reached agreements with us for the reciprocal transit of military aircraft, delivery of strategic materials, and the construction on her soil by the United States of a chain of landing fields. She embargoed oil and scrap iron to Japan when we did. She helped us overcome our labor shortage by permitting the temporary emigration to the United States of about 150,000 agricultural and railroad workers up to the time I left office. When President Roosevelt visited Mexico in 1943 he was given a memorable welcome.

All the American Republics, except Argentina, gave us some form of direct economic assistance. They adopted economic programs to increase their production of strategic materials for us and other United Nations. They cooperated in economic warfare to keep supplies from going to the Axis. They mutually agreed with us upon prices. Many Republics took over the Axis business houses which we had placed on our so-called Proclaimed List. The Republics instituted controls over financial transactions involving Axis interests. They took measures to prevent clandestine trade in industrial diamonds, platinum, and the like which the Axis was doing its utmost to obtain. Those Republics having shipping defied the German U-boats and delivered materials to the United States, some of them losing a number of ships.

It is true, of course, that we ourselves were of great help to the American Republics economically, and that we furnished them Lend-Lease supplies as liberally as we could. It is also true that, if we had not begun in 1940 to adopt the wide range of steps we did to absorb Latin American surpluses, bolster their finances, and maintain sea communications with them, economic chaos might well have resulted. This does not, however, diminish either the value or the spirit of the economic assistance which those Republics rendered us.

All the American Republics, except Argentina, took the necessary steps to rid their territories of Axis agents, including many wealthy and influential persons with strong political connections. They closed down Axis propaganda agencies, while giving open support to the efforts of the United Nations to disseminate propaganda in Latin America. They cut off communications with the Axis, and many Republics permitted United States censorship experts to help them establish satisfactory censorship over mails.

It must not be forgotten that all these steps required considerable courage, especially in those Republics farthest removed from our military and naval protection. The disastrous turn of events in the first half of 1942 which convinced the Argentine Government that the Axis would win, and that it should plan accordingly, was also in the minds of the other Republics. But their appreciation of the risks involved did not deter them from aligning themselves with the United States and the other United Nations, for better or for worse.

I appreciated the courage many Latin American Republics showed in helping to develop and in supporting the policy the President and I maintained toward Argentina. It was not an easy matter for the close neighbors of Argentina, such as Uruguay, Paraguay, and Chile, to join with us in common actions including the recall of ambassadors from Buenos Aires, the refusal to recognize the Farrell regime, and the refusal to recognize the Villarroel regime in Bolivia until it had stripped itself of Axis ties. Since they stood to suffer from economic and other reprisals by Argentina, their cooperation with us was of even greater moral value in emphasizing their condemnation of the course of that Government. It likewise was a striking confirmation of their belief in the efficacy of our policy—not only in its objective of bringing home to the Argentine Government the gravity of its desertion of the United Nations cause, but also in its major objective of preventing the spread of the Argentine nationalist movement to other countries.

As long as I was at the Department, we made it a point not to urge any American Republic to declare war upon the Axis. We did repeatedly state our opinion that all the Republics should sever relations with the Axis, since the continuance of such relations constituted an actual physical danger to us, and since the American Republics had agreed in successive inter-American conferences that an attack upon one American nation would be considered an attack upon them all. Nevertheless, we determined to leave the question of a declaration of war entirely to the American Republics themselves, and we so stated in numerous dispatches to our envoys in South America.

When I left office, six Republics—Uruguay, Chile, Peru, Paraguay, Venezuela, and Ecuador—had not declared war on the Axis. I was determined not to draw any distinction between them and the Republics which had declared war. Some of these six were rendering us far more assistance than some of the Republics at war. Ecuador and Peru gave us the use of bases we vitally needed, and Uruguay was a stalwart outpost against the intrigues of the Argentine nationalists. When we sent out invitations to the United Nations Food Conference at Hot Springs, Virginia, in the spring of 1943, we included the associated as well as the allied Republics.

Shortly before I left office the question began to be raised as to whether the associated Republics should be initial members of the proposed international organization. I believed that they should, without being required to declare war. Russia, however, took the position that only those countries that were actually at war with the Axis should receive initial membership.

The question was still pending when I left the Department. Shortly thereafter the State Department informed the associated Republics of its concern lest the fact that they were not full members of the United Nations prejudice their opportunity to participate in plans for an international security organization. The Department pointed out that it fully recognized the contributions made by those Republics to the war. Nevertheless, it called attention to the advantages to be gained by formalizing their status through a declaration of war against Germany and Japan, although the decision of course remained exclusively in their hands.

In summation, the attitude of the Latin American Republics during the war, with the exception of Argentina, was a striking justification of the Good Neighbor Policy. It fully rewarded the many thousands of hours my associates and I, with the President's approval, had devoted to it in the course of twelve years. It demonstrated that the United States and the Latin American Republics, despite differences in language and origin, have many fundamental interests in common. It made clear that the Good Neighbor Policy must be one of the major tenets of United States foreign policy in the future. The desertion by Argentina does not disprove the rule.

I felt that it was all-important for the American Republics in the future to restore and revitalize the principles on which the great structure of Pan American unity and cooperation had been built up in every way from 1933 to 1943. This effort would embrace the further development of all essential projects designed to improve the mutual welfare of the twenty-one Republics in the political, economic, and cultural fields.

104: France Regained

HAVING CONCLUDED this exposition of our relations with the neutrals as of the time of my resignation, I now pass to a discussion of our relations with our Allies, particularly Britain, Russia, and France, taking up the last-named first.

As the time approached for the Allied landing in northern France, across the English Channel, it had become urgently necessary to reach an agreement with the British and with the French committee of General de Gaulle concerning the civil administration of France as that country was liberated by the Allied armies. The President on March 15, 1944, signed a proposed directive to General Eisenhower on the administration of civil affairs in France, which he sent to Prime Minister Churchill.

Mr. Roosevelt had carried into 1944 the deep-seated suspicions he and I entertained regarding De Gaulle, which he stated as late as November 27, 1943, in his cable to me from Cairo (Chapter 89). His directive to Eisenhower, composed by the interested Government Departments, left it to the General to determine whether he should deal only with representatives of the French Committee of National Liberation or also with other French groups that might be in existence—always excepting the Vichy regime. Our thought was that not until we actually landed in France could we know for certain what percentage of the French people would support De Gaulle as chief of their Government, and the President did not wish to tie Eisenhower's hands to the extent of requiring him to maintain the French committee with American arms if it should prove unacceptable to the French people.

Mr. Roosevelt's feelings toward De Gaulle were not improved when, in an address on March 26, De Gaulle referred to the French committee as the "Provisional Government of the French Republic" and said that that Government need listen only to the French nation, implying that he could ignore his allies.

A few days previously, on March 21, we at the State Department were forced to take cognizance of apparently inspired reports and rumors which periodically issued from French North Africa that the United States Government, upon the liberation of France, intended to deal with the Vichy regime or certain of its members. We pointed out in a public statement that the fact that our Government had kept representatives at Vichy prior to the landing in North Africa for such vital purposes as combating Nazi designs, keeping the French fleet from German hands, and preventing the Nazi occupation of French Africa or the establishment of military bases there, had been falsely represented as founded upon a sympathetic relationship between the American Government and pro-Axis supporters at Vichy.

"No loyal supporter of the Allied cause," we said, "would make the ridiculous charge that the United States Government, while sending its military forces and vast military supplies to the most distant battlefields to prosecute the war against the Axis Powers, would at the same time have any dealings or relations with the Vichy regime except for the purpose of abolishing it."

The President and I agreed to send a special mission to London, headed by Under Secretary of State Stettinius, to explore all existing problems with the British, including the French question. The mission consisted also of Dr. Isaiah Bowman, vice chairman of the Department's Advisory Council on Postwar Foreign Policy; John L. Pratt, Consultant on Commercial Affairs; Wallace Murray, Director of the Office of Near Eastern and African Affairs; and H. Freeman Matthews, Deputy Director of the Office of European Affairs. It left the United States on March 30 and arrived in London on April 7.

Two days later I gave prominent position to France in my address of April 9. I prefaced my remarks by saying we looked with hope and deep faith to a period of great democratic accomplishment in Europe following liberation from the German yoke. "It is important to our national interest," I said, "to encourage the establishment in Europe of strong and progressive popular governments, dedicated like our own to improving the social welfare of the people as a whole—governments which will join the common effort of nations in creating the conditions of lasting peace and in promoting the expansion of production, employment, and the exchange and consumption of goods, which are the material foundations of the liberty and welfare of all peoples."

As for France, I said it was hard to imagine a stable Europe if there were instability in its component parts, of which France was one of the most important.

"Our first concern," I made it clear, "is to defeat the enemy, drive him from French territory and the territory of all the adjacent countries which he has overrun. To do this the supreme military commander must have unfettered authority. But we have no purpose or wish to govern

France or to administer any affairs save those which are necessary for military operations against the enemy. It is of the utmost importance that civil authority in France should be exercised by Frenchmen, should be swiftly established, and should operate in accordance with advanced planning as fully as military operations will permit. It is essential that the material foundations of the life of French people be at once restored or resumed. Only in this way can stability be achieved."

It had always been our thought, I said, that we should look to Frenchmen to undertake civil administration and should assist them in that task without compromising in any way the right of the French people to choose the ultimate form and personnel of the Government which they might wish to establish. That had to be left to the free and untrammeled choice of the French people.

"The President and I are clear, therefore," I said, "as to the need, from the outset, of French civil administration—and democratic French administration—in France. We are disposed to see the French Committee of National Liberation exercise leadership to establish law and order under the supervision of the Allied Commander-in-Chief. The committee has given public assurance that it does not propose to perpetuate its authority. On the contrary, it has given assurance that it wishes at the earliest possible date to have the French people exercise their own sovereign will in accordance with French constitutional processes."

I pointed out, however, that the committee was not the Government of France, and we could not recognize it as such. Nevertheless, the committee would have every opportunity to undertake civil administration and would have our cooperation and help in every practicable way in making this successful. The committee, I added, had been a symbol of the spirit of France and of French resistance. We had fully cooperated with it in all the military phases of the war effort, including the furnishing of arms and equipment to the French armed forces. Our central and abiding purpose, I concluded, was to aid the French people, our oldest friends, in providing a democratic, competent, and French administration of liberated French territory.

Under Secretary Stettinius reported to me in a series of telegrams from London that he had found the President's proposed directive of March 15 to General Eisenhower on civil administration in France still on the Prime Minister's desk. Mr. Churchill indicated that he did not want to bother the President about it at this time; but he seemed unwilling to authorize its acceptance or to have it discussed in the combined United States and British Civil Affairs Committee in London.

The British seemed delighted with the references I had made to France in my address on April 9, but thought they did not entirely coincide with the President's directive. Actually, my speech, which as I have mentioned was read and approved by the President, was a little more strongly in favor of the French committee in that it stated we were disposed to see the committee exercise leadership to establish law and order under the supervision of the Allied Commander-in-Chief.

Stettinius explained to the British that in practice General Eisenhower would deal with the French committee in all his pre-invasion planning and, wherever possible, after the landing in France. Moreover, neither the State Department nor Eisenhower had any intention of encouraging any rival group that might emerge in France. Nevertheless we did not feel that Eisenhower should be forced to maintain the committee in France with American bayonets should the French people refuse to accept it.

Eden said he could not accept the President's directive unless its second article were amended so as to make Eisenhower's dealings with the committee mandatory by changing the word "may" to "should."

In response to this suggestion, which I forwarded to the President, then at Georgetown, South Carolina, he sent me a message on April 15 saying that, in view of the fact that circumstances would differ so much in different areas, General Eisenhower should have complete discretion in the matter of civil government. He therefore disapproved of the substitution of "should" for "may."

The President, after having approved my speech of April 9, had backed away from my statement that we were disposed to see the French committee exercise leadership to establish law and order under the supervision of the Allied Commander-in-Chief. His resentment against De Gaulle was still lively.

The British, Stettinius further reported to me, seemed to want to give to the French committee the fullest possible support and did not wish to approve any document which implied that they contemplated dealing under any circumstances with any group other than the committee. They also indicated that it was contrary to their conception of government to permit important political decisions to be taken by a military commander.

Stettinius said there was much suspicion on the part of the British that after we got into France General Eisenhower might make a deal similar to that made with Admiral Darlan at the time of our landing in North Africa. The British had never more than grudgingly admitted that, however unfortunate the Darlan arrangements might have been from the political point of view, they nevertheless saved many thousands of lives and helped materially to shorten the African campaign. They feared that, for strictly military reasons, Eisenhower might again take some action under the President's flexible directive which would run counter to their determination to give full, undivided support to the French committee.

The British believed that all Frenchmen would rally to the support of De Gaulle and the committee and accept their dictates without question. We on the other hand, while not denying this possibility, thought that it was necessary not to take it for granted, and that it was also possible that, as France was liberated, a period of some confusion and disorder might follow. The British, in any event, stated they did not plan to recognize De Gaulle and the committee as a provisional government until they were established in metropolitan France.

During succeeding days, Prime Minister Churchill requested the President to modify his directive, but the President stood firm. Cables from our Embassy in London then indicated that the British were proposing to write a new formula based on my April 9 address. I spoke strongly on this point to British Ambassador Lord Halifax on May 4, saying that this was dangerous from the viewpoint of working relations between the President and Mr. Churchill, and that it was, in effect, going over the President's head and using my speech as a substitute formula without the President's expressed agreement. Further exchanges between the President and the Prime Minister left the question unsettled on the eve of the invasion.

At a Cabinet meeting about May 20, the President said that Ambassador Winant had raised with him the question of dealing with De Gaulle. He added that he had told Winant that if anyone could give him a certificate proving that De Gaulle was a representative of the French people he would deal with him, but that otherwise he had no idea of changing his mind.

We were now receiving suggestions from London that General de Gaulle should come to Washington to see the President personally, with the hope that his visit would facilitate an agreement. Exactly one week before the landing in Normandy, the President cabled the Prime Minister, on May 31, saying that he would like to make the matter of De Gaulle clear from his point of view beyond peradventure of a doubt. As for the visit to Washington, the President said he had told French Admiral Fénard, who was on the way to Algiers to see De Gaulle, that he had been hoping that the General would send him a message asking if a visit would be welcome. The President, if such a message were received, would answer in the affirmative immediately and cordially.

Mr. Roosevelt said he had explained to Fénard, as he thought he had made his stand clear to many people before, that he, as head of the Government and head of the state, could not well invite De Gaulle, who was not the head of the French Government or the French state, but only the head of a committee.

In general, he said we must of course do everything we possibly could to encourage French national spirit and get it working immediately with us at top speed. What the state of this French spirit was, he observed, we did not definitely know; we should not know until we got to France, but we hoped for the best.

The President informed Prime Minister Churchill, who was about to confer with De Gaulle, that General Marshall would be in London about four days after D-Day, but that we could not give him plenary powers to negotiate with the Prime Minister and De Gaulle jointly, or with De Gaulle singly, since the matter was wholly in the political and not in the military field. He said he could not send anyone to represent him at the conversations with De Gaulle.

In response to Churchill's suggestion that he go to London, the President replied that he hoped at a later date to accept "Dr. Churchill's advice to make a sea voyage"; but conditions here would not permit it shortly after D-Day plus fourteen, as the Prime Minister suggested. (The Democratic Convention of 1944 was now in the offing, and the Presidential campaign would soon get under way.)

Such was the situation when the American and British landing began in Normandy on June 6. General Eisenhower had reached an agreement on the military level with the French committee, but the committee's share in the civil administration of France still remained to be decided.

From the moment of the landing, we carefully scrutinized all developments in France to ascertain as best we could the sentiments of the French people toward the French Committee of National Liberation. It soon became evident that the French were willing to accept the committee as a provisional authority until they could, through popular vote, express their wishes with regard to their future government.

Accordingly, the President approving, my associates at the State

Department began discussions with the War Department and with representatives in Washington of the French committee to perfect arrangements for the administration of civil affairs in France by Frenchmen to be named by the committee.

General de Gaulle, having exchanged with the President the messages the latter desired, arrived in Washington on July 6. I attended a reception for him at the White House that day, and gave a dinner for him that evening at the Carlton Hotel.

I found that De Gaulle was now in a much more reasonable frame of mind. He had visited the Allied bridgehead in Normandy and was filled with admiration for the thoroughness of the invasion preparations and their magnificent execution, and for the fighting qualities of the American troops. His visit to Normandy and his conversations with French leaders there also convinced him that Britain and the United States were far more popular in France than he had thought, and that the old Parliamentary parties in France still had considerable strength. By now he was confident that the Allies would not deal with any group in France other than the French Committee of National Liberation. At any rate, he went out of his way to make himself agreeable to the President, to me, and to other members of the Government, and to assure us emphatically and repeatedly that he had no intention of forcing himself or his committee upon France as her future government.

The President therefore decided, and I concurred, that we should recognize the French Committee of National Liberation as the de facto authority in the civil administration of France. The announcement was made on July 11.

Our negotiations with the French representatives in Washington continued and reached a successful conclusion, which was incorporated in an exchange of letters in London, between General Eisenhower and General Koenig, representing the French committee. This the War and State Departments released jointly on August 24.

Our arrangements embraced civil administration and jurisdiction, currency, captured war matériel and property, publicity, and the distribution of civilian relief supplies. General Eisenhower was authorized to deal with the French committee, whose headquarters were at Algiers, as the de facto authority in France "so long as they continued to receive the support of the majority of Frenchmen who are fighting for the defeat of Germany and the liberation of France." We emphasized that this authorization was based on the understanding that, as Supreme Allied Commander, General Eisenhower had to receive whatever authority he considered necessary for the unimpeded conduct of military operations, and that, as soon as the military situation permitted, the French people would be given an opportunity freely to exercise their will in the choice of a Government.

Following the freeing of Paris, we reestablished our diplomatic mission in the French capital on September 8, 1944.

During the military operations throughout the summer of 1944, as American, British, French, and Canadian troops drove the Germans back to the Siegfried Line, the arrangements we had made with the French committee worked out to our entire satisfaction. As province after province fell into Allied hands, it was clearly proven to us that the great majority of the French people, at least for the period of the emergency, freely accepted the leadership of General de Gaulle and the administration that he had set up on French soil. The French people themselves, particularly the resistance elements of the French Forces of the Interior, made a real contribution to the Allied victory.

By October the military situation made possible the establishment of most of France, including Paris, as a "Zone of the Interior" in which, as our arrangements called for, the conduct of civil affairs became entirely the responsibility of the French authorities. Accordingly, after we had consulted with the British and Soviet Governments, we decided that the French de facto authority established in Paris under the leadership of General de Gaulle should be recognized as the Provisional Government of the French Republic. We announced this decision on October 23, and Britain, the Soviet Union, and other United Nations made similar announcements. With the approval of the French Provisional Government, the President named Jefferson Caffery, who had been our Ambassador in Rio de Janeiro, as Ambassador to France.

The French Foreign Minister, Georges Bidault, sent me a note on November 4, inviting the President and me to visit Paris. I had already left the State Department, however, because of my health and was soon to resign, and the President also was unable to accept.

A week later we, along with the British and Soviet Governments, invited the Provisional Government of the French Republic to full membership on the European Advisory Commission in London. One of the principal questions before the commission was the surrender terms to be imposed on Germany and the postwar treatment of Germany.

Meantime we joined with the British, Soviet, and Chinese Governments at the Dumbarton Oaks conversations beginning in August, 1944, in agreeing that France should be accepted in due course as a fifth permanent member of the Security Council in the proposed international organization for the maintenance of peace.

Thus stood our relations with France at the time of my resignation as Secretary of State. As I left office our policy toward France was based on two primary considerations. The first was to seek to increase France's contribution to the war in every possible way. The second was to assist France to resume her former position of influence and thus assume larger responsibility for maintaining the peace throughout the world following the defeat of the Axis.

In the course of many preceding chapters I have been forced to give considerable attention to General de Gaulle—an attention that sometimes may have seemed disproportionate to the importance of the man himself. The significance of the De Gaulle issue, however, was not limited to the General. It involved relations between the United States and Britain, and between the United States and the Vichy Government and French North Africa. It embraced the basic belief of the President and me that the future of France should not be mortgaged to or by any one man or group, unless the French people themselves so elected.

Not until we occupied large sections of France could we be sure that the French people would accept De Gaulle. The Free French had shown us numerous reports that they said came from the French underground, showing a great majority support for De Gaulle; but we had had other reports from inside France to the opposite effect.

Our military support of De Gaulle had begun early and had never wavered. This was because we were quickly convinced that the Free French could lend some military assistance to the Allies. They were among the first to receive Lend-Lease aid, which was granted them on November 11, 1941.

Our political support lagged behind our military support partly because of De Gaulle's actions in striving to impose himself as the governmental leader of all French elements opposed to the Nazis and of his propaganda which sought to play off Britain and the United States against each other, and the Anglo-Saxon nations against the Russians, and partly because of our uncertainty that he had the approval of a majority of the French people. Once this last point appeared assured, our political backing became cordial and wholehearted.

105: Question of Russia

RELATIONS BETWEEN the United States and Russia, as 1944 began, were closer than they had ever been. Through the Moscow and Tehran Conferences we had brought Russia into a program of real cooperation for the remainder of the war and, we hoped, for the future.

Throughout 1944, my last year in office, our relations continued good on the whole, with Russia joining wholeheartedly in the preparations for the postwar organization to keep the peace. It was obvious, however, that as Germany collapsed and Russia moved in to fill the vacuum in Eastern Europe, problems of a delicate nature would arise. It also was obvious that certain problems already existed that had not been settled.

For one, Russia and another of the United Nations, Poland, were at daggers' points. They maintained no diplomatic relations with each other, and constant recriminations were passing back and forth between Moscow and the Polish Government at London, sharply disturbing to the harmony of the United Nations.

Our submission in August, 1943, of our good offices for the settlement of their dispute had not been accepted; but we tried again in January, 1944, although in general we let the British Government take the lead in endeavors to resolve the dispute. This last was for the reasons that the Polish Government-in-exile was located in London, and that Britain had treaties of alliance both with Poland and with Russia. On January 14 the Polish Government announced its willingness to discuss all outstanding questions with the Soviet Union and indicated that it was approaching the United States and British Governments with a view to their acting as intermediaries.

The President and I quickly agreed to the Polish request. On January 15 I cabled Ambassador Harriman to remind the Soviet Government that, as that Government well knew, we were pledged to the principle of settling disputes by peaceful accord. Without regard to the merits of the case, we hoped that the Soviet Government would give most favorable consideration to the Polish offer to discuss outstanding questions, on the basis presumably of the renewal of official relations between the Governments of Poland and the Soviet Union.

A refusal by the Soviet Government, or any show of hesitancy in this regard at the present time, we added, would adversely affect the cause

of general international cooperation. On the other hand, far-reaching beneficial effects on world public opinion would be brought about by a solution
of the Polish-Soviet differences in conformity with the basic principles
of international cooperation. We likewise pointed to the very considerable
advantages to our war effort which would come from the restoration of
unity in the ranks of the United Nations.

We informed the Soviet Government that, if it found it agreeable
and desirable, we should be glad to extend our good offices toward initiating discussions between the Polish and Soviet Governments, with a view
to the resumption of official relations between them.

In the cable to Ambassador Harriman I stated for his information
that our proposal was intended primarily as an earnest, friendly effort
to help Russia reach a settlement of this difficult problem. The Soviet
newspaper *Pravda* had published a bitter reply to an article by Wendell
Willkie dealing in part with Russia's supposed intentions concerning the
political integrity of states around her borders, Finland, Poland, the Baltic
and Balkan countries. This reply, I said, had had a far-reaching effect on
public opinion here because it was interpreted as an indication that the
Soviet Government proposed to follow a course of unilateral action. Important elements here, I added, viewed the Soviet Government's attitude
and actions with regard to the Polish boundary question as a test of the
reality of friendly international cooperation and respect for the rights of
nations. The Moscow and Tehran Conferences had produced encouraging
results in the United States, I concluded, but we frankly pointed out
the danger to the cause of cooperation in an international security system
which an arbitrary treatment of the Polish-Soviet difficulties would produce.

A week later, on January 24, Soviet Ambassador Gromyko transmitted to me a reply from Molotov stating in effect that conditions were not
yet ripe for mediation. Molotov said it was clear that the Polish Government's aim, in turning to the Governments of the United States and Great
Britain for mediation, was not to achieve agreement with the Soviet Government but to deepen the conflict and involve the Allies therein. It
seemed to him that the exclusion of all pro-Fascist imperialist elements
from the Polish Government and the inclusion of democratic elements
would be a fundamental improvement and would create a favorable
ground for the reestablishment of Soviet-Polish relations and the settlement of the border question between them, as well as for fruitful mediation.

Polish Ambassador Jan Ciechanowski called on me on January 26 and handed me a note from Premier Mikolajczyk to the President. This stated that Prime Minister Churchill had suggested a five-point solution which he would propose to Stalin if the Premier agreed. The five points were:

First, the Polish Government to accept the Curzon Line (roughly equivalent to the limit of Polish territory occupied by the Russians in 1939—this area contained a large percentage of Russians) as a basis for negotiations concerning its eastern frontier. Second, Poland to receive East Prussia, Danzig, and Upper Silesia as far as the Oder River. Third, Poles on the Soviet side of the Curzon Line to have the right to remove to the west of that line. Fourth, all Germans to be removed from the new Poland. Fifth, Britain, Russia, and the United States to guarantee this settlement.

Mikolajczyk asked the President in his note whether the United States Government considered it advisable to enter now upon a final settlement of European territorial problems; whether it would participate in bringing about and guaranteeing a settlement; and whether it supported Churchill's proposals.

I promised Ambassador Ciechanowski I would transmit the note to the President.

The President and I, in talking this over on January 31, agreed that we should not support any definite frontier recommendations during the course of the war. This was in line with the position I had stated on several occasions—namely, that new frontiers should not be fixed during the progress of hostilities except with the free consent of the countries directly concerned. There were more than thirty boundary questions in Europe alone, and an outside attempt to settle any of them would only result in raising all of them, to the detriment of the aggressive prosecution of the war.

We did not believe it possible to give a United States guarantee of the new Poland that might be constituted along the lines of Prime Minister Churchill's suggestions. We felt that all the guarantees necessary would be contained within the new international security organization to which the Russians, British, Chinese, and we had agreed at the Moscow Conference, and that the United Nations organization would get off to a better start if it were not embarrassed by individual arrangements of guarantee.

Accordingly, the State Department drew up answers to the three questions submitted by Premier Mikolajczyk. Mr. Roosevelt approved the answers, and we handed them to the Polish Ambassador.

On the first question—the advisability of entering now upon a final settlement of European territorial problems—the President pointed to the well known basic position of the United States Government that general discussions of European frontier problems during the progress of the war ran the risk of creating confusion and diverting attention from the principal objective of defeating Germany. This attitude, however, did not preclude direct settlement by mutual accord between any two countries that had mutual territorial problems. As for the Russo-Polish problem, the United States recognized that recent developments (Russian troops had crossed the old Polish frontier) might render it desirable for the Government of Poland to reach a solution without delay.

On the second question—participation by the United States in bringing about a settlement and guaranteeing it—the President said this Government would be prepared through the offer of good offices to the Polish and Soviet Governments to assist the Polish Government in freely reaching a settlement of its territorial problems. Although this Government would welcome a friendly solution of the outstanding questions between Poland and the Soviet Union, it was not in a position to guarantee any territorial settlement.

On the third question—supporting Churchill's proposals—the President said the United States was prepared to support the Prime Minister's endeavors to bring about the reestablishment of relations between the Soviet and Polish Governments on the basis of a friendly solution of all outstanding difficulties.

I cabled Ambassador Harriman on February 7 a message from the President to Stalin, which we had prepared in the State Department. Mr. Roosevelt said to Stalin that, in communicating with him on the basis of the conversations they had had at Tehran, he wanted to make it plain that he neither desired nor intended to suggest, much less to advise him in any way, where Russia's interests lay with regard to Poland, since he fully realized that Russia's future security was rightly Stalin's primary concern. He added, however, that the broad principles subscribed to at the Moscow and Tehran Conferences had been enthusiastically welcomed by the overwhelming majority of our people and Congress, and he knew Stalin would agree with him that it was highly important that faith in these understandings should not be questioned. He said he was sure a solution could be found that would fully protect Russia's interests and satisfy Stalin's desire to see a friendly, independent Poland and at the same time not affect the cooperation which the Moscow and Tehran Conferences had so splendidly established.

Foreign Commissar Molotov had stated to Ambassador Harriman on January 18 that it was impossible for the Soviet Government to have any dealings with the Polish Government in London in its existing form, and had suggested that the Polish Government should be reconstituted by including Poles at present in the United States, Great Britain, and the Soviet Union.

Referring to Molotov's statements, the President said to Stalin he fully appreciated the Marshal's desire to deal only with a Polish Government in which he had confidence, and which could be counted upon to establish friendly, permanent relations with the Soviet Union. Nevertheless, he earnestly hoped that, while this problem remained unsolved, neither party, by hasty word or unilateral act, would transform this particular question into one that would adversely affect future international collaboration. He said it was especially necessary to avoid any action that might appear to counteract the achievement of our long-range objectives at a moment when public opinion was forming in support of international collaboration.

The President mentioned that Churchill had informed him that he was urging Premier Mikolajczyk to accept the territorial changes proposed by Russia (the Curzon Line, more or less, in the east, with Poland to move farther west into former German territory). He then asked Stalin whether it was not possible on that basis to leave it to Mikolajczyk to make such changes in his Government as might be necessary without any evidence that a foreign country was pressing or dictating them.

Here Mr. Roosevelt added another paragraph in his own hand stating his opinion that the first consideration at that time should be that Polish guerrillas would work with and not against Stalin's advancing troops.

On the following day, February 8, I sent Ambassador Winant in London a message from the President to Prime Minister Churchill which also had been prepared in the State Department. This was by way of comment on a message that Churchill had sent to Stalin outlining his suggestions for a settlement of the Polish-Russian dispute. The President asked whether the Prime Minister's message might not give "U. J." (the President and the Prime Minister occasionally used this designation, abbreviation for "Uncle Joe," in referring to Stalin) the impression that Mr. Churchill was wedded to the present members of the Polish Government in London and was determined to see them become the future Government of Poland. Stalin, he thought, might interpret this as evidence of a wish on Mr. Churchill's part to see a Government set up along Russian borders which the Russians rightly or wrongly regarded as containing elements irrevocably hostile to them.

The President said he knew that this was not Mr. Churchill's wish, and that the Prime Minister was interested only in preserving the principle of the right of all countries to chose their governments without interference and also in avoiding the creation by the Soviet Government of a rival Polish Government. He suggested that this be made clear to "U. J." by referring to the possibility that, if a real solution of the frontier and other questions with Russia was near, the Polish Government of its own accord would accept the resignation of its members known to be particularly objectionable to Russia.

Mr. Roosevelt sent the Prime Minister a copy of the cable he had dispatched to Stalin.

Nothing came of these exchanges. Premier Mikolajczyk's Government would not accept the Curzon Line as a basis for negotiation with Russia. Stalin on his part said that before Polish-Soviet relations could be resumed, the Polish Government must publicly announce its recognition of the Curzon Line as its eastern frontier; but he added that he wished to have nothing to do with the present Polish Government in London, which, he said, was full of reactionaries who opposed good relations with Russia.

Premier Mikolajczyk had for some time been urging the President to invite him to Washington for a discussion of the Polish situation. Mr. Roosevelt felt, however, and I agreed, that a personal discussion with the Premier would not resolve the difficulty with Russia. We knew the opposition that existed within the Polish Government to any cession of eastern Poland to Russia, however valuable might be the German territory that Poland would receive; and we also knew that Russia would consent to no agreement with Poland that did not involve the reacquisition of eastern Poland which Russia regarded as her own. There was the further objection that a personal conference between Roosevelt and Mikolajczyk, with all the publicity it would naturally receive, might give rise to the impression that the United States had embraced Poland's position versus Russia.

Spring of 1944 was the period of preparation for the greatest military campaign in American history—the landing in Normandy. That landing had to be coordinated with Russian military movements in the east so that the Germans could not draw off too large a portion of their forces to meet us in the west. We could not afford to become partisan in the Polish question to the extent of alienating Russia at that crucial moment.

The President therefore desired to postpone Mikolajczyk's visit. When the Premier wrote him a long letter that Ambassador Ciechanowski sent to the State Department on March 25, stating Poland's position and emphasizing his desire to see the President personally, Mr. Roosevelt, replying on April 3, pleaded the state of his health and other commitments as reasons for postponing the visit at least until May.

The Polish question was now further complicated by the obvious Russian efforts to set up a rival Polish Government in Russia or in that Polish territory which, since the beginning of the year, they had occupied. Soviet Ambassador Gromyko came in on May 27 to inform me that a group of representatives of what was called the National Council of Poland had gone from Warsaw to Russia. They stated that the council was fighting Germans, it needed arms to continue such fighting, it would be willing to work with the Polish Government in London, although it disliked some members of that Government, and it desired to establish relations with the Soviet, British, and American Governments.

When I asked what kind of relations they wanted, Gromyko replied he did not know; but he assumed they meant some sort of political relations short of diplomatic relations.

The President and I had no desire, however, to give any encouragement to the creation of a second Polish Government. We maintained diplomatic relations in London with the Polish Government-in-exile. And we felt, as we did in the case of De Gaulle and the French, that the Poles should be left entirely free, when their country was liberated, to choose their own Government.

In pursuance of the thought Molotov had expressed on January 18 that the Polish Government should be reconstituted by including Poles in the United States, Britain, and Russia, Stalin sent the President a message at the beginning of March asking him to allow two American citizens of Polish descent to go to Moscow for discussions with Soviet officials. These were Professor Oscar Lange (at this writing Poland's delegate to the United Nations) and a Catholic priest, the Reverend Stanislaw Orlemanski, both of whom were known for their pro-Russian views.

Under Secretary Stettinius, who was acting for me during a brief absence from Washington, sent the President, after consulting with me, a memorandum on March 8 in which we opposed Stalin's request. The memorandum stated that Stalin's request raised very serious questions of policy. Orlemanski and Lange represented a heavily slanted view on the Polish-Soviet question which, according to our information, was not shared by American citizens of Polish descent or by American public opinion as a whole. We might become directly involved in the dispute if they went to Russia by our tacit consent and assistance. Their visit would be widely interpreted as the first step in this Government's abandonment of the legal Government of Poland. It was possible that their activities might bring them under the Logan Act, which prohibited American citizens from having any dealings with a foreign Government to defeat the measures of this Government. On the other hand, we concluded, it might be undesirable if not impossible to refuse two American citizens permission to accept an invitation tendered by the Soviet Government.

Despite these objections, the President thought he should accede to Stalin's request. I sent Ambassador Harriman on March 24 a cable for Stalin from the President, which had been drafted in the State Department, saying that Lange and Orlemanski would be given passports in accordance with the Marshal's request. The telegram suggested that the Soviet Union should furnish transportation facilities for the two visitors because of the military crowding of our own transportation facilities. It stated that our Government assumed no responsibility for their activities, and that, if their journey became the subject of public comment, we might find it necessary to emphasize this point.

The visit of the two Polish-Americans to Moscow did arouse, as we knew it would, considerable adverse comment and agitation in the United States. Polish Ambassador Ciechanowski protested on behalf of his Government.

When Soviet Ambassador Gromyko called on me on May 1 I said that this incident had caused great injury to both our Governments so far as public opinion here was concerned.

"I've been spending a large portion of my time," I said, "defending Russia against the attacks made on her mainly on account of these small incidents which in themselves amount to little but which for propaganda purposes of those unfriendly to this Government and to Russia are far-reaching in their damaging effects. If we are to go forward with the movement of international cooperation to preserve peace after the war, it's highly important that we should understand each other's situation and psychology better, so that we can diminish these small incidents."

I added that I would continue in a friendly way to do all possible to clear up these matters, but that frankly I could not do all this work myself.

Ambassador Gromyko said that he thought the criticism would be temporary, and that the matter of Orlemanski and Lange involved fundamental policy of his Government.

I replied that I could scarcely see the force of his last statement.

In any event, Orlemanski's and Lange's visit to Moscow had no effect on the disinclination of the President and me to see the Russians attempt to create a rival Polish Government.

Polish Premier Mikolajczyk's visit was at length arranged, and he arrived in June. He had long conferences with the President, and he came to see me at his request on June 12, along with Ambassador Ciechanowski. As our conversation began, I mentioned that I had happened to sit a little on the inside of the councils during the Wilson Administration, and that Poland had been a constant topic of discussion. I said that every person with whom I came in contact seemed to be consumed with a desire to see Poland once more become a free and independent nation, and that Mikolajczyk would find the American people inherently friendly toward the people of Poland.

"I repeat," I added, "what I have said both to the Russians and to the Poles . . . when two neighbors discontinue speaking terms, the neighbors of each unanimously desire to urge them to find a way to get back on speaking relations. The interests and welfare of each country equally require that they live on friendly terms. There is no way to settle differences that have arisen, and will inevitably arise, between nations hitherto friendly, except by persuasion, reason, remonstrance, and other methods of appealing to another government when it is considered in the wrong."

The Premier said he appreciated these points. He spoke, however, of the difficulties of getting along with Russia. He then brought up the question of credits for Poland, which he had presented to Under Secretary Stettinius several days before. I promised we would give his request every consideration.

As the Premier was about to leave, I said that if it were possible for appropriate Polish and Russian representatives to meet on a conversational basis, it would be of tremendous importance. It would probably mean a discussion in an increasingly friendly spirit of the differences between the two Governments and a solution that each Government would feel was reasonably fair.

"It's true," I commented, "that no country desires to have an unfriendly country living by its side. We Allies feel keenly the unfriendly pro-Axis attitude of the Argentine Government located 7,000 miles away. While it is not essential, though it is preferable, for a next-door neighbor to be thoroughly friendly, yet the purpose of the future welfare of each country is served if one country is not unfriendly toward the other."

The Premier agreed.

The Polish and Russian Governments, I said, had a serious argument over the attempted dictation by the Soviet Government regarding some of the personnel of the Polish Government at London. The Polish Government's resistance to that dictation was based on a sound position. On the other hand, Russia was not required to recognize the Government of any other country, and even then was not required to give any reason for doing so or for not doing so. These two opposing views, each sound, approached each other within a given distance, at which point arose the controversy. Some of these days, I concluded, when both Governments decided to make an equal contribution toward working out such deadlocks as this, they would find ways to do so.

Premier Mikolajczyk smiled and indicated his acquiescence.

In line with this thought that high officials of the two Governments in dispute should meet and talk things over, President Roosevelt communicated to Stalin that Mikolajczyk would be willing to go to Moscow to make a sincere effort to reestablish relations with the Soviet Union. He indicated his interest that Stalin should receive the Polish Premier.

Stalin did not acquiesce in the President's suggestion. Some weeks later, however, at the insistence of Prime Minister Churchill, he consented to receive Mikolajczyk in Moscow, and the visit took place in August, though without concrete results.

In the same month, August, 1944, we had a number of diplomatic exchanges with the Soviet Government in an effort to help the Polish resistance forces in Warsaw who had risen against the Germans as the Russian Army drew near that capital. We sought to obtain permission from the Russians for a shuttle mission of American bombers to drop arms to the Poles in Warsaw who were fighting desperately to hold their capital until the Russian forces could arrive.

On August 15 the Soviet Government refused our request of the 14th, saying that the Warsaw uprising was a "purely adventurist affair" and the Soviet Government would not lend its hand to it, and that, as Stalin had pointed out to Churchill on August 5, it was unimaginable that a few Polish detachments of the so-called National Army could have captured

Warsaw when the Nazis were defending the capital with four tank divisions.

I thereupon sent the President a memorandum on August 16, saying: "I believe for a number of considerations that it is impossible for us or the British to abandon to their fate the Polish underground forces which are actively fighting the Nazi invaders of their country simply because such action might not accord with Soviet political aims."

I attached the draft of a telegram to Ambassador Harriman whereby the President authorized him to associate himself with the British Ambassador in making representations to Stalin, or, if Stalin could not be seen, to Molotov, urging the Soviet Government to reconsider its attitude. The British had already asked our assistance toward this end.

After the President had given his approval, the telegram went out on August 17. We pointed out that, while we sincerely hoped that the Soviet Government would cooperate with us and the British in furnishing assistance to the Polish underground forces and would itself furnish such as might be practicable, the American forces intended, in any case, in so far as militarily feasible, to continue to furnish aid to the Polish underground inside German-occupied Poland. This Government, we concluded, saw no reason to depart from its consistent policy of furnishing all possible aid to any force of the United Nations engaged in fighting our common enemy.

The President himself was keenly interested in this project. From what we could learn, the Poles had gained control of a large part of Warsaw and were valiantly holding out against the Germans. We thought it would be highly advantageous to the general war effort for their resistance to continue until the Russians, who were only a comparatively short distance away, reached the city.

Before this telegram arrived Ambassador Harriman conferred with Foreign Commissar Molotov on August 17, and presented arguments similar to those we had stated. Molotov admitted that Stalin had promised Mikolajczyk, during his visit to Moscow earlier in the month, to give aid to the Poles resisting the Germans in Warsaw. He explained, however, that because of statements emanating from the Polish Government in London, it had become evident by August 12 that the movement in Warsaw was inspired by men antagonistic to the Soviet Union, and therefore the Soviet Government could no longer countenance any association with the uprising. He further said that his Government could not object to British or American planes dropping arms in the region of Warsaw, but they objected to the planes landing in Soviet territory since the Soviet Government did not wish, either directly or indirectly, to associate itself with "the Warsaw adventure."

The President and Prime Minister Churchill made a joint, direct appeal to Stalin on August 20. They said in substance that they were thinking of world opinion if the anti-Nazis in Warsaw were, in effect, abandoned. They expressed the belief that Russia, Britain, and the United States should do their utmost to save as many of the patriots in Warsaw as possible. They hoped that the Soviet authorities would immediately drop supplies and munitions to the Poles or agree to assist our planes in doing so. They stressed the extreme importance of the time element.

The Germans were then bringing overwhelming force to bear against the beleaguered Poles, and it seemed doubtful that the resistance forces could hold out much longer without help.

Stalin finally gave permission for one shuttle flight which was carried out successfully on September 18. He also gave permission for another flight, which, for operational reasons, was not made. The resistance in Warsaw ended on October 2 with the surrender of those Poles who had survived the incessant German attacks.

When Prime Minister Churchill went to Moscow in October for another effort to solve the Polish-Russian dispute, he induced Stalin to receive Mikolajczyk again. The Polish Premier, following his return to London from his second trip to Moscow, tried to persuade the members of his Cabinet to accept the Soviet proposal to use the Curzon Line as the basis for the Polish-Soviet frontier. Encountering difficulties from his colleagues, he appealed to President Roosevelt on October 26 to send a message to Stalin asking the Soviet leader to include the city of Lwów and the oil fields south of that city within Poland's future boundaries.

The President was looking forward at that time to another meeting with Stalin and Churchill within the near future. Consequently he decided not to send the message, preferring to talk the matter over with Stalin personally.

On November 15, after it had become evident that the meeting would be put off—it did not eventuate until February, 1945, at Yalta—the President addressed a letter to Polish Premier Mikolajczyk, which the State Department drew up. This contained four main points.

The first was that the United States Government stood for a strong, free, and independent Polish state in which the Polish people should have the right to order their internal existence as they saw fit.

The second was that we should have no objection to any frontier settlement that was reached in agreement among the Polish, Soviet, and British Governments, but that we could give no guarantee of any specific frontiers.

The third was that, if the Polish Government should desire to transfer population to and from Polish territory, the United States Government would have no objection and would facilitate such transfers as far as practicable.

The final point was that the United States Government, subject to legislative authority, would assist in the postwar economic reconstruction of Poland in so far as practicable.

Ambassador Harriman, who took the letter from Washington to London, was also instructed to discuss Lwów with the Polish Premier and to say that, if the Premier desired him to make a strong appeal to Stalin to have that district included in the future Poland, he would do so.

Premier Mikolajczyk said to Harriman on November 23, however, that he had already decided to resign, since he could not persuade his Cabinet to accept the Russian proposals regarding the eastern frontier. He said he regretted asking the President to take up the question of Lwów because, even if Stalin had agreed, his colleagues still would not have accepted the boundary. As I was in process of resigning, Mikolajczyk himself resigned on November 24.

When I left office, the Polish-Russian dispute was no nearer solution. I have no intention to go into the merits of that dispute. The policy of the President and me was to refrain from stretching the United States upon a bed of nettles. In our diplomatic exchanges with both sides and in our offers of good offices, we repeatedly stated we were not entering into the merits of the differences between Poland and Russia.

We certainly brought all the pressure we logically could on both sides to compose their quarrel. But our broader view of the interests of the United Nations would not permit us to accept the suggestion often advanced that we should cut off Lend-Lease supplies to Russia unless she made a settlement with Poland. Nor could we push our diplomatic approaches to either side to an extent that would injure our relations with the other side. We made it repeatedly clear that we wanted a strong, free Poland; but we were not going to say at that point that Poland's frontiers should be such and such a line, for to have done so would have sprung a Pandora's box of dozens of other frontier questions. We were already helping both Poland and Russia, through Lend-Lease, to the full extent of our ability, and we were willing to go much further in helping Poland transfer

Polish people from one area to another in furtherance of an agreement with Russia.

Poland was only one of a number of countries that entered into the channel of our policy toward Russia. Our relations with Russia were in one sense similar to our relations with Britain, in that there were few diplomatic moves we took toward other countries that did not have some reference to Russia and require consultation with her. I insisted again and again to the President and to my associates in the State Department that we could not have friendly ties with the Soviet Union unless we consulted her on any point or decision that was even remotely of interest to her.

On the other hand, Russia occasionally took a step without consulting us, and friction inevitably arose. Such a step was her sudden establishment of diplomatic relations with the Italian Government on March 13, 1944, without prior notice to us. This move was a stride further than the relations the British and ourselves had established with the new Italian Government. Public opinion naturally resented such a unilateral action; and, for some days following, Russia came in for a bad press in Britain and the United States.

Diplomatic exchanges between ourselves and the Russians straightened the matter out, but when Soviet Ambassador Gromyko came to me on April 13 to give me a second memorandum from his Government explaining its position, I remarked, in thanking him: "This has presented a relatively small question; but in my opinion the handling of this matter publicly has resulted in one hundred times more harm than good to Russia, both in connection with the international movement of cooperation and with public opinion in the United States. I earnestly hope that in future Russia will undertake to talk such matters out, as each of the three great nations should do, rather than go into the press with premature and unilateral decisions."

For three years the United States Government had tried to help Russia by exerting every possible pressure to induce Finland to withdraw from the war. In 1944, as in the preceding three years, we made the strongest of diplomatic representations to Helsinki, pointing out that it was to Finland's best interests to retire, while she still could, and warning her that the responsibility for her continuing in a state of war with Allies of the United States must be borne solely by the Finnish Government.

Finland's aid to Germany was economic as well as military in that Germany received from Finland nickel, cobalt, molybdenum, timber, newsprint, and other products which she needed. The President sent me on May 22, 1944, a memorandum he had received from Leo Crowley, Administrator of the Foreign Economics Administration, pointing out the desirability of cutting off Finnish ferroalloy supplies to Germany; and he asked me to prepare a reply for his signature.

I sent him a draft reply on May 27 in which we pointed out the long efforts we had made to get Finland out of the war, in order to bring to an end the very substantial military and economic aid she had been giving Germany. Apparently, I said, the only practical way to stop Finnish exports to Germany would be through military measures; and I was sure that Britain and the Soviet Union, which were at war with Finland, had this very much in mind. I added, however, that we were considering the early blacklisting of Finnish firms which traded with Germany, and we hoped this would have some effect. We announced the blacklisting of these firms on June 3.

On June 16 the State Department requested Finnish Minister Hjalmar Procopé and three counselors of his Legation to leave the United States because of propaganda activities they were carrying on inimical to our interests. We nevertheless pointed out that this did not constitute a rupture of diplomatic relations with Finland.

The rupture, however, occurred two weeks later, following a visit of German Foreign Minister Ribbentrop to Helsinki and an announcement by the Finnish Government indicating a complete comradeship in arms between the two countries. After consultation with the President, I sent the Finnish Chargé a note on June 30 breaking off relations.

In this we stated that we were not unaware of the fact that the infiltration of German troops into Finland and of Germans into the councils of the Finnish Government had deprived that Government of liberty of action. Nevertheless we had taken every opportunity, publicly and through diplomatic representations, to warn the Finnish Government of the inevitable consequences of its association with Nazi Germany. These warnings had been ignored, and the partnership was now complete.

"The Government of the United States," we said, "must take into account the fact that at this decisive stage in the combined operations of the military, naval, and air forces of the United States and the other United Nations, the Finnish operations have a direct bearing on the success of the Allied effort."

Finland, however, formed only a minor part of our relations with Russia. We were then giving greater attention to the Balkans as Soviet troops advanced into that trouble spot of Europe.

106: Russia—Conclusions

WHEN THE RUSSIAN ARMY began to push into Rumania in April, 1944, the relationship between the Soviet Union and the Balkans came to the forefront of our diplomacy. What were Russia's political intentions in the Balkans? Would she seek to set up a domain of her own in the Balkans? Would she retire completely after victory? Would she work with the other major Allies in solving Balkan questions?

Soviet Ambassador Gromyko came in on April 1 to hand me a statement from his Government relating to the advance into Rumania. This asserted that the offensive was the beginning of a full reestablishment of the border delineated in 1940 by treaty between the Soviet Union and Rumania. At the same time it promised that the Soviet Union did not aim at acquiring any part of Rumanian territory or at changing Rumania's social regime.

In effect, the statement was a reiteration of the position already announced with regard to territorial aims in eastern and southeastern Europe; namely, that the U.S.S.R. would restore its western boundaries as they had existed on June 22, 1941, when Germany attacked Russia. (This stand had been modified slightly when the Soviet Union proposed to establish the frontier with Poland on the basis of the Curzon Line, which in certain parts was a little to the east of the 1941 frontier.) The statement meant that Russia intended to reincorporate all of Bessarabia and all of Bucovina into the U.S.S.R. Bessarabia had formed part of the Russian Empire from 1812 until the end of the First World War. Bucovina had never formed part of the Russian Empire and was incorporated into the Soviet Union only in 1940, at the time Bessarabia was taken over. Its annexation would give the Soviet Union a common frontier with the eastern tip of Czechoslovakia.

A stir of speculation now arose in the press of many countries as to whether Russia's aim was liberation or acquisition. Suddenly British Ambassador Halifax inquired of me on May 30, 1944, how this Government would feel about an arrangement between the British and Russians whereby Russia would have a controlling influence in Rumania, and Britain a controlling influence in Greece. He said that difficulties had risen between Russia and Britain over the Balkans, especially with regard to Rumania.

He handed me a written communication from his Government asking whether we had any objection to an agreement between Britain and Russia whereby, in the main, Rumanian affairs should be the concern of the Soviet Government and Greek affairs the concern of the United Kingdom. This British-Russian understanding would apply only to war conditions and would not affect the rights and responsibilities which each of the three great Powers would have to exercise at the peace settlement.

The British Foreign Office said that the United Kingdom Government was fully alive to the importance of avoiding even the appearance of carving up the Balkans into spheres of influence. A temporary agreement such as they suggested seemed to them the best chance of amicable cooperation between the Allies in the countries concerned during the military period.

After telling Halifax that I would give this serious consideration, I said point-blank:

"At first blush, in view of the many charges and countercharges now rising—and which will certainly rise in the future—about encroachments first by one Government and then by another on the economic, political, military, or other internal affairs of the Balkans and other European countries, it would be a doubtful course to abandon our broad basic declarations of policy, principles, and practice. If these are departed from in one or two important instances, such as you propose, then neither of the two countries parties to such an act will have any precedent to stand on, or any stable rules by which to be governed and to insist that other Governments be governed."

I concluded by saying that, in my opinion, this fact should be carefully studied by all concerned before any definite departures took place. Halifax said he appreciated this thought.

I was, in fact, flatly opposed to any division of Europe or sections of Europe into spheres of influence. I had argued against this strongly at the Moscow Conference. It seemed to me that any creation of zones of influence would inevitably sow the seeds of future conflict. I felt that zones of influence could not but derogate from the over-all authority of the international security organization which I expected would come into being.

I was not, and am not, a believer in the idea of balance of power or spheres of influence as a means of keeping the peace. During the First World War I had made an intensive study of the system of spheres of influence and balance of power, and I was grounded to the taproots in their iniquitous consequences. The conclusions I then formed in total opposition to this system stayed with me.

On the following day, May 31, Prime Minister Churchill, to whom Halifax's cable reporting my remarks was undoubtedly communicated, sent the President a telegram direct in which he argued strongly for our approval of the proposed agreement. He emphasized that Britain did not wish to cut up the Balkans into areas of influence, that the arrangement would apply only to war conditions, and that there would be no change in the present collaboration between the American and British Governments in formulating and executing the policy of the Allies toward Greece and Rumania.

His telegram contained two additional items of information. One was that it was the British Government which had suggested the agreement to Russian Ambassador Gousev in London. The second was that the Russians had informed the British on May 18 that they were in agreement with the suggestion, but before they could give any final assurances they would like to know whether the United States Government had been consulted, and whether we were in agreement with the arrangement.

The Prime Minister said he hoped the President would feel able to give his blessing to the proposal.

Mr. Roosevelt sent this telegram to me for consideration and for the drafting of a reply.

My associates at the State Department agreed with the original attitude I had taken with Lord Halifax; namely, that we could not lend our support to any such agreement and, in fact, should do what we could to discourage it. While we could understand Britain's natural desire to strengthen herself in the Mediterranean through a position of influence in Greece, and to avoid causes of friction with the Russians in the Balkans, we felt that any such arrangement as that proposed, no matter how temporary it might be made to appear, would inevitably conduce to the establishment of zones of influence against which we had been stoutly fighting, and against which I had spoken out at the Moscow Conference.

While this reply was being prepared in the Department, Halifax handed us on June 8 another message from the Prime Minister—this one addressed to him. Mr. Churchill again said there was no question of spheres of influence being involved. But he added that, although we all had to act together, someone must "play the hand." It seemed reasonable to him that the Russians should deal with the Rumanians and Bulgarians, and that Britain should deal with the Greeks, who were in Britain's theater of operations and were Britain's old allies, for whom she had sacrificed 40,000 men in 1941. The same, he added, was true of Yugoslavia.

Mr. Churchill commented that he had kept the President constantly informed, but that Britain had been playing the hand in Greece and had to be very careful to play it agreeably to the Russians. Events, he remarked, moved very rapidly in the Balkans.

Britain, he said, followed the lead of the United States in South America as far as possible, so long as it was not a question of her beef and mutton, on which naturally she held strong views because of the "little folk."

This telegram was important in that it brought in two countries not hitherto mentioned by the British—Bulgaria to be dealt with by Russia, and Yugoslavia to be dealt with by Britain. It therefore seemed more urgent even than before to oppose the arrangement which would bring one set of countries under Russia and another set under Britain.

The President sent our reply to the Prime Minister on June 10. This recalled my conversation with Halifax on May 30 when I communicated to the Ambassador reasons why this Government was unwilling to give its approval. The President acknowledged in his reply that the Government responsible for military actions in any country—Britain was militarily responsible for Greece, and Russia for Rumania—would inevitably make decisions which military developments necessitated. But we were convinced that the natural tendency for such decisions to extend into the political and economic fields would be strengthened by the agreement proposed by the British. The President stated our opinion that this would surely lead to the persistence of differences between Britain and Russia and to the division of the Balkans into spheres of influence, regardless of Mr. Churchill's statement that the agreement would be limited to military matters.

The President concluded that we should prefer to see consultative machinery set up for the Balkans to resolve misunderstandings and to prevent the development of exclusive zones of influence.

The Prime Minister came back the following day, June 11, with a long, forceful telegram saying that the President's message had given him much concern. Action would be paralyzed, he said, if everybody had to consult everybody else before taking action. Events in the Balkans always outstripped the changing situations. Consequently a committee for consultation such as the President had indicated would merely obstruct action and, in emergencies, would always be overridden by direct interchanges between the President and the Prime Minister, or between Stalin and either of them.

Mr. Churchill advanced two examples in which direct action by himself had resolved situations—the mutiny of Greek troops at Easter, and a prospect of trouble in Egypt. If Britain had had to consult other Powers and a system of triangular or quadrangular cables had got under way, chaos or impotence might have resulted.

In the Greek crisis, he commented, the President's telegrams to him had worked wonders. His agreement with the President had been complete, and the result had been entirely satisfactory. He asked why all this efficient direction should be broken up into a committee of mediocre officials such as were being littered throughout the world. He further asked why he and the President could not keep this in their own hands, considering how they saw eye to eye about so much of it.

The Prime Minister finally suggested that the arrangement he had proposed should have a three months' trial, following which it would be reviewed by the three Powers.

When this telegram arrived, I was resting for a few days at Hershey, Pennsylvania. The President, without consulting me or the State Department, replied the following day accepting the Prime Minister's three months' proposal, but adding that care should be exercised to make it clear that no postwar spheres of influence were being established.

The President did not inform the State Department of this action.

I returned to Washington at this juncture. On the day of my return, June 12, not knowing of the President's telegram to the Prime Minister, we sent the British Embassy a memorandum which the President had previously approved in which we outlined our arguments against the proposed Anglo-Russian agreement. In particular, we said it would be preferable to give attention to proposals to establish adequate machinery for frank consultation regarding the Balkan region and thus direct the policies of the Allied Governments along lines of collaboration rather than independent action. We added that we attached particular importance to this policy at the present time when special efforts were being made for concerted action in laying the foundations of a broader system of general security in which all countries great and small would have their part. An arrangement suggestive of spheres of influence, we concluded, could not but militate against the establishment and effective functioning of such a broader system.

Still not knowing of the President's telegram of June 12 to the Prime

Minister, I sent him a letter on June 17, in which I pointed out that Mr. Churchill openly applied his proposition to the entire Balkan region by mentioning Bulgaria and Yugoslavia, in addition to Rumania and Greece, and that he advanced our position in South America as an analogy.

"Mr. Churchill's further exposition of the British case," I said, "did not overcome our objections or seem to us to warrant any change in our views toward this dangerous proposal."

I also called attention to what I termed an "extremely disturbing aspect of this matter"—namely, that the British had not discussed a proposal of this nature with us until after it had been put up to the Russians and the latter inquired whether we had been consulted.

The British Foreign Office had suggested that the whole proposal arose out of a chance remark by Eden to Ambassador Gousev, whereas Mr. Churchill's frank telegram of May 31 said plainly that Britain had suggested to the Russian Ambassador that Britain and Russia should agree between themselves as to Rumania and Greece. The Prime Minister's telegram, I said, "indicated that this Government would have been faced with a concluded spheres-of-influence agreement between the British and Russians if the latter had simply agreed without raising the question of our position."

I suggested that the President might want to call this to Mr. Churchill's attention, and accordingly I attached the proposed draft of a message from the President to the Prime Minister.

Our Ambassador to Greece, Lincoln MacVeagh, whose Embassy was at Cairo, cabled us on June 26 that his British colleague had informed him that the American Government had agreed to the proposal, with the provision that it should be subject to review after three months. This cable was the first intimation we had of the President's decision on June 12.

I wrote the President a letter, enclosing a copy of Ambassador Mac-Veagh's telegram, and asking him whether any changes had been made in our position.

The President replied on June 30, simply enclosing paraphrases or extracts of the messages which had been exchanged between himself and Mr. Churchill. These included his message of acceptance of June 12, to which Mr. Churchill had replied two days later expressing his deep gratitude and stating that he had asked Eden to convey the information to Molotov and make clear that the three months' limitation had been agreed to so that there would be no prejudgment of the question of establishing postwar spheres of influence.

Also among the enclosures was the message to Mr. Churchill which we had drafted in the Department and I had sent the President on June 17. He had dispatched this to the Prime Minister on June 22. In it he said that he was a bit worried, and so was the State Department, concerning the Balkans. He said that frankly we were disturbed that the British took the matter up with us only after they had presented it to the Russians and the latter had asked whether we were agreeable to it. He said that in future he hoped matters of this importance could be prevented from developing in this way.

The Prime Minister replied on the following day, June 23, that he could not admit that he had done anything wrong. Three people in different parts of the world, he remarked, could not work together effectively if each had to keep the third informed of any suggestion to either of the others. He cited as an example the President's message about his conversations with Premier Mikolajczyk of Poland, sent to "U. J." without informing Churchill about it.

In Yugoslavia and Greece, the Prime Minister said, he was struggling to bring order out of chaos and concentrating all efforts against the enemy. With regard to those two countries and to Turkey, he stated, he had been keeping the President constantly informed, and he hoped to have the President's confidence and help in the spheres of action in which Britain had been assigned the initiative.

Mr. Roosevelt replied to this on June 26 by saying that it would seem to him that each of them had inadvertently taken independent steps in a direction which they both now agreed was for the time being expedient. He emphasized that it was essential that they should always be in accord on questions bearing on the Allied war effort. He forthwith sent Mr. Churchill a duplicate of the message he had sent Stalin concerning his conversation with Premier Mikolajczyk.

The Soviet Union now made a direct approach to us to learn our views on Greece and Rumania. On July 1 Ambassador Gromyko sent me an *aide-mémoire* in which he outlined the situation to date, beginning with the initial conversation on May 5 between Eden and Ambassador Gousev and the Soviet reply on May 18.

We replied to this on July 15, after the President had approved our draft. We confirmed the fact that this Government had agreed to the arrangement, for a trial period of three months, our assent having been given in consideration of the present war strategy. Except for this overriding consideration, we pointed out, this Government would wish to make known its apprehension lest the proposed agreement might, by the natural tendency of such arrangements, lead to the division in fact of the Balkan region into spheres of influence.

We said it would be unfortunate if any temporary arrangement should be so conceived as to appear to be a departure from the principle adopted by the three Governments at the Moscow Conference definitely rejecting the spheres-of-influence idea. Consequently, this Government hoped that no projected measures would be allowed to prejudice the efforts toward directing the policies of the Allied Governments along lines of collaboration rather than independent action, since any arrangement suggestive of spheres of influence could not but militate against the establishment and effective functioning of a broader system of general security in which all countries would have their part.

We added that we supposed that the three months' trial period would enable the British and Soviet Governments to determine whether such an arrangement was practicable and efficacious as applying to war conditions only, without in any way affecting the rights and responsibilities which each of the three principal Allied nations would have to exercise during the period of the reestablishment of peace, and afterwards, in regard to the whole of Europe.

Finally we assumed that the arrangement would have neither direct nor indirect validity as affecting the interests of this Government, or of other Governments associated with the three principal Allies.

Events fully justified the apprehensions we entertained over this Anglo-Russian arrangement, which duly entered into effect following the President's acquiescence. When Prime Minister Churchill and Foreign Secretary Eden went to Moscow in October, 1944, to see Stalin and Molotov, they extended the arrangement still further, even reducing to percentages the relative degree of influence which Britain and Russia individually should have in specified Balkan countries. Cables from our Embassies in Moscow and Ankara mentioned that Russia would have a 75/25 or 80/20 predominance in Bulgaria, Hungary, and Rumania, while Britain and Russia would share influence in Yugoslavia 50/50. Later the Russians took it for granted that by the agreement of June, 1944, Britain and the United States had assigned them a certain portion of the Balkans including Rumania and Bulgaria, as their sphere of influence. This assumption had its untoward effect at the Yalta Conference in February, 1945.

Had we made such a determined fight against the Anglo-Russian agreement as we had made successfully against the proposed territorial clauses of the Anglo-Russian alliance in May, 1942 (Chapter 85), it is possible that some of our later difficulties in the Balkans might not have arisen.

As autumn, 1944, approached, my associates and I began to wonder whether Marshal Stalin and his Government were commencing to veer away from the policy of cooperation to which they had agreed at the Moscow Conference, and which, with a few exceptions, they had followed since then. We were beginning to get indications that the Russians were about to drive hard bargains in their armistice agreements with Hungary, Bulgaria, and Rumania, which would give them something in the nature of control over those countries. At the same time we had just been forced to take notice of Russia's strong attitude on the voting question in the United Nations Security Council—which will be taken up in Part Eight.

Accordingly I cabled Ambassador Harriman in Moscow on September 18. Mentioning the voting question that had risen at the Dumbarton Oaks Conference, I said that this, along with other recent developments that he had reported, raised most serious doubts with regard to future long-range Soviet policy. I added that I had begun to wonder whether Stalin and the Kremlin had determined to reverse their policy decided upon at Moscow and Tehran and to pursue a contrary course. I therefore asked Harriman's estimate of the present trend of Soviet policy so that we might decide how to meet this possible change in Russian attitude.

I stated to Harriman that I should find particularly helpful his views as to the causes that had brought about this change in Soviet policy toward the United States and hardening of attitude toward Great Britain. I asked whether he felt that Russia's adverse decisions at Dumbarton Oaks could be ascribed to the fact that her two Allies, Britain and the United States, had just met at the Second Quebec Conference, without Russia being present. I concluded by saying that I need not tell him that questions of the highest import to the future peace of the world were involved.

Harriman replied the following day giving a number of instances of Russia's unilateral actions or apparent unwillingness to collaborate with Britain and the United States. He said we had sufficient evidence to foresee that, if a world organization were established requiring agreement of all permanent members for the consideration of any dispute, regardless of whether or not one of them was involved, the Soviet Government would ruthlessly block consideration by the Council of any question that it considered affected its interests. The Soviet Government would also insist that such a matter be settled by the Soviet Union with the other country or countries involved, particularly any disputes with her neighbors.

Harriman stated his conviction that Stalin and his principal advisers placed the highest importance on the association of the Soviet Union in a major way with the three great Powers, but that they expected their political and military strength would enable them to dictate the conditions. There was no doubt, he said, that the Russian people craved peace and had been led to believe that the intimate relationship developed with Britain and the United States during the war would continue after the war and guarantee a lasting peace.

The Ambassador did not believe that Stalin could forgo the material as well as the psychological value of this association without causing grave concern among the Russian people. Nevertheless, there were powerful elements close to Stalin who were unwilling to give up the right of independent action where Russia's interests were affected or to see Russia depend for her security solely on an untried world organization with associates whom they did not fully trust. Stalin, he thought, liked to have two strings to his bow, and it did not appear inconsistent to the Marshal to pursue simultaneously these two methods to obtain security for his country and to promote its national interests as he envisaged them.

In a later telegram, Ambassador Harriman said he did not believe that the Anglo-American meeting at Quebec without Soviet participation had affected the Russian attitude. He said it was difficult to put one's finger on the causes for the change in the Soviet attitude toward the United States and Great Britain. He thought, however, that when the Russians saw victory in sight they began to put into practice the policies they intended to follow in peace.

In general, he said, Stalin and his principal advisers placed the greatest importance and reliance on the newly won relationship with the British and ourselves, and desired above all else to take a leading role in international affairs. But they were fearful of the antagonism of the world against them and were always conscious of the fact that they were a backward country materially and culturally. Hence they were unduly sensitive and suspicious of our motives and actions. Harriman suggested that we should be understanding of their sensitivity, meet them much more than halfway, encourage them and support them wherever we could, and yet oppose them promptly with the greatest of firmness where we saw them going wrong. He said there was no doubt that the overwhelming majority of the Russian people wanted friendship with us, and he felt that the principal men in the Government held the same view.

In October, 1944, we protested, in numerous diplomatic cables to Russia and Britain, over the nature of the armistice terms Russia was arranging with Rumania, Bulgaria (against whom she had just recently declared war), and Hungary. Prime Minister Churchill and Foreign Secretary Eden, who had gone to Moscow, were carrying on negotiations with the Russians concerning these armistices, and we likewise objected to this fact, stating that the armistice terms should be agreed upon through the European Advisory Commission rather than bilaterally between Russia and Britain. We stated our objection to Russia's inclusion of specific reparation sums in the armistice agreements, since we believed that the reparation settlements with all enemy countries should be decided jointly, after discussion and deliberation, by the United States, the United Kingdom, the Soviet Union, and other interested countries rather than unilaterally, and should be treated as parts of one broad problem.

We further expressed our view that the reparations demanded by Russia of Hungary, $400,000,000, were clearly excessive, from the point of view both of Hungarian capacity to pay and of legitimate Russian claims on Hungary. Furthermore, collection by Russia of the amount demanded might make it impossible for other United Nations that had claims against Hungary to obtain reparations.

We likewise stated our objection to the nature and functions of the Allied Control Commissions for the Axis satellites as outlined by the Russians. We felt that the Control Councils should act under instructions of the Soviet High Command only during the military period, which would come to an end with the termination of hostilities against Germany. Between that time and the conclusion of peace with the satellites, we felt that the three Allied Governments should have equal participation in the work of the commissions, and that their representatives should be able to report directly to their respective Governments.

When I left office the question of our future relations with the satellite countries was still under discussion.

In the summer of 1944 we had begun to receive reports that the Soviet authorities were transferring Lend-Lease supplies or similar goods to third countries, particularly Iran, Yugoslavia, Finland, Poland, and Bulgaria. When the American Embassy in Moscow made inquiries, the Vice Commissar for Foreign Trade denied that American equipment or supplies had been transferred by the Red Army to third parties. He admitted that trucks, grains, and other supplies had been turned over to authorities in liberated areas, but explained that such goods generally were of Soviet origin.

We sent the Soviet Government an *aide-mémoire* on July 6 requesting that this Government be consulted prior to transfers of equipment similar to Lend-Lease. The Russians delayed replying to this request, and at the time I left the State Department in November we had not received the assurances we requested.

In many other instances, however, the Soviet Government kept us fully informed of negotiations in which it was engaged. Soviet Ambassador Gromyko paid me a series of visits to hand me the successive notes his Government was sending to the Finnish Government seeking a basis for peace, and also the Finnish replies.

Gromyko came to me on April 13, 1944, to hand me a note informing us that the Japanese Government had approached his Government with an implied offer to bring about peace between Germany and Russia. Gromyko's note stated that his Government had replied in the negative.

In one of his last visits to me, on September 23, 1944, Gromyko brought me a further note along the same line. The Russians informed us that the Japanese Government had proposed to send a special mission to Moscow to discuss Soviet-Japanese relations. The Soviet Government, believing that the mission had as its aim not so much the relations between Japan and the U.S.S.R. as the possibility of concluding a separate peace between Germany and Russia, had rejected the Japanese proposal.

Our diplomatic exchanges with Russia on postwar subjects leading up to the Dumbarton Oaks Conference were friendly, with the exception of our failure to agree on the inclusion of China in the first phase of the conversations. Some differences of opinion—several of them acute—naturally rose between us during that conference, but in general we were seeing eye to eye.

Patience was the keynote of my attitude toward Russia, but it was a patience fortified and surrounded by principles we were determined to uphold, and activated by a constant effort to understand the Russians and induce them to try to understand us. On several occasions during 1944, when I had basic conversations with Soviet Ambassador Gromyko, I sought to clarify this attitude.

When I saw him on March 19, I said I had remarked to Molotov a number of times that our two peoples differed in many ways in their customs, habits, and psychology. "It will take time," I said, "for them to become really acquainted with each other in all these respects to enable them to function more harmoniously in the part each must play in helping carry forward the organized movement of international cooperation."

Small or temporary mistakes, I added, would often be made by both Governments, and by Great Britain. But we should be patient with each other, and in a friendly spirit discuss and work out amicable solutions of these small incidents.

"Soviet Russia," I said, "has been considerably injured by some small occurrences that have been magnified out of all proportion by persons either unfriendly to this Government or unfriendly to Russia, or by some who were precipitant in concluding that a small incident appeared to determine the whole future course of world cooperation."

When Gromyko mentioned Russia's unilateral establishment of diplomatic relations with the Italian Government under Marshal Badoglio, without prior consultation with us and Britain, and said he would send me a statement on this question the following day, I remarked that this was a case illustrating what I had just said. "It is these small matters involving a combustible psychology," I commented, "which enable troublemakers and sinister influences to expand them like balloons and create a surprising amount of coolness toward Russia among people here and in Europe."

I therefore proposed that Russia should reiterate fairly often her interest in the Four-Nation Declaration of the Moscow Conference and in carrying forward her full participation in the movement of international cooperation. This, I concluded, would help to clear the air and protect both the United States and the Russian Governments from excessive criticism over minor matters.

Gromyko said he agreed with this and would communicate it to Molotov.

Ten days later he came back to me and said that Molotov had agreed that this would be a fine and timely thing to do, but had suggested that, instead of Russia making the statement herself, she should join with the United States and Great Britain in a joint statement reiterating their interest in and support of the Four-Nation Declaration.

We took this under advisement. Actions took the place of words in succeeding weeks in that we began preparing for the Dumbarton Oaks Conference to carry out the agreement we had reached in the Four-Nation Declaration to assist in creating an international organization to maintain the peace.

During 1944 I held a number of off-the-record conferences with members of the House and Senate and with groups of editors and clergymen, in which Russia was naturally a prominent subject of comment and questioning. In general, my remarks pursued the following theme, which I give here because it expressed my thoughts as to Russia at the moment I left office:

In the summer of 1943 it became increasingly necessary to ascertain Russia's views on some most important international questions: Would she make a separate peace with Germany? Would she drive the enemy to Russian borders and stop, leaving the Allies to finish the job? What was her attitude toward Japan? Would she cooperate with China? Would she abandon isolationism and cooperate internationally?

On these questions Russia was like a "closed book," "a complete sphinx."

At the beginning of the Moscow Conference Russia was interested only in discussing measures for shortening the war—that is, a second front in the west. But the time had come when the three powerful nations had to indicate what they would do in the future.

Russia held a deciding vote on whether the world would take the road to destruction or the road toward security and human welfare. Although the three most powerful nations might not be able to settle all major international questions if they acted together, no one or two of them, acting alone, could hope to resolve these fundamental problems.

In the end, Russia did put her name to the Four-Nation Declaration.

Some time after the Moscow Conference, difficulties appeared. Russian habits, customs, and manners are as inexplicable to us as ours are to them. It takes time to get acquainted.

We must remember that the Russians were locked up and isolated for a quarter of a century. During that time, whenever they heard somebody on the outside say something about Russia, it was generally a violent epithet. They became very seclusive and more suspicious than usual, and vituperative in return. They got into the habit of slashing back at anybody who attacked them, and sometimes much more savagely than the offense justified. Such sudden, sporadic acts and utterances became part of the Russian custom.

Nevertheless, I believe that the Russians are peacefully inclined people. I believe also that the attitude of the Soviet Government on religion is softening. We must not forget that the Russians have many qualities similar to our own. I believe that in a reasonable time they will work together with other nations in the projected international organization, but that it will take time for them to get into step internationally.

We must not let Russian unilateral action—for example, her recognition of Badoglio without previously consulting Britain and the United States—be magnified out of proportion to its importance. Narrow-minded people may continue to irritate Russia to a point where she will draw back into extreme isolationism and nationalism. Then we should have to arm to the teeth.

We must be patient and forbearing. We cannot settle questions with Russia by threats. We must use friendly methods. We are constantly conferring with the Russians in a friendly way.

When I was a boy I had to handle a number of mules in plowing on my father's farm in Tennessee. One of them could outkick any three mules. When he did I would lay my whip on him. That just gave him fuel, and he would kick all the more. I therefore had to give up and let him cool off. Then I would start quietly moving forward in the plow, whereupon he agreed to work. But whenever he kicked and I fought him with the whip he kicked all the more.

We must ever remember that by the Russians' heroic struggle against the Germans they probably saved the Allies from a negotiated peace with Germany. Such a peace would have humiliated the Allies and would have left the world open to another Thirty Years War.

As I left office, the policy I advocated toward Russia rested on two bases. The first was: Continue in constant, friendly discussion with the Russians. Consult them at every point. Engage in no "cussin' matches" with them. Explain to them, again and again if necessary, the principles upon which we felt peaceful international relations would prosper. Show them as clearly as possible the superior advantages to Russia of whole-hearted cooperation with other nations as compared with the minor advantages of predominance in neighboring states. Make it clear to them that we did not object to a nation's preaching the merits of its form of government, whether Communism or Democracy, but that we did object to a nation's interfering in the internal affairs of other nations.

On many occasions I had made our policy on nonintervention clear to Russian representatives—including Molotov and the four Ambassadors who represented Russia to the United States during my tenure of office—right from the time of our establishment of diplomatic relations in 1933. I had said that if Russia after the war adopted a policy of relying for security on interfering with her neighbors she would not have a friend on earth. I reemphasized again and again the significance of the Four-Nation Declaration, which precluded policies of intervention. This stated specifically that the four nations would not employ their troops in other countries except for the purpose of carrying out the objectives of the Declaration.

I strongly stated to the Russians our policy toward the liberated areas, as I had presented it at the First Quebec Conference. This was that, as our Allied Governments liberated territory from the enemy, we would keep military supervision during the continuance of the war, and we would preach democracy to the people. When it became possible for the people to assume control of their Government we would authorize them to hold an election to choose their own form of government.

I repeatedly made clear to the Russians the nature of our policies in the Pan American field, where we had given up the thought of intervention, and where our little neighbors like Haiti and Salvador enjoyed parity, equality, and security with the larger countries. It was my plan, with regard to the Russians, to stand definitely on this policy of non-interference, and to show them that there was nothing more absurd than the pretension of any nation to a right to prowl about over the world and stick its nose into the affairs of other nations. I hoped, if my health permitted me to remain in office, to persuade Russia to adopt the policy of cooperation and nonintervention that prevailed in the Western Hemisphere, and to make this a solid world policy to which all nations subscribed. Under this Pan American policy transplanted to Europe, Russia could have the friendliest political relations and the liveliest economic exchanges with her neighbors while refraining from interference in their internal affairs.

The second premise of our policy toward Russia was: By our own actions give Russia a concrete example of how we thought she should act. Therefore I opposed the view of our Joint Chiefs of Staff that the Pacific islands we would take from Japan should become United States property. I felt strongly that there should be no exception to my view that all the colonial territories wrested from the Axis should be placed under a United Nations trusteeship system. It was not hard to see that Russia would not oppose our outright acquisition of these islands, but it also was not hard to see that Russia would thereupon use this acquisition as an example and precedent for similar acquisitions by herself. Our acquisition of these islands estopped us from objecting to similar acquisitions by other nations.

Therefore I likewise opposed the project later put through in the Act of Chapultepec at the Mexico City Conference in March, 1945, after my resignation, whereby the American Republics agreed in effect to intervene militarily in any one of them in certain circumstances. Once we had agreed to this new position on intervention, Russia had more excuse to intervene in neighboring states, and we had less reason to oppose her doing so.

President Roosevelt and I saw alike with regard to Russia. We both realized that the path of our relations would not be a carpet of flowers, but we also felt we could work with Russia. There was no difference of opinion between us that I can recall on the basic premise that we must and could get along with the Soviet Government.

The President did not confer with me regarding any phase of his Yalta Conference with Stalin and Churchill, nor did I know of the concessions made there to Russia until they were published. Yalta was the only international conference attended by Mr. Roosevelt when I was not in office. My views relating to the questions arising among the major nations were fully set forth in the State Department record of conferences and conversations. As I left office I was still opposed to any change in the vote to be given Russia, any more than the vote for our own country. My view was that each major country possessed such powerful prestige and influence generally that it would have little difficulty in securing a full representation of its rights and interests at all times, without any need to have more than one vote.

On the occasions when the President came to see me at the hospital after my resignation, including his last visit only a few days before his death, he said nothing about any fears he might have that Russia would abandon our cooperative movement for peace or would block or destroy it.

It might be said that the President and I were taken in by Russia's promises and written pledges, that we should have realized it was impossible to do business with Soviet Russia, that we should have come to the conclusion that the democratic United States could not be friendly with a Government founded on Communism, and consequently that we should have adopted the policy of the mailed fist toward Russia right from the beginning.

But as we went back over our relations with Moscow I felt, and President Roosevelt did too, that there was ample reason for the policy of friendship that we adopted. Since 1917 Russia had been wrestling with many nations that had refused to recognize her, more or less on account of her policy of conducting subversive activities from Moscow. By constant effort, she had gradually increased the number of recognitions—being obliged in connection with virtually all acts of recognition to agree not to practice subversive activities against the countries establishing relations wth her.

That she did not abandon these activities completely is a matter of record; but it was our view that the other governments, by steadily organizing and building up and strengthening world opinion against such activities, would make as nearly certain as possible Russia's abandonment of interference in the affairs of other countries. It is of record that the President and I had been hammer and tongs at the Russian Government many times during the years from the recognition in 1933 until we approached the Moscow Conference in 1943. I never lost an occasion to point out to the Russians the advantage to themselves of abandoning their thorny policy of intervention.

Before I went to Moscow I naturally looked backward and scrutinized to the utmost possible extent the Soviets' course, attitude, and utterances, together with their implications. This survey of the preceding years revealed Russia as having sought and secured admission to the League of Nations, and as having established herself as a reasonable and working factor at Geneva in promoting peace and suitable international relations for an improved state of affairs among the different peoples and nations of the world. There also stood out the fact that the Soviet Government and other leading governments raised no question about the inability of nations with basic differences in their forms of government to function in the League. All other governments proceeded to function along with a Russia that was apparently making conspicuous peace efforts during the years from her admission to the League in 1934 until her expulsion in 1939 following her invasion of Finland.

It was in the light of these facts and conditions that I proceeded in my conversations with the Russians to revive talk of a postwar peace organization. It seemed to me that, if Soviet Russia could function in the League of Nations, she could also function in the new international security organization which we hoped to create. But even as I sought to bring Russia into that organization, I made every effort to keep the situation entirely clear by pointing out to the Russians that international cooperation would necessitate the abandonment of interference in the internal affairs of other nations. The Russians, in turn, gave me their solemn assurances that they had abandoned this practice.

During the later years prior to the Moscow Conference in 1943 I began to emphasize my belief that, on account of the great difference in customs and habits and the entire lack of understanding between countries like my own and Russia, much time, patience, and education would be required for developing the trust and friendliness necessary to make effective a world organization, which would be based especially on the more powerful nations such as the United States, Russia, Great Britain, and China. When I returned from Moscow I continued to keep the American people reminded of the absolute necessity for such patience, education, and understanding.

When it was agreed among the four big nations to call a conference at Dumbarton Oaks, the favorable and cooperative attitude of each of them, including Russia, was encouraging. It was not until the meeting at Dumbarton Oaks, when the deadlock rose between us and the Russians over the voting procedure in the council and when the Russians confidentially made known to us that they desired sixteen votes in the organization, representing as many Soviet Republics, that any question developed in the minds of the President and myself about Russia's failing to go forward as a cooperative and working member of the proposed United Nations organization. Nevertheless, Russia had agreed on virtually all other important points with us, and it should be made clear that our difference was not over the veto as such, to which the United States was as much committed as Russia, but over the question whether a member of the Security Council concerned with a dispute should be permitted to vote in a balloting on the dispute.

My associates and I further reminded the American people, along with the representatives of other countries, that our own Constitution and the other great documents of liberty or those relating to more effective cooperation among nations had always been more or less imperfect or inadequate at the beginning. We were convinced that we had prepared the first draft of the postwar peace organization on a basis as broad and comprehensive as we could possibly prevail on all the nations to subscribe to. We depended on additions, amendments, and further developments, as time went on, to perfect it.

The President and I were convinced that it was eminently to the self-interest of Russia to be a full-fledged member of the United Nations security organization and to cooperate wholeheartedly with it, and that the Russian leaders would recognize this fact. We believed, as I believe today, that the United Nations would ultimately evolve into a unified, effective organization thoroughly adequate to maintain the peace. We recognized that there would be difficulties, that some of these would come from Russia, and that the United Nations would have to pass through uncertain, delicate periods; but we were certain by the end of 1944 that we and the nations working with us had laid the basis for a projected organization within which Russia and the United States could work together.

In our relations with Russia, the President and I also had constantly before us the emphatic advice of our military leaders, given on several occasions, that friendship with Russia after the war was vitally essential from their military point of view. On one occasion, May 16, 1944, the Joint Chiefs of Staff sent me a memorandum, replying to my request for their views on British informal proposals for the disposition of Italian overseas territory, in which they pointed out that such proposals might lead to conflict between Britain and Russia. They then said: "From the point of view of national and world-wide security, our basic national policy in postwar settlements of this kind should seek to maintain the solidarity of the three great powers and in all other respects to establish conditions calculated to assure a long period of peace, during which, it may be hoped, arrangements will be perfected for the prevention of future world conflicts. The cardinal importance of this national policy is emphasized by a consideration of fundamental and revolutionary changes in relative national military strengths that are being brought about in Europe as a result of the war."

During the Dumbarton Oaks Conference our military advisers held strongly to the same view, and were willing to go farther than many of the political advisers in agreeing to Russia's position that the veto should be applied without exception.

When I left office in November, 1944, we had had a promise from Stalin that Russia would enter the war against Japan as soon as the war against Germany ended. We had given him no promises of territory and made him no concessions in return. We had agreed to no Russian acquisition of territory by reason of the war. We had unfortunately agreed, through the President and over the opposition of the State Department, to a temporary delineation of military spheres of influence in the Balkans between Russia and Britain, proposed by the latter. We had induced Russia to cooperate in the future development and administration of the world security organization. We had rejected the Russians' claim, made at Dumbarton Oaks, to more than one vote in that organization. The Soviet Government had dissolved the Communist International encharged with the promotion of Communism in other countries.

As 1944 approached its close, it was easily apparent that many difficulties would inevitably rise between Russia and ourselves in the future. But it was also apparent that, with good will and understanding on both sides, and with the support of other nations, these difficulties could be solved and an era of fruitful working together come to pass.

107: Working with Britain

AS I COME TO WRITE a final chapter on our relations with Britain during my tenure as Secretary of State, and as I look back over those relations, I am struck by the fact that there was scarcely any point of our contact with the outside world at which we were not talking and working along with the British. Whether we were dealing with Spain or Russia, the Far East, the Middle East, or Latin America, Britain almost always entered into the ken of our negotiations and conclusions.

This was true before the outbreak of war in Europe; it intensified after the historic date of September 1, 1939; and it rose to its climax after Pearl Harbor.

I have devoted fewer chapters to our direct relations with Britain than to our relations with several other countries for the simple reason that Britain appears prominently in all those chapters. We were in constant discussion with the British, but the major portion of our discussions related to other countries.

From Pearl Harbor until my resignation, our policy toward Britain embraced three objectives. First, to arrive at the maximum cooperation in the prosecution of the war. Second, to work closely with the United Kingdom, the Soviet Union, China, and other countries toward creating institutions to deal with problems arising from the war and problems that would face us after the war. Third, to solve specific Anglo-American postwar problems by direct negotiation before the end of hostilities.

On the military side, the efforts of the two countries were integrated to a degree probably never previously reached by any two great allies in history. This was owing in large measure to the operation of the Combined Chiefs of Staff, the unified commands, and the combined boards for the allocation and distribution of munitions, certain strategic materials, and shipping. It was also owing to the close personal relations and frequent, friendly contact between President Roosevelt and Prime Minister Churchill. There were at times basic differences of opinion, as, for example, the President's desire to invade northern France and Churchill's to invade the Balkans; but they were ironed out with good will.

On the diplomatic side, it is probably true that never before in history have two great powers tried to coordinate so closely their policies toward all other countries. In this effort toward a virtual unification of

our foreign policies, so as to present a common front to encourage our
Allies and dishearten the enemy, it was inevitable that we should have
to solve problems of unprecedented magnitude. We did not always succeed to the degree we both should have liked, but it is a fact that we
reconciled to an astonishing extent our diverging interests, some of which
were based on geographic and national grounds.

Relations with Britain during the war period meant, to a considerable
degree, relations with Winston Churchill. In my opinion Mr. Churchill,
while a strong Conservative or Tory, showed great vision and sound states-
manship on many critical occasions. I had heard him crying out for arm
ments almost alone while Hitler was strenuously rearming Germany. I had
heard him inveigh against isolation after the disarmament movement
failed in the years 1934 and 1935. He had been in the forefront of every
movement to warn and arouse the people of Great Britain to the dangers
ahead from Germany.

After the war came and after he became Prime Minister, he promptly
went forward with every kind of leadership called for. When the supreme
crisis arrived during the Dunkirk period, involving life or death to Britain,
Churchill's was the one single voice that could be heard above the din
at home and abroad, instilling into every man, woman, and child in Britain a determination to resist German invasion to the last breath.

After Pearl Harbor I naturally saw Mr. Churchill many times in
connection with developments of joint or individual interest to our respective countries. He seemed to me to be one of the most approachable
of men, entirely agreeable in conversation even when we were discussing
points at acute issue between us. He could use the harshest language, but
in a tone and manner that disarmed any umbrage that might otherwise
be taken.

In a large sense he was the modern British Tory at his best. Nevertheless, in reviewing modern British statesmen, I found myself in the
opposite camp embracing the views of the Gladstone Liberals.

Numerous important points of difference rose between us—Mr.
Churchill on the one hand and the President and me on the other; for in
all these clashes of ideas with the Prime Minister, except the question
of spheres of influence in the Balkans, the President and I thought alike.
We differed with the Prime Minister over De Gaulle and the future of
France; over the extent of pressure to be brought upon European neutrals
to prevent their assisting Germany; over Italy and the Italian King; over

the treatment of dependent peoples; over India; and over the continuance of imperial tariff preferences.

The President and I considered social welfare to be a general policy. Wherever a situation presented itself for practicing sane and practical liberalism in our foreign relations we sought to apply it as conditions called for it. Mr. Churchill's conservatism, on the other hand, seemed to constitute a sort of cleavage between us.

I was in constant contact with Mr. Churchill's thought by reason of the fact that the President was, in general, accustomed to sending me the telegrams and messages he received from the Prime Minister on subjects involving foreign relations rather than military affairs. He asked me to prepare and recommend to him suitable replies, or to reply direct for him. This he did at almost all times in the case of messages to him from the chiefs of other governments as well, or when he wished to originate a message to a foreign statesman.

With Foreign Secretary Eden my relations were in general most satisfactory. He possessed an agreeable personality and a high order of intelligence. He was always on the alert when any matter pertaining to Great Britain or peace was involved. In a few instances, as in the case of De Gaulle, we had more opposition from him than from Mr. Churchill; but we could usually count on his understanding, and at the Moscow Conference I found him thoroughly cooperative and broad-minded. I considered Eden a person of unusual promise in the political field, barring the changes of fortune implicit in politics.

In all the differences with Britain our policy was based primarily on our desire that the war should be prosecuted in the most effective way possible, that the peoples of the countries occupied by Germany should have the full right, when liberated, freely to choose their own form of government and their leaders, and that the future peace should not be endangered by the development of rival spheres of influence in Europe.

Britain's policy, while motivated to a great degree by these same considerations, also took into account her greater preoccupation with her future political and commercial relations with the western European countries, her strategic and political position in the Mediterranean, and her wish to restore her prestige and reduced power relative to the Soviet Union and the United States.

Despite these diverging viewpoints, we were nevertheless able to achieve substantial coordination.

We differed with Britain over policy toward Argentina during my last two years in the State Department. Britain's dependence on Argentine meat and her desire to maintain her influence and commercial ties with Argentina made her reluctant to recognize as fully as we thought necessary the prime interest we and the other American Republics had in preventing the growth of Nazi ideology and methods in this hemisphere. Even in this sphere, however, Britain went along with us to a degree, though not nearly so far as the President and I felt the situation called for.

In another area of the Western Hemisphere, the Caribbean, we achieved a high and fruitful degree of cooperation with the British through the Anglo-American Caribbean Commission of which Charles W. Taussig was the United States co-chairman.

In the Far East Britain cooperated with us militarily to the full extent that she could spare her forces from the battle for Europe; and in that area we received wholehearted and valuable assistance from her Dominions, Australia and New Zealand. The British Government permitted us to occupy needed bases in British islands such as the Fijis. Prior to the outbreak of the European War, when transoceanic aviation increased the importance of Pacific islands, we asserted our claim to a number of such islands, and Britain vigorously contested some of these claims. We continued to press our position until the fall of France, but we then, at Britain's request, set the entire subject aside without prejudice until after the war, while agreeing with Britain on the joint use of some of the islands.

We declined to permit American Civil Affairs officers to serve under Lord Mountbatten in the Southeast Asia Command, because we wished to dissociate ourselves from British colonial policy as much as we could.

With regard to China, we were more determined than Britain in striving to treat that country as a great nation, bring her into the councils and agreements of the big three Western nations, and persuade Russia to adopt the same policy; but at moments of decision the British gave us valuable support.

In the Near East, to which the British for many generations have paid special attention, we had excellent cooperation with Great Britain on questions directly related to the war. Nevertheless, we had to take account of a somewhat contradictory attitude on the part of Britain in that she did not wish us to seek a predominant postwar position in any part of that area, while, on the other hand, she did not want us to lose interest there entirely.

We received the closest possible cooperation from Britain in working out the bases for international institutions to handle problems arising out of the war and the peace, including the United Nations organization. We at the State Department were careful, however, to work with the Governments of the United Kingdom, the Soviet Union, and China rather than separately with any one of them. All the ideas we developed and all the moves we took with regard to the United Nations were meticulously coordinated with these three Governments, rather than with the British alone. This was my approach during the preparations for the Moscow Conference and at the conference itself, and similarly in preparations for the Dumbarton Oaks Conference and at the conference itself.

In addition to these general discussions for postwar institutions, scarcely a week passed during my last years in office that we were not talking with the British toward laying a broad basis for continuing sound and friendly Anglo-American relations after the war. We engaged in technical conversations on such subjects as petroleum, double taxation, rubber, and commercial policy. The operation of the Lend-Lease policy, which Winston Churchill called "the most unsordid act in history," even though it too had its difficulties, brought our economic relations with Britain as close as they had ever been in our history.

But commercial policy was one of our most delicate meeting grounds with the British. After long negotiation we had induced the British to sign the Lend-Lease Agreement of 1942, of which Article VII pledged them in effect to give up preferential arrangements in the British Empire after the end of the war. Thereafter, however, it frequently became apparent to me that Prime Minister Churchill, despite this pledge, was determined to hold on to imperial preference.

I brought this subject up with Ambassador Halifax on May 4, 1944, when I complimented him on a speech he had recently made. "As I view it," I said, "your speech was quite in contrast with recent utterances of Mr. Churchill which give the impression that he favors the preservation intact of Empire preferences, while at the same time preaching closer relations among the three large Western nations and advocating a tightening up of the British Commonwealth. All of this, taken together, has discouraged many people in this country and many small nations which are growing more fearful that the three large nations in the West will come closer and closer together and practice the worst forms of imperialism, while neglecting the small nations."

I added that I was merely stating a situation which it seemed to me Mr. Churchill was overlooking. I repeated what we had done to keep alive our formula relating to future international commercial policy and economic cooperation and added that, unless we could have more cooperation now from the British, the future would become dangerous. I said that the President and I had made a fight in this country for more liberal commercial policy against overwhelming odds and that if we had faltered, as Mr. Churchill seemed to be faltering, we should have gotten exactly nowhere.

Richard Law, British Parliamentary Under Secretary of State for Foreign Affairs, came to me on July 20, 1944, to make a special request that further discussions of commercial policy based on Article VII of our Lend-Lease Agreement of 1942 be postponed until the autumn because of British economic difficulties and preoccupation with the war.

I said I could appreciate the situation of his Government and country, but I stressed the indispensable necessity for a broader and more liberal commercial policy after the war if we were to increase and broaden production and consumption. I emphasized that this course would require Herculean efforts such as Britain had put forth during the years following the British-French commercial treaty in the 1860's.

"Unless the business people in our two countries," I said, "recognize that we have to turn over a new page in economic affairs and go forward as resolutely as Britain did at that time, there will simply be no foundation for any stable peace structure in the future. On the contrary, there will be the inevitable seeds of future wars in the form of vast unemployment and hunger throughout the world."

I added that if we postponed such a tremendous undertaking, many of its supporters would take entirely too much for granted and would become inactive—which would be fatal. I suggested that Britain should now start a real revival and awakening in support of the long-view program of liberal commercial policy. The British Government and the majority of the British people, I said, might be submerged by high-pressure selfish or prejudiced minorities unless that Government organized and fought for such a program as we had fought for here through the trade agreements to make the first serious inroads on international economic isolation.

We had definite ideas with respect to the future of the British colonial empire, on which we differed with the British. It might be said that the future of that Empire was no business of ours; but we felt that unless dependent peoples were assisted toward ultimate self-government and were given it when, as we said, they were "worthy of it and ready for it," they would provide kernels of conflict.

Both the United States and Great Britain became committed, in the course of our conversations, to the progressive development of dependent peoples toward self-government, including their political, economic, social, and educational advancement. We both recognized, moreover, that other countries than the parent or administering country might have political, economic, or strategic interests in certain dependent areas, and that the economic development of such areas should be in the interests of the world as a whole.

The American Government advocated the eventual self-government of all colonial peoples. Both the President and I repeatedly said we considered the Atlantic Charter applicable to all such peoples throughout the world. The British Government, on the other hand, made it clear that self-government in British colonial areas should be achieved within the British Commonwealth. Prime Minister Churchill repeatedly maintained that Point Three of the Atlantic Charter (the right of self-determination) applied only to the occupied countries of Europe.

In my conversation with Richard Law on July 20 I remarked—in no spirit of criticism but in illustration of what I thought was a drifting policy in Great Britain—that for some time we had seen the two opposite extremes of thought in Britain badgering each other about dependent peoples. The leftists would go their own distance and take charge of colonies and supervise the treatment of their populations by the parent governments. On the other hand, Prime Minister Churchill merely stood on the policy that the British Empire, including India, would not be dismembered while he was in office.

"If all nations having special relations with backward peoples," I said, "would proceed simultaneously with an awakening and a general forward movement to give them more opportunities, more facilities, more encouragement, and any other feasible material cooperation to help all dependent peoples make greatly increased efforts to improve their levels of existence, this would be a wonderful thing in the end for all. It would increase production, employment, and purchasing power for surplus-producing countries. The United States' policy toward the Philippines is a case in point."

I concluded by saying it would be very hazardous to wait until the war was over, when political chaos set in and emotions got out of control, to undertake this great task and that of establishing liberal economic relationships.

In summation, our policy toward the United Kingdom had this primary objective, to work out the closest possible coordination of the material and political strength of the two countries so as to secure and maintain a just and lasting peace. Militarily, this meant the integration of strategy, forces, and resources. Economically, it meant the joint stimulation of the maximum flow of international trade, transportation, and communications. Politically, it meant the maintenance of friendly relations between us and also the coordination, wherever possible, of our policies toward all other countries.

As I have pointed out throughout these memoirs, we had numerous problems and difficulties with the British in my nearly twelve years as Secretary of State. But, had we not approached each other in the spirit of friendship sustained at a high level during all those years, our differences would have magnified in number and size. Napoleon said, in effect, "Give me a coalition to fight," because he knew how fragile such temporary alliances had proven. But the coalition of which the United States and Great Britain were a part proved it could not only stick together for the duration of a victorious war but also plan for the future.

In my efforts toward this end I was fully aided by the spirit of understanding and friendship unfailingly demonstrated by British Foreign Secretary Anthony Eden and by British Ambassadors Lothian and Halifax as well as by the efforts of Ambassador Winant in London. Both countries, too, were immeasurably aided by the British Dominions, in particular Canada, who had a fundamental interest in seeing that the two major English-speaking nations moved forward in the same way toward the same goal.

Throughout my twelve years at the State Department no sector of our foreign policy gave me more satisfaction or brought more fruitful results than our relations with Canada. In 1933 cooperation between the two countries had sagged to a low point; the depression, the Smoot-Hawley Tariff Act, and the Ottawa agreements had slashed their trade; and there was no adequate expression of the natural identity of the two countries, especially in the strategic and economic spheres. As I left office, we had built a solid economic relationship through two trade agreements and a truly wonderful industrial cooperation during the war; we had assured the strategic interdependence of the two countries through the establishment of the Permanent Joint Board of Defense; and our relations in general had increased in extent and importance. They offered to the world the highest example of nations, bordering on each other and cherishing the same free institutions, working together for their mutual advantage.

The masterly leadership and sincere friendship of Canada's true statesman, Prime Minister Mackenzie King, contributed enormously to revitalizing the relations between the two countries. Canada is one of the few countries that have practiced in a model way the rules governing the right living together of nations.

As I left office Canada flourished as an independent entity, fourth in industrial and military power among the United Nations, enjoying representation on an equal basis with the United States and the United Kingdom on certain of the key war boards and international agencies. We willingly agreed to the "functional policy" stated by Prime Minister Mackenzie King providing that small nations should be represented along with the great powers in those fields in which they could make a major contribution. In November, 1943, we recognized Canada's heightened stature by increasing the rank of our representative Ray Atherton from Minister to Ambassador, while thoroughly capable Minister Leighton McCarthy became Canada's Ambassador to the United States.

Before I left office we had already begun to take up problems of postwar reconversion, such as the orderly disposition of defense projects in Canada, and the removal of wartime barriers such as our visa requirements for Canadian visitors, Canadian labor exit and foreign exchange controls, and Canadian and American export and import controls. We appreciated the fact that the unique relationship between the two countries stemmed largely from the traditional free movement of people and ideas across our border, and therefore that the wartime restrictions should not continue into the peace.

Throughout, we had been careful to recognize Canada as a completely sovereign and independent nation, while at the same time taking no position that would affect her special ties with the United Kingdom and the other British Dominions. The question of Canada's becoming a member of the Pan American movement of cooperation was not much discussed or specially urged either by Canada or by the United States, both having in mind the fact that, although Canada is free to make her own decisions, she gets in and fights alongside the British when the United Kingdom becomes involved in war. This did not prevent virtually the same close-in relations and cooperation to every practical extent in the Western Hemisphere as would have occurred had Canada been a member of the Pan American system. Further steps should and doubtless will be taken to extend and strengthen these thoroughgoing cooperative relations.

108: Independence for India

WHEN JAPAN STRUCK at Pearl Harbor, the importance of India in the pattern of the war suddenly increased many times. The Japanese soon overran Burma and stood at the borders of the subcontinent. Tension between the Indians and Britain, and tension among the religions and factions in India, offered Japan an opportunity if she were able to use it. India was on the highroad to what I considered the most fateful possibility of the war—a juncture of German and Japanese forces in the Indian Ocean, severing the United Kingdom from the Middle East and the Pacific Dominions. That great peninsula, with a population of 400,000,000, was a source of materials essential to our own defense and our aid to Britain. Working wholeheartedly with the British, it could be of immense assistance in Britain's defense. Working against the British, it could be a frightful danger.

The President and I, both before and after Pearl Harbor, were convinced that the Indians would cooperate better with the British if they were assured of independence, at least after the war. We at the State Department were already working on our proposal for positive steps to raise dependent peoples to political and economic levels where they could begin to govern themselves, after the manner of our policy toward the Philippines. The people of India were among those we had in mind.

Nevertheless, we recognized that any change in India's constitutional status could be brought about only if Great Britain were in agreement, and we realized full well that, with Britain fighting for her life, we should take no step and utter no words that would impede her struggle. We also knew that the British Government, and Prime Minister Churchill in particular, considered India their own problem, and that an attempt by the United States to bring pressure to solve it might give rise to controversy between our two Governments and peoples. It was therefore a delicate question how far we could go in any representations to the British to grant independence, or in any actions that might encourage the Indians to demand it immediately.

At the same time there was a danger that doing nothing would have unfavorable repercussions both on the general war effort and on ourselves. After Pearl Harbor we felt that failure to solve the Indian problem would hamper military operations in the Far East and might later constitute a threat to peace when the war was over. And we also felt that our own position among the Asiatic peoples would be adversely affected by a belief on their part that we were helping Great Britain maintain her imperial policy in the Orient.

With these two viewpoints in mind, we had to keep our discussions with Britain on the subject of Indian independence on as informal a basis as possible. In publicly stating our conviction that subject peoples should be assisted toward self-government and eventual independence, we kept our statements general, without making specific reference to India. But in private conversations the President talked very bluntly about India with Prime Minister Churchill just as I was talking with British Ambassador Halifax. The President was entirely of the same mind as myself. While for the sake of good relations with Britain we could not tell the country what we were saying privately, we were saying everything that the most enthusiastic supporter of India's freedom could have expected, and we were convinced that the American people were with us.

Even before Pearl Harbor we had begun to see the need for more direct ties with India. Following a proposal delivered to me by Halifax on April 18, 1941, that an Indian official with the rank of Minister be attached to the British Embassy, we reached an agreement that a quasi-diplomatic American Mission should be established in New Delhi, and an Indian Agency General in Washington. Previously we had been represented in India by consuls rather than by diplomatic officers. The American mission was set up in October. Halifax presented to me the first Indian Agent General, Sir Girja Shankar Bajpai, on November 25, a fortnight before Pearl Harbor.

In 1941 we held discussions for a treaty of commerce and navigation with the Government of India. Early in 1942, however, the British indicated that they preferred that discussions on the treaty be suspended until after the war; and we accordingly left it in abeyance.

As early as the spring of 1941 I raised the question of Indian independence with Ambassador Halifax, when I saw him on May 7. I simply asked, in a general way, whether the British found it feasible to consider further acts of liberalizing the relations of the United Kingdom to India. Nothing came of this approach.

Ambassador Winant advocated in a cable of August 1 that our Government suggest to the British that they reach an agreement on Dominion status for India. Assistant Secretary Berle and Wallace Murray, Chief of the Near Eastern Division, supported this recommendation, but Under

Secretary Welles, in a memorandum to me on August 6, took the position that our Government was not warranted in suggesting officially to the British Government what the status of India should be, and that, if the President wished to raise the question, he could discuss it in a very personal, confidential way directly with Prime Minister Churchill. I agreed with Welles's view.

A few days later the President and the Prime Minister held their historic meeting on the Atlantic and agreed to the Atlantic Charter, Article 3 of which said: "Third, they respect the right of all peoples to choose the form of government under which they will live; and they wish to see sovereign rights and self-government restored to those who have been forcibly deprived of them."

Mr. Churchill, however, in an address to the House of Commons on September 9, specifically excluded India and Burma from the application of the Atlantic Charter. He said that Article 3 applied only to European nations under Nazi occupation and had no effect on British policy as previously enunciated relative to the development of constitutional government in India, Burma, and other parts of the Empire.

Ambassador Winant had tried to persuade the Prime Minister to eliminate this passage from his speech—without success. Mr. Churchill took the position that this was a question of internal British policy, and that the passage had the support of the Cabinet.

Although neither the President nor I and my associates accepted this interpretation, we had no desire to engage in an altercation with the British. Nevertheless then and in succeeding years we took appropriate occasions to state to the public and to the British Government our position that the Atlantic Charter applied to all peoples alike seeking independence in every part of the world.

In my radio address of July 23, 1942, I had India in mind, among other peoples, when I said:

"We have always believed—and we believe today—that all peoples, without distinction of race, color, or religion, who are prepared and willing to accept the responsibilities of liberty, are entitled to its enjoyment. We have always sought—and we seek today—to encourage and aid all who aspire to freedom to establish their right to it by preparing themselves to assume its obligations. We have striven to meet squarely our own responsibility in this respect—in Cuba, in the Philippines, and wherever else it has devolved upon us. It has been our purpose in the past—and will remain our purpose in the future—to use the full measure of our influence to support attainment of freedom by all peoples who, by their acts, show themselves worthy of it and ready for it."

On August 8, 1942, in connection with an Office of War Information suggestion for an exchange of messages between the President and the Prime Minister on the anniversary of the signing of the Atlantic Charter, British Minister Sir Ronald Campbell wrote me saying that Foreign Secretary Eden hoped that any such messages, if they were to deal with the interpretation of the Charter, would be carefully concerted, and that any reference to India or Burma in the messages or in any public statements by this Government would be consistent with the Prime Minister's statement of September 9, 1941.

While the anniversary message sent by the President to the Prime Minister on August 14, 1942, and published, did not go into the question of interpretation of the Charter, I discussed this point-blank with Ambassador Halifax on August 24. I said to him that, according to my idea of the Charter's proper construction and practical application, it should be universally applied to all nations and peoples—to all peoples, whatsoever their condition, and whatsoever shade of independence and freedom they might aspire to.

Halifax replied that some high officials of his Government were in the act of preparing an interpretation and application of the Atlantic Charter as it would relate to the British Empire.

I commented that, while it was not my business except in a general sense, in my judgment the application of the Charter should be made universal, and the British Empire would probably run into constant difficulties if it should seek to have the Atlantic Charter applied in separate compartments, so to speak.

Some of the hesitation we had in taking up with the British the subject of independence for India vanished after the Japanese attacked at Pearl Harbor and began to overrun the Far East. Prior to that time India could be considered a purely British object of concern. From then on India became an object of concern to us as well, from the viewpoint of winning the war. We were rendered more uneasy by the fact that the political situation in India seemed to be deteriorating.

President Roosevelt discussed India with Prime Minister Churchill during his visit to Washington in December, 1941, but no conclusions were arrived at. The President sent Ambassador Winant in London a telegram on February 25, 1942, saying that the situation in India gave him some concern, particularly in view of the possible necessity of retiring slowly from Burma to India. He said he gathered that the people of India would not give sufficiently enthusiastic support to the British defense. He therefore requested the Ambassador—or W. Averell Harriman, who was then in London on an official mission—to give him a "slant" on what Prime Minister Churchill thought relative to new Anglo-Indian relationships. The President concluded that he was hesitant to send the Prime Minister a direct message because it was not, strictly, our business; but, from the viewpoint of the conduct of the war, it was nevertheless of great interest to us.

Harriman replied on the following day that the Prime Minister told him the picture with regard to India was not yet definite, and that the Prime Minister intended to cable the President himself within a few days. A fortnight later Mr. Churchill announced the mission of Sir Stafford Cripps to India to lay before Indian leaders proposals of the Cabinet looking toward the eventual attainment of self-government. During Cripps's stay in India the President made every possible effort to prevent the negotiations from failing. I thought the British proposals were a far-reaching step in the right direction, but the Indian leaders turned them down. Mr. Roosevelt still sought to keep matters from reaching an open break by persuading Mr. Churchill to delay Cripps's return to Britain; but without success. Colonel Louis Johnson, formerly Assistant Secretary of War, whom the President had appointed his personal representative to India, had arrived in New Delhi during the stay of the Cripps mission, and he also had made earnest efforts to facilitate a satisfactory settlement.

The situation in India worsened instead of improving, and on June 3, 1942, I asked Ambassador Halifax to come to see me and discuss it. I said we had received disquieting news from India that explosive conditions might make their appearance during coming weeks and months. Halifax asked whether, in my opinion, an impartial commission should be sent to India to investigate and report. I said I was not sufficiently informed to discuss this definitely.

To Indian Agent General Bajpai, who came to see me on June 15, I said that Mahatma Gandhi to all intents and purposes was playing into the hands of the Japanese by preaching nonresistance, and that no practical steps of resistance were being advocated by the other leaders, including Nehru. When the Agent General replied that Gandhi's influence was strong only when he went to certain cities and called upon the people to adopt his nonresistance policy, I commented that Gandhi could go within a short time to many populous areas and get deadly results by his preaching.

Ambassador Halifax called again on June 18 to give me the substance of a telegram from the British Secretary of State for India, Leopold S. Amery. This suggested that Halifax might think it desirable to let me, or also the President, know that the British Government would be forced to take "drastic measures" against Mahatma Gandhi and the Indian Congress Party if the civil disobedience movement were launched which Gandhi was apparently contemplating to hasten Britain's withdrawal from India.

I asked Halifax whether he had any further thoughts on the impartial commission he had suggested at our previous meeting. He said Amery's opinion was that a mission of one or more persons sent by an American university to India to investigate and report on India's constitutional future, with suggestions as to a solution, might be beneficial in an educational way to America and might also have some advantageous effect on the Indian situation. He himself, however, did not think such a mission could have any effect on the immediate situation in India.

Chiang Kai-shek had cabled the President, asking our help in an effort to solve the Indian problem. My associates and I assisted in preparing the President's reply, which was given to the Chinese Ambassador on August 13:

"I think," said Mr. Roosevelt, "your position and mine should be to make it clear to the British Government and to Mr. Gandhi and his followers that we have not the moral right to force ourselves upon the British or the Congress Party; but that we should make it clear to both sides that you and I stand in the position of friends who will gladly help if we are called on by both sides.

"At the same time I think we should intimate to both sides that because both of them and China and the United States and all the other United Nations are in a struggle for existence, the assistance of India is vital to the common cause, including the cause of the people of India themselves."

The President remarked that he had delivered the same opinion at a meeting of the Pacific War Council the day before. He cited the thirteen American colonies in 1775 as an example for India, saying: "Each Colony was a separate sovereignty. They set up differing republican forms of government. They had a loose Confederation, but when their independence was acknowledged in 1783 they realized they must have a breathing spell

before they could set up a permanent constitutional form of federal government. They, therefore, went through a six-year period of trial and
error and discussion. Finally, they adopted a Federal Constitution which
is in existence today—one hundred and fifty-three years later."

British Minister Sir Ronald Campbell gave me on August 8 a copy
of a message to the President from Clement Attlee, in Mr. Churchill's
absence, stating the British Government's intention to arrest Gandhi and
certain other Indian leaders if the program for civil disobedience went
into effect. This would be done to render the movement abortive by removing and detaining its leaders and to prevent widespread demonstrations and disorders. Mr. Attlee expressed the confidence of his Government that the President would agree that there was no other course open
to them either from the viewpoint of the war effort or from that of orderly
political advance in India itself.

I inquired of the Minister with some emphasis whether his Government had prepared a succinct statement showing the essential conditions
and preparations necessary to enable India to set up the complete structure of an independent Government if independence should be granted at
once. This might also show equally clearly the difficulties the Indians
would experience in an attempt immediately to establish and carry into
successful operation an entirely independent government—if not the impossibility of their doing so.

Sir Ronald seemed very much interested in the point I had raised
interrogatively, especially in its psychological aspect in both the Empire
and in other parts of the world.

The President on August 13 sent me the Attlee message along with
a short memorandum saying: "This came in five days ago from Attlee in
the absence of his chief. Frankly, I think it is best not to reply to it.
What is your view?"

Answering on August 15, I said: "You and other officials of this
Government during past months earnestly laid before Prime Minister
Churchill and other British officials the unequivocal attitude of yourself
in favor of an adjustment on a basis that could and should be mutually
agreed upon in the relations between the home Government of Great
Britain and either officials or certain political leaders headed by Mr.
Gandhi in India."

Referring also to my conversations with Halifax and the efforts made
by Colonel Johnson, I said our attitude had not been one of partisanship
toward either contender, and in these circumstances there was scarcely

more to add in relation to the Attlee message. I concluded, however, with the following suggestion:

"It would seem that if the British Government would repeat with full emphasis its proposal of independence to India at the end of the war, and accompany it by a statement of the adjustments to be made prior to the announcement of independence, including some reference to the equal interest of India with the twenty-eight nations in resisting the Axis Powers, it would clarify public opinion and might lead to the resumption of discussions between Great Britain and the Indian leaders. In any event, it ought to have the effect of reducing the feeling of tension in India."

We were now preoccupied with an additional development, of direct concern to ourselves. As part of the United States' operations in support of China, American military units, particularly air and supply forces, had been sent to India. Disturbing indications reached us that Congress Party supporters were tending to believe that American forces were in India for the purpose of supporting British rule. A telegram from Lauchlin Currie, special envoy of the President, prompted a memorandum which I sent the President on August 12, after consulting the War Department, with a draft of appropriate instructions to be sent the American forces in India and to be published.

The President having approved the draft of instructions I attached, we made these public on the following day, August 12. We stated that the sole purpose of the American forces in India was to prosecute the war of the United Nations against the Axis Powers, primarily to aid China. American forces were not to indulge to the slightest degree in any other activities unless India should be attacked by the Axis Powers, in which event they would aid in defending India. They were to exercise scrupulous care to avoid the slightest participation in India's internal political problems, or even the appearance of participating. In the event of internal disturbances they were to resort to defensive measures only if their own personal safety or that of other American citizens was threatened or if American military supplies and equipment required protection.

Meantime the President had received an appeal for assistance from Gandhi, to which he asked me to prepare a reply. Our response stated in effect that this Government had consistently striven for and supported policies of fair dealing and fair play and all related principles looking toward the creation of harmonious relations between nations. Nevertheless, now that war had come as a result of Axis dreams of world conquest and enslavement, we, together with many other nations, were making a

supreme effort to defeat the enemies of mankind. The letter concluded
with the hope that "our common interest in democracy and righteousness
will enable your countrymen and mine to make common cause against a
common enemy." It attached a copy of my address of July 23.

This letter went forward to our Mission in New Delhi on August 5
for delivery to Gandhi. By the time it arrived, however, Gandhi had been
put in jail. We then faced a decision as to whether to ask the British to
deliver it to Gandhi, whether to deliver it to the only Congress Party
leader not then in prison, who was antagonistic to Gandhi, or to retain
it in the Mission's files until it could be delivered to Gandhi directly. I
recommended the third choice to the President, who agreed. The letter
could not be delivered until two years later.

With the unleashing of the campaign of civil disobedience, and with
the arrest of the Indian leaders, India now became a scene of violence
and unrest. The President and I were keenly perturbed lest this situation
promote Japanese conquest and Chinese discouragement.

I raised the question of India with Ambassador Halifax on September 17, 1942, and asked if there were any prospect of a resumption of
conversations between the United Kingdom and the Indian leaders. Halifax replied that this would have to wait until Indian violence and resistance had ceased. I thereupon remarked that during this deadlock there
was in prospect in the United States a general movement of agitation
against Great Britain and in favor of independence for India which might
create complications later on.

Prime Minister Churchill and Mr. Amery, the Secretary of State for
India, having made strong speeches concerning India a few days before,
I said I was wondering if speeches adequately firm to meet resistance, but
at the same time expressing sympathy for India and calling attention to
the British policy which gave such former colonies as Canada, Australia,
New Zealand, and South Africa the equivalent of independence and to
the continuance of this policy looking toward independence for India,
might not be preferable to speeches of a blunt nature.

"More moderate and sympathetic speeches," I said, "could make it
clear that the British Government desires to resume its course of going
forward with its program for Indian independence just as quickly as this
movement of violence ceases, and at the same time remove any impression
that the British Government is being moved by undue pressure or threats.
If the British could reach a point where they could announce that Indian
resistance had definitely terminated, and that the British Government

was therefore moving back to the resumption of further consideration of its original plans for granting independence to India, and if this step soon could be followed by conferences between even one person representing Great Britain and one person representing India, so as to make it appear that the situation was on the move in the right direction, this, in my judgment, would have a most wholesome psychological effect on the public opinion of other nations and India as well."

The Ambassador did not take issue with my views.

The Indian situation, however, grew more bitter as Gandhi and the other leaders stayed in jail and the passive resistance movement went on.

At that juncture I recommended to the President that he send William Phillips, former Under Secretary of State and Ambassador to Italy, one of our most competent diplomats, to India as his personal representative. (Colonel Johnson had returned to the United States.) The President agreed.

I cabled Phillips, then in London with the Office of Strategic Services, comprehensive instructions on November 20, 1942, which the President had approved. I said that the President and I and the entire Government earnestly favored freedom for all dependent peoples at the earliest date practicable. Our course in dealing with the Philippines offered, I thought, a perfect example of how a nation should treat a colony or a dependency in cooperating with it to make all necessary preparations for freedom. We offered this as a strong example to all other countries and their dependencies.

The President and I had not become partisans of either Great Britain or India, I added, and to do so would seriously handicap us in dealing with the other side. We had sought fellowship freely and in a thoroughly friendly way with both British and Indian peoples, especially their leaders, without making ourselves partisans in our acts and utterances to the extent of generating friction and ill feeling.

Therefore, I went on, we could not bring pressure to bear on the British, but we could in a friendly spirit talk bluntly and earnestly to appropriate British officials so long as they understood that it was our purpose to treat them in a thoroughly friendly way. Objectionable pressure upon either side would probably result not in progress but only in exasperation and, with the British, in a possible disturbance of our unity of command and of cooperation both during and after the war.

I concluded that the settlement of the Indian problem had an added interest for us by reason of its relation to the war. This fact probably

gave us an opportunity to speak more freely and earnestly than we otherwise could, so long as we made it clear that we were speaking from a
genuine friendship and will to cooperate both during the war and after it.

Shortly after Phillips arrived in New Delhi he found India confronting a dangerous situation. Gandhi, who had been in jail for some months,
was apparently on the verge of death as a result of his prolonged fast. It
seemed likely that, if Gandhi died in jail, India would explode in a revolution that would require extraordinary efforts to contain it and might invite
the Japanese to invade the subcontinent.

Phillips cabled on February 16 asking whether, if he learned that
Gandhi's death was imminent, the President and I would approve of his
informally approaching the Viceroy of India, Lord Linlithgow, to express
the deep concern we felt over the political crisis in India. The following
day I cabled Phillips that the President and I concurred in his suggestion,
and that he might also, at his discretion, express our hope that a way
might be found to avoid the deterioration in the Indian situation which
was almost sure to follow the death of Gandhi.

On the day I received Phillip's cable, February 16, I said to Ambassador Halifax that I had a feeling that if Gandhi should die during
his fast acute conditions might arise which it would be important to foresee and prepare against. He said his Government was giving this the
closest attention.

I then raised with him the question whether the British might find
it possible and advisable to consider certain additions to the Cripps proposals made to the Indian leaders. I emphasized this possibility by again
expressing my fear of the dangers which might arise from the sudden death
of Gandhi.

Four days later, February 20, I saw Halifax again, and this time said
that the President desired me to take up the matter of Gandhi's fast and
express his view that Gandhi should not be allowed to die in prison.

Halifax said his Government was very desirous that Phillips should
avoid any public reference to the Gandhi matter at this time.

I replied that Phillips was in a very difficult and unsatisfactory situation in this connection, and that the Viceroy of India had forbidden him
to call on him just then on the ground that it would be exceedingly dangerous to the British-Indian situation. I referred again to Phillips's instructions from the President and myself to the effect that he would not be
expected to remain absolutely quiet and nonvocal, and said that the

President now went much further and emphasized his position that the British should not allow Gandhi to die in prison.

"A vital question for the British to consider from their standpoint," I said, "would seem to be whether they cannot deal more effectively with the situation with Gandhi alive than if he were dead and his supporters were claiming martyrdom."

The Ambassador said he would get this message to his Government without delay.

Two days later he brought to Under Secretary Welles, in my temporary absence, a telegram from Prime Minister Churchill asking Halifax to make it clear to me and to his contacts that the British Government would not in any circumstances alter the course it was pursuing about Gandhi. Therefore great embarrassment between the British and American Governments would be created by any American intervention. Mr. Churchill earnestly hoped that Britain's difficulties would not be added to at so critical a moment, and said the Ambassador could be sure there would be no weakness in London. He asked Halifax to lay the whole matter before Harry Hopkins.

Welles communicated the matter to President Roosevelt, who replied that the United States Government would say nothing further now, but that, in the event that Gandhi died, he would have some statement to make. The President also suggested, that, in that event, I make clear the fact that this Government had expressed its concern over the possibility of Gandhi's death and its belief that the difficulties in the Indian situation would be less great if he were alive than if he were permitted to die.

The following month, during the visit of Foreign Secretary Eden to Washington, I pointed out to him on March 22 that we had made a real effort to keep down anti-British sentiment in this country growing out of the situation in India, and that we had done our best to prevent the question from becoming a matter of serious contention.

The President asked Phillips to return to the United States by the end of April or the beginning of May for a month's visit to report to us on the situation in India. Developments in India during Phillips's visit here were such that he did not return to New Delhi; another important post was awaiting him, on the staff of General Eisenhower in London. His appointment as the President's personal representative in India, however, continued in effect.

On April 19, 1943, Phillips sent me a copy of a letter to the President summing up his impressions on the situation in India. He said in his covering letter that the impressions did not make very pleasant reading, but nevertheless he felt he ought to send them to the President and me for whatever they were worth. He said India was in a state of inertia, prostration, divided counsels, and helplessness, with growing distrust and dislike for the British, and disappointment and disillusion with regard to Americans. The British had been completely successful in their policy of "keeping the lid on" and suppressing any movement among the Indians that might be interpreted as being toward independence. British armies dominated the picture; twenty thousand Congress leaders remained in jail without trial.

Phillips said it was hard to discover, either in New Delhi or in other parts of India, any pronounced war spirit against Japan, even on the part of the British. Rather, the British seemed to feel that their responsibility lay on the Indian side of the Burma-Assam frontier. Unless the present atmosphere changed for the better, we Americans should have to bear the burden of the coming campaign in that part of the world and could not count on more than token assistance from the British in British India.

Our inability to influence British policy in India, coupled with the presence of our troops in that area, gradually gave rise toward the end of 1943 to considerable anti-American feeling among the Indians, who felt that we were buttressing the British Empire. The President, seeing this in numerous dispatches, sent me a memorandum on January 17, 1944, saying: "What would you think of my telling the press something like the enclosed if I am asked? I think it would clear up a good deal of anti-American feeling in India."

I replied two days later, after consulting with my associates, saying that I thought the proposed statement would be very helpful, and suggesting two changes in wording proposed by Wallace Murray, Chief of the Near Eastern Division. The President made the statement on February 1. "The American objectives in India or elsewhere in continental Asia," he said, "are to expel and defeat the Japanese, in the closest collaboration with our British, Chinese, and other Allies in that theater. . . . No matter what individual or individuals command in given areas, the purpose is the same. . . . Nobody in India or anywhere else in Asia will misunderstand the presence there of American armed forces if they will believe, as we do at home, that their job is to assure the defeat of Japan, without which there can be no opportunity for any of us to enjoy and expand the freedoms for which we fight."

We took all steps we could to dissociate our activities in India, which merely served as a base for our operations in aid of China, from those of the British. We likewise took care to keep all American propaganda work based in India, other than that of a purely psychological warfare nature directed against the enemy, completely separate from similar work by the British.

In the summer of 1944 an unexpected and serious issue rose between us and the British when an American columnist published a large portion of the previously mentioned letter which Phillips had written to the President on April 19, 1943. This publication created excitement in the United States and resentment in Britain. Beginning with a visit to me by British Minister Campbell on the day of publication, July 25, 1944, the British repeatedly protested and requested our Government to issue a statement dissociating ourselves from the views expressed in the letter.

On August 15, however, we sent the President a memorandum stating: "It is the Department's feeling that it would be impossible to issue a statement satisfactory to the British inasmuch as we share in general the views expressed in the Ambassador's letter. Unless you feel that we should comply with the British request, I would appreciate having your permission to tell the British that we consider it preferable to make no public statement on the subject." The President went along with this view.

The question received considerable airing in Congress, particularly when Phillips's resignation from Eisenhower's staff was announced. We made a statement, however, to Representative Sol Bloom, chairman of the House Committee of Foreign Affairs, showing that there was no connection between Phillips's resignation, given on July 19, and the publication of the letter, made on July 25.

The British did not easily let the matter drop. Ambassador Halifax called on me on September 8 and very pressingly urged that the President at an early press conference refer to the Phillips letter without mentioning it and speak well of the Indian military forces, and then correct any impression that the British were not aiding in the war against Japan.

I talked this over with the President, who said he could and would make such a statement. He did not make it; but he joined with Prime Minister Churchill a week later in making a joint statement at the Quebec Conference that all the nations concerned with the war in the Orient were "ardent" to engage against the Japanese the massive forces which they were marshaling.

Throughout these years of political disturbance, we gave India what economic assistance we could. In March, 1942, the President appointed Henry F. Grady, former Assistant Secretary of State, to head an economic mission to India to study the subcontinent's needs. The mission proposed a program of assistance which, however, could be implemented only in small part because of the shortage of shipping.

When a serious famine developed in Bengal in 1943, we made efforts to secure from the all too inadequate rice stocks in the Western Hemisphere an allocation of rice for India. The British representatives on the Combined Food Board in Washington insisted, however, that the responsibility for Indian food requirements be left to Britain, and we perforce had to agree.

When I left the State Department at the end of November, 1944, the situation in India was still acute. The United Nations' military progress in the Pacific had largely removed the danger of a Japanese attack; but the danger of internal explosions was still ever present. We had taken every occasion we legitimately could to make clear our view that India should receive independence, but we had also proceeded with great caution so as not to antagonize either the British or the Indians. India continued to be one of the principal foci of our general policy on dependent peoples. And we had the conviction that, soon after the war ended, India must, and would, be granted independence.

Toward India's neighbor to the north, Afghanistan, our policy assumed a new importance with our entry into the war and with the manifest plans of the Germans to penetrate into western Asia en route to India. The mountain country's strategic position on the northwest frontier of India, the hostility of its people to both the British and the Russians, and the pro-German sentiment existing there, made it imperative for us to develop our relations with the Afghans. In February, 1942, we assigned a Foreign Service officer to Kabul, their capital, with instructions to open a Legation; and the President on May 2 appointed Cornelius Van H. Engert our Minister to Afghanistan. In June, 1943, the Afghans opened a Legation in Washington.

We forthwith lent what assistance we could in both a cultural and an economic way. Grants-in-aid were given to American teachers accepting posts in Afghanistan's higher schools. Assistance was given the Government in employing American engineers to develop irrigation projects. We tried to support the country's economy by continuing the importation into the United States of karakuls and other Afghan produce, and facilitating the export of manufactured articles to Afghanistan.

Toward the end of my years at the State Department, when it became apparent that the Germans could no longer carry out their plans of driving into the Middle East and effecting a juncture with the Japanese, we nevertheless continued our policy of cooperation with Afghanistan. We had in mind the possibility that a breakdown in Afghanistan's internal economy might lead to serious political disorders along the northwest frontier of India which would tie down a number of Allied troops. We also believed that the prestige we might acquire in Afghanistan would favorably affect our position in other Moslem areas in the Middle East. And we thought that, if it ever became economically feasible to develop oil and mineral resources in Afghanistan, a friendly attitude there toward the United States would be helpful.

On only one occasion did we take political action with regard to Afghanistan. This was in May, 1943, when we received reports that the British and Russians might be planning a joint demand on the Afghan Government that it expel the German and Italian diplomatic staffs. We felt that the Government's compliance with this demand might result in its overthrow by the tribes and in the creation of disorder. We accordingly informed the British Government that if any such demand were made the United States Government would openly disassociate itself from the *démarche*. The British replied that they had no present intention of asking for the expulsion of the Axis representatives, and that a request they had made for a reduction in the number of such representatives was not in the form of a demand. The Afghan Government brought about the departure of a few Axis representatives and arrested certain Axis agents.

Partly as a result of our efforts, Afghanistan throughout the war presented no element of trouble. The northwest frontier of India was secured against becoming a sore spot of disorder and a base for propaganda and other operations by the Axis.

109: The Near East Looms Big

THE NEAR EAST, in which our Government had evinced only a slight interest for a century and a half, became through the demands of World War II a vital area in the conduct of our foreign relations. Those legendary and, to the average American, somewhat shadowy countries of Asia Minor, whose names were linked with Bible lore and ancient history, suddenly presented us with concrete problems of the moment, requiring almost daily decisions and affecting our ties with other major nations. Iran (once known to us as Persia), Iraq, Saudi Arabia, Lebanon, and Syria began to appear more and more in American print, not as lands of the ancients but as cogs in the machine of war. Palestine, already known not only as the Holy Land but also as the goal of the Zionists and the kernel of the struggle between Jews and Arabs, took on new significance because of the war. The cities of Tehran, Bagdad, Beirut, and Damascus, which had heard the tread of armies of long-past centuries, now quivered under the roar of tanks or bombers.

Prior to June, 1941, when Hitler became engrossed in his struggle with Russia, the Near East was one of the immediate points of German ambition. British and Free French troops had to invade Syria in 1941 to prevent the Germans, with Vichy France acquiescing, from using it as a base to penetrate into the Middle East and support a rebellion in Iraq. In my eyes the Near East offered the greatest danger of the war, the possible juncture of German and Japanese forces, effectively cutting the world in two.

After the Nazi invasion of the U.S.S.R., the Near East became to the British and us a corridor for sending supplies to the embattled Russians, Iran being our major highway. We had to negotiate with Iran and other Near Eastern countries, and with Britain and Russia, for this purpose. At the same time we were in frequent diplomatic contact with Moscow and London to prevent dissension from rising between them over the Near East, and to forestall any thought on their part of dividing that region into spheres of influence.

Our policy was predicated on our belief that all the countries of the Near East should eventually be fully independent. Toward that end we furthered the legitimate aspirations of the Arab states toward an Arab federation, and we fought the attempt of General de Gaulle's committee to prevent the peoples of Syria and of Lebanon from achieving independence. We also worked hard to bring the Near Eastern states into the United Nations.

We likewise had our own interests to protect, principally the vast oil concessions in Saudi Arabia, held exclusively by American companies, as well as our large oil interests in Iraq and Kuwait, held jointly with citizens of other countries.

In pursuit of all these objectives we had to be ready to lend financial and other assistance to the countries of the Near East, including the sending of economic, military, and other missions, to establish closer diplomatic relations with them, and to exert our diplomatic influence, when necessary, upon them or upon our major Allies.

President Roosevelt and I agreed, in August, 1942, on a plan of procedure in the Near East and on a basic statement of our policy in that region, after the State Department and the Joint Chiefs of Staff had carefully studied the whole situation. I thereupon cabled Ambassador Winant in London to show our plan to the British and obtain their concurrence.

In support of our proposed plan we stressed the serious consequences the loss of the Near East would have for the United Nations, and we emphasized that every possible political and military effort had to be made to retain that vital area. The United States, we said, continued to have a unique position in the area, where our influence and prestige were still high because the Near Eastern peoples realized that we had no vested political or territorial interests there. This widespread good will toward us had developed into a deep-seated belief to this effect among the Near Eastern peoples, principally as a result of a century of American philanthropic, educational, and missionary efforts that no material interests or motives had ever tarnished. Such a position was occupied by none of the other United Nations.

We suggested therefore that we take specific steps with regard to the Near East: the appointment to Syria and Lebanon of a diplomatic agent; the issuance of a policy declaration by our Government with respect to the Near East; and the sending of an American mission, partly economic, partly military, to that area, although we recognized that the military responsibility for the region continued to be primarily British.

Finally we proposed that the American mission should use four main arguments in its approach to the Near East: first, the United Nations' military power and potentialities; second, the inevitable political and economic enslavement that the Near Eastern peoples would suffer, as had those in all the occupied countries, in the event of an Axis victory; third, the Near Eastern peoples' own interest and their better prospects for economic and political development in a United Nations victory; fourth, the assurance of this country's support, after the war, for their aspirations toward independence if, in line with the Atlantic Charter and American foreign policy, the peoples of the Near East actively assisted in winning the war.

I likewise sent Winant the text of the proposed basic statement of policy, built around and quoting my radio address of July 23, 1942, when I said: "It has been our purpose in the past—and will remain our purpose in the future—to use the full measure of our influence to support attainment of freedom by all peoples who, by their acts, show themselves worthy of it and ready for it."

The British reaction was more unfavorable than favorable. Eden welcomed our proposal to appoint a diplomatic agent to Syria and Lebanon, but Mr. Churchill opposed the wording of our proposed declaration. The British, in an *aide-mémoire*, saw "considerable dangers" in it; they thought the emphasis on "freedom" and "liberty" inappropriate in so far as the independent countries of the Near East were concerned, and apt to have dangerous repercussions in so far as Palestine and the Levantine states—Syria and Lebanon—were concerned. The *aide-mémoire* also deprecated the dispatch of an American mission of the character outlined, but indicated that the assignment of American specialized personnel to work with the British in those fields would be welcomed.

In consequence of this reaction, we did not pursue our proposal for a declaration of policy, and we did not take up the matter with the French National Committee, as we had intended. We did not, however, drop the idea of greater American participation in the affairs of the Near East, but took numerous steps relating to the countries of that region.

Iran probably attracted more of our attention than any other country in the Near East. With the British and the Russians occupying portions of that country, and with Americans using Iranian routes for the dispatch of supplies to Russia, Iran became the only common meeting place of the three major nations where they might work out a plan for the treatment and development of small nations. This was particularly important because Iran for more than a century had been a diplomatic battleground for predominance between Britain and Russia. The President believed, and I with him, that Iran, possibly because of the very difficulties inherent in the problem, offered us a unique opportunity to see what an unselfish American policy could do in raising the status of her national life.

Prior to the war our relations with Iran had never been of great importance. Iranian foreign relations had been oriented toward Russia and Britain. In the 1920's German technicians entered Iran by the hundreds, and Germany flooded the country with cheap goods. This German penetration later proved unfortunate for Iran, since it caused the British and Russians to invade her in 1941. The Iranian Government, under the hardheaded, ultrasensitive dictator, Shah Reza Pahlavi, from 1925 to 1941, had itself been an obstacle in the way of better American-Iranian relations. Reza Pahlavi, while trying to shut the door to any foreign influence, periodically complained to other Governments against any comment in the foreign press he considered injurious to Iran. He closed the Iranian Legation in Washington in 1936 because his Minister was unfortunately arrested in a traffic incident in Maryland, and opened it again only after a personal visit to Tehran in 1938 by Wallace Murray, Chief of the Division of Near Eastern Affairs.

At the time the British occupied southern Iran and the Russians northern Iran in August, 1941, both the British and the Iranian Government requested our support. The British wanted us to back the Anglo-Soviet representations to Tehran demanding the expulsion of most of the large German colony in Iran, which seemed to be a danger to the Allies particularly because Iran lay just to the south of the Russian oil fields toward which the Germans were then driving hard. Though refusing to associate our Government with these joint representations, I instructed Minister Dreyfus at Tehran to express to the Iranians our sincere hope that all the requisite measures were being taken by the Iranian Government to prevent Nazi activities from spreading—a development that would inevitably be disastrous to it.

The Iranian Minister, Mohammed Shayesteh, on the other hand, called on me on August 22 to ask on behalf of his Government what we should be disposed to do to prevent the threatened British invasion. I emphasized to him then and in later conversations the global nature of the conflict with the Axis and my belief that Iran should take all possible steps to avoid being of any assistance to the Axis and to aid the Allies.

Shah Reza Pahlavi, however, blindly pursuing a narrow policy of neutrality and nationalism, and refusing to heed our friendly advice to look at the war from a broader viewpoint, temporized until it was too late. The British and Russians invaded his country on August 25. The

Shah thereupon cabled President Roosevelt, asking for his intervention "to put an end to these acts of aggression." The President sent this to me on August 30 for a reply. Our response, which went out on September 2, followed the line of my conversations with the Iranian Minister, placing the Anglo-Soviet-Iranian dispute in its true light as one small element in the vast effort to stop Hitler's ambition of world conquest. The President also informed the Shah that we had noted the British and Russian statements to Iran that they had no designs on the independence or territorial integrity of that country. He added that we had already sought information from the British and Soviet Governments as to their immediate as well as long-range plans and intentions in Iran, and had suggested to them the advisability of a public statement to all free peoples of the world reiterating their assurances cencerning Iran's independence.

I had made these approaches in conferring on August 27 with Soviet Ambassador Oumansky and British Chargé d'Affaires Campbell, and I took this suggestion up again in cables to London and Moscow on September 4. A fortnight later, the stubborn Shah Reza Pahlavi abdicated and was succeeded by the Crown Prince, Mohammed Reza Pahlavi, who was more disposed to cooperate with the Allies. Although the British and Russians did not at that time issue the declaration of assurances I had suggested, they did, in the Anglo-Soviet-Iranian Treaty signed on January 29, 1942, undertake to respect the territorial integrity, sovereignty, and political independence of Iran and to withdraw their troops not later than six months after the end of hostilities.

Prior to the signature of this treaty our Legation in Tehran had reported that the Soviets were said to be giving at least sympathy to separatist movements in their zone in northern Iran. I had this report taken up strongly with the Russians, and Soviet Deputy Foreign Commissar Vishinski denied any knowledge on the part of his Government of political or propaganda activities in northern Iran looking toward separatist movements.

Nevertheless, alarmed by continuing reports of Soviet separatist activities in northern Iran, the Iranian Government asked us to become a joint signatory to the treaty of January 29. We contented ourselves, however, with taking note of the Anglo-Soviet assurances contained in the treaty, in a telegram from the President to the new Shah on February 6.

In the spring of 1942 Iran's strategic position became of great importance to all the United Nations because of a threatened German attack in the Near East and Japanese successes in the Far East. Iran was also providing the major supply route for the U.S.S.R. Despite the Anglo-Soviet-Iranian treaty, continuing anti-British and anti-Soviet sentiment in Iran prevented any wholehearted support of the United Nations' war effort. The Iranian Government appeared extremely apprehensive over Soviet objectives in northern Iran and resentful of British interference in Iranian internal affairs. The war had cut off Iran's export trade and made it difficult for her to obtain essential imports, while the continued presence of British and Soviet troops had produced internal difficulties both political and economical.

The Iranians, disliking the British, fearing the Russians, resentful against both because of their occupation of Iran, and looking upon the United States as the only disinterested large nation able to help them, turned to us for aid.

The President accordingly declared Iran eligible for Lend-Lease supplies on March 11, 1942. We likewise began to send economic, military, and other advisers to Iran, always at her own request. At the time I left office we had some seventy-five Americans in these advisory missions, to which the Iranian Government had granted a considerable degree of authority. The largest mission was of an economic and financial nature, headed by Dr. Arthur C. Millspaugh, with an authorized strength of sixty Americans. The Iranian Parliament granted these missions plenary powers to supervise and direct such vital activities as finance, internal revenue, customs, price stabilization, rationing, distribution, collection of harvests, public domains, and road transport. A military mission headed by Major General Clarence S. Ridley worked toward the reorganization of the Quartermaster Corps of the Iranian Army. Another military mission under Colonel H. Norman Schwarzkopf reorganized and administered the Iranian rural police.

The work of these missions was attended with many difficulties. Sharp disputes rose between some of the advisers, particularly Dr. Millspaugh, and some Iranian officials, and the latter interfered from time to time with the work of the advisers. We had to iron out the difficulties through diplomatic representations to the Iranian Government and through counseling the advisers; we had to keep Britain and Russia assured that we were not attempting to take control of the Iranian Government; and we had to keep in frequent contact with other Departments and agencies of our own Government in order to obtain their cooperation.

I recommended to the President on August 16, 1943, that the United States should adopt "a policy of positive action" in Iran, so as to facilitate not only the United Nations' war operations in that country but also a sound postwar development. In the memorandum I sent him, which was prepared in the Near Eastern Division under Wallace Murray, I said: "We should take the lead, wherever possible, in remedying internal difficulties, working as much as possible through American administrators freely employed by the Iranian Government. We should further endeavor to lend timely diplomatic support to Iran, to prevent the development of a situation in which an open threat to Iranian integrity might be presented."

We pointed out that the success of this proposed course of action was favored by the exceptionally high regard in which the United States was held by the Iranian people. We also had reason to believe that the British Government would acquiesce, or even lend its active support. The attitude of the Soviet Government was doubtful, but we felt we should be in a position to exert considerable influence on that Government if the occasion arose. We stated that the safeguarding of legitimate British and Soviet economic interests in Iran ought to be a basic principle of American action.

Our recommendations, we said, were rendered necessary by the deterioration of the political and economic situation in Iran. We felt that the geographical, political, and economic bases of the century-old ambitions of Britain and Russia in Iran still remained unchanged. The attitudes of the British and Soviet Governments gave us strong reason to fear that their rivalry would break out again as soon as the military situation eased. This danger was greatly increased by the economic and political weakness of the Iranian Government and the presence of British and Soviet armed forces on Iranian soil. If events were allowed to run their course unchecked, it seemed likely that either Russia or Britain, or both, would take action that would seriously abridge, if not destroy, effective Iranian independence. The best hope of avoiding such action, we believed, lay in strengthening Iran to a point where she could stand on her own feet, without foreign control or "protection," and in calling upon Britain and Russia, when necessary, to respect their general commitments under the Atlantic Charter and their specific commitments to Iran under the Treaty of Alliance of 1942.

The President was in agreement with the policy we suggested. The War Department joined with us in its implementation.

Iraq, one of Iran's neighbors, having declared war on the Axis, had been admitted to the ranks of the United Nations in January, 1943. Immediately the Iranian Government sought a like status. After exchanges of views the London, Moscow, and Chungking Governments joined with us in stating to the Iranian Government that when Iran entered the war against one or more of the Axis nations she would become eligible. Iran declared war on Germany on September 9, 1943, and adhered on the following day to the United Nations Declaration through an exchange of notes between the Iranian Minister and myself.

At the Moscow Conference in October, 1943, Eden, Molotov, and I discussed the question of a declaration by the three major nations concerning Iran. Eden had taken up with us the substance of such a declaration prior to the Moscow Conference, and I was in general agreement with it. This pronouncement stated that, so long as Iran complied with her obligations under the Anglo-Soviet-Iranian Treaty of Alliance and gave the Allies the aid they desired in the economic and financial fields, they had a moral obligation, in making use of Iranian facilities, to do the least possible harm to Iran's economy and to do all possible to safeguard the Iranian people against the privations that war must inevitably bring.

During one of my conferences with Eden in Moscow, I suggested on October 24 that the declaration be expanded to include a promise of support for the foreign advisers and domestic agencies working to improve conditions in Iran, and that separate declarations be made stating the intentions of the three Powers to withdraw their armed forces from Iran after the cessation of hostilities.

Eden agreed, and throughout our subsequent discussions at the conference the British and we were in substantial agreement. Molotov and his assistants, however, opposed the issuance of any declaration asserting that the assurances and undertakings involved were already covered in the Anglo-Soviet-Iranian Treaty and in a draft agreement we had drawn up relative to American troops in Iran, and that a reiteration of them might alarm rather than reassure the Iranians.

At that time we were discussing with the Iranian Government a draft agreement relative to American troops already in Iran. Following the establishment of the Persian Gulf Command in Iran late in November, 1942, and the arrival of American technical troops to superintend the transport of supplies to Russia, the Iranian Government had proposed that the United States become a party to the Anglo-Soviet-Iranian Treaty to clarify the status of our troops there. Not considering it feasible to become a party to a treaty of alliance with Iran, we proposed to the Iranians a separate agreement to cover the presence of our troops on their territory.

In our draft we undertook to "respect, in the future as in the past, the territorial integrity, sovereignty, and political independence of Iran." The Iranians, however, desired still broader guarantees, and difficulties also rose over certain of the economic clauses in the agreement. These negotiations were suspended by the Iranian Government in December, 1943.

The proposed three-Power declaration on Iran which Eden and I were supporting at Moscow ran aground on the rocks of Soviet opposition. Eden, Molotov, and I thereupon agreed to recommend that the declaration be further considered at the forthcoming Roosevelt-Stalin-Churchill meeting, although Eden and I should have preferred to continue the discussions at Moscow.

While returning to Washington from Moscow, I stopped at Tehran and received a visit from the Iranian Prime Minister, Ali Soheily, and the Foreign Minister, Mohammed Saed, who expressed their Government's desire for the early withdrawal of the British and Soviet troops in Iran, even before the end of the war. They contended that Iran's situation had radically changed since the Anglo-Soviet-Iranian Treaty of 1942; the Germans were no longer a threat; the Axis agent problem had been disposed of, and, most important, Iran was now at war with the Axis and a member of the United Nations.

The War Department, however, indicated to us on December 21, 1943, that it did not wish to see the British and Soviet troops leave Iran at that time, principally for manpower reasons. Our Chargé at Tehran, Richard Ford, also opposed the proposal on the grounds that it was highly unlikely that all Axis agents had been eliminated from Iran, that the presence of foreign troops exercised a deterrent influence on the unruly tribes that continued to menace the security of the supply line to Russia, and that the Persian Gulf Command and the American advisers to the Iranian Army desired to see the existing arrangement continued, with the British responsible for security in the south and the Russians in the north. We accordingly did not support the Iranian request.

Meantime the President, Marshal Stalin, and Prime Minister Churchill had signed at Tehran, on December 1, a declaration on Iran. This was prepared by our Legation at Tehran with the assistance of General Patrick J. Hurley, whom the President had sent on a special mission to the Near East, and was presented by Mr. Roosevelt. The declaration acknowledged Iran's contribution to the common war effort, recognized the special economic problems created for Iran by the war, pledged such economic assistance to Iran as might be possible, promised consideration of Iran's economic problems in the postwar period, and expressed a desire for the maintenance of Iran's independence, sovereignty, and territorial integrity.

This declaration was of the highest importance to Iran because, in addition to the pledges it contained of economic assistance, it gave the Iranians what they had so much wanted; namely, a formal expression of American desire for the maintenance of Iran's sovereignty and territorial integrity, and a renewal of the assurances previously given by Russia and Britain.

After the President returned to Washington from the Tehran Conference, I recommended to him on December 22 that we raise our Legation at Tehran to an Embassy. Mr. Roosevelt agreed and, on the Department's recommendation, appointed Leland B. Morris, then our Minister to Iceland, to be our first Ambassador in Tehran.

The President's personal interest in Iran was keen. He had sent General Hurley on one mission to the Near East and on another to Iran, and had closely read Hurley's reports and recommendations, in addition to numerous State Department dispatches and memoranda. On January 12, 1944, in a memorandum to me about a very interesting letter from Hurley, he wrote:

"Iran is definitely a very, very backward nation. It consists really of a series of tribes, and 99 per cent of the population is, in effect, in bondage to the other 1 per cent. The 99 per cent do not own their land and cannot keep their own production or convert it into money or property.

"I was rather thrilled with the idea of using Iran as an example of what we could do by an unselfish American policy. We could not take on a more difficult nation than Iran. I should like, however, to have a try at it. The real difficulty is to get the right kind of American experts who would be loyal to their ideals, not fight among themselves and be absolutely honest financially.

"If we could get this policy started, it would become permanent if it succeeded as we hope during the first five or ten years. And incidentally, the whole experiment need cost the taxpayers of the United States very little money."

Hurley was critical of British policy in Iran, which he considered imperialistic, and one of his recommendations was that the Lend-Lease Administration should take complete control of the distribution of our own Lend-Lease supplies in the Near East. These had been distributed largely through a British agency, primarily because of the difficulty of recruiting and transporting American personnel for the purpose. This recommendation, among others, was approved by the President and was gradually carried out, except in a very few cases where it proved impracticable.

In 1944 our assistance of all kinds to Iran increased. Nevertheless dissension intensified between some Iranian officials and a few of our advisers. Iranian officials at times resented or objected to the projects and procedures recommended by some of the advisers, and on the part of the latter, absorbed as they were in their specialized fields, there was often an inadequate realization of the need for diplomacy in conducting their relations with the Iranian Government.

When Mr. Abol Hassan Ebtehaj, governor of the National Bank of Iran, who according to our Embassy in Tehran was in "open warfare" with Dr. Millspaugh, visited the United States in June, 1944, he expressed great dissatisfaction with the trend of American-Iranian relations, basing his position on a series of minor incidents. I suggested to him that his chief complaints, about which he had allowed himself to become so much exercised, could well be brushed aside in the face of the more important questions and policies that our two peoples and Governments had to solve. I said that the United States Government was making an immense contribution toward bringing defeat to the Axis Powers, all of which protected the liberty of Iran. I was told later that this conversation had the effect of placating the irate governor.

Iran being one of the great oil-bearing countries of the Near East, one facet of our diplomacy consisted in supporting the efforts of American companies to obtain petroleum concessions there. The War and Navy Departments, alarmed by statistics tending to prove the depletion of the United States oil fields, and feeling that the oil of the Near East, because it lay closer to the Far East than the Western Hemisphere fields, might be vitally necessary in the war against Japan, strongly urged that the Near Eastern potentialities be developed.

When the Standard-Vacuum Oil Company asked the Department's views on its desire to enter into an arrangement with the Iranian Government to produce petroleum in Iran, we replied that we favored the development of all possible sources of petroleum because of the importance of the product both for war purposes and from the long-range point of view, and saw no objection to the company's undertaking negotiations with the Iranian Government. I approved this reply at a meeting with my associates on November 15, 1943. The British already had extensive oil concessions in Iran, but I said that, since we had no agreement with the British not to seek oil concessions there, I saw no reason why the company should not go ahead with its plans. We cabled our Legation in Tehran accordingly.

The Standard-Vacuum Company sent a representative to Tehran early in 1944, and the Sinclair oil interests did likewise. At the same time a representative of a British oil company was in Tehran trying to obtain further oil concessions. Then on February 28 Chargé Ford in Tehran reported that the Soviet Embassy had stated to the press that the U.S.S.R. had prior rights to the exploitation of any oil in northern Iran, a claim apparently based on an old concession never approved by the Iranian Parliament.

The negotiations of the American and British oil interests with the Iranian Government continued satisfactorily through the summer of 1944 until, in September, a Soviet delegation arrived in Tehran and requested the immediate concession to the Russian Government of exclusive rights for a five-year period to explore for petroleum and other minerals in an area of 200,000 square kilometers in northern Iran. All other foreigners were to be excluded from such exploitation.

Iranian Prime Minister Saed, therefore, informed Ambassador Morris on October 9 that his Government had decided to postpone all oil negotiations until after the war. We cabled Morris on October 16 to inform the Iranian Government that we had taken note of its decision; that, although the two American firms involved were naturally disappointed at its decision, we were confident that the Iranian Government had acted in good faith in carrying on the previous negotiations; that we should naturally expect, when and if the Iranian Government was ready to consider applications for oil concessions, that the applications received from Americans would be given no less favorable treatment than those received from the Government or nationals of any other country; and that we should also expect the Iranian Government to inform us or the American companies concerned as soon as it was ready to consider such applications.

The British took a similar position, but the Soviet reaction was quite different. The Russian press immediately began a campaign against the Saed Government, and the Soviet officials in Tehran expressed their displeasure. Ambassador Harriman in Moscow, acting on our instructions, thereupon informed the Soviet Foreign Office of our instructions to Ambassador Morris on October 16 and said that these were based on our recognition of an independent nation's sovereign right to withhold or

grant commercial concessions on a nondiscriminatory basis. We called attention to the Tehran Declaration on Iran and said we could not agree
to any action constituting undue interference in Iranian internal affairs.

Nevertheless, Soviet pressure brought about the fall of the Saed
Government on November 9, three weeks before my resignation. While
Soviet demands for the desired oil concession thereafter relaxed somewhat,
this was a basic question involved in the crisis in Soviet-Iranian relations
in 1946.

110: Near East and Oil

OIL LUBRICATED THE DIPLOMACY of the major nations toward the Near East. When it became apparent in the twenties and thirties that the petroleum deposits in that area represented one of the greatest reserves in the world, the attention of the larger nations turned toward the Near Eastern production of a commodity whose importance to industry and transport was becoming ever more marked.

In Saudi Arabia the element of oil entered into United States diplomacy to a greater extent than in the case of any other Near Eastern country. With that comparatively unknown land, consisting largely of Arabian desert, under the rule of King Ibn Saud, the greatest single influence among the Arabs, we had had only unimportant relations in the years before the war. In 1933 we had signed with Saudi Arabia a provisional agreement for diplomatic and consular representatives, juridical protection, commerce, and navigation. In the same year the Standard Oil Company of California obtained a concession to develop the Saudi Arabian oil fields, which it began to do, in conjunction with the Texas Company, through a jointly owned subsidiary, later called the Arabian American Oil Company. The company had obtained the concession on its own initiative, in competition with various foreign interests. King Ibn Saud, suspicious of governmental diplomatic processes, had preferred to deal directly with company officials.

During the next few years the company did not require our diplomatic protection and, in view of Ibn Saud's attitude toward diplomacy, we felt it better to remain in the background. Later, as tests revealed the Saudi Arabian oil fields to be among the most important in the world and as many more American technicians went to Saudi Arabia, we thought it advisable to establish diplomatic relations with the King. In 1939 Minister Bert Fish, already accredited to Egypt, was accredited also to Saudi Arabia.

Following the outbreak of the European War, King Ibn Saud began to experience serious financial difficulties primarily owing to the curtailment of the pilgrim traffic to Mecca and Medina as a result of the war. In June, 1941, he requested a $10,000,000 credit from the United States Government. The President agreed but found there were legal difficulties in the way. The British Government having recommenced payment of cash and goods subsidies to Saudi Arabia, the President also felt that there was more reason for the British, with their greater strategic and political interests in the Near East, to attend to Ibn Saud's financial needs.

After our entry into the war, however, the preservation of law and order in the Near East became of great concern to us. The planning and carrying out of the campaign in North Africa, where the Arab population predominated, and the establishment of important American supply lines to Russia through the Near East, showed the necessity for stability in the Near East, toward which end stability in Saudi Arabia was essential.

In January, 1942, we took up with the President and with Secretaries Ickes of Interior and Wickard of Agriculture a request from the Saudi Arabian Government for the services of American experts in irrigation and agriculture, and obtained their approval. A mission, headed by Mr. K. S. Twitchell, who had acted in the United States as an informal representative of King Ibn Saud, went to Saudi Arabia in May, 1942, remained until December, and received the commendation of Ibn Saud in a letter to the President.

We opened an American Legation on May 1, 1942, at Jidda under a Chargé d'Affaires, who, in July, 1943, was appointed Minister Resident. Early in January, 1943, the State Department recommended that Saudi Arabia be made eligible for Lend-Lease assistance, and the President so declared on February 18, 1943.

These steps were taken in recognition of the importance of King Ibn Saud and Saudi Arabia to the United Nations' war effort. Ibn Saud had granted our air forces fly-over privileges, and the War Department had evinced an interest in obtaining aircraft landing rights there. Both the War and Navy Departments were interested in securing oil reserves in Saudi Arabian ground. Furthermore, King Ibn Saud exerted great influence upon the Arab countries of the Near East, where American troops were stationed.

The President himself was drawn to the powerful personality of King Ibn Saud, and looked forward eagerly to making his personal acquaintance. We drafted for him in July, 1943, a message to the King inviting him to visit the United States in the near future, or, if he were unable to come, to designate a member of the Royal Family to make the visit on his behalf. The King accepted the latter part of the invitation, designating his son, Amir Faisal, Foreign Minister of Saudi Arabia, to represent him.

The news of the invitation and acceptance leaked out and became twisted to indicate that Ibn Saud's son was coming to the United States for propaganda purposes in connection with the Jewish problem in Palestine. The President sent me a tart note on August 15, attributing the leak to the State Department, and adding: "Of course, I have no sympathy with those Jews who object to my seeing the son of Ibn Saud any more than I have any sympathy with those Arabs who are starting anti-Semitic prejudices in this country."

I replied to the President three days later, saying I did not believe any leak had occurred in the State Department. I remarked that a member of the British Embassy had called on an officer of the Department about the time the invitation was sent to Ibn Saud and said he had learned through Zionist contacts in New York that an invitation was to be extended. So far as Arab propaganda activities in the United States were concerned, I added, our Minister Resident at Jidda had reported that the British Legation there had advised the Saudi Arabian Government to undertake such propaganda to counteract Zionist propaganda in the United States.

The Arab princes, Faisal and his brother Khalid, arrived in Washington in the autumn of 1943 and, during my absence at the Moscow Conference, held a series of conferences with officers of the Department on economic aid for Saudi Arabia, development of Saudi Arabian petroleum resources, and American policy in the Near East generally.

Meantime, by arrangement between the State and Treasury Departments, a Treasury representative, John W. Gunter, had gone to Saudi Arabia to explore with that Government the Saudi Arabian financial situation. As a result of this visit, we signed an agreement on October 3, 1943, to loan Saudi Arabia over 5,000,000 ounces of silver. At the end of the year an American military mission, headed by Major General Ralph Royce, visited Saudi Arabia, at King Ibn Saud's invitation, to survey Saudi Arabian military requirements, and in the spring of 1944 a small United States Army training mission went to the desert kingdom.

Rivalry with Britain in Saudi Arabia sharply disturbed us in the first half of 1944. Although the British Government, in an *aide-mémoire* of October 30, 1943, had expressed to us their anxiety to coordinate their policy in the Middle East with that of this Government and their hope for close collaboration with us in that area; although they had accepted, early in 1944, our proposal for discussion of Saudi Arabian fiscal and currency problems; and although British Ambassador Halifax had called on me on March 20, 1944, to characterize as entirely erroneous a statement attributed to General Hurley that the British were opposed to American development of oil interests in Saudi Arabia, the State Department, in March and April of 1944, received reports of increasing British activity in Saudi Arabia potentially prejudicial to American interests there.

I could credit the British Government with acting in good faith and friendship, but there was no blinking the fact that they had at Jidda an overzealous Minister, S. R. Jordan, who was working in numerous ways to supplant American interests in Saudi Arabia by British interests. Britain had been subsidizing King Ibn Saud for several years, and Minister Jordan was making full use of this fact to exalt British prestige by lowering our own.

Our Minister in Jidda, James S. Moose, Jr., informed us on March 31, 1944, of reports that Jordan had persuaded King Ibn Saud to remove certain key officials known to be friendly to the United States and to agree to appoint a British economic adviser and possibly a British petroleum adviser as well. He had also reported that Jordan, without consulting him, had arranged for certain road work in Saudi Arabia to be undertaken under the supervision of the British military, although General Royce, during his visit to Saudi Arabia in December, 1943, had discussed the construction of two military roads with King Ibn Saud, and the King had given his permission for United States military forces to make a survey toward this end.

It seemed to my associates and me that we should meet these developments in two ways. One was to increase our own economic assistance to King Ibn Saud so that he would not lean too heavily on Britain for aid. The other was to talk the situation over frankly with the British and reach an arrangement with them whereby our national interest in the petroleum resources of Saudi Arabia would be protected and Ibn Saud would not have an opportunity to play Britain and the United States off against each other with respect to the granting of help.

I outlined the situation to the President in a memorandum on April 3, 1944, stating our belief that we should extend additional financial and economic assistance to Saudi Arabia so as to safeguard our national interest in her petroleum resources. Pointing out that the Government of Saudi Arabia had relied principally upon British subsidies during the previous few years, I informed the President that we had now ascertained that the British Government proposed in 1944 to subsidize Saudi Arabia to the extent of nearly $12,000,000, which was approximately six times the value of Lend-Lease aid our Government contemplated extending in 1944.

After citing the activities of the British Minister in Jidda, I said: "If Saudi Arabia is permitted to lean too heavily upon the British, there is always the danger that the British will request a *quid pro quo* in oil. To obviate this danger, it is recommended that this Government share the subsidy on an over-all equal basis with the British."

The President wrote his O.K. on this memorandum, and we entered into negotiations with the British. These were conducted by Wallace Murray, Chief of the Office of Near Eastern Affairs, who had accompanied Under Secretary Stettinius on a special mission to London. The British assured us there had never been any intention on their part to undermine or to prejudice American oil rights in Saudi Arabia, and they agreed to investigate the possibility of an Anglo-American goods subsidy program for Saudi Arabia on as nearly an equal basis as possible.

The British proposed that a joint Anglo-American military mission, headed by a British officer, should be sent to Saudi Arabia. After obtaining the concurrence of the War Department, we agreed to this proposal since we recognized that the primary military responsibility in the Near East was British. We made our approval contingent, however, upon the Foreign Office's agreeing that an American should head any economic or financial mission sent to Saudi Arabia at Ibn Saud's request in view of the preponderant United States economic interests in that country.

The Foreign Office hedged on this reservation, saying that the leadership of an economic and financial mission should be determined according to which country had the preponderant interest in Saudi Arabian economy and finance at the time the mission were sent. We rejected this idea, saying that our proposal was based on the fact that the preponderant interest in the economy of Saudi Arabia was without any question American and presumably would continue to be so for a long time to come since the Saudi Arabian economy would be based on the oil produced by reason of substantial American capital investments. The British came back with the assertion that our claim to a preponderant American interest in Saudi Arabian economy was based on a "misconception of the facts" and stated that they would be very willing to reconsider the position when oil production had increased and Saudi Arabia no longer depended primarily on her economic relations with sterling-area countries.

We could reach no agreement. We were willing to agree that the British should head the joint military mission, but they sought to keep open the possibility of heading the joint economic mission as well, which we could not accept.

In July, 1944, however, we did agree to participate during 1944 equally in a joint supply program for Saudi Arabia which would make up the difference between inadequate imports and consumption. King Ibn Saud had appealed in June to both countries for assistance in alleviating a very grave economic situation in Saudi Arabia, and this agreement was a major step in putting the relations of Britain and the United States toward Saudi Arabia on a better footing.

Although our relations with Britain in regard to Saudi Arabia were now on a better basis, the activities of British Minister Jordan in Jidda continued in what we regarded as a definitely anti-American direction. On June 26 I had asked British Ambassador Halifax to call in order to raise with him the question of Jordan. I said to him that our officials in the Middle East were convinced beyond peradventure of doubt that Jordan was doing his level best to injure the United States Government's relations with King Ibn Saud, and was endeavoring in other ways to undermine our position in Saudi Arabia, and that we just could not put up with these activities without making constant and louder complaint to the British Government.

I cabled our Legation at Jidda on July 12 that the joint supply and financial program of aid to Saudi Arabia agreed upon between the British and American Governments was to be considered as expressing a single combined policy toward Saudi Arabia in this field. I instructed Minister Moose to treat all proposals relative to financial and supply aid to Saudi Arabia jointly with the British Minister, cooperating with him closely and wholeheartedly and making all approaches to the Government of Saudi Arabia on such matters jointly with him. I added that similar instructions were being sent by the British Government to Minister Jordan.

We continued to receive from our Legation at Jidda, however, dispatches showing that Minister Jordan refused to cooperate. We therefore informed the British Embassy that the continuance of Mr. Jordan in Saudi Arabia was unacceptable so far as we were concerned. Eventually, some time after my resignation, Jordan was transferred.

Saudi Arabia and her vast oil deposits provided one of the reasons for the negotiations we undertook with the British in 1944 for a worldwide agreement to cover the production and distribution of oil, in which other nations subsequently would be invited to join.

Throughout most of 1943 we at the State Department had been giving intensive study to the problem of oil reserves outside the United States. We had before us the statements of many experts that reserves inside the United States were dwindling and that the demands for oil during the war and the postwar period would be greatly augmented. I had set up a Committee on International Petroleum Policy within the State Department, with Economic Adviser Herbert Feis as its chairman, and had created the position of Petroleum Adviser. On Dr. Feis's recommendation, I appointed Max W. Thornburg to it. When we later learned, however, that Thornburg still was connected with an American oil company, I immediately requested his resignation, and in December, 1943, named as his successor Charles Rayner, who had been an independent petroleum producer for twenty-five years and had had no connection with a major oil company during that time. Rayner carried out his functions with marked efficiency.

Dr. Feis's committee submitted a report to me on March 22, 1943, saying that both Secretary of the Navy Knox and Secretary of the Interior Ickes had repeatedly indicated to the committee their eagerness that some action be taken to safeguard our petroleum reserve situation. After two meetings with the committee to consider their report, I sent copies of it on March 31 to Secretaries Stimson, Knox, and Ickes and suggested that they and I meet to discuss the situation. The report proceeded on the assumption that the future American demand for oil, both for defense and for essential economic requirements, would be in excess of production within the United States. It added: "Unless our ability to derive required supplies from abroad at all times (tranquil, overshadowed, or critical) is safeguarded, the United States will be in hazard (*a*) of having to pay an economic or political toll to secure the oil, or (*b*) actually fail to secure it."

The committee therefore recommended that, while continuing to study the possibility of concluding an international petroleum agreement, our Government should organize a Petroleum Reserves Corporation. This corporation would negotiate option contracts with companies (American or foreign, privately or publicly owned), holding petroleum concessions in foreign countries. The contracts would give the Government the right to procure specified amounts of petroleum for delivery to it at times to be agreed upon. They would be negotiated only with the consent of the Government in whose territory lay the reserves. The board of directors of the corporation might be composed of representatives of the State, War,

Navy, and Interior Departments, with the State Department representative as chairman.

We now began exchanges of views with those Departments. Stimson, Knox, and Ickes were of the opinion that the United States Government should become part owner, probably majority owner, of the American company producing Saudi Arabian oil. Admiral Leahy sent me a memorandum dated June 11, 1943, recommending that our Government should make immediate efforts to obtain from Saudi Arabia oil concessions for the United States Government for the purpose of establishing a naval oil-fuel reserve similar to those then existing in the United States. The Joint Chiefs of Staff, in a memorandum to the President, had emphasized the crisis in oil and proposed that the Reconstruction Finance Corporation be directed to organize a corporation specifically for the purpose of acquiring proven foreign petroleum reserves, including the immediate acquisition of a controlling interest by the United States Government in Saudi Arabian oil concessions. The President had directed Leahy to take up these recommendations with me personally.

During a series of meetings presided over by James F. Byrnes, Director of War Mobilization, the interested Government Departments reached the conclusion that a Petroleum Reserves Corporation should be set up.

A clear-cut difference of opinion developed during the conversations we were having with other Government Departments. Ickes believed, as he stated in a letter to the President, that the Government should purchase a controlling stock interest from the two parent companies in the American company developing oil in Saudi Arabia. The Joint Chiefs of Staff recommended the negotiation of a new oil concession with Ibn Saud by our Government. My associates and I, on the other hand, believed that the Government should not itself enter the oil business; it should merely contract with the American company owning the oil concessions in Saudi Arabia—ultimately known as the Arabian American Oil Company—for the creation of oil reserves to be delivered when called for. Moreover, we considered the problem of oil a delicate element in the more important question of our over-all foreign relations.

Accordingly, I sent the President a memorandum on June 14, 1943, which Feis, at my direction, had prepared. After stating our attitude that the task of proceeding in the petroleum field with the development and construction needed for war purposes was primarily one for the War and Navy Departments, the Petroleum Administrator for War (Ickes), and other interested Government agencies, with such cooperation as the State Department had given in many previous cases, we said:

"Experience clearly shows that the acquisition and maintenance of foreign concessions requires carefully directed negotiations with foreign Governments, and these negotiations are always closely connected with other questions in the political and economic field being dealt with at the same time.

"In each and every negotiation the Department has had to reckon with many and variable factors such as (a) the frequent tendency for foreign governments to seize control of oil resources or restrict their development to their own nationals; (b) rival efforts on the part of foreign countries and governments; (c) fears of imperialism; (d) the interplay of diplomatic bargaining."

We added that the principles on which our Government based its efforts to obtain control of petroleum reserves, and the use of such reserves, would affect every phase of our relations with foreign governments in the postwar period—including territorial settlements and matters affecting international political relations.

"It will be recalled," we said, "that in many conferences after the last war the atmosphere and smell of oil was almost stifling. It is essential that our own efforts in the period ahead be so directed as to achieve our ends without stimulating new restrictive moves on the part of other countries and creating intense new disputes."

We therefore thought the State Department should occupy an important place in the Petroleum Reserves Corporation and have prime responsibility for its negotiations with foreign governments.

As for Ickes's recommendation that the United States Government acquire controlling interest in the American company developing oil in Saudi Arabia, we stated our belief that, if it were approved, it would be necessary to notify King Ibn Saud of this intention and that it was not known what attitude he might take toward the entrance of the American Government into the business of developing oil reserves located within his domain. We also referred to a provision in the agreements between the company and Ibn Saud prohibiting the company, without the consent of the Saudi Arabian Government, from assigning to anyone its rights and obligations under its contract.

As to the Joint Chiefs of Staff recommendation that the United States Government negotiate with King Ibn Saud for oil concessions for itself, we pointed out that the most promising oil-bearing land in Saudi Arabia was already included within the concessions held by the American company. We added that any negotiations that disturbed the present concession might have adverse results and possibly lead to new demands either upon the company or upon our Government under penalty of reducing the present concession or of admitting representatives of other countries.

Representatives of the State, War, Navy, and Interior Departments next held a series of meetings in the office of Under Secretary of War Patterson to reconcile the views of the several Departments. This group drew up a report which I sent to the President on June 26, with a letter signed by Stimson, Ickes, Acting Secretary of the Navy Forrestal, and myself. This first recommended the establishment by the Reconstruction Finance Corporation of a Petroleum Reserves Corporation. It then submitted to the President the two conflicting views as to the method of obtaining Saudi Arabian oil for the Government—Ickes's proposal that our Government acquire 100 per cent of the stock of the company owning the oil concessions in Saudi Arabia, and the State Department's proposal that the Government contract with the company for the purchase of oil. The report stipulated that the Petroleum Reserves Corporation should not embark on any major projects without receiving the prior approval of the Secretary of State and that all major negotiations with foreign Governments should be conducted through or under the supervision of the State Department.

The President seemed to lean toward the recommendation that the Government acquire 100 per cent of the company's stock.

The Petroleum Reserves Corporation was set up. I stated I did not want to be chairman of it, and Feis, on my behalf, said he thought the logical choice should be Ickes, who was, in fact, elected president of the Board of Directors on August 9, 1943.

Under Ickes's impetuous leadership, the Corporation began to develop sweeping plans for the injection of the Government into oil fields not only in Saudi Arabia but in other areas as well. It drew up projects for expanding the operations of the Anglo-Iranian Oil Company, a wholly British-owned concern, for a new pipeline to the Mediterranean from the British-controlled Iraq oil fields, and for a refinery in British India. At the same time Ickes began negotiations with the Standard Oil Company of California and the Texas Company to purchase 100 per cent of the stock of the company—Arabian American—they had set up to produce oil in Saudi Arabia. The two companies, however, refused to permit the Petroleum Reserves Corporation to acquire 100 per cent of the company's stock, a controlling share, or even one-third.

As new reports began to be published about the failure of these negotiations, and about the ambitious plans of the corporation, I wrote Ickes, its president, on November 13, 1943, pointing out that its activities were already causing us embarrassment in the Near East, and might well weaken in the eyes of King Ibn Saud the position of the American company which held the oil concession in Saudi Arabia since there was now no assurance that its holdings would be substantially developed in the near future.

"This Department," I said, "believes that there should be a full realization of the fact that the oil of Saudi Arabia constitutes one of the world's greatest prizes, and that it is extremely shortsighted to take any step which would tend to discredit the American interest therein, whether that interest be of a public or private character."

We also objected to the corporation's seeking to aid the expansion of British oil interests, and pointed out that the expansion of American facilities should have priority over any further expansion of British facilities in the Near East area. "We believe," my letter stated, "that strong criticism will develop if British petroleum facilities in the Middle East are further expanded for American purposes and with American materials, for to do so will retard the development of American enterprises, jeopardize their holdings, and so tend to make this country dependent on British oil in the future."

We in the State Department had, in fact, been considering for some months a possible agreement between the United States and British Governments with respect to Near Eastern oil reserves. On December 2, 1943, I addressed a note to British Ambassador Halifax proposing that informal and preliminary oil discussions be undertaken between the two Governments. I sent the President a memorandum on the 8th reemphasizing that the full development of Near Eastern oil resources was of tremendous wartime and long-range importance. "Because of the complex problems involved," I said, "those resources, which are held to a substantial extent jointly by American and British interests, cannot be adequately developed unless the United States and British Governments reach an agreement providing for close cooperation." I suggested that, in view of the delicate political situation in the Near East and the close connection between foreign oil questions and the general conduct of our foreign relations, it was extremely desirable that any conversations with the British on oil be under the clear supervision and guidance of the State Department.

Ickes, however, wrote the President a letter—of which Mr. Roosevelt sent me a copy on December 29—stating, "This is my baby," and insisting that he himself be one of the negotiators. We in the State Department thought the negotiations should be begun by experts of the State and Interior Departments, but Ickes contended that they should be on a Cabinet level, and would not name a representative to sit for him.

We also suggested that any further negotiations with American oil companies whereby the Government would obtain an interest in the American company in Saudi Arabia should be postponed until it was seen what direction the negotiations with Britain would take, but Ickes objected. The President, in a memorandum to Ickes and me on January 10, adopted Ickes's position. "It is, of course, true," he said, "that the State Department should handle, in general, matters relating to foreign affairs—but at the present time I think it vital that we should go ahead with some speed in negotiating with the American companies, in order to find out just where the United States stands before we take the matter up with the British. . . . I feel that time is important—because after the war the American position will be greatly weaker than it is today. Can't we agree on a policy and on the method of putting it into effect?"

Ickes continued his negotiations with the American oil companies and reached an agreement late in January, 1944, for government construction of a pipeline from the Persian Gulf to some point on the eastern Mediterranean and for the establishment of a billion-barrel oil reserve in Saudi Arabia and in the sheikdom of Kuwait for the use of our armed forces. The President approved this agreement. I acquiesced in it with reservations. I did not want to see government ownership of the pipeline. I was willing to go along to the extent of government ownership during the period of the war, after which it would revert to private companies; Ickes on the other hand wanted permanent government ownership. Nor did I want to see the pipeline operated by the Government. Ickes compromised to the extent of agreeing that the pipeline should be privately operated and that at the end of the war the question of ownership should be reviewed.

Ickes, however, still wanted personally to conduct the negotiations with the British Government. During my brief absence from Washington early in February, he induced the President to make him chairman of the negotiating group, with the Under Secretaries of State, War, and Navy, and Charles E. Wilson, vice chairman of the War Production Board, as the other members. Under Secretary Stettinius, after telephoning me, informed the President of my view that it would be a great mistake to deprive the State Department of leadership in the negotiations, and that the discussions should be conducted on a working level with technical and political experts who could devote full time to the many intricate problems involved. I had already advised the British, with the President's approval, that the conversations would be conducted at the working level with the American group headed by Charles Rayner, Petroleum Adviser of the State Department, the other members being Paul Alling, Deputy Director of the Office of Near Eastern and African Affairs, and a representative of Secretary Ickes. I had likewise so advised the American petroleum industry.

The President thereupon, on February 15, suggested a compromise solution, whereby I would be chairman of the group, and Ickes vice chairman, the other members being the Under Secretaries of War and Navy and Wilson and Rayner.

The British, however, immediately protested this decision. They said it would be impossible to send representatives of Cabinet rank to Washington at that time in view of the coming invasion (of Normandy).

The President's reaction, which Stettinius communicated to Ambassador Halifax, was that the whole matter of mutual agreement on petroleum problems was of such extreme importance to both countries and to international security that high ranking representatives of both Governments should constitute the negotiating groups.

Thereupon Prime Minister Churchill cabled the President on February 20, stating that certain British quarters were apprehensive that this country wished to deprive the British of their Near Eastern oil interests. He added that any announcement of a conference on Near Eastern oil, with the American delegation led by the Secretary of State, was sure to raise questions in Parliament which the Prime Minister would be unable to answer with an assurance that no transfer of property was involved—although he himself was sure there was no ground for such suspicions so far as the United States Government was concerned.

President Roosevelt replied to this message two days later, saying he had particularly noted the Prime Minister's concern that a wrangle over oil between the two Governments be avoided. While the Prime Minister, the President said, had pointed to British apprehensions with respect to United States aims in the Near East, he himself was concerned over a rumored British desire to "horn in" on the oil reserves of Saudi Arabia. Mr. Roosevelt said that questions and problems that occasioned apprehensions and rumors of this kind clearly showed the great need for a basic Anglo-American understanding relative to the oil of the Middle East, from which should develop oil agreements more extensive in scope. He insisted on the negotiators being of Cabinet rank because of the importance of the negotiations, and said that he himself wished to preside at the first meeting of the joint discussion group, which would be held in the Cabinet room in the White House.

Following further exchanges of messages between the President and the Prime Minister, involving primarily an exchange of assurances with respect to British oil interests in Iran and Iraq and American interests in Saudi Arabia, they agreed that an announcement should be made of the forthcoming discussions, first on a technical, then on a higher, or Cabinet level. The President was very anxious to have this announcement made— it was issued March 7, 1944—because of press intimations of Anglo-American discord on oil.

The President was also concerned over opposition that had risen in the Senate following Ickes's announcements at the beginning of February concerning the pipeline agreement he had reached and his big oil expansion program throughout the Near East. This opposition in general stemmed from anxiety, on the one hand, over the extent—as indicated by Ickes's announcements—to which the Government was becoming involved in the oil business, and, on the other, over the extent of the major oil companies' control of government policy in this field. The implications with respect to our future foreign policy also aroused apprehension.

Following the passage of a resolution on March 13, the Senate established a special Committee to Investigate Petroleum Resources. After discussions between members of this committee and the State and Interior Departments, we informed our Legation at Jidda on June 27 that there was within our Government an informal understanding that no further action would be taken on the pipeline as a government project until after the British and American Cabinet-level discussions to take place shortly, and such public hearings as the Senate special committee might wish to hold subsequently. The plan for a government-constructed pipeline was not revived while I remained in office. When an Arabian American Company reconnaissance group desired to go to Saudi Arabia in the autumn of 1944 to survey a pipeline to be constructed by the company itself, the Department cabled our Legation at Jidda on October 16 that, if the question were raised by King Ibn Saud or officials of his Government, the position to be taken was that this was solely an Arabian American Company matter not involving this Government, although we had no objections to the company's plans of which we were fully informed. Subsequently, the company was successful in obtaining from certain of the governments directly concerned permission for the construction of the pipeline through their territories.

Meantime preliminary conversations on a technical level had been held in Washington between the British and ourselves, looking toward an Anglo-American oil agreement that subsequently would be joined by other nations. The British committee of Cabinet rank, headed by Lord Beaverbrook, arrived in Washington in July to conclude the discussions. I presided over the first meeting on July 25 and thereafter turned the meetings over to Ickes as vice chairman. An Anglo-American petroleum agreement was reached following a series of conferences, and was announced on August 8, 1944.

This agreement embraced five principles of cooperation between Britain and the United States with regard to international trade in petroleum. These were:

(1) Adequate petroleum supplies should be made available to the nationals of all peaceable countries at fair prices and on a nondiscriminatory basis, subject to such collective security arrangements as might be established.

(2) Petroleum resources should be developed in such a way as to encourage the sound economic advancement of the countries in which the petroleum deposits lay.

(3) There should be equal opportunity to acquire exploration or development rights in areas not already under concession.

(4) There should be respect for valid concession contracts and lawfully acquired rights. (This was designed to put an end to the suspicion that had beclouded Anglo-American relations in the Near East for many years.)

(5) The operations of the petroleum industry should not be hampered by restrictions inconsistent with the purpose of the agreement. (This principle restated the basic purpose of the agreement; namely, that the international petroleum trade should be conducted in an orderly manner on a world-wide basis so that ample oil supplies would become available in international trade to meet the economic needs of all coun-

tries, subject always to considerations of military security and to the provisions of international security arrangements.)

The Anglo-American agreement also provided for the establishment of an International Petroleum Commission. This would prepare long-term estimates of world petroleum demand and suggest how this demand might best be satisfied by production equitably distributed among the various producing countries. It would analyze short-term problems. It would make reports and recommendations to the two Governments.

The agreement was intended to be voluntary in nature, with no executive authority vested either in it or in the International Petroleum Commission to be established under it. It was preliminary to the negotiation of an international agreement to which the Governments of all producing and consuming countries interested in the international petroleum trade would become parties and which would establish a permanent International Petroleum Council.

I sent this agreement to the President on August 22, and he transmitted it to the Senate two days later.

Much adverse reaction followed the publication of the agreement. The American petroleum industry felt that the accord was so worded that it could be construed to cover operations of the domestic petroleum industry, and they were already apprehensive that Secretary Ickes was seeking to control these operations. It thought the agreement gave mandatory powers to the proposed International Petroleum Commission.

Such was the situation when I resigned at the end of November, 1944. In January, 1945, the President, at the suggestion of the State Department, asked the Senate to return the agreement for revision. Subsequently certain provisions were reworded so as clearly to limit its scope to the international and not the domestic trade in petroleum, and further to define the functions of the International Petroleum Commission as advisory and recommendatory only. Ickes went to London, obtained British approval of the revised agreement, and it was again submitted to the Senate, where it lies at this writing. The agreement in its final form embraced all the principles contained in the original agreement.

I continue to believe, as I have consistently advocated, that the United States Government should confine itself to the role of negotiator and mediator in the international petroleum field, and should not itself enter into the business of producing, transporting, or selling oil. It was from this viewpoint that I advocated an international agreement on petroleum.

Oil has become so important a commodity in international trade; it has so often in the past provided the spark for disputes between nations; it will continue so strong a temptation for the domination of small countries by strong nations, that I strongly believe that an international accord such as we negotiated is all-essential. For many years I have seen the problems of oil assume greater and greater importance in our foreign relations until I am convinced that an acceptable international understanding on the principles by which so vital a commodity is to be handled in world commerce has become an essential factor in the establishment and preservation of lasting peace.

111: The Problem of Jews and Arabs

FEW PROBLEMS of a more delicate nature faced us during the war than the question of the Jewish National Home in Palestine. On the one hand we had the burning aspirations of a great percentage of the Jews to establish a state for their people in Palestine, coupled with the fact that the barbaric Nazi persecution was forcing the Jews to flee the charnel house of Central Europe. On the other hand we had the fierce opposition of the Arabs to the establishment of a Jewish state in Palestine and to the continued immigration of Jews into Palestine, plus the fact that the decision in the case was the function of the British Government, not ours. We were constantly being pressed for action by the nearly five million Jews in the United States, while at the same time our representatives in the Near Eastern Arab countries, plus our own military officials here, were informing us of the danger of antagonizing the sixty million Arabs there at a moment when their help in a strategic area of the war was so vital.

Our own relations to Palestine rested on the American-British Mandate Treaty of December 3, 1924, whereby the United States had recognized Britain's mandate over Palestine confided to her by the League of Nations. This provided for nondiscriminatory treatment in matters of commerce; nonimpairment of vested American property rights; permission for Americans to establish and maintain educational, philanthropic, and religious institutions in Palestine; safeguards with respect to the judiciary; and, in general, equality of treatment with all other foreign nationals. We had no right to prevent the modification of the terms of the mandate, but we could refuse to recognize the validity of any modification as it affected American interests.

The Roosevelt Administration's diplomatic interest in Palestine began during the first term. A conflict having broken out in Palestine between Jews and Arabs in the spring of 1936, an investigation of the situation by the British Government gave rise to reports that Jewish immigration into Palestine might be suspended, severely curtailed, or completely eliminated. On July 27, 1936, I cabled Ambassador Bingham in London that influential Jewish groups here had informed the President that Britain was thinking of suspending Jewish immigration into Palestine. Saying that Jewish leaders here feared that such action might prove hard to revoke and might close the German and Polish Jews' only avenue of escape, I asked Bingham to mention this entirely unofficially and personally to Foreign Secretary Eden.

The following year, on April 27, I sent Bingham another telegram of similar tenor. I added that Bingham might mention to Eden that large groups of Jews here were of the opinion that, because of their experience under certain European Governments, Jews throughout the world had logically become the supporters of democratic institutions and looked naturally to the democratic Governments to give them equitable and fair treatment.

Then on October 12, 1938, shortly before the British Government's Palestine Partition Commission was due to report, I cabled Ambassador Kennedy, who had succeeded Bingham, to inform Eden's successor, Lord Halifax, that the White House and the State Department had received thousands of letters and telegrams of protest from all over the country. These messages inveighed against the British Government's alleged intention to eliminate or curtail Jewish immigration and thereby jeopardize the policy that the Balfour Declaration of 1917, with respect to the Jewish National Home in Palestine, had established.

In each of these telegrams to London, however, I instructed our Ambassador to make it entirely clear to the British that we were not in any way questioning Britain's responsibility for Palestine's administration or presuming to interfere in that administration.

Two days later we issued a long public statement of our position toward Palestine. In this we said: "As is well known, the American people have for many years taken a close interest in the development of the Jewish National Home in Palestine. Beginning with President Wilson, each succeeding President has on one or more occasions expressed his own interest in the idea of a National Home and his pleasure at the progress made in its establishment." I also referred to the joint resolution of Congress on September 21, 1922, of the same nature.

Finally the British Government, in May, 1939, released its White Paper on Palestine. Among other provisions, this eliminated immigration into Palestine after March 31, 1944, unless the Arabs agreed to its continuance. I had an analysis made of this document and sent it to the President.

Mr. Roosevelt strongly objected to the British White Paper in a memorandum he sent me on May 17, saying: "I have read with interest and a good deal of dismay the decisions of the British Government regarding its Palestine policy." He continued:

"Frankly, I do not believe that the British are wholly correct in saying that the framers of the Palestine Mandate 'could not have intended that Palestine should be converted into a Jewish state against the will of the Arab population of the country.'

"My recollection is that this way of putting it is deceptive for the reason that while the Palestine Mandate undoubtedly did not intend to take away the right of citizenship and of taking part in the Government on the part of the Arab population, it nevertheless did intend to convert Palestine into a Jewish home which might very possibly become preponderantly Jewish within a comparatively short time. Certainly that was the impression that was given to the whole world at the time of the Mandate. The statement on your Page 6, Paragraph 2, quoting the White Paper of 1933, bears out my contention."

The President, after noting that the new White Paper admitted that the British Mandate was "to secure the development of self-governing institutions," said: "Frankly, I do not see how the British Government reads into the original Mandate or into the White Paper of 1922 any policy that would limit Jewish immigration.

"My offhand thought is that while there are some good ideas in regard to actual administration of government in this new White Paper, it is something that we cannot give approval to by the United States.

"My snap judgment is that the British plan for administration can well be the basis of an administration to be set up and to carry on during the next five years; that during the next five years the 75,000 additional Jews should be allowed to go into Palestine and settle; and at the end of five years the whole problem could be resurveyed and at that time either continued on a temporary basis for another five years or permanently settled if that is then possible. I believe that the Arabs could be brought to accept this because it seems clear that 75,000 additional immigrants can be successfully settled on the land, and because also the Arab immigration into Palestine since 1921 has vastly exceeded the total Jewish immigration during this whole period."

This memorandum coincided also with the thoughts of the State Department. The President, however, did not want it communicated to the British Government, and we limited ourselves to a cable to Kennedy on May 23, 1939, instructing him to mention informally and orally to Foreign Secretary Halifax that disappointment here, especially in Zionist circles, over certain of the White Paper's provisions was rather wide-spread, particularly over those that foreshadowed a marked reduction eventually in Jewish immigration into Palestine. A flood of protests was, in fact, pouring into the State Department.

War came to Europe only three months later. Following the outbreak of fighting, Zionist agitation in this country lay comparatively dormant for a period, although several delegations of Zionists and also Dr. Chaim Weizmann, president of the World Zionist Organization, called on me during 1940 and discussed the development of Palestine as a Jewish refuge after the war.

In the spring of 1941, however, the American Palestine Committee was organized under the chairmanship of Senators Wagner and McNary and with Cabinet members Ickes, Wickard, and Jackson, along with prominent members of Congress and other public figures, as members. The British Embassy thereupon made several representations to us to the effect that if speeches were made in the United States by persons high in the Government advocating the immediate opening up of Palestine to Jewish resettlement planners in the event of a British victory, very great unrest would be created in the Arab world, particularly in Iraq, where a highly critical situation already existed. A rebellion had broken out in Iraq, which the British later had to quell.

I took the occasion of the twenty-fifth anniversary of the Balfour Declaration of 1917 to make a public statement relating to Palestine on October 31, 1942. A group of rabbis having presented to me a memorandum on Palestine, I pointed to the fact that the United States had followed with interest and sympathy the work that had been done under the Balfour Declaration, in which work American citizens had played a useful part.

"Of all the inhuman and tyrannical acts of Hitler and his Nazi lieutenants," I said, "their systematic persecution of the Jewish people—men, women, and children—is the most debased." But I put the solution of the Jewish problem on a broader basis than merely that of the National Home in Palestine. "The Jews," I said, "have long sought a refuge. I believe that we must have an even wider objective; we must have a world in which Jews, like every other race, are free to abide in peace and in honor."

The continuing Zionist agitation in the United States began to have increasingly serious repercussions among the Arab states in the Near East, according to reports we were receiving in the State Department late in

1942 and early in 1943. The Prime Minister of Iraq, Nuri Pasha, pro-tested to our Minister at Bagdad about the pro-Zionist statements emanat-ing from the United States. The heir to the Egyptian throne, Prince Mohammed Ali, raised the same point with Minister Kirk in Cairo.

Lieutenant Colonel Harold B. Hoskins, who, speaking Arabic fluently and knowing the Near East well, had been sent to that area in the autumn of 1942 on a mission for the Joint Chiefs of Staff, reported to us from Cairo on January 23, 1943, his fears that unless some action were taken to reduce the tension, Arab-Jewish conflict might soon break out again in Palestine, even before the end of the war, and throw all the Arab Near East into turmoil. Egyptian Minister Mahmoud Hassan Bey called on me on February 3, 1943, to hand me an *aide-mémoire* from his Government calling attention to "the deplorable effect on the Arab and Mohammedan world" of the Zionist activities, and to their possible repercussions with respect to this Government and the Allied war effort.

King Ibn Saud of Saudi Arabia sent President Roosevelt a message in April and a letter in May. He expressed his personal interest, as an Arab and Moslem leader, in the Arab question, with particular reference to Palestine and Syria. He said, however, that, although urged to make representations to the United States Government respecting Palestine, he had refrained from doing so only because of his desire not to embarrass the United States at this time or to prejudice the United Nations cause by taking a step likely to increase Arab-Jewish antagonisms. He wanted to know whether the President approved of his attitude of silence and, if so, whether he would be advised in advance of any steps of an affirma-tive character contemplated by the American Government with respect to Palestine.

On May 26, 1943, I sent to Cairo for delivery to the King a message from the President voicing his appreciation of the King's helpful coopera-tion and sympathetic understanding. He expressed his complete agreement with the King's policy of silence as being most helpful to the United Nations. If, however, the President said, a friendly understanding on Palestine should be reached by the interested Jews and Arabs through their own efforts before the end of the war, a development of that nature would be highly desirable. In any event, he assured the King, it was our Government's view that no decision altering the basic situation of Pales-tine should be reached without fully consulting with both Jews and Arabs.

The President felt strongly that, if the Arab and Jewish leaders could be brought together for friendly conversations, they might be able to settle their basic differences. In a further message to Ibn Saud in June, Mr. Roosevelt said: "It appears to me highly desirable that the Arabs and Jews interested in the question should come to a friendly understanding with respect to matters affecting Palestine through their own efforts prior to the termination of the war."

The following month I instructed Colonel Hoskins, at the President's direction, to pay a personal visit to King Ibn Saud and ask him whether he would enter into discussions with Dr. Chaim Weizmann or some representative selected by the Jewish agency. The President had already talked this project over with Dr. Weizmann. The King, whom Hoskins saw in August, 1943, refused to see Weizmann, giving as one of several reasons that, despite his position of leadership in the Arab world, he could not, without prior consultation, speak for Palestine, much less "deliver" Palestine to the Jews, even if he were willing for even an instant to consider such a proposal.

In this connection the President had already invited Ibn Saud to come to the United States, hoping that, among other objectives, they might be able in personal conversation to solve some of the problems connected with Palestine.

During the spring and summer of 1943, we discussed with the British a suggestion by Colonel Hoskins that a joint declaration be issued by the United Nations stating that no final decisions regarding Palestine would be taken until after the war, and that any postwar decisions would be taken only after full consultation with both Arabs and Jews. To these points we added another; namely, that, if the interested Jews and Arabs found it possible to arrive at a friendly understanding through efforts of their own prior to the war's end, such a development would be extremely desirable. The President approved this text, and the British did likewise. As a result of objections from the War Department, however, the issuance of the statement was postponed, and President Roosevelt and Prime Minister Churchill decided at the First Quebec Conference, on August 22, 1943, that the question of the statement should be held in abeyance and be discussed further between the two Governments from month to month.

When Colonel Hoskins returned to the United States from his mission to King Ibn Saud, and saw the President on September 27, 1943, Mr. Roosevelt said to him that his own thinking leaned toward a wider use of the idea of trusteeship for Palestine. He thought Palestine should be made a real Holy Land for all three religions, with a Jew, a Christian, and a Moslem as the three responsible trustees. While I was at the Moscow Conference, the State Department gave serious study to this idea; but the impossibility of bringing the Jews and Arabs together on a common, friendly ground at that time, and the danger of stirring the sands of the Near East by a premature attempt to settle the question of Palestine made it wiser to postpone action until a more propitious time.

Beginning with a conversation I had with British Ambassador Halifax on December 13, 1943, we made numerous efforts to induce the British to relax the decision they had made in 1939 to terminate immigration of the Jews into Palestine after March 31, 1944. On that occasion I said to Halifax, who had called at my request, that the United States Government had been exerting itself in every possible way to render all aid and relief to the persecuted Jewish people. "The President and I and other officials of this Government," I said, "in the light of our international interest in the Jewish situation, are in earnest sympathy with the Jews' proposal that immigration into Palestine be extended by the British Government beyond March 31 and that in every other possible way relief and aid be given to the Jewish people." I mentioned that the only question in my mind was how I could best define the attitude of our Government publicly without seriously embarrassing the British in dealing with the military situation in the Near East.

Following several further conversations I had with Halifax, during which he assured me that Eden was giving urgent consideration to my suggestion, the British stated their intention of continuing immigration into Palestine for a certain period after March 31, 1944, inasmuch as the immigration quota for the preceding five years lacked being filled by about 30,000 immigrants.

Early in 1944 we were suddenly confronted by an alarming situation developing in the Near East as a result of resolutions introduced in the Senate and House of Representatives stating that "the United States shall use its good offices and take appropriate measures to the end that the doors of Palestine shall be opened for free entry of Jews into that country, and that there shall be full opportunity for colonization so that the Jewish people may ultimately reconstitute Palestine as a free and democratic Jewish commonwealth."

At the State Department we felt that the passage of these resolutions, although not binding on the Executive, might precipitate conflict in Palestine and other parts of the Arab world, endangering American troops and requiring the diversion of forces from European and other combat areas.

It might prejudice or shatter pending negotiations with Ibn Saud for the construction of a pipeline across Saudi Arabia, which our military leaders felt was of utmost importance to our security. And it would stimulate other special interests to press for the introduction of similar resolutions regarding controversial territorial issues relating to areas such as Poland and Italy.

The reaction in the Near East to the mere introduction of the resolutions had been, as we feared, sharply antagonistic. We received protests from the Governments of Iraq, Egypt, and Lebanon, from King Ibn Saud and from Imam Yahya of Yemen. We assured them that the resolutions, even if passed, were not binding on the Executive. The President on March 13 renewed his previous assurances to the King that it was our Government's view that no decision should be reached changing Palestine's status without full consultation with both Jews and Arabs. The Department sent assurances along the same line to the Egyptian Government and to Imam Yahya.

In the latter notes the Department said: "Although Palestine is primarily a British responsibility, it is the view of the Government of the United States that no decision altering the basic situation of Palestine should be taken until an appropriate time is reached, and that at such a time the Governments responsible for the establishment of peace and the maintenance of law and justice in the world should come to an equitable settlement of all the questions involved, in full consultation with both Arabs and Jews." This continued to be our position throughout the remainder of my period in office.

We were also considering what steps we could take to induce both Houses of Congress not to consider the resolutions. At my request, Assistant Secretary Breckinridge Long met with a group of Senators in Senator Connally's office and orally expressed the Department's views. I had a memorandum drawn up which I intended to give the President to be sent to Congress. At that point, however, Secretary of War Stimson wrote a letter to Senator Connally in the latter's capacity as chairman of the Senate Committee on Foreign Relations. Stimson forthrightly pointed out that the Senate resolution was a matter of deep military concern to the War Department since its passage, or even public hearings on it, would be apt to provoke dangerous repercussions in areas where we had many vital military interests. General Marshall testified in identical vein before the Senate Foreign Relations Committee in executive session. In consequence of the position taken by the State and War Departments, the resolutions were not then reported out of the Senate or House committees.

The apprehensions of the Arabs, however, were further aroused when the President gave two Jewish leaders, Dr. Stephen S. Wise and Dr. Abba H. Silver, an interview on March 9, 1943. The press reported the President as having authorized them to announce that "when future decisions are reached full justice will be done to those who seek a Jewish National Home," that this Government "has never given its approval to the White Paper of 1939," and that the President was "happy that the doors of Palestine are today open to Jewish refugees."

Two days later Minister Kirk in Cairo reported that he had received an inquiry from the Egyptian Prime Minister, Nahas Pasha, regarding this reportedly authorized statement. On March 14 I sent the President for his approval two proposed replies, one to Kirk in Cairo, the other to Minister Loy Henderson in Bagdad. The President approving, these went out to Kirk and Henderson, informing them that the Zionist leaders' statements had in fact been authorized by the President substantially as reported in the Near East. The Ministers were to point out that a Jewish National Home, rather than the Jewish commonwealth referred to in the Congressional resolutions, was mentioned in this statement and that, although the American Government, it was true, had never approved the White Paper, our Government, it was also true, had never taken a position relative to it. Our Ministers were also to renew assurances that it was our Government's view that no decision changing Palestine's basic situation should be arrived at without full consultation with both Jews and Arabs.

Prime Minister Nahas Pasha replied that the Arabs were reassured, although not entirely, by the clarification of the President's statement to the Zionists.

In general the President at times talked both ways to Zionists and Arabs, besieged as he was by each camp. Rabbis Wise and Silver believed that the President had made pledges to them. The State Department made no pledges.

When Under Secretary Stettinius went to London on a survey mission in the spring of 1944, I sent Wallace Murray, Chief of the Office of Near Eastern and African Affairs, with him to discuss Palestine, among other problems, with the British Foreign Office. Murray took with him the draft of a possible joint statement on Palestine by the two Governments similar to that we had prepared the year before. In London it was agreed, however, that the draft should be held in reserve.

During the Republican and the Democratic conventions in 1944, planks were inserted in both platforms urging free immigration into Palestine and the creation there of a Jewish state. The Iraq Government forthwith expressed its deep concern. I sent the President a memorandum on July 26, 1944, saying: "I believe that it would be advisable for leaders of both parties to refrain from making statements on Palestine during the campaign that might tend to arouse the Arabs or upset the precarious balance of forces in Palestine itself."

Fortunately Palestine did not become an issue in the 1944 campaign.

As I left office our policy toward Palestine was one of constantly being on the alert to prevent that explosive area from touching the match to the powder train of the Near East. We could not resolve the questions of the relationship of the Jews to the Arabs, the immigration of the Jews into Palestine, and the creation of a Jewish state in Palestine since these were primarily the responsibility of the British. We had, however, made clear our interest in the solution of the Palestine question; we had induced the British to relax their decision to cut off Jewish immigration into Palestine, and we had made serious, albeit unsuccessful, efforts to bring the Arabs and Jews together for friendly discussion of their differences.

At the same time we had been eminently successful, through unremitting diplomacy, in preventing the already dangerous issue of Palestine from embroiling the whole of the Near East and from stirring up the Moslems in India. The strategic Near East continued to furnish the British and ourselves with much needed oil and to serve as the southern gateway for supplies to Russia without requiring the dispatch of any troops to that area from the vital combat zones in Europe and Africa. It is easy to see the serious consequences to the United Nations cause that might have followed from any diversion of Allied troops to the Near East because of Palestine when the British were thrown back to El Alamein or when we and the British were grappling with the Germans in North Africa. The effect of such German machinations as led to the uprising in Iraq and the British and Free French invasion of Syria would have been multiplied had fighting broken out between Jews and Arabs.

Palestine was but one facet of the unremitting effort of the State Department for over a decade to assist the Jews caught by the unspeakable Nazi persecution. In the 1930's we had made innumerable representations to the Germans and taken concrete steps to evince our condemnation of this persecution and to induce the Nazis to desist. We had likewise brought every possible influence to bear on countries adjacent to Germany to receive, feed, and clothe the Jews of Germany, and on other countries to afford them refuge. This Government took the initiative in creating the Inter-Governmental Refugee Committee, of which Myron C. Taylor became president. In the State Department we began to fill the German, Austrian, and later Czech immigration quotas almost entirely with Jews, and in addition we issued scores of thousands of visitors' visas to Jews in the hope that after coming to this country they could find refuge in other countries or could eventually be received here permanently.

From 1933, when Hitler's persecution of the Jews began, until I resigned at the end of November, 1944, we took into the United States from Germany and Nazi-occupied Europe approximately 600,000 persons, mostly refugees from persecution for racial, political, or religious reasons. In one year alone, that ending in June, 1941, we granted enough visas to save 135,000 refugees. We had made special efforts to get out rabbis, professors and students in rabbinical colleges, Jewish writers, and others who were the light of the Jewish Church. Many came out through Russia and went to Japan, where we issued visas for them.

After the closing of our consulates in Germany and German-occupied areas in June, 1941, our efforts to save the Jews became much more difficult, and the difficulties increased after Pearl Harbor. We could no longer send Americans into Germany to try to induce the Nazi officials to permit the Jews to leave. Shipping was much harder to obtain. Finding it impossible to issue visas to Jews in German-held countries, we concentrated on granting visas to Jews who escaped from that area into adjacent countries.

In 1942 however, we and people throughout the world were horrified to learn that Hitler and his Nazis were inflicting on the Jews the most fiendish outrage that savages or demons could commit against human beings—their inconceivable effort to exterminate utterly the entire Jewish race within their reach. As these menacing developments gradually revealed themselves, the American Government and people, especially the Jewish people, gave the most serious attention to the problem of thwarting Hitler's designs. We exhausted all efforts authorized by law to grant visas or in any feasible way to aid in securing the exit of Jews or to assist their escape from the Hitler area of savagery. And we officially and emphatically, along with Britain and Russia, called to the attention of the

Nazi authorities the condign punishment that would await any of them guilty of such atrocities.

During the war, with the cooperation of the British, Portuguese, and Spanish Governments, and the French National Committee of Liberation in North Africa, we got out of Spain some 30,000 refugees who had trickled over the Pyrenees to that country. We sought places of refuge for them ranging from Madagascar, Cyrenaica, Palestine, and French North Africa, to the Dominican Republic and Ecuador.

President Roosevelt and I had many conferences on the subject of Hitler's attempt to exterminate the Jews. We eagerly studied all ideas and information that might be in the least helpful in relieving their inconceivable situation.

The inescapable fact was, however, that Jews could not leave German-occupied Europe unless they escaped across borders into neutral Spain, Switzerland, or Sweden, or unless the German authorities permitted them to leave. And the Germans permitted Jews to leave only when they were amply paid to do so. We were reluctant to deposit sums of money to the credit of the Nazis, even though the deposits were to be made in Switzerland, were to be liquidated only after the end of the war, and apparently could not be used by the Nazi leaders. Moreover, the State Department did not have the large amounts of money and the personnel needed to carry out a plan of reaching and bribing the German officials in charge of the extermination program.

We also found that the Nazi authorities were sending out intelligence agents in the guise of refugees, and the Federal Bureau of Investigation was called upon to handle a number of such cases. We accordingly set up a control commission in the Department to screen refugee applications, consisting of representatives of the State, War, Navy, and Justice Departments, and the President appointed a little group to serve as an appeals board from this commission.

In 1944 the President created the War Refugee Board to handle the work of aiding refugees, and the State Department fully cooperated in its institution and administration.

Naturally the more extreme sympathizers in this country, especially among the Jews, and some in high positions such as Secretary of the Treasury Morgenthau, found grievous fault with the State Department and especially with every official handling the refugee problem. It was but natural that, in their anguish over the projected extermination of their race in Europe, they should feel that even the strenuous efforts we were making were inadequate. Nevertheless, it can be safely said that the results accomplished by the State Department, up to the time of the creation of the War Refugee Board, at least equalled those of all other countries combined, and that some hundreds of thousands of Jews are now alive who probably would have fallen victim to Hitler's insane enmity had not the Department begun so early and so comprehensively to deal with the refugee problem. President Roosevelt at no time complained to me that the Department had not done enough.

Our interest in the establishment of a Jewish national home in Palestine was paralleled, especially during the war years, by our interest in seeing that independence should eventually come to all the Arab countries and also by our sympathy with the aspirations of Arab leaders toward the creation of an Arab federation. The Arab national movement had begun in the nineteenth century in an effort to achieve independence from Turkey, and it had been no little encouraged by the liberal ideas imparted by American educators in the Near East. Woodrow Wilson expressed the sympathy of this country toward Arab national aspirations by stating in the twelfth of his Fourteen Points that "the other nationalities which are now under Turkish rule should be assured an undoubted security of life and an absolutely unmolested opportunity of autonomous development."

After the First World War, however, the League mandates granted to Britain and France in the Near East seemed to the Arabs a negation of their hopes for the independent Arab empire they believed had been promised them. Their primary objective in the postwar period became the termination of French and British control. They felt that until the Arabs both in the mandated areas and in the nominally independent states could achieve complete independence, any movement toward unity among the various Arab countries was impossible.

After Iraq became independent in 1932, the Arabs concentrated on obtaining independence for the Levantine states of Syria and Lebanon, which were under French mandate. France agreed in 1936 to grant independence to these two mandates, but did not carry out her agreement.

Syria became of keen concern to us in June, 1941, when the British and Free French were forced to invade the mandate after finding that the Germans, with acquiescence of the Vichy Government, were using it as an air base. At that time both the French and the British promised independence to Syria and Lebanon. At the conclusion of the fighting, the British expressed their disinterest in the Levant states and acknowledged the "predominant" French position there. The Free French General Catroux proclaimed Syria independent with certain conditions. We were asked to take a position on this question when the British, after officially recognizing Syrian independence on October 28, 1941, informally urged us to do likewise on the ground that such action would bring greater stability to the Near East and would also strengthen the position of the Allies in the Arab countries.

We demurred, however, on the grounds that recognition without the negotiation of a new treaty might jeopardize the rights we had under the 1924 treaty with France, guaranteeing us nondiscriminatory treatment in Syria and Lebanon; that we were still maintaining relations with the Vichy Government; and that the British acknowledgment of France's "predominant" position and an assertion made by General de Gaulle that France had a "preeminent and privileged position" raised serious complications. We also suggested that our delay in recognizing the independence of Syria might well support British policy since the United States would remain in a position to insist on clarification of the special privileges sought by the French, whereas the British were precluded from doing so by the fact that they had already acknowledged these special privileges.

General Catroux, the Free French Delegate to the Levant states, proclaimed Lebanon independent on November 26, 1941, but emphasized that France did not renounce her "tutelary friendship" or privileged position acquired over the centuries. We thereupon issued a public statement on November 29, 1941, expressing the sympathy of our Government and people with the natural and legitimate aspirations of the peoples of Syria and Lebanon, including the full enjoyment of sovereign independence, which we had endorsed in principle in the treaty with France in 1924 consenting to the French mandate. We added that this treaty guaranteeing American rights must be regarded as continuing in effect until a new treaty could be concluded.

This statement was welcomed by the Syrian and Lebanese authorities, but they, along with the British and Free French, continued to press for formal recognition. We thought it wiser, however, to hold such recognition in abeyance for the time being, to see how the declarations of independence were being implemented. This attitude was amply justified in the spring of 1942 when a serious conflict developed between the French and the British as a result of the latter's insistence that elections be held in Syria and in Lebanon to choose representatives to replace the handpicked appointees placed in power by the French at the time of their "independence" proclamations. Relations between General Spears, the British Minis-

General de Gaulle our concern, as a country participating in the common war effort, that there be scrupulous fulfillment of the assurances that had been given the Levant states. If this were not so, we said, the Arab world and all peoples asked to believe in our sincerity would feel justifiable doubts relative to the assurances given by any of the Allied nations or groups.

We ourselves made a gesture toward encouraging the peoples of Syria and Lebanon when, on the recommendation of the State Department, the President approved of our giving our Consul General in Beirut the additional rank of Diplomatic Agent, a designation reserved for representation in semi-sovereign states. Mr. Roosevelt named George Wadsworth, a Foreign Service officer, to the new office, the appointment being announced on October 2, 1942.

The British and Free French continued to quarrel over British insistence that the French live up to the assurances they had given with regard to the independence of the Levant states, although relations became temporarily less strained following an exchange of correspondence between Prime Minister Churchill and De Gaulle in the autumn of 1942. Finally the French gave in on the question of holding elections, which were conducted in July and August, 1943, in Syria and Lebanon, respectively. Nationalist regimes were elected in both states, and a crisis was soon precipitated as the new Governments indicated their intention to secure control of the governing powers still exercised by the French.

In view of the potential gravity of the situation the British handed us an *aide-mémoire,* dated September 10, in which they reiterated their willingness to recognize France's "predominant position" in the Levant states. They added, moreover, that they would not oppose treaties between the Free French authorities and the Syrian and Lebanese authorities if such treaties, defining their relationship, were desired by both parties.

In our reply on October 25 we made it clear that our Government "was not a party to the agreements concluded prior to the invasion of the Levant states by British and Free French forces in 1941, and is not prepared to admit that France should enjoy a 'preeminent and privileged position' in Syria and the Lebanon." However, we added, should the French and the Levant states desire to enter into free and voluntary negotiations, we were in substantial agreement with the British provided that the interests of the local populations and of the United States were adequately safeguarded and that the treaties would only be applied provisionally pending formal ratification.

As it became apparent that the situation was mounting to a climax in Lebanon, we instructed Counselor Robert D. Murphy at Algiers on November 9, 1943, to advise the appropriate French authorities that the United States Government was of the opinion that practical steps should be taken to implement the "independence" promised Syria and Lebanon. Failure to do so, we said, would cast doubt on the announced principles of the United Nations.

Before Murphy could act on these instructions, however, the French on November 11 arrested the President of Lebanon, Sheik al-Khuri, and the Cabinet, and installed a government of their own choosing. Riots broke out in Beirut.

We immediately sent out two cables, one to Diplomatic Agent Wadsworth in Beirut, the other to Murphy in Algiers. We instructed Wadsworth to have no official relations with the regime just set up by the French. We instructed Murphy urgently to inform the French National Committee in Algiers that our Government had learned with surprise of the repressive action taken by their authorities in Lebanon. We said it was "difficult to understand how the French, whose country is now groaning under the heel of the invader, can be unmindful of the aspirations toward independence of another people"; that the French action in Lebanon "must cast the gravest doubt upon the sincerity of the avowed declarations of all the United Nations"; and that the United States Government could not "permit itself to be associated in any way with such acts of repression."

We further said that unless the French National Committee took "prompt steps to restore the duly elected Government of the Lebanese Republic and to implement the solemn promises of independence given to the Lebanese people" in 1941 in the name of the French National Committee, our Government would be "obliged publicly to announce its complete disapproval of the acts of the French authorities in the Lebanese Republic and to take such further steps as may appear appropriate." We added that we would take such action with the utmost reluctance but that we felt "it would be less detrimental to the united war effort than for us by silence to appear to accept a situation which is contrary to the aims and principles for which the liberty-loving nations are fighting."

We repeated this telegram to London, Beirut, and Cairo, for the information of the appropriate authorities, and used it as the basis of our replies to protests over the French action we received from the Egyptian, Iraq, Syrian, and Saudi Arabian Governments.

I kept President Roosevelt, who was on his way to Cairo, informed of the situation, and he discussed it with Prime Minister Churchill, whose Government was taking a strong position similar to ours. I received a message from the President on November 20 saying: "I think we should back up the British position in Lebanon and try to make it even more positive."

The British, who commanded the defense forces in Lebanon, informed the French National Committee that they would declare martial law unless the duly elected Lebanese Government were reinstated by November 22. The French at first tried to compromise by reinstating only the President and not the Cabinet, but the British and we continued to insist on the reinstatement of the entire Lebanese Government. The French thereupon gave in, and the crisis—a crisis not only for the Near East, but for relations with the French National Committee and for the principles of the United Nations—ended. We issued a press release on November 26 noting with approval the remedial action taken by the French National Committee and expressing "the earnest hope of this Government that friendly negotiations can now proceed in an atmosphere of good will on both sides for the solution of the underlying issue of the independence of the Levant states."

In December, 1943, General Catroux concluded a series of informal accords with the Syrian and Lebanese Governments providing for the transfer to them of the powers formerly exercised by the French in their joint behalf. In succeeding months these accords were gradually given practical application, and in August, 1944, we concluded that the Governments of Syria and Lebanon could now be considered representative, effectively independent, and in a position satisfactorily to fulfill their international obligations and responsibilities. Thereupon, with the President's approval, we informed the Governments of Lebanon and Syria on September 7, 1944, that we were prepared to extend full and unconditional recognition of their independence and to exchange Ministers with them upon receipt from them of written assurances that the existing rights of the United States and its nationals (embracing nondiscriminatory treatment) would be fully recognized. The Syrian and Lebanese Governments having given these assurances, the President nominated George Wadsworth as our first Minister to those countries. In a public statement on September 19, 1944, I said:

"I am confident that the free nations of Syria and Lebanon will play a helpful part in the cooperative task of international peace and progress which lies before us."

At that moment the French were pressing the Levant Governments for the conclusion of treaties of alliance with France. We received reports that the French desired that recognition be given to a "special position" for France in Syria and Lebanon, and that the Syrian and Lebanese Govern- ments were resisting this pressure. We accordingly informed the French National Committee, in a memorandum of October 5, 1944, that our Government could "not agree that France or French nationals should enjoy discriminatory privileges in independent Syria and Lebanon." Sub- sequently in a telegram to Wadsworth we took the position that, while we would not approve a treaty under which France or her nationals ob- tained discriminatory privileges, we were of the opinion that it would be well for those Governments to consider seriously the arguments the British had made in favor of negotiations between them and France, particularly the desirability of obtaining formal and clear confirmation by the French of the independence of Syria and Lebanon before the withdrawal of British forces by reason of the favorable progress of the war.

As Syria and Lebanon took long but troubled steps toward independ- ence, the movement toward a Pan Arab Federation in the Near East gathered impetus. Foreign Secretary Eden had declared to the House of Commons on February 24, 1943, that the British Government would view with sympathy any move among the Arabs to promote their economic, cultural, or political unity. Eden said, however, that the initiative would clearly have to come from the Arabs themselves, and that, so far as he was aware, no such scheme which would command general approval had yet been worked out.

This declaration induced Nuri Pasha, Prime Minister of Iraq, to write Nahas Pasha, Prime Minister of Egypt, urging the latter to take the initiative in calling an Arab congress. Nahas Pasha soon began a series of individual conferences with representatives of Iraq, Trans-Jordan, Saudi Arabia, Syria, Lebanon, and the Yemen, regarding an Arab union, preliminary to convening an Arab congress.

It was during this series of conferences that our Government stated its sympathetic attitude toward the formation of an Arab union or federa- tion. The Saudi Arabian representative, while conferring with Prime Minister Nahas Pasha, addressed a query to Minister Kirk in Cairo to learn the attitude of the United States Government toward an Arab union.

On October 26, 1943, the Department (I was then in Moscow) replied, in paraphrase:

"This Government desires to see the independent countries of the Near East retain their freedom and strengthen their economic and social condition, and fully sympathizes with the aspirations of other Near Eastern countries for complete liberty.

"If the peoples of the Near East should find it advantageous to unite of their own free will, it naturally follows from this Government's basic attitude that such a development would be viewed with sympathy, always on the understanding that it should take place in accordance with the principles of the Atlantic Charter and in harmony with the declarations of Secretary Hull, notably those of July 23, 1942, and September 12, 1943.

"It is realized that the countries concerned will shape their own decision, but it seems to this Government that the events and problems of the war years have shown that the Near Eastern countries need greater strength in the economic, social, and cultural domains, and that first steps toward unity might well have these ends in view."

We repeated this reply to our diplomatic missions in the Arabic-speaking countries for their information.

Our attitude, therefore, was that we fully favored the concept of an Arab federation, but we took the realistic view that the Near Eastern countries should move toward this objective gradually and should take the first steps in the economic, social, and cultural fields before proceeding to political federation.

When the convening of a preliminary Arab conference was under discussion in July, 1944, the Saudi Arabian Government again sought our Government's views. We replied in substantially the same terms as in October, 1943. We also referred, however, to the position we had taken on the Palestine question in March since this question obviously would have to be solved before any true Arab unity could be achieved.

As I left office, I entertained the strong hope that the Arab states of the Near East would soon begin to take the economic, social, and cultural steps we believed necessary as an approach toward political unity, that they would be able to compose the conflicting ambitions of various of their leaders, and that, not too many years after the conclusion of the war, they would be able to bring stability, unity, and economic development to that historic corner of the world.

112: Italy: Enemy and Friend

PRESIDENT ROOSEVELT and I believed almost from the time of Mussolini's declaration of war against the United States, four days after Pearl Harbor, that we should draw a distinction between the Italians on the one hand and the Germans and Japanese on the other. In the discussions I had with the President on this subject in 1942 we reached two conclusions. The first was that Americans had always been friendly with the Italians, despite our opposition to the Fascist regime, and that Mussolini had led the people of Italy into an unpopular war without in the slightest consulting them. The other was that it might be possible to withdraw Italy from the war before the surrender of Germany and Japan, and that this withdrawal would in fact hasten that surrender. Italy's retirement, we felt, would be accelerated if we were to adopt an attitude toward the Italians different from that toward the Germans and the Japanese.

In consequence of this position, Attorney General Biddle announced on Columbus Day, October 12, 1942, that Italian aliens in the United States would no longer be classed as "alien enemies." The following day Assistant Secretary of State Berle, recalling in a public address the pledge in the Atlantic Charter that all peoples had the right to choose the form of government under which they would live, said that this pledge would be redeemed when Italy had rid herself of her Fascist government. He said that no punitive peace for Italy was envisaged, and that Americans did not desire to destroy Italy as a nation.

Three years of war, punctuated by defeat after defeat, which reached a climax with the Western Allies in full possession of Italy's African possessions and Sicily and about to put foot on the Italian mainland, brought the Italians to the end of their resistance. After exchanges of telegrams, in which the State Department took part, President Roosevelt and Prime Minister Churchill agreed on a joint message to the Italian people which they made public on July 16, 1943. In this they stated: "The sole hope for Italy's survival lies in honorable capitulation to the overwhelming power of the military forces of the United Nations. If you continue to tolerate the Fascist regime which serves the evil power of the Nazis, you must suffer the consequences of your own choice."

Nine days later Mussolini resigned, and King Victor Emmanuel III entrusted the Government to Marshal Pietro Badoglio. On July 31 I sent the President a memorandum suggesting that, since it was obvious that the Soviet Government was becoming concerned over the Italian situation, a joint Anglo-American message should be sent to that Government informing it of developments and asking for any suggestions the Russians might care to offer. I attached a draft of a message which stated that this Government continued to share the view that it was essential that the United States, British, and Soviet Governments keep one another fully informed regarding military and political developments in the various areas in which their respective armed forces were operating.

The President agreed to this approach.

During the following weeks negotiations for surrender were conducted in Lisbon between representatives of the Anglo-American Combined Chiefs of Staff and representatives of Marshal Badoglio. The State Department had little share in these discussions, which were of a military nature. We saw to it that the Russians were kept informed of the terms of surrender, and the British did likewise. On August 28 Admiral Standley, our Ambassador in Moscow, cabled us that the Soviet Government approved the terms and empowered General Eisenhower to sign on their behalf, a special representative of the Soviet Government not being required in this instance.

On the same day I sent the full draft instrument of surrender and a summary outline to the Governments of Russia, the British Dominions, Brazil, Ethiopia, Greece, and Yugoslavia and to the French Committee of National Liberation. The Greek Government had informed us of its interest in two regions then occupied by Italian forces—Epirus and the Dodecanese Islands—but, with the approval of the President, I informed Greek Ambassador Cimon P. Diamantopoulos on September 15 that it was the policy of this Government that territorial questions be left for settlement until after the war.

A plenipotentiary of Marshal Badoglio signed the terms of surrender in Sicily on September 3, and Eisenhower and Badoglio announced them on September 8, the day they became effective. Two days later President Roosevelt and Prime Minister Churchill sent a joint message to Marshal Badoglio and the Italian people urging them to strike hard alongside their American and British friends to drive the Germans out of Italy.

During the discussions between the British and ourselves on the terms of surrender for Italy, which were drawn up by the Combined Civil

Affairs Committee of the Anglo-American Combined Chiefs of Staff in Washington, a basic cleavage of opinion had developed over the status of the Italian Crown and the Badoglio Government. The British had strenuously objected to American proposals to limit the scope and duration of authority of the Badoglio Government and to suspend the power of the Crown in Italy. This cleavage later became deeper and more pronounced.

I myself was not at all sympathetic to the idea of keeping King Victor Emmanuel on the throne. He had, to all intents and purposes, gone along with Mussolini. We had hoped that the King would keep Mussolini from going to war, but he had done nothing, possibly because he could do nothing. In any event, his name had been associated with that of Mussolini in aligning Italy militarily with Germany against Britain and France, and later against Russia, and still later with Germany and Japan against the United States. I felt that Italy was virtually without a chief of state after the King had diminished himself and his position to such an extent.

As for Badoglio, he was the appointee of a King with whom we had no sympathy. He was adequate for the purpose of signing the terms of surrender, but I did not consider him adequate for the purpose of governing Italy. I felt that, as soon as feasible, the people of Italy, represented by the parties in opposition to Fascism, should be permitted to express their choice of the form and personnel of the Government they wanted.

As I talked over these ideas with the President, I found he was fully of the same opinion.

The British, on the other hand, and Prime Minister Churchill in particular, would have been glad to see the Italian royal family continue its rule. They wanted the royal family kept in power at least temporarily, but with the idea in mind that during this temporary period the King could strengthen his position and render his rule or that of his family permanent.

I sent a telegram on September 22 to Robert D. Murphy, the State Department representative on General Eisenhower's staff, giving him and Eisenhower the President's and my thoughts on the policy he should carry out with respect to Italy and the Italian Government. This stated that Eisenhower should make recommendations from time to time to lighten the provisions of the Italian armistice in order to permit the Italians to wage war against Germany within the limit of their capacities. If the then Government of Italy declared war on Germany it would be permitted to carry on as the Government of Italy and treated as a cobelligerent. It had to be clearly understood, however, that these concessions were not in any way to prejudice the untrammeled right of the Italian people to decide on the form of government they would eventually have. And no final form of government for Italy would be decided upon until the Germans were driven from Italian territory. Finally, Eisenhower should encourage the vigorous use of Italian armed forces against Germany.

On October 13, 1943, the Italian Government declared war on Germany. Badoglio's proclamation to this effect, in the name of the King, stated that the Government he headed would shortly be completed, and that representatives of every political party would be asked to participate so that it might be a truly democratic Government. This arrangement, he said, would in no way impair the untrammeled right of the Italian people to choose their own form of democratic government when peace was restored. On the same day, Roosevelt, Churchill, and Stalin issued a joint statement accepting Italy as a cobelligerent.

At that time I was en route to the Moscow Conference. I have already recounted how, at that conference, Molotov, Eden, and I agreed upon a policy to restore democratic institutions and practices in Italy. We likewise agreed to establish the Advisory Council for Italy, consisting of representatives of the Governments of Great Britain, the United States, the Soviet Union, Greece, and Yugoslavia, and the French Committee of National Liberation. The Council provided a channel for the expression of United Nations policy toward Italy, and made recommendations concerning this policy to the Allied Commander-in-Chief in Italy, General Sir Henry Maitland Wilson. Those United Nations who were not actively taking part in the fighting in Italy but who had an interest in Italian affairs were allowed a voice in Allied policy in Italy through the Advisory Council.

As I returned from the Moscow Conference on November 10, Marshal Badoglio was having difficulty incorporating the other political parties into his Government as he had promised in his October 13 proclamation. Generally they did not relish serving under the King; they thought he should abdicate; and they did not consider Badoglio himself a shining emblem of democracy.

The center of this opposition to the King was Carlo Sforza, who had been Italian Foreign Minister prior to the advent of Mussolini to power. He had spent some years in the United States lecturing and writing, and was the acknowledged leader of Italian anti-Fascists in North and South America. Sforza came to see me on August 16 and expressed his desire to return to Italy. Following an exchange of letters he had with Assistant Secretary of State Berle, in which he agreed to support Marshal Badoglio or any other Italian Government acceptable to the United Nations in fighting against Germany, our Government aided his return to Italy. Passing through London en route to Italy, Sforza had luncheon with Prime Minister Churchill and repeated to him the same promise.

After Sforza returned to Italy and consulted other anti-Fascist leaders, he balked at the prospect of entering an Italian Government as long as Victor Emmanuel remained on the throne. Both the King and Badoglio sought personally to induce him to enter their Government, but he refused. He drew up papers of abdication for the King's signature, naming the Prince of Naples, the King's grandson, as his successor, with Badoglio as Regent. These would have passed over the King's son, Prince Humbert of Piedmont, who seemed as unacceptable as his father to the anti-Fascist parties. The King refused to sign.

Generally we in Washington thought Sforza's formula a happy solution. The British, however, thought otherwise. We took a less serious view of the consequences of abdication than the British, who felt that so fundamental a decision should not be made at that time.

In November, 1943, when the Italian political situation was critical, General Eisenhower recommended a compromise solution to which the President agreed. This was that, if the King failed to form a liberal Government but refused to abdicate, the existing arrangement with the King and Badoglio should continue until Rome was in Allied hands. Eisenhower made this recommendation, believing that the occupation of Rome was imminent.

Following the Allied landing at Anzio, I cabled the acting American representative on the Advisory Council for Italy, G. Frederick Reinhardt, on January 25, 1944, the thoughts of the President, my associates, and myself concerning the Italian situation. I said that the State Department had concluded that there should be no further delay in reorganizing the Italian Government on a broad political basis, and that liberal forces in Italy should be allowed to proceed at once to set up a representative Italian regime to function until the full liberation of the country.

We had also concluded, I said, that no political reconstruction under King Victor Emmanuel was possible. We believed he would never abdicate of his own free will, and that the longer his abdication was postponed the more difficult it would be to bring it about. We were definitely opposed to the King's return to Rome, believing that his arrival there would strengthen his determination to remain on the throne. Nevertheless, I said, it was not our intention to go into the constitutional question of the monarchy as an institution and form of government; in line with our announced policy, that question should be left to the determination of the Italian people when Italy was freed of the Germans.

We had also communicated this position to the British. Mr. Churchill, however, did not like it. On January 23 he cabled the President urging that we should hold on to Badoglio and the King until we could be sure of something better and more effective for our purpose, and do nothing to weaken them in the interval. On the contrary, he said, should we become masters of Rome in the near future the early return of Badoglio and the King to the capital would be beneficial. He thought that, after Rome was occupied, we could at leisure survey the scene and see what other alternatives were in sight.

The same month the British and we stated there was no objection on our part to the return from Russia to Italy of Palmiro Togliatti, alias Ercole Ercoli, the leading Italian Communist who had spent many years in Russia and had risen to a high position in the Communist International. We stated, however, that this had to be agreeable to the Italian Government and to Allied Forces Headquarters at Algiers. Togliatti went to Italy soon thereafter.

The expectation of Allied military authorities that Rome would soon be occupied proved vain. The Germans established a strong defensive line between Naples and Rome and also contained our landing at Anzio. Moreover, Allied troops were already being diverted from the Mediterranean theater to the British Isles for the landing in Normandy.

At the beginning of February, Mr. Churchill cabled the President that he was much concerned at any attempt to work with Sforza and the Italian Junta at this critical moment in the battle. He accused Sforza of having completely broken his undertaking to support the Badoglio Government, and asked that no decisions be taken without Britain being consulted and without the President and the Prime Minister trying to reach agreement. He believed we were in for a very heavy struggle on the Italian front.

I talked the situation over with British Ambassador Lord Halifax on February 9 and informed him that, when the State Department recommended that the King not be permitted to go to Rome but that consideration be given to other elements in the political situation, it appeared that the Allied Armies would be in Rome within a few days, whereas it now appeared that they would not be there for some time to come. I said that the application of our attitude toward the King was not of the same urgency as it had appeared a short time before.

Later in the day I discussed the matter with the President in the same vein. Accordingly he sent me a memorandum on February 10, saying: "Please take such action as is necessary and feasible in the Department of State to insure that no effort is made by the United States Government to effect any change in the existing Government of Italy at the present time, and until our military situation in the Italian campaign is sufficiently improved to warrant risking disaffection of those Italians who are now assisting the Allied Armies."

I had left Washington that morning for a short vacation, and Stettinius communicated this to our representatives in Italy.

The Executive Junta of the six opposition parties in Italy, however, formally requested Allied support for its program of obtaining the King's abdication and preparing the formation of a Government with full powers to govern until general elections could be held after the liberation of all Italy. The Supreme Allied Commander for the Mediterranean theater, General Wilson, recommended support of this program.

American concurrence in this recommendation was submitted to the British members of the Combined Civil Affairs Committee of the Combined Chiefs of Staff on February 23. Our agreed position was that General Wilson should be authorized to inform the Junta that their program would have Allied support; to confirm that support to the King if necessary; and so to inform the members of the Advisory Council.

British concurrence, however, was never given. A few days later, on February 29, Prime Minister Churchill publicly stated to the House of Commons that Britain opposed any change in the Italian Government at present. This statement received an adverse reaction from all the anti-Fascist parties in Italy and was construed by them as a negative Allied reply to the Junta's proposal. We hastened to state to our representatives in Italy on March 2 that the Prime Minister's statement was not to be considered as a reply to the Junta, that the subject was still being considered by the Combined Chiefs of Staff, and that only from them could come any agreed Allied reply.

We had already stated our attitude directly to Marshal Badoglio in a letter from the President dated February 21, which was drafted in the State Department. This answered a letter to the President from Badoglio in which the latter pleaded that Italy be given full status as an ally. The

President rejected this appeal "until the Government of Italy can also include the articulate political groups of anti-Fascist liberal elements." He referred to the existing plan "for the reconstruction of the Italian Government on a broad political basis as soon as the present critical military situation will permit and not later than the liberation of Rome."

That same day the King, up to that moment stubbornly determined to prolong himself on the throne regardless of the political turmoil his decision was producing, weakened. He informed British General MacFarlane, chief of the Allied Control Commission for Italy, that, since his position had become almost untenable "because the Allies had permitted him to be openly discredited and attacked through the Psychological Warfare Board and lax censorship," he proposed to nominate Crown Prince Humbert as his lieutenant with full powers as soon as Rome was reached, and to make an announcement to that effect immediately. He did not, however, carry out this latter intention.

During March the President and Prime Minister Churchill exchanged numerous cables seeking in vain to compose the divergent American and British viewpoints. On March 7 the President reiterated to Mr. Churchill our view that liberal groups must be brought into the Italian Government at the earliest opportunity. The following day the Prime Minister gave the President his opinion that it would be a serious mistake "to yield to agitation, especially when accompanied by threats on the part of groups of politicians who are seeking office," and that action should be postponed until the battle had been gained, or, best of all, until Rome had been taken.

The political situation in Italy was deteriorating, however, to the disadvantage of the Allied war effort, and the President cabled the Prime Minister on March 8 asking for his suggestions as to how it could be remedied in a way acceptable to the British. Five days later the President cabled again, urging action on the basis of the plan approved both here and by the Allied commander in Italy and his British and American advisers. The Prime Minister replied on March 15 that the six anti-Fascist parties were not representative of Italy or Italian democracy and that they could not now replace the existing Italian Government, which had "loyally and effectively" worked in our interests, but that the question of timing would, of course, have to be reviewed if the capture of Rome were unduly delayed. He said the War Cabinet felt that nothing could be worse for our joint interests and for the future of Italy than to set up a weak democratic Government which "flopped."

In his cables the Prime Minister pointed out that Britain had suffered 232,000 casualties in her war with Italy which had lasted since June, 1940, as well as extensive ship losses. He therefore felt that his views toward Italy should receive the President's consideration. He pleaded that the divergence which had risen between the two Governments be kept quiet.

The President cabled Mr. Churchill on March 17, agreeing that the divergence of views should not be divulged "particularly at this time," but saying that the situation should be carefully watched and the matter be kept continually before the Advisory Council for Italy.

Suddenly, while these numerous exchanges of cables between the President and the Prime Minister were occurring, the Soviet Government out of a clear sky announced that it was exchanging diplomatic representatives with the Badoglio Government. Simultaneously the Communist Party in Italy deserted the six-party front and declared its support of the King and Badoglio.

This unilateral action, taken without advance consultation with the British or ourselves, was highly disconcerting. It tended to undermine the authority of the Advisory Council for Italy through which the United Nations carried on relations with the Badoglio Government. Neither the British nor ourselves had diplomatic representatives accredited to that Government.

I instructed Ambassador Harriman in Moscow on March 16 to see Molotov and explain to him that all the complicated machinery of control for Allied government in Italy was designed to support and secure the supreme authority of the Allied Command, and that any development outside the established machinery of control over Italian administration, economy, and resources must be brought into relationship with the Allied military authorities responsible for that major theater of operations.

I added that at the Moscow Conference the United States and Great Britain, in accordance with Soviet desires, had welcomed and agreed to full Soviet participation in all matters of policy with regard to Italy. The Moscow Conference had thus established the principle of Allied as against individual approach to particular questions in the liberated areas of Italy, including relations with the Italian Government. Up to the present time, I said, the Soviet Government had given us no indication that these arrangements were in any way unsatisfactory, and it was a fact that the Soviet representatives on the Advisory Council and on the Control Commission were afforded means of contact with the Italian authorities identical to those enjoyed by the British and American representatives.

In conclusion I pointed out that the supreme responsibility for matters relating to the Italian theater continued to be vested in the Allied Commander-in-Chief, and that no special arrangement between the Italian Government and one of the Allied Governments could modify in the slightest degree that responsibility.

We informed Badoglio, moreover, that the Italian Government was not entitled to make any arrangements with any foreign Power, whether Allied or neutral, without the consent of the Supreme Allied Commander.

Molotov sought to justify the Soviet action on the ground that Russia had not been sufficiently consulted concerning developments in Italy—this despite the fact that we had made every effort to keep Russia thoroughly informed.

I instructed Ambassador Harriman on March 24 to say to Molotov that we expected that, during the period of our active military operations against Germany, any further developments in the relations of the Soviet Union with Italy would be referred to the Advisory Council for consideration and appropriate action.

The President and Prime Minister Churchill had agreed in their early discussions concerning Italy that, the Mediterranean being in general a British theater of operations, Britain should have the major degree of control in Italy. This applied to the command of the military operations there and also to the conduct of the Allied Control Commission and Allied Military Government. The British occupied most of the key posts in the military command and in civil affairs.

Nevertheless, when Badoglio, in a conversation with Samuel Reber, our political adviser on the Allied Control Commission, expressed his regret on March 22, 1944, at what seemed to him a decision by the United States Government to "pull out of" the Mediterranean, both politically and militarily, leaving the dominant role to others, I took sharp exception to his statement. I cabled Reber on April 3 that, if any suggestion came up that we were "pulling out," he should state that the policy of this Government had undergone no change whatever from the time we undertook the campaign in Italy with the Anglo-American landing in Sicily. We had, I added, just as much interest as before in the Italian situation, and we had just as much hope that Italy would be restored to the family of nations and that the Italian people would, as soon as military exigencies permitted, be free to choose their own leaders and Government.

ter to the Levant states, who was a personal friend of Prime Minister
Churchill, and General Catroux, the Free French Delegate, deteriorated.

We sent instructions on April 24 to our Consul General at Beirut,
Cornelius Van H. Engert, to say to the local British and French com-
manders, Generals Spears and Catroux, that our Government would be
very glad to assist in any way we could to achieve a better understanding among the French, the British, and the peoples of the Levant states.
As the situation worsened, we took the question up with the British Foreign Office.

General de Gaulle, by agreement with Foreign Secretary Eden, went
to Beirut in August in an effort to clarify the situation. We immediately
began to receive reports, however, that his presence in the area was having
exactly the opposite effect. De Gaulle emphatically and repeatedly told
our Consul at Beirut, William M. Gwynn, who was then in charge, that
he was determined to bring about an immediate showdown with the British in the Levant. He complained that, through General Spears's intervention in Levantine internal affairs, the British had broken their promises
to acknowledge the predominance of the Free French. He said that if the
British did not agree to remove Spears all collaboration would end. De
Gaulle was apparently convinced that the British intended to eliminate
the French from Syria and Lebanon. He told Gwynn that France would,
when possible, grant independence to the Levant states, but that this
could not be done until the peoples were ready for it, which might not be
for many years.

I cabled this information to Ambassador Winant in London on August 21, 1942, instructing him to discuss the situation with Eden again.
I authorized Winant to say that we were unable to support in their en-
tirety either the Free French or the British positions, but we could not
remain indifferent to a dispute that had an important effect on the common war effort. I said we thought that De Gaulle's statement that the
Levant states might not be ready for independence for many years was
not in harmony with the statements made by the Free French and the
British just before they occupied Syria when, primarily for its propaganda
value with the Arabs, they had announced that the Allies were bringing
independence to the two areas, or with the later proclamations by General
Catroux that the two Levant states had begun an independent existence.
On the other hand, I said, General Spears seemed to be exceeding the
functions of a foreign diplomatic representative.

I cabled Consul Gwynn at Beirut on the same day to point out to

Since the President and the Prime Minister were unable in their exchanges of telegrams to resolve the differences between our two Governments over whether and when the Italian Government should change or the King go out, I instructed the acting American representative on the Advisory Council, G. Frederick Reinhardt, on March 24, to place the question on the Council's agenda to be worked out by that body.

The British Embassy had left with us an *aide-mémoire* on March 6 containing Eden's suggestion that both Governments watch developments without declaring for any solution, and that the Combined Chiefs of Staff inform General Wilson to this effect. In reply we referred to a statement by the President in his telegram to Mr. Churchill on March 13 when he said he had not at any time intended to convey to the Prime Minister his agreement that all political decisions should be postponed until after Rome had been taken. We stated that this Government favored the proposal presented by the Junta of the Italian anti-Fascist parties involving the abdication of the King and the delegation of all or some of the royal powers to a lieutenant. We desired an immediate solution along these lines. The mere policy of preserving the status quo until after the liberation of Rome favored the position of one group, and we could not avoid the responsibility of supporting one of the various solutions. We said we were opposed to a policy calculated to suppress normal political activity in those areas of Italy restored to Italian administration.

As a result of our initiative, the Advisory Council began a discussion of the question of the Italian Government. Since the King's stubborn determination to keep his throne still seemed to be the major obstacle, the American representative, Robert D. Murphy, obtained the agreement of his British colleagues that he should inform the King personally and unequivocally that the time had come for him to retire.

Murphy saw the King on April 10 and demanded his acceptance by the following day. Apparently relying on the support of the Italian Communist Party, the King refused to go further than announce his intention to withdraw in favor of Crown Prince Humbert after Rome was occupied. The British representative would not agree to press the matter further, and Murphy therefore consented to the formula which the King announced on April 12. The Soviet representative had no part in this *démarche*, but he was kept fully informed, and the Soviet Government went along with it.

The Executive Junta of the opposition parties decided on April 16 to accept the King's plan and to enter immediately a new Government composed almost entirely of the representatives of the six anti-Fascist parties. The new broad-based Government under the premiership of Badoglio was announced on April 21, and for the first time in two decades that part of Italy which had been liberated from German and Fascist domination had a truly representative Government.

At this time Marshal Badoglio sent the President a personal letter asking for "a full reexamination of the very harsh terms made to us six months ago" with a view to Italy's transition from cobelligerency to alliance. He made the same request of the British.

For three months we had been exchanging cables with the British on the subject of an Italian Government request of December 27, 1943, that it be permitted to make formal announcement of its desire to adhere to the principles of the Atlantic Charter. We saw no objection to this wish, but the British were opposed. Finally, British Ambassador Halifax came to see me on March 31 and handed me a memorandum from his Government sustaining the British position and pointing out that it would be most inexpedient to take any action that would give even the appearance of creating an obligation to maintain Italian territories intact. The matter rested in abeyance.

The British now made known to us on April 20 their views concerning Italy's plea for the status of an ally. The British felt that, while Italy's position as a cobelligerent entitled her to better treatment than as merely a defeated enemy, she must not forget her position as a defeated enemy nor claim the privileges of an ally. The greater the concessions now made, they thought, the more difficult would it be to impose such sanctions as the Allies might wish when all Italy had been freed, and at the end of the war. The British said they planned to seek Soviet agreement to a positive stand that Allied status for Italy could not be considered at the time, but before drafting the note they asked that we coordinate our views.

We agreed with this position, and so informed the British. I cabled Murphy on April 29 that, should the matter be raised in the Advisory Council, he should make it clear that the Department had no intention of agreeing to Allied status for Italy.

Since agitation for Allied status continued, I cabled Murphy again on May 16, stating that the plight of Italy had the full sympathy of the Department and that this Government should take with the Allies all feasible steps to strengthen the new Italian Government and assure its position until Rome was reached. Nevertheless, I added, the Department considered it premature to raise the question of Allied status. This was not only because of the far-reaching consequences this would have toward breaking down the entire machinery of the Allied Control Commission and the armistice terms far in advance of the date when Italy, as a defeated Power, would inevitably sign a peace treaty, but also because of the unfavorable impact it would have on the Yugoslavs, the Greeks, and the French, sufferers from Italy's aggression.

The Allied armies were now in full campaign to capture Rome. For eighteen months the question of whether Rome might be preserved from bombing had been a subject for diplomatic exchanges among ourselves, the British, and the Vatican. The British, whose capital, London, had been bombed by Italian planes, did not wish to renounce the possibility of bombing the Italian capital.

Myron Taylor, the President's representative to the Vatican, had suggested to Mr. Roosevelt on November 30, 1942, that this Government adopt an independent course. The President asked me the following day to prepare a reply. I sent the President a memorandum on December 3, stating my own view that it would be inadvisable for us to adopt an independent course from that of our principal associate in the war. "It seems to me," I said, "that if we disagree with the policy of the British Government in regard to the bombing in Italy, we should communicate with them and endeavor to reach a meeting of minds and a common policy."

The President replied to Taylor in this sense.

The Apostolic Delegate in the United States, Archbishop Cicognani, left a memorandum with Assistant Secretary Berle on December 4, requesting this Government to use its good offices so that the Pope might be assured, at least informally and confidentially, that Vatican City and the city of Rome might be spared the horrors of aerial bombardment. Taylor sent the President on December 17 a further message from the Vatican stating that the Vatican had undertaken negotiations with the Italian Government to remove Axis military installations from the Eternal City, and that the Italian Government had given on December 13 oral assurances that the Supreme Command and the General Staff, together with Premier Mussolini, were about to leave Rome.

The day following this memorandum from Taylor to the President, Mr. Roosevelt sent me a note, dated December 18, in which he said:

"I really think that England and the United States could agree not to bomb Rome on condition that the city itself, outside of the Vatican, be not used in any shape, manner, or form either by the Germans or the Italians for war purposes.

"I understand that today most of the Italian Departments have left Rome with their civil and military personnel, but that Germans, who are of course all military, are using Rome as central headquarters.

"I should think that we might consider that it is up to the Vatican itself to propose that Rome be demilitarized. If that is accomplished, there is no reason for us to bomb it."

British Ambassador Halifax took up with me on December 21 the question of stating certain conditions which, if carried out, would relieve Rome of the risk of being bombed. These included the removal of the Italian Government and all German organizations from the Rome area within a certain time limit, the removal to be verified by Swiss officials.

"This Government," I replied, "has been approaching the matter the other way around, so to speak. Instead of presenting what is really an ultimatum as to the evacuation from Rome of all military agencies, including the King, the German officials and others, this Government feels, and has so indicated to the Vatican and others, that we do not want to bomb Rome or see it bombed. At the same time we have inquired why Italians and those at the Vatican who do not want Rome bombed are not proceeding to cause objectionable military agencies, properties, and interests to be cleared out of Rome before making pointed and unqualified requests that Rome be not bombed."

I said we were also calling attention to the fact that many of the United Nations, like Britain, had been and were being bombed to the limit of endurance in the most inhuman, uncivilized, and unauthorized manner.

"Instead of an ultimatum in effect," I concluded, "this Government prefers to keep alive all its rights with respect to the possible bombing of Rome and in the meantime from week to week inquire of those opposing such bombing why they are not more fully and actively paving the way for their objective by causing a removal from Rome of objectionable interests and agencies."

I also had the British Embassy informed, through Ray Atherton, Chief of the Division of European Affairs, that we doubted whether the Italians had the power to agree to an ultimatum and to force the Germans to leave Rome. If the ultimatum were not accepted, we should then be in a position either of having made an empty threat or of being forced to bomb Rome. The implications of the latter step and its effect on the war effort might be serious in the extreme.

The President, having received a further letter from Myron Taylor, urging that we take some action, sent it to me with a notation: "What do we do about this next?" I replied on January 5, 1943, stating that we were awaiting the reaction of the British to our negative position on a possible ultimatum, and suggesting that we continue to wait for it.

"The memorandum from the Apostolic Delegate," I said, "indicates that the military objectives, both Italian and German, are actually being transferred from Rome and that the initiative for this action has been taken by the Holy See. This confirms the position which we took with respect to the British proposals, that is, that those officials, both Vatican and Italian, interested in saving Rome from bombardment should more fully and actively pave the way for their objective by causing the removal from Rome of the objectionable military agencies, properties, and interests."

Ambassador Halifax sent me a memorandum on January 12 stating that his Government had decided, somewhat reluctantly, to abandon its idea, partly as a result of our attitude. The British also felt it would be well to keep the Italian Government and the Vatican guessing about our policy toward the bombardment of Rome. Moreover, the British Government had promised Egypt that Rome would be bombed if Cairo were bombed by the Axis.

Harold H. Tittmann, Jr., who represented us at the Vatican in the absence of Myron Taylor, cabled us on January 12 that he was stating to questioners that he had received no instructions from his Government on the subject of the bombing of Rome, and that we must be reserving our right to bomb should the military situation require it. Tittmann asked our approval of this position, which I gave. The War Department also agreed with this attitude.

This continued to be our policy until the taking of Rome. The initial effort of the Italians to remove their military installations from Rome was not followed by the Germans. Following a statement by Pope Pius XII appealing again for the safety of Rome, I stated publicly on March 13, 1944, that the Allied military authorities in Italy were dealing primarily with considerations of military necessity forced on them by the activities and attitude of the German military forces. Naturally, I added, we were as much interested as any Government or any individual in the preservation of religious shrines, historic structures, and human lives. "If the

Germans," I concluded, "were not entrenched in these places or were they as interested as we are in protecting religious shrines and monuments and in preserving the lives of innocent civilians and refugees, no question would arise."

The President the following day stated to the press that the Germans were using the Holy City of Rome as a military center, whereas we had tried scrupulously—often at considerable sacrifice—to spare religious and cultural monuments, and we would continue to do so.

After receiving an appeal from Irish Prime Minister de Valera on April 3, the President replied on April 19 that, if the German forces were not entrenched in Rome, no question would arise concerning the city's preservation.

The center of Rome was, in fact, not bombed, although Allied planes dropped bombs on the city's railroad yards. The Allied advance on Rome was carried out so as to encircle the city and force the Germans to retire without contesting the capital street by street, which would have wrought great destruction. When the Allies reached Rome they found the city comparatively untouched, with the exception of the fact that the Germans, on leaving, had crippled its water supply.

On June 5, the day after the fall of Rome, King Victor Emmanuel carried out his promise and transferred his powers to Crown Prince Humbert. The King had wanted to go to Rome, but I cabled Kirk and Murphy on May 31 that we felt that under no circumstances should he be permitted to return to Rome at that time.

Crown Prince Humbert entrusted Badoglio with the task of forming a new Government, but the latter was unable to do so. A new Cabinet was then constituted, with Ivanoe Bonomi, a prominent anti-Fascist leader, who had been in hiding in Rome during the German occupation, as premier.

Almost immediately difficulties rose between us and the British over the new Government. General MacFarlane, head of the Allied Control Commission, insisted to Bonomi that Count Sforza should not be appointed Foreign Minister. Since he undertook to speak in the name of the British and American Governments, we instantly protested to the British that MacFarlane had no right to speak in our name on a matter of this nature; and we requested General Wilson, the Allied commander, to inform Bonomi that MacFarlane's position did not represent the views of the United States Government since the appointment of Sforza would be entirely agreeable to this Government.

More basically, Prime Minister Churchill objected to the formation of the Bonomi Government itself. In an irate telegram to the President on June 10, 1944, he gave his opinion that Badoglio's replacement by "this group of aged and hungry politicians" was a great disaster. He said Badoglio, from the time he had safely delivered the fleet into our hands, had been a useful instrument, and he added that he had thought it was understood that Badoglio was to carry on, at least until the democratic north could be brought in and a thoroughly sound Italian Government could be formed. He objected that the Advisory Council for Italy had not been consulted. He said he was not aware that we had given the Italians, who had cost us so dearly in life and material, the right to form any government they chose without reference to the victorious powers.

The President sent me this cable for the preparation of a reply. I sent him a preliminary memorandum on June 13, suggesting that we should not be unduly influenced by Mr. Churchill's precipitate action, that the latter's alarm might be unwarranted, and that his attitude toward the political developments in Rome did not appear to accord with American policy. I indicated further that, pending the liberation of all Italy, no better indication of the popular will had appeared than that expressed through the parties of the Italian Committee of National Liberation. I said our policy had been to welcome political solutions worked out by the Italian people themselves, that such a solution seemed to lie in the present Italian Government, and that its anti-Fascist and democratic character should be welcomed and supported by this Government and the other democracies. I concluded that any interference on our part at this time to change the complexion of a Government which we had every reason to believe was friendly to the Allies and bitterly anti-Fascist and anti-Nazi would appear to be contrary to the Moscow Declaration and to our general policy of encouraging the development of a truly democratic, representative Government, and would be generally misunderstood.

After obtaining the views of the Advisory Council for Italy and General Wilson, we prepared the President's reply to the Prime Minister, which he duly sent. In this Mr. Roosevelt said he had reached the conclusion that it would be a grave mistake not to permit the prompt installation of the Bonomi Cabinet. Badoglio's withdrawal, while regretted, might be of distinct advantage, allaying criticism at home and abroad and pointing to the implementation of our proclaimed policy. The surrender terms, hitherto associated with Badoglio's person, would become the obligation of the most representative men today available in Italy, forming a Cabinet regarded as 100 per cent anti-Fascist. The intention to broaden the Government when Rome was reached, the President continued, had long been foreseen, and negotiations were held, following the fall of Rome, with the approval of and in constant consultation with the Allied Control Commission. The parties represented in the Rome Committee of National Liberation, which seemed to be the best available channel existing in Italy for the expression of the popular will, had chosen Bonomi unanimously, while they were divided on Badoglio. Interference on our part at this late moment, the President feared, would have serious repercussions both at home and in Italy, to the detriment of the military situation, and would directly violate our announced policy to let the Italian people choose their own Government.

Prime Minister Churchill now agreed to the installation of the Bonomi Cabinet without delay. Later, arriving in Rome in August for an inspection, he stated to Ambassador Alexander Kirk, then the American representative on the Advisory Council for Italy, that some mark of confidence should be given to the Bonomi Government short of a "preliminary peace" with Italy.

Premier Bonomi soon sent a series of messages to our Government outlining the numerous difficulties that confronted Italy in the economic and political field during her period of cobelligerency, and asking for alleviation of the armistice conditions. I dispatched a comprehensive reply to Rome on August 23, 1944. I said our Government would be glad to receive any specific proposals for revision of the armistice terms, but I reminded Bonomi that those terms were applied by the Allies solely to further our common primary objective of Germany's total defeat. We understood and appreciated, I added, Italy's wish to participate more actively in the war, and, within the limits of military needs and supply possibilities, would continue to give sympathetic consideration to this wish. I likewise expressed our full sympathy with Italy's desire to participate in international organizations.

"Patience, understanding, and hard work will be needed," I said, "to overcome the crimes Fascism committed in Italy's name, but any efforts in this direction will meet with this Government's sympathy and support." We were continuing to give constant, careful study, I added, to Italy's economic problems. Until victory was won, the Allied theater commander must retain full authority, but the recent return of seven provinces in central Italy to the authority of the Bonomi Government was proof of the Allied desire to restore liberated areas to Italian administration when military conditions permitted. Italy's aims, I concluded, were in harmony with ours, and our friendship and cooperation in achieving them could be counted on.

I had a number of cable exchanges with Kirk in September on the subject of Italian diplomatic representation abroad. On September 16 I stated our willingness to receive unofficially a technical Italian representation in the United States. I added that I did not favor continuance of Italian relations with the Argentine Government, the only American Government which had not severed its relations with Fascist Italy; that Italian prestige would not be enhanced if Italy continued to maintain diplomatic relations with the one American Government which had isolated itself from the United Nations; and that I favored unofficial Italian representation to the United Nations. I concluded that the Italian Foreign Office should make careful choice of its representatives abroad, especially in the Western Hemisphere, so that they would have clear records as regarded Fascism.

A few weeks later Mr. Churchill discussed the question of Italy with the President at Hyde Park, following the Second Quebec Conference. They announced on September 26 that an increasing measure of control would be gradually handed over to the Italian Administration, and that, to mark the change, the Allied Control Commission would be renamed "the Allied Commission." The British High Commissioner in Italy would assume the additional title of Ambassador, which the United States representative (Kirk) already held. The Italian Government would be invited to appoint direct representatives to Washington and London.

The Roosevelt-Churchill statement devoted much attention to the economic rehabilitation of Italy. In doing so it took account of exchanges of views we had been having with the British, which revealed another divergence of opinion between us. We had proposed that the dollar equivalent of the lire issued as pay to American troops in Italy be credited to the Italian Government to enable the latter to finance the procurement of relief and rehabilitation supplies. Generally we had proposed a more generous treatment of Italy in the field of supply policy than had hitherto been the agreed Anglo-American practice.

British Ambassador Halifax gave me on August 22, 1944, an *aide-mémoire* from his Government maintaining that to depart from the minimum standard agreed to and to embark on a program of general rehabilitation for Italian industry would be most difficult to justify to the Allies still subject to Axis domination, and especially difficult to justify to the victims of Italian aggression. The British thought that any concessions now made to Italy would bring requests from our Allies for more favorable treatment than that given to this ex-enemy.

Believing that the situation in Italy was serious, however, we went ahead with our plan to give the Italian Government the dollar credit we had in mind, which would amount to about $100,000,000 as of September 30.

At Hyde Park the President and the Prime Minister agreed that the first steps should be taken toward the reconstruction of an Italian economy, but that they should be taken primarily as military measures to put the full resources of Italy into the struggle to defeat Germany and Japan.

The day before the issuance of the Roosevelt-Churchill statement, I sent a circular message on September 25 to our diplomatic missions in all the other American Republics except Argentina, telling them of the new decisions reached. I said we were considering the establishment of full diplomatic relations with the Italian Government as being of material aid in the successful conclusion of the war and the reestablishment of democratic government. I requested the opinion of the foreign ministers as to the attitude of their Governments.

The American Republics forthwith stated their desire to resume diplomatic relations with Italy, and agreed to make an announcement to that effect along with us on October 26.

The Soviet Union reached the same decision, but the British, with whom we had disagreed more than once on the subject of Italy, took a different position. The British Embassy handed us a telegram of October 20 from the Foreign Office stating that British public opinion would react most unfavorably to an announcement at that stage of the war of any intention to resume full diplomatic relations with the Italian Government. The Foreign Office stated that it would not be clear how "full-blown" diplomatic relations between the Allies and Italy were compatible with the continued existence of an armistice regime, and also that the British public would consider it derogatory to the dignity of the King if he were to address a letter to the head of a state with whom he was still legally at war. It would be curious, to say the least, they commented, to accredit Ambassadors to Italy while refusing to accredit Ambassadors to the French Government in Paris. The Italian precedent would give rise to claims from Bulgaria, Rumania, and so on, for similar exchanges of diplomatic representatives.

We nevertheless went ahead on our own, along with the American

Republics and the Soviet Union, and announced on October 26 that full diplomatic relations with the Italian Government would be resumed. The President submitted to the Senate the nomination of Alexander Kirk as American Ambassador to Italy.

Basically we felt that, while the British arguments were cogent, the need to encourage the Italians to evolve a democratic form of government was a still more cogent argument. We pointed out that the resumption of diplomatic relations with Italy did not reestablish peace, nor did it settle the many questions that would have to be settled before a formal state of peace was declared—which required Senate consent. But it was intended to facilitate our return to a state of peace, which was an objective of our Italian policy. And it was designed to recognize the efforts of the Italian people during the preceding year to establish a healthy political basis for government and to cooperate with the Allies in the struggle against the common enemy.

Understandably, the British, and particularly Prime Minister Churchill, looked at Italy with different eyes. It was not easy for the British to be lenient toward Italy, for they had suffered far more casualties and damage in a much longer war against Italy than had we. Moreover, the British did not have among them millions of citizens of Italian origin, as we had, whose natural sympathy for their distant friends and relatives could not but affect our thinking.

As I left office at the end of November, 1944, the Bonomi Government was plunged into another Cabinet crisis. Again the State Department was forced to protest to Great Britain over the fact that the Foreign Office had once more vetoed the appointment of Count Sforza as Foreign Minister. We expressed our regret that the Foreign Office, without prior consultation with us, felt it necessary to intervene in an internal political crisis in Italy, and we stated our position that the composition of the Cabinet was a purely Italian problem, and that any objection made by the Supreme Allied Commander had to be based solely on important military reasons.

The policy we had pursued toward Italy from the time of the Italian armistice until my resignation assisted in bringing about a natural evolution toward democratic forms of government, as against the possibility of a revolution marked by civil war and chaos. King Victor Emmanuel, tainted with his long years of association and concurrence with Mussolini, left his throne. Marshal Badoglio, who had no democratic affiliations, remained in office for a period of emergency, and then gave way to a

Government with a broader base. The Bonomi Government, with the exception of a few émigrés, embraced men who had lived and suffered under Fascism and then Nazism, who represented varying political parties, from Right to Left.

We opposed King Victor Emmanuel, but we did not seek to influence the Italians relative to the institution of the monarchy itself. We considered that to be their own concern. The Italian Government undertook to call a constituent assembly when all Italians had been liberated and to postpone a decision on the monarchy until then. That decision has since been rendered through a plebiscite, which decided against the retention of the monarchy.

In addition to supporting the development of a representative Government in Italy, we took many steps to restore self-respect to Italy. We assumed the lead in trying to modify the prisoner-of-war status in which large numbers of Italian soldiers continued to be held in United Nations territory. We suggested inviting the Italian Government to send a representative to the Bretton Woods Financial and Monetary Conference, although the suggestion failed of implementation because of strong British and French opposition. We early agreed to receive an Italian technical mission to discuss economic and financial problems of concern to Italy.

Bearing in mind the terrific demands for shipping to support our Army in France and our armed forces in the Pacific, we sent all the relief we possibly could to Italy. From the time of the armistice until my resignation, Allied military authorities had spent about $158,000,000 for civilian supplies for Italy, of which the United States' share was $120,-000,000.

At the time I left office, the President and I felt that Italy, after more than two decades of Fascist domination, had made gratifying progress toward embracing the concepts and forms of democracy. We had no illusions that the task would be easy in a country economically prostrate, but we did have hopes that the basic good sense of the Italians, plus the lesson of the terrible catastrophe into which Fascism had plunged them, would keep them headed in the right direction. During the three years that have followed, Italy has made excellent advances toward improving her internal conditions as well as toward achieving political stability on democratic lines.

Having concluded this exposition of our policies toward our Allies, plus Italy, I turn now to our policies toward our enemies, particularly Germany and Japan.

113: Unconditional Surrender

THE PRINCIPLE of unconditional surrender overshadowed our policy toward the Axis and their satellites and our planning for their future.

Originally this principle had not formed part of the State Department's thinking. We were as much surprised as Mr. Churchill when, for the first time, the President, in the Prime Minister's presence, stated it suddenly to a press conference during the Casablanca Conference in January, 1943. I was told that the Prime Minister was dumbfounded.

Basically, I was opposed to the principle for two reasons, as were many of my associates. One was that it might prolong the war by solidifying Axis resistance into one of desperation. The people of the Axis countries, by believing they had nothing to look forward to but unconditional surrender to the will of their conquerors, might go on fighting long after calmer judgment had convinced them that their fight was hopeless.

The President himself had qualified his unconditional surrender phrase by stating at Casablanca that this did not mean the destruction of the people of Germany, Japan, and Italy, but the ending of a philosophy based on the conquest and subjugation of other peoples. Nevertheless the phrase itself spread more widely than the qualification, and it became a weapon in the hands of Nazi propagandists.

The second reason was that the principle logically required the victor nations to be ready to take over every phase of the national and local Governments of the conquered countries, and to operate all governmental activities and properties. We and our Allies were in no way prepared to undertake this vast obligation.

I thought that our principle of surrender should be flexible. In some cases the most severe terms should be imposed. I had Germany and Japan in mind in this connection. In other cases we would have preliminary informal conversations that would result in substantial adjustments away from the terms of unconditional surrender. Here I had in mind Italy and the Axis satellite states, Rumania, Hungary, Bulgaria, and Finland.

In our postwar planning discussions in the State Department, which had begun more than three years prior to the Casablanca Conference, we had not embraced the idea of unconditional surrender. In the United Nations Declaration of January 1, 1942, each Government simply pledged

itself not to make a separate armistice or peace with the enemies. Nevertheless, after the President had stated the principle so emphatically at
Casablanca, there was nothing we could do except to follow it at least in
form. It was to rise on numerous occasions to plague us and to require
explanation.

The President became aware of this after his return to the United
States from Casablanca. His first statement on the subject, made in the
course of his address to the White House Correspondents Association,
February 12, 1943, was still strong as he said: "The only terms on which
we shall deal with any Axis Government or any Axis factions are the
terms proclaimed at Casablanca: 'unconditional surrender.' In our un-
compromising policy we mean no harm to the common people of the Axis
nations. But we do mean to impose punishment and retribution in full
upon their guilty, barbaric leaders."

He softened this somewhat a few months later when, in his message to
Congress on August 25, 1943, transmitting a report on Lend-Lease operations, he said: "Except for the responsible fascist leaders, the people of
the Axis need not fear unconditional surrender to the United Nations. . . .
The people of Axis-controlled areas may be assured that when they agree
to unconditional surrender they will not be trading Axis despotism for
ruin under the United Nations. The goal of the United Nations is to
permit liberated peoples to create a free political life of their own choosing and to attain economic security."

In line with this thought, the surrender of Italy the following month,
although ostensibly on an unconditional basis, was actually, as I have
previously mentioned, a negotiated surrender, and the terms of the armistice were agreed to in discussions in Lisbon, Portugal, between representatives of the Anglo-American Combined Chiefs of Staff and Marshal
Badoglio.

With the President's definition in mind, Molotov, Eden, and I used
the term "unconditional surrender" in the preamble to the Four-Nation
Declaration we agreed to at the Moscow Conference in October. This
had been approved by the President in advance of my departure for
Moscow. The four nations declared their determination to continue hostilities against those Axis powers with which they respectively were at war
until such powers had laid down their arms on the basis of unconditional
surrender.

Following the Tehran Conference, I received a cable on December
17, 1943, from William Phillips in London, who was then a member of

General Eisenhower's staff, stating that it seemed that at the Tehran Conference Marshal Stalin had objected to the principle of unconditional surrender, and that Prime Minister Churchill had agreed with him. Phillips said there appeared to be no record of what the President thought, although it was reported in London that he had not dissented from Stalin's view.

Phillips informed us that the British Foreign Office had suggested that the term "unconditional surrender" be avoided until a final decision was reached, and that meanwhile the phrase "prompt surrender" be used.

The British Embassy handed us an *aide-mémoire* on December 22, 1943, which stated that the Tehran Conference had considered the question of a joint declaration to the German people on the basis of unconditional surrender. Marshal Stalin, it added, informed President Roosevelt on November 29 that he thought this would be bad tactics toward Germany and suggested instead that the Allied Governments concerned should work out terms together and make them generally known to the German people.

Foreign Secretary Eden suggested to us that the matter be dealt with as soon as possible by the European Advisory Commission. He hoped we would send appropriate instructions in this sense to our representative on the commission.

I sent the President a memorandum on December 22, informing him of the contents of this *aide-mémoire*, and adding: "As I have no information on this question of a joint declaration, and as I have not been under the impression that the European Advisory Commission would undertake political discussions of this character, I would be glad to know what your views are with regard to avoiding the use of the term 'unconditional surrender.' "

The President replied that this matter had not been brought up in any way at Tehran in his presence, and he felt that Ambassador Winant in London should take the matter up with Churchill as soon as the Prime Minister returned to London. I so cabled Winant on December 24.

That night, Christmas Eve, the President delivered a radio address in the preparation of which the State Department assisted. He said: "The United Nations have no intention to enslave the German people. We wish them to have a normal chance to develop, in peace, as useful and respectable members of the European family. But we most certainly emphasize that word 'respectable'—for we intend to rid them once and for all of

Nazism and Prussian militarism and the fantastic and disastrous notion that they constitute the 'master race.' "

At the end of December the British Embassy handed us an *aide-mémoire* informing us that peace feelers had come to the British Government through Sweden from a prominent member of the German Foreign Office and from Heinrich Himmler, Hitler's police chief. The feelers were in the nature of a statement that Himmler was ready to send an army officer and a Nazi Party official to meet British representatives to obtain a definition of "unconditional surrender." The British informed us that their plan was to reply only that the United Nations demanded unconditional surrender of Germany, without further interpretation. We assented to this reply.

Unconditional surrender was next raised with us by the Russians during a conversation between Molotov and Ambassador Harriman on December 31. In consequence of this approach, and after discussing it with my associates, I sent the President a memorandum on January 14, 1944, informing him that Molotov on his own initiative had brought up with Harriman the definition of "unconditional surrender" and had inquired as to the attitude of this Government.

"It is my understanding," I said, "that the Soviet interest in this matter is not based on any desire to weaken the principle of unconditional surrender or to offer milder terms to enemy countries but rather on the belief that the present undefined term 'unconditional surrender' affords enemy propaganda an opportunity to play on the natural fear of the unknown in the minds of their people and consequently stiffens their will to fight.

"As I understand it, the Soviet Government believes that some definition, however general and severe, of the conditions of surrender which will be imposed on the enemy countries would deprive the enemy of this propaganda advantage and consequently weaken the morale of their armed forces and people. In view of the Soviet interest in this matter, do you approve of discussions with the Soviet and British Governments to explore the desirability of some public definition for propaganda exploitation of the terms of unconditional surrender to be imposed on the respective enemy countries?"

Three days later the President, on January 17, sent me a memorandum in reply which he began by saying:

"Frankly, I do not like the idea of conversation to define the term 'unconditional surrender.' Russia, Britain, and the United States have agreed not to make any peace without consultation with each other. I think each case should stand on its own merits in that way."

He then continued:

"The German people can have dinned into their ears what I said in my Christmas Eve speech—in effect, that we have no thought of destroying the German people and that we want them to live through the generations like other European peoples on condition, of course, that they get rid of their present philosophy of conquest. I forget my exact words but you can have them looked up.

"Secondly, the German people and Russia should also be told the best definition of what 'unconditional surrender' really means. The story of Lee's surrender to Grant is the best illustration. Lee wanted to talk about all kinds of conditions. Grant said that Lee must put his confidence in his [Grant's] fairness. Then Lee surrendered. Immediately Lee brought up the question of the Confederate officers' horses, which belonged to them personally in most cases, and Grant settled that item by telling Lee that they should take their horses home as they would be needed in the spring plowing."

(The President had a comprehensive knowledge of American history, which he had studied thoroughly and intensively. It was not at Appomattox, however, that Grant demanded unconditional surrender, but at Fort Donelson in 1862, when he received the surrender of General S. B. Buckner.)

"A few little incidents like the above," the President concluded, "will have more effect on the Germans than lots of conversations between the Russians, British, and ourselves trying to define 'unconditional surrender.' Whatever words we might agree on would probably have to be modified or changed the first time some nation wanted to surrender."

I communicated the substance of this memorandum to Ambassador Harriman in Moscow on January 25. I added that Harriman might inform Molotov that our Government would rather deal with the case of each individual enemy country as it arose because we did not consider it wise to attempt at this time to make any general public definition of "unconditional surrender."

A few weeks later the Russians were themselves modifying the principle of unconditional surrender in their discussions with the Finns directed toward reaching a peace. Instead of demanding unconditional surrender from Finland, they offered to negotiate on certain specified subjects. As to Germany, Marshal Stalin had already stated that Russia had no desire to destroy that country but only Hitlerism.

Foreign Secretary Eden made the Russian approach to Finland the basis of a proposal to us to soften the principle of unconditional surrender so far as the minor Axis states as a whole were concerned. On March 20, 1944, British Ambassador Halifax handed me a telegram from Eden to this effect, dated March 17, 1944.

Eden suggested that, while it might be desirable to continue to apply unconditional surrender to Germany and Japan, we could achieve better results by dropping it either tacitly or openly with regard to the minor Axis states. Rigid application of the principle, he argued, was likely to hinder our desire to get them out of the war as soon as possible. We might wish to give them some assurance that their desertion of Germany and any contribution they might make toward hastening Germany's defeat would earn them some reward. Also, we would want to be able to discuss with them such questions as military cooperation, future frontier claims, or the possibility of our giving them assistance against the Germans.

Five days later I recommended to the President that we follow the British suggestion in order to obtain more flexibility with regard to the Axis satellites. In a memorandum of March 25 to Mr. Roosevelt, attaching the note from Eden, I said:

"While the British telegram correctly points out that the Soviet terms to Finland definitely do not impose unconditional surrender, such terms are not required under the joint Four-Nation Declaration for the reason that Finland is not a member of the Axis, whereas the other satellites are. Although the premise of the British reasoning may not be strictly correct, I recommend, however, that we concur in the proposal in order to obtain more flexibility vis-à-vis the Axis satellite states.

"The events of the past few days make it unlikely that the question of surrender terms for Hungary and Rumania will have any immediate importance. [This referred to Russia's advance into Rumania and Germany's occupation of Hungary.] Furthermore, Mr. Molotov has indicated that he is not yet prepared to discuss Bulgarian surrender terms in the European Advisory Commission currently meeting in London. Nevertheless, for the purpose of handling either propaganda or peace feelers, I think it would be advantageous now to free ourselves from the Moscow decision on the unconditional surrender of Axis satellite states."

While I was awaiting the President's response to this recommendation, I received a memorandum from Soviet Ambassador Gromyko indicating that his Government was in agreement with the position the British Government and the State Department were taking; namely, that the principle of unconditional surrender should be modified. This stated that the Soviet Government had received a communication on the subject from the British—this was Eden's telegram of March 17—and that it had replied on March 29 that under certain circumstances it considered it possible not to apply the principle to the satellites of Germany. To apply unconditional surrender, the memorandum said, might strengthen rather than weaken the bonds of the satellite countries with Germany. The principle would still be preserved to the full extent with regard to Germany. The Soviet Government asked our views.

Before I had a chance to communicate this to the President I received his reply, dated April 1, to my recommendation of March 25.

"I think this should be handled differently," he said. "It would be a mistake, in my judgment, to abandon or make an exception in the case of the words 'unconditional surrender.' As a matter of fact, whom do we mean those words to apply to? Evidently our enemies.

"In August, 1941, at the time of the Atlantic Charter, and in January, 1943, at the time of Casablanca, Hungary, Bulgaria, Rumania, and Finland were the Axis satellites. But they were not our enemies in the same sense that Germany and Italy were. These four little satellite states were enemies under the duress of Germany and Italy.

"I think it a mistake to make exceptions. Italy surrendered unconditionally but was at the same time given many privileges. This should be so in the event of the surrender of Bulgaria or Rumania or Hungary or Finland. Lee surrendered unconditionally to Grant but immediately Grant told him that his officers should take their horses home for the spring plowing. That is the spirit I want to see abroad—but it does not apply to Germany. Germany understands only one kind of language."

On the copy of Eden's March 17 telegram, which the President returned to me, he had written: "No—the British Foreign Office has always been part of this and it is N.G.—F. D. R."

Following the receipt of the President's response, various of my associates strongly recommended in memoranda to me that I take the matter up with Mr. Roosevelt again. After some discussion, I sent the President a letter on April 4 saying: "Upon further reflection, I am very much afraid that the Soviets will not understand our refusal to accede to the desire of both the British and Soviet Governments on this point.

Since the Soviet Government itself has to some extent laid down without objection from us definite conditions in the case of Finland, I am sure they will not understand why there should be any objection to doing the same in the case of Rumania and Hungary as in their opinion there is a definite military advantage to be gained. We might find ourselves in the position of being accused of having rendered more difficult the Soviet military task."

I asked the President to let me have his views in the light of these considerations and said that meantime I would withhold replying to the British and Soviet Ambassadors.

The President at this time was confined to bed in the White House with a severe attack of bronchitis, and it was not possible to talk to him personally; hence the series of written messages. He replied the following day.

"I understand the problem thoroughly," he said, "but I want at all costs to prevent it from being said that the unconditional surrender principle has been abandoned. There is real danger if we start making exceptions to the general principle before a specific case arises.

"We all know that this would happen if we were to make any exceptions to the principle which would thereafter apply in all cases.

"I understand perfectly well that from time to time there will have to be exceptions not to the surrender principle but to the application of it in specific cases. That is a very different thing from changing the principle.

"If the Soviet and British Governments will advise us of any case of this kind, I am quite sure that we will agree with them. This should be made clear to both of these Governments. Then they cannot accuse us of having rendered more difficult the Soviet military task."

In consequence of this note, I replied to both the British and the Soviet Embassies on April 11 saying that this Government had come to the conclusion that it was undesirable to make any general departure from the doctrine of unconditional surrender. Such a departure might serve as a precedent for all future cases. We would prefer that the general principle of unconditional surrender be retained intact, and that consideration be given to any modification on the basis of specific cases. We concluded that, rather than abandon the principle with respect to the satellite countries as a group, we were prepared to give favorable consideration to modifying the principle in the specific case of any one satellite when either the British or the Soviet Government believed it would be advantageous to the common cause to do so.

The question, however, would not die. Only two days later it was strongly raised from another quarter, the military. On April 13, 1944, I received a cable from Under Secretary Stettinius, who was then in London, conveying recommendations made to him by General Eisenhower and General Bedell Smith, Eisenhower's Chief of Staff. Stettinius said both generals had brought up the question with him and expressed their considered opinion that the term "unconditional surrender" should be clarified by announcing the principles on which the treatment of a defeated Germany would be based. He said this seemed highly desirable to them because of the accumulated evidence that German propaganda was interpreting the words "unconditional surrender" to strengthen the morale of the German Army and people.

The generals thought it was necessary to create certain conditions through our own propaganda to offset this. One condition to be created was a mood of acceptance of unconditional surrender in the German Army such as would make possible a collapse of resistance similar to that in Tunisia. The other was a mood in the German General Staff whereby a German Badoglio would undertake the necessary political steps for unconditional surrender.

Toward this end Eisenhower and Smith suggested that an American-Anglo-Russian statement be issued to define unconditional surrender and to guarantee the promotion of law and order. They likewise suggested that, once an Allied bridgehead were established in France, the Commander-in-Chief should make a statement calling for surrender and at the same time recapitulate the terms of other declarations clarifying unconditional surrender.

General Smith, Stettinius reported, felt that, in default of such statements, it would be impossible to exploit the crisis in the German Army to which a successful Allied landing in France would undoubtedly give rise.

Stettinius stated that William Phillips, the American political adviser to General Eisenhower, was in hearty accord with these views, and that the British political officer corresponding to Phillips had been asked to express the same views to the Foreign Office.

I sent this cable on to the President, who was then resting from his recent illness at the estate of Bernard M. Baruch at Georgetown, South Carolina. On April 15 I cabled Phillips stating that the President held very strongly to the maintenance of the principle of unconditional surrender for Germany, as Phillips knew. I said I felt that the case for action should be given every consideration, but before going further I suggested that it should be ascertained whether the European Advisory Commission had progressed in its work to arrive at a tripartite declaration upon a military government for Germany. I also questioned whether we should proceed on this subject by other means than through the European Advisory Commission unless the British and Russian Governments were willing to do so.

Later in the day I received a brief message from the President which, referring to Stettinius's cable of April 13, said: "Any reply thereto should have my approval before being sent."

I cabled Phillips on April 17 asking him to inform all concerned that the President wished that the subject be given no further consideration without his approval.

I telegraphed the President on the same day that, since Stettinius's cable had raised the question of a tripartite statement to define unconditional surrender, I had thought it well to send a message immediately to the effect that the President was holding very strongly to the principle of unconditional surrender for Germany. I also informed him of the further points we had raised with Phillips and of the second message just sent him on April 17.

The British and Russian Governments continued strongly to press the point that some modification of unconditional surrender, at least in the case of the Axis satellites, should be made. Since March we at the State Department had been working on the draft of a proposed statement to the satellites which the British, Russian, and American Governments might issue.

The President having returned to Washington on May 7, I sent him a memorandum on the subject three days later. I said the State Department had been informed by the British Embassy that the British Government considered it important that Allied propaganda to the satellite states should be reenforced. With special reference to Hungary and Bulgaria this propaganda should henceforth omit use of the term "unconditional surrender" in order to attain the maximum military advantage in strengthening resistance to Germany. Abandonment of the general principle would be avoided.

After referring to my letter of April 4 to the President and his reply directing that the general principle of unconditional surrender be retained, though exceptions might be made in its application in specific cases, I said:

"In making this proposal, the British Embassy has pointed out that the Soviet Government had not applied the principle to Finland, and the same could be said for Rumania, if the Rumanians should come to terms along the lines proposed for their surrender. It is supposed that the propaganda agencies will take these considerations into account in preparing their directives. As for Hungary and Bulgaria, the Department thinks that advantages can in fact be gained from energetic action at this time in propaganda operations, and I should therefore be grateful if you would indicate whether you would approve our taking parallel action with the British and the Russians in authorizing a degree of latitude for propaganda purposes, having it clearly understood that the exception is authorized to enable the propaganda services to omit reference to the term, though of course there would be no public recantation of the principle as applicable to these countries."

The President sent this back to me with his O.K. written on it.

As a result of further diplomatic exchanges among London, Moscow, and Washington, we agreed upon a joint statement which the three Governments made simultaneously on May 12, 1944. In this we stated that Hungary, Rumania, Bulgaria, and Finland "still have it within their power, by withdrawing from the war and ceasing their collaboration with Germany and by resisting the forces of Nazism by every possible means, to shorten the European struggle, diminish their own ultimate sacrifices, and contribute to the Allied victory."

We gathered some fruits of this position several months later, when Rumania, Finland, and Bulgaria asked for and obtained an armistice. Hungary was in the hands of the Germans.

As for Germany, we now sought to concentrate on a statement that Roosevelt, Stalin, and Churchill might issue addressed to the German Army, designed to weaken the German will to resist, especially at a moment when that Army felt the impact of the Anglo-American invasion in northern France. In May the President agreed to the extent of submitting a draft to Churchill, stressing the inevitability of the German defeat, the stupidity of the Germans continuing the struggle, and the wisdom of their throwing overboard the philosophy of their leaders. Churchill and his War Cabinet, however, did not like the draft.

The Department accordingly sent the President a new draft in June, and then on July 11 I sent him a later and shorter draft. This recited the overwhelming power of the United Nations and stated that every German life lost was a needless loss. Germany's only hope lay in unconditional surrender, but the draft went on to say that, while we promised nothing, the Allied leaders—Stalin, Churchill, and Roosevelt—had made it abundantly clear that they did not seek the destruction of the German people.

The President wrote me, however, on July 17, 1944: "It does not appear to me that Allied progress on all the fronts has yet been sufficiently impressive to promise the best results that might be obtained from such a tripartite statement. Later, when our combined attack shall have made further and more impressive advances, an approach to Churchill and Stalin suggesting a tripartite statement may give better promise of agreement and more prospect of advantage to our attack."

The following month, on August 21, I sent the President a further memorandum on the subject. I attached this to a letter to me from Admiral Leahy, transmitting a telegram the Supreme Headquarters, Allied Expeditionary Forces had sent to the Combined Chiefs of Staff to recommend the issuance of synchronized orders of the day by General Eisenhower, Marshal Stalin, and General Wilson, addressed in effect to the German Army. SHAEF said the psychological climax of the war was approaching and that a decisive demonstration of military unity between the Western, Eastern, and Southern Fronts might rapidly demoralize the already flagging German morale. They thought this could be true not only of the German home front but of the German Army which recently had shown significant signs of slackening in its relatively high fighting morale.

In my memorandum, I said: "I see no objection to this proposal from the political point of view and consider it primarily a military matter. If you approve the proposal, you will no doubt wish to take it up with Churchill and Stalin."

Three days later, however, Admiral Leahy wrote me that he had been directed by the President to tell me that Mr. Roosevelt did not consider the time appropriate for issuing such a statement.

The public statements made at different times by the leaders of the three major Allies to soften the interpretation of unconditional surrender did not conduce to the early surrender of Germany. The Nazi propaganda machine continued until the last to stress its drastic interpretation of unconditional surrender. The police hold by Hitler and his Nazis over the German people was too strong to permit of any successful reaction, and Germany went on fighting needlessly and hopelessly until her total collapse in May, 1945. Whether the Germans would have surrendered at an earlier date had there been no enunciation of the principle of unconditional surrender or had easier terms been agreed upon and stated by the United Nations will remain a question.

In any event, the continued application of unconditional surrender to Germany did have this effect, that no future propaganda machine in Germany could ever claim, as did the Nazis during the twenties and thirties, that the German armies had not been defeated and that Germany surrendered because of the weakness of the civilian government and people behind the lines.

As for our Oriental enemy, Japan surrendered three months later when she perceived that the principle of unconditional surrender could be applied conditionally.

114: Toward Victory in the Orient

OUR DIPLOMATIC EFFORTS directed toward Europe during the last years of my period at the State Department were naturally of greater intensity than those directed toward Asia. There were more nations to deal with in Europe, whereas in the Orient, with Japan an enemy, there was only one major nation left, China. Nevertheless, a large part of the attention of my associates and myself centered on the Far East, as we attempted to solve problems of real magnitude.

Toward China we had two objectives. The first was an effective joint prosecution of the war. The second was the recognition and building up of China as a major power entitled to equal rank with the three big Western Allies, Russia, Britain, and the United States, during and after the war, both for the preparation of a postwar organization and for the establishment of stability and prosperity in the Orient.

In 1943 we had taken three major steps to demonstrate our recognition of China as a great power. I signed on January 11, 1943, the treaty relinquishing our extraterritorial rights in China. At the Moscow Conference I was successful in introducing China as one of the signatories of the Four-Nation Declaration which called for the creation of an international organization to maintain the peace. On December 17 Congress, at the suggestion of the Administration, passed an Act repealing the Chinese Exclusion Laws and permitting Chinese citizens to enter the United States as immigrants. This last had been one of my projects for a number of years, just as it had been in the case of the Japanese. Believing it unwise and unfair to exclude Chinese and Japanese as immigrants, I felt they could be placed under a quota system like citizens of other nations, and I considered repeal of the Exclusion Laws necessary as one means of improving our relations with the Orient. The quota for Chinese immigrants, worked out on the same proportional basis as that assigned to other countries, would be very small indeed, but the principle was important. Especially after Pearl Harbor it seemed anomalous to strive for complete cooperation with our Chinese Ally while barring her citizens from our shores. When the matter came before Congress, I repeatedly conferred with members of both Houses to urge their support of repeal. Following the enactment, the President on February 8, 1944, set a quota of 105 Chinese immigrants annually.

As our military pressure on Japan became ever stronger in 1943, the Japanese overlords sought to make a separate peace with China so as to free themselves for the major conflict in the Southwest Pacific. The Government of Chiang Kai-shek, however, although sorely tried by China's growing exhaustion after six years of unremitting resistance to the invader, repulsed all such attempts. I cabled the President in Cairo on November 29, 1943, that our Embassy at Chungking had informed us that Japan was continuing to make peace offers to the Chinese Government, but without success.

President Roosevelt and Chiang Kai-shek made great progress in friendship and cooperation at the Cairo Conference. There the President agreed that all territory taken from China by Japan should be returned, including Manchuria, Formosa, and the Pescadores Islands.

The President did not consult with me before this agreement; nor did he consult with me before agreeing with Chiang Kai-shek and Prime Minister Churchill on a statement that independence would be restored to Korea "in due course." I considered this statement unwise for several reasons. One was that the Koreans wanted their independence immediately Korea was liberated, and not in due course. They did not welcome the Cairo Declaration, and they feared that their country would be placed under the control of China. Another reason was that the Soviet Union should have been consulted first. Although Russia was not at war with Japan, she was our Ally in Europe, and she had an interest in Korea.

The United States supplied China with every possible military assistance considering the enormous difficulties of transportation and our immense commitments elsewhere. This help ranged from the establishment of an air force of American volunteers in China and an air transport service into China to the operation of a staff school for higher Chinese officers.

Nevertheless, we encountered a feeling from time to time on the part of the Chinese Government that we were not giving it sufficient representation in our Allied military councils. This was the burden of a conversation I had with Chinese Foreign Minister Dr. T. V. Soong when he called on me September 22, 1943, shortly before returning to Chungking. He said his Government had one matter most strongly in mind; namely, more recognition in connection with the work of the Combined Chiefs of Staff. Dr. Soong had already taken this up with the President directly.

I told Dr. Soong that the President was a great friend of China, as everyone knew, and that I was sure he desired to do the proper thing.

The United States did, in fact, make every effort to give China adequate representation in Allied military deliberations.

On the economic side, this Government took many steps—in addition to Lend-Lease, which was for direct military purposes—to assist China's economy, endangered by the long-continued strain of war. The assistance ranged from a credit of $500,000,000 and the facilitation of China's import and export trade, to technical advice in organizing a Chinese War Production Board under the direction of the President's representative, Donald M. Nelson.

We lost no opportunity to bolster China's own consciousness of her position as a major Power. In addition to her recognition at the Moscow Conference, to our relinquishment of extraterritorial rights, and to our admission of Chinese immigrants, China was encouraged to play a prominent part in the United Nations Relief and Rehabilitation Administration, in the Bretton Woods Monetary Conference, and finally in the Dumbarton Oaks Conference for the establishment of the United Nations organization.

At the same time, we took every opportunity we could to state to China that we felt justified in expressing our expectation that she would solve her internal problems and achieve political stability. The tense relations between the Chinese Communist organization in the north, and the Kuomintang Party in Chungking were of persistent concern to us. We decidedly wanted China to assume a position of influence alongside the three big Western powers, but we knew this was impossible if China were torn by internal strife.

Vice President Wallace went to China in 1944 with the idea of converting both parties to this point of view. This was his own idea, and when I became aware of it I sent Joseph W. Ballantine, one of the Department's Far Eastern experts, to try to dissuade him from it. It seemed to me that a special mission of this nature might harm instead of help the situation.

I never at any time favored excursions into foreign affairs by Wallace, especially through trips abroad such as he made to Latin America in 1943 and to China in 1944. A network of questions and conditions existed in our international affairs, especially during the war period, which necessarily had to be handled with extreme care and delicacy. I was convinced that no person outside the State Department and the White House could break into these affairs without serious risk of running amuck, so to speak, and causing hurtful complications. For this reason I always opposed suggestions that raw materials, as I called them, should be recruited from the outside to go abroad and undertake seriously to handle important phases of our foreign affairs.

But when Ballantine saw Wallace the latter had already got to the President and secured his permission. Ballantine had to present the points I had given him as pitfalls to be avoided rather than as arguments to dissuade him from the trip. So far as I could see, Wallace's trip was without beneficial effect.

When Lord Beaverbrook, British Minister of Production, came to see me on July 24, 1944, we discussed the Chinese situation, and I remarked that it sometimes worried us. "I myself believe," I said, "that China has only a fifty-fifty chance to reestablish herself as a great power. But if she's rebuffed now by the other major Allies even that chance might be lost, and the Chinese Government would tend to dissolve. In that case it's quite likely that the Soviets might have to assume responsibility for the whole situation—if they would."

There had been some thought, I said, in certain business circles here that the Pacific situation could be stabilized by agreement among London, Washington, and Tokyo, and some Britishers shared this view. But by now, I concluded, it was plain that Japan was out of it, and if China went out too there was no stabilizing means at all.

Beaverbrook agreed. He said there was, however, a feeling in Britain that the Government of Chiang Kai-shek was not a real fighting Government but was "something plastered on top of China like a button on a coat."

Chiang Kai-shek, in my opinion, had followed faithfully in the footsteps of Sun Yat-sen in attempting the task that many considered next to impossible, the creation of a real Republic out of the innumerable divisions and subdivisions composing the vast territory of China. He was wise and patriotic. He knew the Chinese people.

Nevertheless, we had great difficulty in our relations with China during my last years in office because of the loose procedure followed by Chiang Kai-shek in dealing most irregularly with our Government through the Treasury, War, and Navy Departments, and other agencies of the Government. He sent numerous cables direct to different officials of this Government, taking up political subjects that should have been handled through the State Department. His brothers-in-law, H. H. Kung and T. V. Soong, were in Washington dealing on political matters with officers, for example, of the Treasury, War, and Navy Departments. They were circumventing the State Department and our Ambassador in China. The President unfortunately permitted this condition to continue.

I felt rather strongly that if the State Department had been permitted to hold a stiff rein on the Chinese situation, and require the Chinese Government to deal directly with it alone, it might have induced that Government to rely far more on itself and to pursue a stable, resolute course instead of bumping along expecting aid of all sorts from other countries, particularly the United States.

I felt that American aid to China could not be effective by itself without the cooperation of the Chinese Government. That Government was dominated by the reactionary groups in the Kuomintang, which were devoted to their own selfish interests and were afflicted with much corruption and little efficiency. I felt we could have had more military cooperation. Chiang Kai-shek kept some of his best divisions near himself, traffic continued between the Chinese and Japanese zones, and the Government seemed more interested in the blockade against the Communists than against Japan.

Nevertheless, I never faltered in my belief that we should do everything in our power to assist China to become strong and stable. It was obvious to me that Japan would disappear as a great Oriental power for a long time to come. Therefore, the only major strictly Oriental power would be China. The United States, Britain, and Russia were also Pacific powers, but the greater interests of each were elsewhere. Consequently, if there was ever to be stability in the Far East, it had to be assured with China at the center of any arrangement that was made.

At this point I should say that, after my resignation, President Roosevelt gave me not the slightest hint of his plans for the Yalta Conference, at which he made decisions of great concern to China. The day before his departure for Yalta, the President came to the hospital to see me. He had hardly sat down when I began to state the thoughts I had in mind. I restated the most pertinent doctrines and policies we had been standing for, which more and more had become part of our postwar policies. These policies would have negated some later developments, such as a few decisions at Yalta. After talking with Mr. Roosevelt thirty-five minutes, I apologized for taking so much of his time. He said he was glad to hear my views; but he did not indicate what he would take up at Yalta, nor did he seek my views on such points.

Toward China's neighbor to the south, Thailand (Siam), our policy after Pearl Harbor revolved around the fact that we refused to consider her as an enemy, regardless of the fact that the Thai Government had declared war against us on January 25, 1942. We did not declare war, but took the position that the Government at Bangkok, under the domination of the Japanese, did not represent the desires of its people; and we continued to recognize the Thai Minister in Washington as the Minister of his country.

Our desire being to see Thailand restored as an independent nation, we held discussions on this point with the British Government in 1944. The British, however, stated that they regarded Thailand as an enemy country which had to work its passage toward independence. Foreign Secretary Eden assured us that Britain desired the ultimate restoration of Thai sovereignty, but he made reservations with regard to security and economic collaboration by Thailand and to strategic guarantees in the Kra Isthmus which cuts across Thailand.

We on our part agreed that the new territories Thailand had acquired through Japanese "mediation," principally from French Indo-China, should be restored to their former owners, although this was to be without prejudice to eventual adjustments or transfers of territories by orderly, peaceful processes.

The President requested the Department on November 3, 1944, to instruct American representatives and to inform the British, French, and Dutch Governments, that the United States expected to be consulted on any arrangements as to the future of Southeast Asia. This included Thailand.

As I left office, our policy with regard to Thailand was to favor its restoration as a sovereign country, with an independent Government representing the free will of the people. We did not recognize the Government then existing. We were sympathetic to the "Free Thai Movement" which had been started here and in other countries, but we did not intend to make any political commitment to it, since we desired to leave the choice of government to the Thai people themselves.

With regard to Japan, the work of the State Department during my last years in office followed three main lines. The first was an unceasing effort to obtain humane treatment for prisoners of war and civilian internees in Japanese hands and to hasten the repatriation of these civilians. The second was a constant use of diplomacy to concert with our Allies all efforts toward prosecuting the war in the Orient to victory. The third was to prepare a plan for the postwar treatment of Japan.

Through the Swiss Government, which ably represented our interests toward Japan, we made literally scores of representations to Japan to induce her to accord proper treatment to Americans in her hands. Right after Pearl Harbor we took care to give the Japanese in our hands humane treatment, hoping that the Japanese Government might follow our example. Although Japan was not a signatory of the Geneva Prisoners of War Convention, we obtained from that Government a commitment to apply the provisions of the convention to American prisoners of war and, so far as adaptable, to civilian internees.

When, however, the first group of Americans repatriated from Japan, including Ambassador Grew, arrived on the first exchange voyage of the *Gripsholm,* they told stories of outrageous treatment by the Japanese. We made their accounts the basis of a vigorous, comprehensive protest to Japan.

As succeeding reports came in, it was obvious that Japan was flagrantly violating its commitment to carry out the provisions of the Geneva Convention. The hideous treatment of many American prisoners of war and civilian internees revealed a barbarism among the Japanese military which shocked the civilized world.

This mistreatment reached one of many climaxes when the Japanese executed the American aviators who fell into their hands after General James Doolittle's raid over Tokyo. We made this the subject of a vigorous protest on April 12, 1943. Calling again upon Japan to carry out its agreement to observe the Geneva Convention, we bluntly warned that the United States Government would punish all Japanese officers who participated in such atrocities.

I wish I could say that the many steps we took, and the valid support we received from the Swiss, had some effect. It did not seem that they had; Japanese barbarism was too deeply rooted; and our protests were still continuing when I left office. We were able, however, to build up a vast record of substantial evidence against individual Japanese which was of later aid in bringing these criminals to the punishment they amply deserved.

In 1943, and particularly in 1944, my associates and I devoted much time to the subject of the future treatment of Japan as a whole. We had frequent discussions among ourselves and with the War Department. In May, 1944, we in the State Department arrived at certain basic conclusions which we submitted to the War Department.

One was that Japan should be treated as a whole; it should not be partitioned, although the territories it had wrested from other nations should be returned to them.

Another was that the Japanese Government as a unit should be suspended during the period of armed occupation. That is, its policy-making functions should cease. The Privy Council, the Cabinet, the Diet, the Board of Field Marshals and Fleet Admirals, and the Supreme Military Council should go. The Ministries of War, Navy, Munitions, and Greater East Asia Affairs should be liquidated; routine administrative functions of the Ministry of Foreign Affairs should be performed under the direction of Allied Civil Affairs officers, with policy matters referred to the State Department.

Administrative Departments, such as the Ministries of Home Affairs, Finance, Justice, Transportation and Communications, Agriculture and Commerce, Education and Welfare, could continue under Civil Affairs officers in the top policy-making positions. We also believed that the municipal and prefectural administrative machinery could be retained, at first under Civil Affairs supervision.

A third point in our thinking was that all the principally interested United Nations who had taken part in the war against Japan, should participate in the occupation and control of Japan. We felt it was undesirable to assume the sole onus for future Japanese resentment. We believed it more effective to show the Japanese people, through the presence of other nationalities in the forces of occupation and control, that the condemnation of Japanese aggression was world-wide. We wished to see the presence in Japan of the armed forces of other nations, even if only token forces, and we were particularly anxious to have forces of other Asiatic peoples in evidence, such as Chinese, Indians, and Filipinos, so as to impress the Japanese with the fact that this had been not merely a white man's war against them.

We divided our thinking with regard to Japan into three postwar periods. During the first, comparatively short, period, Japan should be deprived of her prewar colonial empire and be completely demilitarized.

During the second, and longer, period, we proposed the establishment of permanent bases from which Japan could be militarily policed so as to prevent a revival of Japanese aggression; the establishment of control systems to prevent Japanese rearmament and the development of a war potential; the encouragement of democratic thought, with the help of Japanese moderate elements; the elimination of ultranationalistic organizations; and Japan's gradual participation in world economy.

During the third period, of indefinite duration, we proposed the establishment of a Japanese Government that would carry out its proper functions in a peaceful manner.

The Emperor of Japan and his future naturally occupied a considerable portion of our thinking. Should the institution of the Emperor, hallowed in Japanese history, be continued, or should it be abolished? The opinion of the State Department on this point was requested at various times by the War and Navy Departments. It proved to be one of our most difficult questions to answer, because it was impossible at the time to prophesy accurately the effects of an attempt by the United Nations to eliminate the institution of the Emperor.

We summed up our conclusions, however, and gave our recommendations in a memorandum on May 9, 1944. In this we pointed out that, since the Japanese then showed an almost fanatical devotion to the Emperor, an attempt from the outside to abolish the institution of the Emperor would probably be ineffective. The mere dethronement of the Emperor would not abolish the Emperorship if the Japanese were determined to maintain it, and an indefinite military occupation of Japan might be necessary if the United Nations wished to prevent its revival. We called attention to the unique position of the Japanese Emperor in that he was considered as the source, sacred and inviolable, from which all authority emanated.

Accepted governmental procedure had allowed the Emperorship to be made an instrument of the Japanese military, we pointed out; and accordingly this close relationship would probably have to be severed if we were to wipe out militarism in Japan. In any event, the supreme authority in Japan must be the Allied military Government.

If the Emperor were retained, we said, there were three choices—redelegate to him none, all, or only some of his functions. We argued against the first in that it might create a difficult situation for the occupation authorities. Japanese functionaries considered the throne as the source of their authority, and they might refuse to serve under foreign masters if the Emperor were deprived of his rights of sovereignty. We questioned whether a sufficient number of Allied Civil Affairs personnel could ever be trained to operate by themselves the entire administration of Japanese government and the essential functions of Japanese economy.

We argued against the second on the grounds that it might infringe too much on the authority of the occupation forces, it might imply that the latter were supporting the continuance of the throne, and it would probably encounter the opposition of American public opinion.

We felt that the third choice, to redelegate to the Emperor some of his functions, offered the best possibilities. The Allied governor would permit the Emperor to exercise only those functions that related to the assignment of administrative duties to subordinate officials. Without impairing the essential authority of the theater commander, this would tend to assure the good behavior of the Japanese people and to keep in office the maximum number of Japanese officials willing to serve directly under the supervision of Civil Affairs officers.

We did not think the Japanese would interpret this procedure as support of the Emperorship and its symbolic value, in view of the fact that foreign military forces would have apprehended the imperial family and would be using some of the Emperor's functions for their own ends. Moreover, the Japanese would be uncertain as to the eventual disposition of the Emperor.

It might well be possible, we thought, for the Civil Affairs administration to diminish even the limited use it might make of the institution of the Emperor as the administrative machinery of military government functioned more effectively. We considered this desirable politically. And, if a substantial movement developed among the Japanese people to abolish the imperial institution, the Allied military authorities should take no action against that movement, except to maintain law and order, and should cease to utilize the Emperor as a political instrument.

Generally, we recommended that the Allied military authorities adopt as flexible a course as possible. If they decided to permit the Emperor to exercise certain limited functions, we then made five recommendations.

The first was that the Emperor should be kept in seclusion, after being removed from the Imperial Palace and taken to a location which was comparatively easy to guard. But his personal advisers should have reasonable access to him, and he should be accorded normal courtesies. The Japanese people could therefore be assured of the Emperor's safety and welfare and of the fact that he was under surveillance.

The second was that the authority and responsibility of the theater commander should supersede that of all officials and organs in the occupied territory. The military governor would permit only those functions of the Emperor to be exercised which related to the assignment of administrative duties to subordinate officials. He should suspend those functions of the Emperor relating to the enactment of laws and to the armed forces. This would show to the Japanese people that the authority of the occupation government was superior to that of the Emperor.

The third was that, if retaining the Emperorship did not facilitate the use of Japanese personnel under the supervision of Civil Affairs officers, it might become advantageous to suspend all the functions of the Emperor, but the occupation authorities would have to be prepared to take charge of the actual operation of all Japanese governmental activities. We requested that, before such action were taken, the State Department be given an opportunity to express its opinion.

The fourth was that, if a portion of Japan were occupied for any length of time prior to unconditional surrender of the entire country, the occupation authorities should be prepared to operate directly most of the functions of government in the occupied area. This for the reason that it would probably be difficult to obtain the services of any Japanese officials of significance in that area.

The fifth was that the occupation authorities, in all their treatment of and contact with the Emperor, should refrain from any action that would imply recognition of or support for the Japanese concept that the Emperor was different from and superior to other temporal rulers, that he was of divine origin and capacities, that he was sacrosanct, and that he was indispensable. They should permit absolute freedom of discussion of political as well as other subjects, except where there might be incitement to breaches of the peace.

In general, we felt we should not make advance commitments that would prejudice the situation in favor of the Emperor institution or against it. We did not want to come out against the institution lest this give the Japanese militarists live coals to blow upon and bring up a flame of last-man resistance. Nor did we wish to come out for the institution lest this discourage whatever popular movement there might be in Japan to erase it.

Just before Secretary of State Byrnes left for the Potsdam Conference in July, 1945, he telephoned me at my apartment and gave me the substance of a draft statement which he said President Truman had given him. This proposed statement, for issue by the United States, Britain, and Russia at the Potsdam Conference, contained a declaration by the Allies to Japan that the Emperor institution would be preserved if Japan would make peace. Byrnes asked my opinion. He said that high officials of the State, War, and Navy Departments had approved it.

I replied that, since he was leaving in a few minutes, there was no time to write anything for him, but that the statement seemed too much like appeasement of Japan, especially after the resolute stand we had maintained on unconditional surrender. I pointed out that, as it was worded, it seemed to guarantee continuance not only of the Emperor but also of the feudal privileges of a ruling caste under the Emperor. I said that the Emperor and the ruling class must be stripped of all extraordinary privileges and placed on a level before the law with everybody else.

I then sent Byrnes a cable on July 16, through the courtesy of Under Secretary Grew, to outline my thoughts in further detail. I said that the support of the statement by the chief people in the State, War, and Navy Departments called for the most serious consideration. Nevertheless I pointed out that the central point calculated to create serious difference was in the paragraph relating to a proposed declaration by the Allies now—I underlined "now"—that the Emperor and his monarchy would be preserved in the event of an Allied victory. The proponents of this promise, I added, believed that somehow the influences and persons who paid allegiance to the Emperor and his religious status would fight and resist less hard and so save Allied lives and shorten the war.

The other side, however, I concluded, was that no person knew how the proposal would work out. The militarists would try hard to interfere. Also, should it fail, the Japanese would be encouraged and terrible political repercussions would follow in the United States. I therefore asked whether it would be well first to await the climax of Allied bombing and Russia's entry into the war.

The following day I received a message from Secretary Byrnes agreeing that the statement should be delayed, and that, when it was issued, it should not contain this commitment with regard to the Emperor.

When the Potsdam Declaration concerning Japan was issued, it contained no commitment with regard to the Emperor. The Japanese Government stated it would accept the Potsdam Declaration provided the right of the Emperor to rule were accepted. In line with the conclusions we had previously reached at the State Department, however, President Truman and Secretary Byrnes agreed to retain the Emperor only if his right to rule were subject to the Allied Command in carrying out the terms of surrender agreed to at Potsdam. The Japanese agreed.

The Potsdam agreement differed from the State Department recommendations made under me in that it permitted the continuance of the Japanese Government as such. We had recommended that certain sections of that Government be retained for administrative purposes; but at Potsdam it was agreed that the Government as a whole should continue along with its policy-making functions. Our recommendation that Allied Civil Affairs officers be stationed in all Government Departments likewise was not followed.

Concerning the vast area of the Southwest Pacific, my associates and I had been doing considerable thinking and, along with the President, had arrived at certain conclusions during my last years in office. This area embraced such important territories as the Dutch East Indies and the Philippines, and could be taken to include Malaya and French Indo-China.

These enormous lands entered into the intensive discussions we had been holding on the subject of dependent peoples. Without being specifically mentioned, they were included in the projects I had presented to the British and Russians under that heading.

We believed that the time had come when all parent countries should begin to plan and prepare for the self-government of these peoples, to be given them when they were ready for and worthy of it. Before us we always had the example of the Philippines, whom the United States had been preparing for independence almost since the day of our acquisition of the islands, and for whom an independence date had been formally set by national legislation in the Tydings-McDuffie Act of 1934.

The President was in thorough agreement with our proposals. He himself entertained strong views on independence for French Indo-China. That French dependency stuck in his mind as having been the springboard for the Japanese attack on the Philippines, Malaya, and the Dutch East Indies. He could not but remember the devious conduct of the Vichy Government in granting Japan the right to station troops there, without any consultation with us but with an effort to make the world believe we approved.

From time to time the President had stated forthrightly to me and to others his view that French Indo-China should be placed under international trusteeship shortly after the end of the war, with a view to its receiving full independence as soon as possible.

When British Foreign Secretary Eden came to the United States in March, 1943, he and I attended a conference with the President at the White House on March 27. William Strang (Assistant Under Secretary of State in the British Foreign Office), Harry Hopkins, Welles, British Ambassador Halifax, and Ambassador Winant, who was here on leave from London, were also present.

One of the first subjects brought up was whether China was to be one of the four controlling powers after the war, and whether the British and ourselves were in agreement on this point. The consensus was Yes on both points.

Another question related to our postwar policies regarding Manchuria, Korea, Formosa, and Indo-China. The President suggested that a trusteeship be set up for Indo-China, that Manchuria and Formosa be returned to China, and that Korea might be placed under an international trusteeship, with China, the United States, and one or two other countries participating.

He said that the Japanese mandated islands should be internationalized for the purpose of keeping the peace. Eden indicated he was favorably impressed with this proposal.

The President went over this subject again in the conference my associates, Admiral Leahy, and I had with him at the White House on October 5, 1943, two days prior to my departure for the Moscow Conference. On that occasion he said the British might, as a gesture of generosity, return Hong Kong to China while China might, in return, immediately declare Hong Kong a free port under international trusteeship.

He added that Indo-China and the Japanese mandated islands in the Pacific might be placed under international trustees, along with security points in many parts of the world. He mentioned Truk, the Bonin Islands, the Kurile Islands (although he thought the Kuriles should really go to Russia), Rabaul or some point in the Solomons, appropriate points in the Dutch East Indies, Ascension Island in the South Atlantic, Dakar, and some point in Liberia.

Ambassador Halifax came to me on January 3, 1944, and remarked that information had come to him from the Foreign Office that the President, during his visit to the Near East for the Cairo and Tehran Conferences, had rather definitely stated to the Turks, Egyptians, and perhaps others his views to the effect that Indo-China should be taken away from the French and put under an international trusteeship. Halifax said he had heard the President make remarks like this during the past year or more, but it was important to know whether his utterances represented final conclusions, in view of the fact that they would soon get back to the French.

I replied that I knew no more about the matter than the Ambassador. I said I had heard the President make these remarks occasionally just about as he had heard them. I added that, in my judgment, the President and Prime Minister Churchill would find it desirable to talk the question over fully, deliberately, and perhaps finally at some future stage.

I informed the President of this conversation in a note to him on January 14. I enclosed two brief memoranda citing the more important public statements or commitments we and the British had already made with regard to the future of French territory after the war. These were: the August 2, 1941, statement relative to the French-Japanese agreement; the President's letter to Pétain in December, 1941; a statement on New Caledonia made on March 2, 1942; a note to the French Ambassador on April 13, 1942; the President's statements and messages at the time of the invasion of North Africa; a letter from Robert D. Murphy to Giraud on November 2, 1942; and the Clark-Darlan agreement of November 22, 1942. Generally these looked toward the restoration of French territories after the war.

Ten days later the President sent me a memorandum, dated January 24, which began by saying: "I saw Halifax last week and told him quite frankly that it was perfectly true that I had, for over a year, expressed the opinion that Indo-China should not go back to France but that it should be administered by an international trusteeship. France has had the country—thirty million inhabitants—for nearly one hundred years, and the people are worse off than they were at the beginning."

He then went on: "As a matter of interest, I am wholeheartedly supported in this view by Generalissimo Chiang Kai-shek and by Marshal Stalin. I see no reason to play in with the British Foreign Office in this matter. The only reason they seem to oppose it is that they fear the effect it would have on their own possessions and those of the Dutch. They have never liked the idea of trusteeship because it is, in some instances, aimed at future independence. This is true in the case of Indo-China.

"Each case must, of course, stand on its own feet, but the case of Indo-China is perfectly clear. France has milked it for one hundred years. The people of Indo-China are entitled to something better than that."

In August, 1944, the British, in an *aide-mémoire,* raised with us the question of a French role in military operations in the Far East, with particular reference to Indo-China. They requested our concurrence in steps looking toward French participation in the liberation of Indo-China and in the war against Japan, for which the French had requested British approval. I sent this to the President on August 26, and commented, in a memorandum that, while these steps were "ostensibly military in character, they have wide implications and for this reason they are being referred to you for decision."

The President informed me orally that he planned to discuss these French proposals with Mr. Churchill at Quebec, where he was shortly going. He and the Prime Minister were unable, however, to reach any agreement. We subsequently received reports that the British were going ahead with the proposal to attach a French military mission to the Southeast Asia Command headquarters, though the mission, in the absence of American agreement, would at first be "ostensibly unofficial."

After learning that a French military mission had gone to Kandy to consult with the Southeast Asia Command regarding military operations affecting Indo-China, the President on November 3, 1944, gave instructions that American approval must not be given to any French military mission being accredited to the Southeast Asia Command, and that no American representatives in the Far East, whether civilian or military, were authorized to make any "decisions on political questions with the French mission or anyone else."

When we sent Mr. Roosevelt another memorandum on October 13 relative to an Office of Strategic Services proposal to assist resistance groups in Indo-China, he sent me a memorandum three days later, saying: "In regard to the Indo-China matter, it is my judgment on this date that we should do nothing in regard to resistance groups or in any other way in relation to Indo-China. You might bring it up to me a little later when things are a little clearer."

The President's opposition to the return of Indo-China to France continued at the time of my resignation the following month.

My own thought was that Indo-China should fall within the general category of dependent peoples, to whom the mother countries should be pledged to grant eventual independence. I favored this method rather than placing Indo-China under a trusteeship. Though the Vichy Government had betrayed Indo-China to Japan, I felt that an international agency would have great difficulty handling so large an area and population unless it were exceptionally well equipped. If France were prepared to restore her own popular institutions and to deal properly with the colonies, I favored the return of Indo-China, with France's pledge of eventual independence as soon as the colony became qualified for it, along the lines of our pledge to the Philippines. If France were not prepared to do full justice to Indo-China in accordance with this example, then it would be necessary to look to an international trusteeship; but I did not underestimate the terrific undertaking that administration by a trusteeship would represent, both in service and in money.

Our prime difficulty generally with regard to Asiatic colonial possessions, of course, was to induce the colonial Powers—principally Britain, France, and The Netherlands—to adopt our ideas with regard to dependent peoples. Britain had refused to go along with us on the idea of eventual independence for her colonies, believing instead that they should in time achieve self-government within the Empire. We had frequent conversations with these parent countries, but we could not press them too far with regard to the Southwest Pacific in view of the fact that we were seeking the closest possible cooperation with them in Europe. We could not alienate them in the Orient and expect to work with them in Europe.

At no time did we press Britain, France, or The Netherlands for an immediate grant of self-government to their colonies. Our thought was that it would come after an adequate period of years, short or long depending on the state of development of respective colonial peoples, during which these peoples would be trained to govern themselves. Our cause was harmed, not helped, by some vociferous persons in the United States, including Vice President Wallace, who argued for an immediate grant of independence or for the total separation of colonies from their mother countries.

These persons disregarded the magnitude of the problem that would thereupon face all nations. When a certain Texan argued with me along the line of separating all colonies from their mother countries and particularly urged that Britain should return Hong Kong to China, I retorted that Hong Kong had been British longer than Texas had belonged to the United States, and I did not think anyone would welcome a move to turn Texas back to Mexico.

We also encountered resistance from our own War and Navy Departments, which felt that our ideas conflicted with their desire to acquire sovereignty of Japanese islands in the Pacific for use as United States bases. We were accordingly not able to bring before the Dumbarton Oaks Conference our dependent peoples project, embraced within a plan for a trusteeship system to be set up under the United Nations organization. To me this was a keen disappointment.

As Allied, principally American, forces began the reconquest of the Southwest Pacific islands, we summed up our thinking with regard to the Netherlands Indies in a letter of February 28, 1944, to the Director of the Civil Affairs Division of the War Department. We began this by saying that arrangements for the civil administration of liberated Netherlands Indies territory should be predicated on the assumption that the exercise of all attributes of sovereignty would be resumed by the Netherlands Government as soon as the situation, in the judgment of the Supreme Commander of the Allied Expeditionary Force (General Douglas MacArthur) permitted. We then said:

"However, in any military agreement of the nature under consideration no commitments should be made which would prejudice the right of the Government of the United States to bring up either prior to or after the resumption of sovereign rights by the Netherlands Government certain proposals for discussion and agreement of a general character which it may believe to be of rightful concern to the United States Government and to all Governments which have subscribed to the principles of the Atlantic Charter, and to the Four-Nation Declaration at Moscow, and certain particular proposals which may be of special mutual concern to the people of the Netherlands Empire and the people of the United States."

In brief, we did not want agreements made between our military commander and Netherlands authorities which would militate against our presentation of proposals relating to the eventual independence of the Netherlands Indies.

We summarized our thoughts on colonial areas in Southeast Asia generally in a Department memorandum which I sent to the President on September 8, 1944. In this we suggested the value of "early, dramatic, and concerted announcements by the nations concerned making definite commitments as to the future of the regions of Southeast Asia." We added:

"It would be especially helpful if such concerted announcements could include (1) specific dates when independence or complete (dominion) self-government will be accorded, (2) specific steps to be taken to develop native capacity for self-rule, and (3) a pledge of economic autonomy and equality of economic treatment toward other nations.

"Such announcements might well be accompanied by . . . a pledge to establish a regional commission. . . . The value of such concerted announcements would be still further enhanced if each of the colonial powers concerned would pledge a formal declaration of trusteeship under an international organization for the period of tutelage; but it might be unwise for the United States to attempt to insist upon such a declaration of trusteeship by one country if similar declarations could not be secured from the others. In addition to their great value as psychological warfare, such announcements would appear to be directly in line with American postwar interests."

The President warmly approved these ideas. He subsequently directed that instructions be sent to American officers at home and abroad, and that the British, Dutch, and French Governments be informed as well, that the United States expected to be consulted on any arrangements as to the future of Southeast Asia.

Such was our policy toward the Southwest Pacific as I left office. It might be thought that we were presumptuous in seeking to present our ideas to the British, French, and Dutch Governments as to what they should do with their own Pacific possessions. We had, however, two rights to take such action. One was the fact that the liberation of those possessions would not have been achieved—and possibly never could have been —except by United States forces. The other was our interest in seeing that peace in the Pacific, restored by our forces, should continue. And we could not help believing that the indefinite continuance of the British, Dutch, and French possessions in the Orient in a state of dependence provided a number of foci for future trouble and perhaps war. Permanent peace could not be assured unless these possessions were started on the road to independence, after the example of the Philippines. We believed that we were taking the long-range view, and that a lasting peace in the Pacific was of greater ultimate benefit to Britain, France, and The Netherlands—as well as to the whole world—than the possible immediate benefits of holding on to colonies.

115: Plan for Germany

WHEN THE PRESIDENT decided to meet with Prime Minister Churchill for the Second Quebec Conference, in September, 1944, he asked me whether I wished to accompany him. The conference, however, was intended to be largely military. I was not well, the Dumbarton Oaks Conference was in progress, and I told him I preferred to remain in Washington but would be available if he needed me.

Shortly before the conference was to assemble, the President was prevailed upon to permit Secretary of the Treasury Morgenthau to attend the meeting. Morgenthau and his friends had been working for some time on a drastic plan for the postwar treatment of Germany, and the leaders of groups who had been justly wrought up by German outrages requested the President to invite him to go to Quebec primarily to present his plan for Germany.

My associates and I at the State Department had spent hundreds of hours working on a plan for Germany. We had had frequent conferences on the subject with the War Department. I had presented a preliminary plan, which had the full approval of the President, at the Moscow Conference. There it received the general approval of Eden and Molotov, and was referred to the European Advisory Commission in London to be worked out in detail. That Commission had done considerable work in setting up arrangements for the postwar government and control of Germany, and numerous exchanges of views had taken place among the United States, Britain, and Russia.

To Morgenthau, however, our plan (which I have outlined in Chapter 92 on the Moscow Conference) was too mild. He insisted to the President that Germany should be stripped of all industries and converted into an agricultural country.

The President himself leaned to the idea that the German people as a whole should be given a lesson they would remember. On August 26, 1944, he had sent a long memorandum to Secretary of War Stimson, a copy of which was sent to me, protesting against the handbook drawn up for the guidance of military government officials in Germany.

"It gives the impression," he said, "that Germany is to be restored just as much as The Netherlands or Belgium, and the people of Germany brought back as quickly as possible to their prewar estate.

"It is of the utmost importance that every person in Germany should realize that this time Germany is a defeated nation. I do not want them to starve to death, but, as an example, if they need food to keep body and soul together beyond what they have, they should be fed three times a day with soup from Army soup kitchens. That will keep them perfectly healthy, and they will remember that experience all their lives. The fact that they are a defeated nation, collectively and individually, must be so impressed upon them that they will hesitate to start any new war."

After quoting from several of the handbook's pages to which he particularly objected, he concluded:

"There exists a school of thought both in London and here which would, in effect, do for Germany what this Government did for its own citizens in 1933 when they were flat on their backs. I see no reason for starting a WPA, PWA, or CCC for Germany when we go in with our army of occupation.

"Too many people here and in England hold to the view that the German people as a whole are not responsible for what has taken place— that only a few Nazi leaders are responsible. That unfortunately is not based on fact. The German people as a whole must have it driven home to them that the whole nation has been engaged in a lawless conspiracy against the decencies of modern civilization."

With regard to the disposition of the German Navy, the President advanced a new idea. The Joint Chiefs of Staff wrote me on September 4, 1944, stating that they wanted the complete destruction of the German fleet except for a limited number of ships that could be retained for experimental purposes. If no agreement could be reached with the Russians and British on this basis, they said, the United States should press for either a one-third share in each category of vessel, or an agreement that all capital ships, such as battleships, pocket battleships, heavy cruisers, and submarines, be destroyed, while smaller craft would be shared equally by the United States, Russia, and Great Britain.

After I sent this letter to the President, he wrote me a memorandum on October 13 in which he accepted the views of the Joint Chiefs of Staff with regard to the complete destruction of the German fleet, but had one amendment to make.

"Destruction in the past," he said, "has meant taking the ships to sea and sinking them. I think that in some cases surrendered ships have been destroyed by converting them into scrap metal. I do not like the idea of complete destruction by the sinking of thousands of tons of steel.

"Recently a new use for such ships has been discovered. We have used sunken ships as breakwaters for the formation of new harbors. This has been done in Italy, and it has been done on the coast of Normandy. It is a relatively cheap way to build a breakwater. I think that the United Nations should be in a position to pass on applications by Allied nations for these ships for the definite and specific purpose of sinking them as breakwaters to improve or create safe anchorages. It is rather a nice thought to use them for such peaceful purposes.

"In any such cases, the ships should be sunk at a designated place as quickly as possible and under the eyes of a United Nations Committee. Once sunk it would be practically impossible to raise them and restore them to war purposes."

We cabled Ambassador Winant in London on October 19 instructing him to guide himself according to the President's memorandum in the discussions of the European Advisory Commission.

Harry Hopkins came to me on September 1, 1944, and informed me of the President's desire to establish a "Cabinet Committee on Germany." He said the President had asked him to give his undivided attention to this matter in the next few weeks. Hopkins at this time also explained Morgenthau's interest in the question, arising from his disagreement with certain sections of the plans for Germany which already had been prepared.

My associates at the State Department, particularly H. Freeman Matthews and James W. Riddleberger, went over with Hopkins in detail the studies concerning postwar Germany made at the State Department and by the European Advisory Commission in London. They prepared a memorandum, which I approved, explaining the work that already had been done and setting forth the State Department's views on the treatment of Germany. This Matthews and Riddleberger presented at a meeting of representatives of the State, Treasury, and War Departments called by Hopkins in his office at the White House on September 2.

Morgenthau's, or the Treasury's, plan was presented at this session by Dr. Harry White. This plan proposed, among other things, that parts of Germany should be given to neighboring countries and the remainder split into three units.

Poland should get southern Silesia and that part of East Prussia which did not go to Russia. France should get the Saar and the adjacent territories bounded by the Rhine and Moselle rivers. Denmark should get territories north of the Kiel Canal, between her present borders and an International Zone.

This International Zone would be one of the three units into which Germany would be partitioned. It would contain the Ruhr and the surrounding industrial areas and the Kiel Canal, and would be run by the proposed United Nations organization. The remaining portion of Germany would be divided into two autonomous, independent states—a South German state comprising Bavaria, Württemberg, Baden, and some smaller areas, and a North German state comprising a large part of the old state of Prussia, Saxony, Thuringia, and several smaller states. There would be a customs union between the new South German state and Austria, the latter to be restored to her pre-1938 borders.

Industrial plants and equipment situated within the International Zone and the North and South German states would be removed and distributed among devastated countries. Forced German labor would be used in such countries.

Dr. White explained that no trade would be permitted between the International Zone and the remainder of Germany. He emphasized that the productivity of this zone would in no way be permitted to contribute to German economy.

Later the Treasury inserted in its plan this paragraph with regard to the Ruhr and surrounding industrial areas:

"This area should not only be stripped of all presently existing industries but so weakened and controlled that it cannot in the foreseeable future become an industrial area—all industrial plants and equipment not destroyed by military action shall either be completely dismantled or removed from the area or completely destroyed, all equipment should be removed from the mines and the mines shall be thoroughly wrecked."

The Treasury plan stated that the United States would have military and civilian representation on whatever international commission might be established to carry out the German program, but that the primary responsibility for the policing of Germany and for civil administration in Germany would be assumed by the military forces of Germany's continental neighbors, specifically Russia, France, Poland, Czechoslovakia, Greece, Yugoslavia, Norway, The Netherlands, and Belgium. United States troops could be withdrawn within "a relatively short time."

It was obvious on its face that this plan was drastic. It would leave Germany with practically no industry, and would force the population to live entirely on the land, regardless of the fact that there was not enough land on which the large German population could live.

Essentially, this was a plan of blind vengeance. It was blind because it failed to see that, in striking at Germany,. it was striking at all of Europe. By completely wrecking German industry it could not but partly wreck Europe's economy, which had depended for generations on certain raw materials that Germany produced.

The Treasury recommendation that the German mines be ruined was almost breath-taking in its implications for all Europe, because various other countries relied upon German coal for their industries. After the Allied occupation of Germany began, the Allied authorities there did, in fact, have to bend every effort to restore German mines to the fullest production so as to improve Europe's economy generally.

At the State Department we had drawn up on September 1 a memorandum to emphasize our views on this point. "If a far-reaching program of industrial destruction or dismantlement is agreed upon," we stated, "it is apparent that, if put into effect, it will bring about extensive and important changes in European economy as a whole.

"Germany is a deficit country in foodstuffs, and it is doubtful if a plan of making Germany predominantly agricultural can be put into effect without the liquidation or emigration of X millions of Germans.

"Germany is furthermore an important producer of certain raw materials—namely, coal and bauxite—for Europe as a whole, not to speak of the vast amount of industrial goods which Germany normally exports. If we advocate a 'wrecking program' as the best means of assuring our security, we may face considerable European opposition on account of its effect on European economy; and if we desire continuing reparations out of Germany, we shall eliminate any such program by a policy of destruction of German industry."

We were also agreed at the State Department to oppose Morgenthau's ideas of a partition of Germany. We stated in our memorandum:

"The State Department is, in general, opposed to the forcible partition of Germany into two or more separate states as has been advocated as a practical means of forestalling any renewal of German aggression. Such a measure, however drastic in itself, would not offset the necessity of imposing and enforcing far-reaching security controls upon Germany for an indeterminate period, whether Germany is left united or is divided. Moreover, because of the high degree of economic, political, and cultural integration of Germany, it must be anticipated that partition would not only have to be enforced but also maintained by force.

"The victor powers, by imposing partition, would take on themselves a burdensome and never-ending task of preventing surreptitious collaboration between the partite states and of restraining the nationalistic determination to reunite, which would, in all probability, be the response of the German people. Finally, the disruption of German economic unity would carry with it grave dangers for the economic stability of Europe as a whole, and not merely to Germany."

On the other hand, we said that we should not oppose any spontaneous German movement for partition.

We recommended that, in place of partition, every effort be made to promote a federal system of government in Germany, and a division of Prussia into a number of medium-sized states. We pointed out that Prussia in 1938 included five-eighths of the area and two-thirds of the population of Germany, and it might well be that in reaction to the Nazi overcentralization many Germans would want to return to a considerable degree of federal decentralization, including the break-up of Prussia.

The War Department representatives at the meeting on September 2, Assistant Secretary McCloy and General Hilldring, pointed out the difficulties that would arise for the Army under any such plan as that advanced by the Treasury.

Following the presentation of the Treasury plan, Matthews and Riddleberger presented the State Department views and explained how they fitted into British and Russian ideas in so far as these had been communicated to us. The conferees thereupon requested Riddleberger to draw up a further memorandum attempting to reconcile the views of the three Departments, which the Secretaries of State, Treasury, and War might be willing to sign and submit to the President as their recommendation.

After Assistant Secretary of War McCloy said it was essential that General Eisenhower be given an interim directive for the treatment of Germany, Hopkins thought it most important that this directive be prepared as soon as possible, and urged McCloy to hasten the work. McCloy said that the State and War Departments had both been working on this directive, and that there were only minor differences between them which could easily be adjusted, but that the Treasury memorandum obviously ran counter to some major provisions of the directive. It was thereupon decided that a meeting be held, in which Treasury representatives would participate, to hasten the completion of the directive.

Harry Hopkins met on September 3 with James C. Dunn, the State Department's Political Adviser on European Affairs, Matthews, and Riddleberger, on which occasion Dunn emphasized to Hopkins the supreme importance of working with our Allies, particularly Britain and Russia, on the whole question of the postwar treatment of Germany. He pointed out the impossibility of obtaining the concurrence of Russia and Britain to some of the provisions advocated by the Treasury. He explained the tripartite control of Germany envisaged in proposals submitted to the European Advisory Commission by the United States and Britain, which would have to be modified extensively if the Treasury's ideas were accepted. Hopkins seemed to realize the validity of these contentions, and remarked that in his opinion it was essential that the President and the Secretary of State keep in step on all plans that might be developed for Germany.

I held the first meeting of the "Cabinet Committee" in my office on September 5, with Hopkins, Morgenthau, and Stimson attending. I laid before them a memorandum my associates and I had prepared, dated September 4, containing suggested recommendations the Cabinet Committee might present to the President.

This suggested the appointment, as soon as possible, of an American High Commissioner for Germany, who would meet with equivalent representatives of Britain and Russia immediately upon the occupation of Germany. We proposed the complete demilitarization of Germany, the dissolution of the Nazi Party and all affiliated organizations, the maintenance of extensive controls over communications, press and propaganda, and education, and the breaking up of the great Junker estates. These proposals had appeared in our previous plans and also in the Treasury plan.

We differed with the Treasury, however, on the partition of Germany. We said that no decision should be taken on this point, as distinguished from territorial cessions to neighboring countries, until we saw what the internal situation in Germany and what the attitude of our principal Allies would be. We should, however, encourage a decentralization of the German governmental structure, and, if any tendencies toward spontaneous partition arose they should not be discouraged.

We differed also on making Germany an agricultural country. In this connection we said that the American Government had no direct interest in obtaining reparations from Germany and consequently no interest in building up German economy in order to collect continuing reparations. However, the United Kingdom and the U.S.S.R., along with a number of small states, might have claims on German production which they would require for purposes of reconstruction. Consequently, we should not take a fixed position on reparations at this time but await the views of Governments more directly interested.

We stated three primary objectives of our economic policy in Germany. The first was that the standard of living of the population should be held down to subsistence levels. The second was that Germany's economic position of power in Europe must be eliminated. The last was that German economic capacity must be converted in such a manner that it would be so dependent on imports and exports that the country could not by its own devices reconvert to war production.

Secretary Stimson agreed with virtually all this memorandum, except the point that the standard of living of the German population should be held down to subsistence levels. Secretary Morgenthau also seemed to agree with large sections of the memorandum, but he would not commit himself to it. Harry Hopkins sent me a note on September 5 in which he said that, with minor reservations about language which did not affect the content of the document, he approved it.

On the following day our little group met with the President at the White House. I presented our memorandum of September 4, with the statement that it had not been agreed to by the other members of the committee, but might serve as a basis for discussion. Stimson presented a War Department memorandum that was very largely in line with our memorandum. Morgenthau, however, presented the original drastic Treasury memorandum.

The discussion that followed was inconclusive. The distance between the views of the State and War Departments on the one hand and of the Treasury on the other was so great that no meeting of minds ensued.

Secretary of War Stimson sent me a copy of a memorandum he addressed to the President on September 9. In this, after citing Morgenthau's proposal that industrial plants and equipment in the Ruhr and surrounding areas be dismantled, removed, or completely destroyed and the mines thoroughly wrecked, he said he was unalterably opposed to such a program. These resources, he said, constituted a natural and necessary asset for the productivity of Europe. In a period when the world was suffering from destruction and from want of production, the concept of the total obliteration of these values was to his mind wholly wrong. His insistence was that these assets be conserved and made available for the profit of the whole of Europe, including Great Britain particularly.

Stimson recommended that the President accept a program generally in accord with the memorandum I had submitted on September 5. He added suggestions for several modifications, and canceled out our provision that the standard of living of the German population be held down to subsistence levels.

Thus the matter stood when the Quebec Conference met on September 11. We had been able to achieve no further reconciliation of views. As I have already stated, the President was induced to permit Morgenthau to attend the conference, at which the latter intended to advocate his extreme plan before the President and the Prime Minister. I requested Ray Atherton, our Ambassador to Canada, to represent us at the meetings.

Four days after the conference began, I was astonished to receive from the President a memorandum addressed to me, dated September 15, which indicated that he and Churchill had largely embraced Morgenthau's ideas. The memorandum set forth that the President and the Prime Minister felt that an essential feature of the best measures to prevent renewed rearmament by Germany was the future disposition of the Ruhr and the Saar. The ease with which the metallurgical, chemical, and electric industries in Germany could be converted from peace to war had already been impressed upon us by bitter experience. It had also to be remembered that the Germans had devastated a large portion of the industries of Russia and of other neighboring Allies, and it was only just that these injured countries should be entitled to remove the machinery they required in order to repair the losses they had suffered.

The memorandum then stated:

"The industries referred to in the Ruhr and in the Saar would therefore be necessarily put out of action and closed down. It was felt that the two districts should be put under somebody under the World Organization which would supervise the dismantling of these industries and make sure that they were not started up again by some subterfuge.

"This program for eliminating the war-making industries in the Ruhr and in the Saar is looking forward to converting Germany into a country primarily agricultural and pastoral in its character.

"The Prime Minister and the President were in agreement upon this program."

In his note to me introducing this memorandum, the President said this seemed eminently satisfactory to him, and he thought I would approve the general idea of not rehabilitating the Ruhr, Saar, and so on.

I could not, however, approve any program "looking forward to converting Germany into a country primarily agricultural and pastoral in its character." Seventy million Germans could not live on the land within Germany. They would either starve or become a charge upon other nations. This was a scheme that would arouse the eternal resentment of the Germans. It would punish all of them and future generations too for the crimes of a portion of them. It would punish not only Germany but also most of Europe.

The President also said in his note to me that he thought he had worked out the locations of the occupying forces in Germany. He had been hoping to get the northwestern portion of Germany as the American zone of occupation, but finally agreed with Churchill that Britain should have it, while the United States would have most of southern Germany, including Bavaria.

Thus was settled a difference of opinion between the President and the Prime Minister which had remained unsolved for some seven months. The original plan of the Combined Chiefs of Staff had been to make the British sphere of occupation (if occupation were necessary in all these areas) northwestern Germany, Norway, Belgium, Luxemburg, Holland, and Denmark; the United States' sphere southern Germany, France, and possibly Austria; Russia's sphere the area to the east of the British. After the United States Chiefs of Staff, however, proposed that the British and American spheres be exactly reversed, Mr. Churchill cabled the President in February, 1944, strongly urging that the original plan continue. He said Britain was better equipped and situated to ensure the naval disarmament of Germany; close liaison had already been established between the Royal Air Force and the Norwegian and Netherlands Air Forces which the British had trained, and it was desirable to continue this liaison after the war, which would be difficult if Norway and the Netherlands were outside the British zone. The United States, on the other hand, had had major responsibility for reequipping French forces. Mr. Churchill further argued that the plans for the invasion of Normandy had already been agreed to, placing the British on the left flank going toward Germany, with bases in the Havre-Cherbourg area, and American forces on the right flank, with bases in the Brittany ports. A reversal of the spheres would involve crossing the lines of communication, and it was obviously too late to replan the invasion so as to reverse the British and American forces.

The President, who had the whole matter much at heart, sent a memorandum on February 21, 1944, to Under Secretary Stettinius, while I was briefly absent from Washington, strongly stating his own arguments. "I do not want the United States," he said, "to have the postwar burden of reconstituting France, Italy, and the Balkans. This is not our natural task at a distance of 3,500 miles or more. It is definitely a British task in which the British are far more vitally interested than we are."

Our principal object, he pointed out, was not to take part in the internal problems in southern Europe "but is rather to take part in eliminating Germany at a possible and even probable cost of a third World War." He said the British argument about the difficulties of transferring our forces from a French front to a northern German front—what was called "leap-frogging"—was "specious" because, no matter where British and American troops were on the day of Germany's surrender, it was physically easy for them to go anywhere, north, east, or south.

"I have had to consider also," he said, "the ease of maintaining American troops in some part of Germany. All things considered, and remembering that all supplies have to come 3,500 miles or more by sea, the United States should use the ports of northern Germany—Hamburg and Bremen—and the ports of The Netherlands for this long-range operation."

He therefore thought that the American policy should be to occupy northwestern Germany, the British to occupy the area from the Rhine south and also be responsible for the policing of France and Italy if this should become necessary.

As for the long-range security of Britain against Germany, he commented, this was not a part of the first occupation period, and the British would have plenty of time to work that out, including Helgoland, airfields, and the like. "The Americans by that time," he said, "will be only too glad to retire all their military forces from Europe."

He concluded by saying: "If anything further is needed to justify this disagreement with the British lines of demarcation, I can only add that political considerations in the United States make my decision conclusive."

These arguments were duly communicated to the British, but without visible effect, the President and the Prime Minister continuing at opposite poles on the subject.

After Under Secretary Stettinius went to London in April, he cabled me on April 14 that General Eisenhower was deeply convinced that the British and American zones in Germany should be combined in one Anglo-American zone of occupation. Eisenhower argued to Stettinius that it would be very difficult from a military point of view to split up in two distinct occupation commands, after Germany surrendered, what amounted to a unified combined Anglo-American command. Various combined Anglo-American boards were slated to direct shipping and supply for western Germany; and to set up each zone with its own transportation and supply programs in separate American and British zones would be very confusing administratively. Eisenhower's suggestion, however, had possible political implications that negatived its acceptance.

In August the question of the zones again came to a head when the Russians indicated that they did not wish to continue discussions concerning the Allied zones of control in Germany until we and the British had settled the location of our respective zones.

On August 3, 1944, the President, who was on a trip to Hawaii, the Aleutians, and Alaska, cabled the Department asking us to inform Ambassador Winant in London that he was awaiting an agreement by the Prime Minister that American troops would police northwestern Germany and would not police southern Europe. "It is essential," he said, "that American troops of occupation will have no responsibility in southern Europe and will be withdrawn from there at the earliest practicable date. . . . No possible difficulty with England is foreseeable in regard to her naval problems in northwestern Germany. They can march hand in hand with the supply of our troops; but in consideration of our 3,000 miles of transport I want to be able to carry this out through Holland and Hamburg and Bremen."

We cabled Winant accordingly, but it remained for the personal meeting of the President and the Prime Minister at Quebec to iron out their differences. The President accepted the southern section of Germany as the American zone of occupation, but his insistence on having the use of northern ports was met by assigning an enclave to us which included Bremen.

On the same day, September 15, that the President sent me the memorandum embracing the Morgenthau plan and the decision on the zones of occupation, he sent me another memorandum which informed me that Morgenthau had presented at Quebec, in conjunction with his plan for Germany, a proposal of credits to Britain totaling six and a half billion dollars. This might suggest to some the *quid pro quo* with which

the Secretary of the Treasury was able to get Mr. Churchill's adherence
to his cataclysmic plan for Germany.

The President said in his memorandum that he had agreed that, after
the defeat of Germany and while the war against Japan went on, Britain
should continue to receive munitions assistance from us to the extent of
$3,500,000,000 and other assistance of $3,000,000,000. He concurred in
Churchill's statement that if the United Kingdom were once more to pay
her way it was essential that her export trade, which had shrunk to a
very small fraction, should be reestablished. Naturally no articles obtained
on Lend-Lease or identical thereto would be exported or sold for profit;
but it was essential that the United States should not attach any conditions to supplies delivered to Britain on Lend-Lease which would jeopardize the recovery of her export trade.

This struck me amidships. It tended to shatter negotiations we had
been conducting with the British for three years. It derogated from Article VII of our basic Lend-Lease agreement with Britain, signed in 1942,
which provided that Britain would adopt a nondiscriminatory commercial
policy after the war, meaning that she would give up imperial tariff
preferences.

This whole development at Quebec, I believe, angered me as much as
anything that had happened during my career as Secretary of State. If
the Morgenthau plan leaked out, as it inevitably would—and shortly did
—it might well mean a bitter-end German resistance that could cause the
loss of thousands of American lives.

Morgenthau returned to Washington from Quebec, while the President went first to Hyde Park, where Prime Minister Churchill paid him a
visit. Morgenthau was wildly enthusiastic over what he had accomplished,
and came rushing to Stimson and me and others with the latest copies of
his plans.

I held a meeting of the Cabinet Committee in my office on September
20 to go over these developments, with Morgenthau and Stimson, Harry
White of the Treasury, Assistant Secretary of War McCloy, and H.
Freeman Matthews of the State Department. I made no effort to hide my
stupefaction at what the President and Mr. Churchill, at Morgenthau's
insistence, had agreed to at Quebec. I considered it a tragedy for all
concerned. I emphasized that I did not regard the matter as closed.

Morgenthau said that the President's invitation to him to go to
Quebec had been a complete surprise to him, and he did not want people
to think he had engineered it. He then went into a long explanation of

what had happened at Quebec. He said that Mr. Churchill had at first been violently opposed to the Morgenthau policy toward Germany. The Prime Minister had bluntly inquired whether he had been brought over to Quebec to discuss a scheme that would mean "England's being chained to a dead body."

Morgenthau turned to Stimson and said, in effect, "He was even more angry than you, Harry." Stimson had been as angered as I was over Morgenthau's high-handed procedure in conducting negotiations at Quebec on a matter of primary concern to the State and War Departments, without consultation with us; and he made no effort to conceal the fact.

Morgenthau said he then took up the subject with Lord Cherwell, personal assistant to the Prime Minister, and apparently convinced him. Cherwell discussed it with Churchill and won him over. The proposal apparently appealed to the Prime Minister on the ground that Britain would thus acquire many of Germany's iron and steel markets and eliminate a dangerous competitor. Morgenthau said they then made several attempts to put the understanding on paper, none of which pleased the Prime Minister, who thereupon called in his secretary and dictated his understanding of what had been agreed to. This was the document initialed by the President and the Prime Minister and dispatched to me on September 15. Morgenthau said it was drafted entirely by Mr. Churchill.

Stimson asked Morgenthau point-blank whether there had been any connection between Churchill's acceptance of this policy and his eagerness to obtain the credits that Morgenthau was offering him. Morgenthau answered No, but he said that the credits were clearly the Prime Minister's principal nonmilitary objective at Quebec.

The following day, Morgenthau said, Foreign Secretary Eden arrived at Quebec and became very much upset at the agreement reached by the President and the Prime Minister concerning Germany. Eden had a heated discussion with Mr. Churchill, who instructed him not to take it up in the War Cabinet until the Prime Minister returned, for he was bent on pushing it through.

Morgenthau said he was surprised at Eden's opposition, since he had gained a contrary impression when he talked with Eden in London a short time before. This statement disclosed to us that the Secretary of the Treasury, even prior to Quebec, had been discussing with British officials a matter of primary concern to the State and War Departments.

As for the credits side of the picture, Morgenthau said he had found the President prepared to accept the Prime Minister's views without question, but that he, Morgenthau, had insisted that a committee be set up to work out the project. Morgenthau himself did not seem to feel that the committee would be any too effective in obtaining British cooperation toward liberal economic policy, but he felt that at least it gave us a foot in the door. He said that the President had not raised any question as to what economic policy the British should pursue in return for our assistance.

Without cushioning my words, I said I was acutely shocked at the way such vital matters had been settled without any consultation with the appropriate experts of our Government and without any regard for the policy we had been trying to pursue in the past.

While awaiting the President's final ruling on the decisions reached at Quebec, representatives of the State, Treasury, and War Departments met in the War Department on September 22 to draw up an interim directive for Germany. After an all-day session they agreed tentatively on a directive, to which I gave my formal approval a few days later. During this meeting the Treasury representatives made it plain that they expected to be consulted henceforth not only on financial matters relating to Germany but on all other questions as well. They said this was the purpose behind the establishment of the Cabinet Committee, and they also indicated that the views set forth in the original Treasury memorandum on Germany had received the President's approval.

I sent the President a memorandum on September 25 suggesting that we should have the firm agreement of the British and Soviet Governments to the policy he had outlined in his memorandum of September 15 before going any further. "We have thus far," I said, "acted on the basis that every action followed with respect to Germany, particularly in the post-hostilities period, would be on an agreed tripartite basis. It has also been our understanding that the Soviet Government has also acted on this general assumption, and of course the European Advisory Commission, established by the Moscow Conference, was set up for the purpose of working out the problems of the treatment of Germany. We must realize that the adoption of any other basis of procedure would enormously increase the difficulties and responsibilities not only of our soldiers in the immediate military occupation period but also of our officials in the control period following."

I concluded by saying: "Our information up to the present has been to the effect that the British Government no doubt has ideas of its own with respect to the application of economic controls to Germany, and we have not yet had any indication that the British Government would be in favor of complete eradication of German industrial productive capacity in the Ruhr and Saar. We have no ideas as yet what the Soviet Government has in mind. Would it not be well at this time for the State Department to sound out the British and Russian views on the treatment of German industry either through the European Advisory Commission or otherwise?"

Shortly after the President returned to Washington I went to see him at the White House. I took his memorandum of September 15 and the Morgenthau plan with me.

I said bluntly to the President that Morgenthau's plan was out of all reason, and that no experts, no appropriate officials of our Government or the President, and no other Governments had had anything to do with its preparation. Morgenthau's plan, I added, would wipe out everything in Germany except land, and the Germans would have to live on the land. This meant that only 60 per cent of the German population could support themselves on German land, and the other 40 per cent would die.

I remarked that with regard to the postwar treatment of Germany I would bear in mind two controlling points. The first was that Germany should be kept under military control for twenty-five or fifty years, as necessity might require, until she experienced an absolute change of heart away from all theories and notions of Nazism and the absurd idea that Germans were a superior race and had a right to govern other races. The second was that the standard of living of the German population should be kept below the average of neighboring populations but should be raised gradually in proportion to the rate of change on their part away from Nazism, racial superiority, and the like, toward ideas of human rights, individual liberty, freedom, and peace.

I concluded that I was satisfied that the British at Quebec had joined in on this extreme starvation plan in order to get Morgenthau's help in obtaining the six-and-a-half-billion-dollar credit proposed by the Secretary of the Treasury. I particularly inveighed against this credit.

For one reason, I said, negotiations with Britain should be conducted primarily through the State Department, the organ of the Administration set up to negotiate with foreign Governments. For another reason, Morgenthau's proposal had attached to it no conditions whatever. There were numerous questions pending between us and Great Britain on which we should seek settlement or action, and the credits would be needed as a part of our bargaining position with her. Morgenthau had brushed aside or ignored these considerations, and made an unconditional offer of six and a half billion dollars without consulting any appropriate official of the Government either in the State Department or in Congress.

I concluded that, apart from all the other serious objections, if Morgenthau's proposals became known and the President were connected with them, it would greatly injure him politically. He was then in the midst of the 1944 Presidential campaign.

The President said very little during this conversation except to indicate that he had not actually committed himself to Morgenthau's proposals. In fact, he did not seem to realize the devastating nature of the memorandum of September 15 to which he had put his "O.K.—F.D.R."

I now asked my associates at the State Department to assist me in preparing a further memorandum for the President. This, dated September 29, I handed to him personally on October 1, and went over its major points with him.

"The Cabinet Committee," the memorandum said, "has not been able to agree upon a statement of American policy for the postwar treatment of Germany. The memorandum presented by the Secretary of the Treasury is decidedly at variance with the views developed in the State Department. In the meantime, I have received your memorandum of September 15, with the statements of views respecting the Ruhr, Saar, etc., and the conversion of Germany into an agricultural and pastoral country, which was formulated at Quebec. This memorandum seems to reflect largely the opinions of the Secretary of the Treasury in the treatment to be accorded Germany. I feel that I should therefore submit to you the line of thought that has been developing in the State Department on this matter."

We pointed out that the instrument of unconditional surrender of Germany had been recommended by the European Advisory Commission and had been formally approved by this Government, and we expected that British and Russian approval would be forthcoming. The European Advisory Commission, we continued, was going ahead on plans for tripartite control machinery and military government for Germany during the occupation period. All three Governments had submitted similar proposals. Our proposal contemplated a Supreme Authority consisting of the three commanding generals of the United States, United Kingdom, and U.S.S.R., which would coordinate Allied control of Germany and supervise the centralized governmental functions and economic activities they deemed essential. A Control Council, composed of representatives in equal numbers from the three Allied Governments, would be established by the Supreme Allied Authority. It would coordinate the administration of military government throughout Germany, including detailed planning for the execution of directives received from the three Governments.

We then set forth the objectives we had stated in the memorandum of September 4, such as demilitarization of Germany, dissolution of the Nazi Party, and control of communications, press and propaganda, and education. No decision should be taken on the possible partition of Germany, but we should encourage a decentralization of the German governmental structure, and if any tendencies toward spontaneous partition of Germany arose they should not be discouraged.

We stated our economic objectives to be, first, to render Germany incapable of waging war, and, second, to eliminate permanently German economic domination of Europe. A shorter-term objective was to require the performance by Germany of acts of restitution and reparation for injuries done to the United Nations.

We made five specific recommendations to achieve the first two objectives. First, destroy all factories incapable of conversion to peaceful purposes and prevent their reconstruction. Second, enforce the conversion of all other plants to peaceful manufacture. Third, eliminate self-sufficiency by imposing reforms that would make Germany dependent upon world markets (that is, annul the Nazi plan of economic autarchy or self-sufficiency). Fourth, establish controls over foreign trade and key industries for the purpose of preventing German rearmament. Fifth, eliminate the position of power of large industrialists and landowners.

We concluded the memorandum by stating: "It is of the highest importance that the standard of living of the German people in the early years be such as to bring home to them that they have lost the war and to impress on them that they must abandon all their pretentious theories that they are a superior race created to govern the world. Through lack of luxuries we may teach them that war does not pay."

The following day I received from the President a memorandum he had written me on September 29, that is, before my talk with him on October 1. This was by way of reply to my memorandum to him on September 25, and it clearly revealed that he had not realized the extent to which, at Morgenthau's urging, he had committed himself at Quebec.

"I do not think," he wrote, "that in the present stage any good purpose would be served by having the State Department or any other Department sound out the British and Russian views on the treatment of German industry. Most certainly it should not be taken up with the

European Advisory Commission which, in a case like this, is on a tertiary and not even a secondary level.

"The real nub of the situation is to keep Britain from going into complete bankruptcy at the end of the war." This last sentence he emphasized by inking a double line alongside it.

The press during the last week had come out with a number of articles indicating the drastic nature of the postwar treatment of Germany discussed at Quebec. This furnished Nazi propaganda agencies with wonderful ammunition to spur the Germans on to fight to the end.

"Somebody," the President said in his memorandum, "has been talking not only out of turn to the papers or [sic] on facts which are not fundamentally true.

"No one wants to make Germany a wholly agricultural nation again, and yet somebody down the line has handed this out to the press. I wish we could catch and chastise him."

(Secretary Stimson later informed me that the President thought the news leak had occurred in the State Department. By showing the President the article of the columnist who first came out with the story, and who was in close contact with certain officials in the Treasury, Stimson said he convinced the President that the leak had not occurred in the State or War Department.)

"You know," the President continued, "that before the war Germany was not only building up war manufacture, but was also building up enough of a foreign trade to finance rearming sufficiently and still maintain enough international credit to keep out of international bankruptcy.

"I just cannot go along with the idea of seeing the British Empire collapse financially, and Germany at the same time building up a potential rearmament machine to make another war possible in twenty years. Mere inspection of plants will not prevent that.

"But no one wants 'complete eradication of German industrial productive capacity in the Ruhr and Saar.'

"It is possible, however, in those two particular areas to enforce rather complete controls. Also, it must not be forgotten that outside of the Ruhr and Saar, Germany has many *other* areas and facilities for turning out large exports."

Turning to Russia, apropos of my insistence that the Soviet Government must be consulted regarding any plan for Germany, he said:

"In regard to the Soviet Government, it is true that we have no idea as yet what they have in mind, but we have to remember that in their occupied territory they will do more or less as they wish. We cannot afford to get into a position of merely recording protests on our part unless there is some chance of some of the protests being heeded.

"I do not intend by this to break off or delay negotiations with the Soviet Government over Lend-Lease either on the control basis or on the proposed Fourth Protocol basis. This, however, does not immediately concern the German industrial future."

My conversation with the President on October 1 had obviated the need to take any action on his memorandum. This latter showed me, however, the line of thought he had been pursuing. In his mind the future of Britain was linked inversely with the future of Germany. Britain needed to get back her export trade after the war, but he felt that she could not do so if Germany were permitted to develop an extensive export trade in competition. Therefore he embraced Morgenthau's plan. But he forgot, despite Churchill's initialing of the agreement, that the British Government was the last to desire the conversion of Germany into a pastoral country, because Britain's livelihood would be impaired if Europe's economy collapsed because of a wrecked Germany.

The President's memorandum also showed plainly that he had not understood the meaning of what he had agreed to at Quebec. At about this time Secretary Stimson had a talk with the President, from which Stimson drew the same conclusion. He informed me that he had thereupon read to the President several sentences from the President's memorandum of September 15, concluding with the phrase "looking forward to converting Germany into a country primarily agricultural and pastoral in its character."

Stimson informed me that the President was frankly staggered at hearing these sentences and said that he had no idea how he could have initialed the memorandum, and that he had evidently done so without much thought.

In any event, the President, after my conversation with him, ceased to embrace Morgenthau's ideas on Germany. Three weeks after my memorandum of September 29 he sent me a reply dated October 20 which he began by saying: "I think it is all very well for us to make all kinds of preparations for the treatment of Germany, but there are some matters in regard to such treatment that lead me to believe that speed on these matters is not an essential at the present moment. It may be in a week, or it may be in a month, or it may be several months hence. I dislike making detailed plans for a country which we do not yet occupy."

He said he agreed with our proposals for the demilitarization of Germany and suggested they include everything having to do with air-craft. He was "in hearty agreement" with our proposals for the dissolution of the Nazi Party and its affiliated organizations, and for extensive con-trols over communications, press, and propaganda. He agreed with our suggestion that no decision should be taken on the possible partition of Germany. With regard to our section on economic objectives, he said: "I should like to discuss this with the State Department in regard to some of the language. I agree with it in principle, but I do not know what part of it means. Much of this subhead is dependent on what we and the Allies find when we get into Germany—and we are not there yet."

Such was the situation when I left office. The American, British, and Soviet Governments had approved an instrument of unconditional sur-render for Germany. They had also agreed to the plan for tripartite control machinery and military government of Germany. The President had appointed Robert D. Murphy as Political Adviser for Germany to General Eisenhower, with the rank of Ambassador. Work had been com-pleted on a directive outlining the policies to be followed in German territory during the period prior to surrender or the collapse of armed resistance. An interim directive was in preparation covering the post-hostilities period.

The ideas my associates and I had stated in the memoranda of September 4 and 29, to which the War Department generally subscribed, and to which Britain and Russia later agreed, became to some degree those that were carried out when Germany was occupied. Nevertheless, Morgenthau did not cease to press his philosophy of crushing Germany to the dust, and his ideas had an adverse effect on the Allied program for that country, resulting in a more drastic plan than what we had in mind at the State Department prior to my resignation. The experience of several years' occupation of Germany, however, coupled with a realization of the validity of our argument that Germany's economy was interconnected with that of Europe, eventually required the American and British Gov-ernments to move away from Morgenthau's vengeful philosophy.

My talk with the President on October 1 was my last important item of business in his office. I was now on the verge of the collapse that necessitated my resignation.

Part Eight

PEACE AND AFTER

(1939–1945)

116: We Begin to Plan

THE SIX AND A HALF YEARS of my tenure as Secretary of State up to the outbreak of war in Europe on September 1, 1939, had been a spectacle of the futility of existing methods for maintaining the peace, whether by the League of Nations or by the efforts of individual nations working singly or together. War had come despite all the earnest endeavors of many nations to prevent it. And policies of neutrality had not served to keep nation after nation from being drawn into the vortex.

From the moment when Hitler's invasion of Poland revealed the bankruptcy of all existing methods to preserve the peace, it became evident to us in the State Department that we must begin almost immediately to plan the creation of a new system. This, profiting by the failures of the past, had to erect a viable and practical structure by which the peace of the world could be successfully maintained. Thus it was that, in an address on which we in the State Department had worked with him, the President at the very outset stated on September 3, 1939, the night of the day Britain and France declared war on Germany:

"It seems to me clear, even at the outbreak of this great war, that the influence of America should be consistent in seeking for humanity a final peace which will eliminate, as far as it is possible to do so, the continued use of force between nations."

The United States was thus committed from the very moment when chaos descended upon Europe to devote her influence toward developing a postwar world in which peace could be assured.

In this country and elsewhere in the world, the horror aroused by the advent of the war almost immediately produced thoughts along the same line. The Council on Foreign Relations in New York proposed on September 12 to amplify its studies and make them available to the State Department. We forthwith accepted. The Federal Council of Churches of Christ in America and a number of other organizations made similar offers of help. To each we stated we should be glad to receive its views.

From Europe we also began to garner indications that nations there, likewise spurred by the thought that the holocaust must not be permitted to occur again, were dedicating some of their energies to postwar studies. The British Foreign Office early organized a group of experts toward this end, and Pope Pius XII on October 20, 1939, advocated the necessity of founding a stable international organization after the war.

President Roosevelt's exchanges of messages with the Pope, the President of the Federal Council of Churches, and the President of the Jewish Theological Seminary of America on December 23, 1939, were a step in the direction of enlisting the assistance of the churches in parallel endeavors for a righteous peace.

Immediately after Hitler's invasion of Poland, I asked my principal associates in the Department to begin giving attention to long-range problems, and the Department's actual work on postwar questions may be said to have begun about that time. In connection with this work I asked Leo Pasvolsky, an economist and specialist in international affairs, to return to the State Department and resume his position as Special Assistant to the Secretary of State, from which he had retired some time before. His capacities were splendid, his service exceedingly valuable. I requested him specifically to work on long-range problems bearing on the postwar future.

Late in December, 1939, after consultation with my principal associates, I decided to organize postwar preparations within the State Department and to establish a Department committee for this purpose. In formulating this decision, the importance of which was manifest, I called to my office on December 27 Welles, R. Walton Moore (Counselor of the Department), Assistant Secretaries of State Berle, Messersmith, and Grady, Legal Adviser Hackworth, Leo Pasvolsky, Economic Adviser Feis, Political Adviser Hornbeck, and Chief of the European Division Moffat, to discuss the question with them.

We agreed upon a memorandum outlining the work we would undertake. At that time I had also thought to create a special division within the Department to study the problems of peace and reconstruction and to assemble and analyze information and views with regard to international economic relations, territorial, political, and armaments problems, neutral rights and duties, and the whole machinery of international cooperation. This, however, would have required a staff of Department officers, and our personnel were even then working night and day because of the many problems the war had thrust upon us.

The committee we set up was divided into three subcommittees. One was to handle political problems, chiefly the organization of peace. Another was to deal with the limitation and reduction of armaments. The third was to embrace economic problems. I stated my thought that the committee should make recommendations on immediate problems arising from the war as well as analyze postwar questions.

We publicly announced, on January 8, 1940, the creation of this committee, called the Advisory Committee on Problems of Foreign Relations, of which I named Welles chairman and Hugh Wilson, formerly Ambassador to Germany, vice chairman. The other members, in addition to those who had met with me on December 27, were Assistant Secretary of State Breckinridge Long, Political Adviser James C. Dunn, Norman Davis (who had so often assisted me in many valuable ways in the past), and George Rublee, director of the Inter-Governmental Committee on Political Refugees. The chairmen of the three subcommittees were: George Rublee for political problems; R. Walton Moore for armaments; Pasvolsky for economic problems.

The Advisory Committee had fifteen members in all. With the exception of Davis and Rublee, it was composed entirely of Department officials. Because of Rublee's illness, Welles carried on most of the work of presiding over the subcommittee for political problems.

The President stated in his message to Congress on January 3, 1940, the aim with which we began to work when he said, "We can strive with other nations to encourage the kind of peace that will lighten the troubles of the world."

The committee undertook to study means whereby the war might be limited and possibly ended, the foundations of a peaceful world order laid, and the defense of the Western Hemisphere strengthened. The three subcommittees began to work intensively despite the fact that their members were largely Department officers already heavily engaged in other duties. The work in the beginning had to be informal and exploratory. Individual members presented papers outlining their views. The respective subcommittees considered these views and, if agreement were reached, sought to state them in the form of recommendations, which were considered by the Advisory Committee as a whole and were then communicated to me.

During the spring of 1940 the political subcommittee began to consider the organization of world order after the war. Naturally it had to make its views tentative, because so much depended on the outcome of the war. Should the United States be a member of a world organization, or should we advocate regional organizations? Should the League of Nations be retained, should we join it, or should a new organization be set up?

As early as January 15, 1940, the economic subcommittee outlined the bases for an economic settlement that we hoped might be presented at a conference of neutral nations which we then had in mind. The subcommittee had to take into consideration the probability that, however the war in Europe ended, its conclusion would find many countries in desperate economic need. Should such needs be neglected, recovery in all countries might be retarded and social upheavals might follow that would seriously impair postwar reconstruction.

On February 9 and 10 we began diplomatic conversations with forty-seven neutral Governments looking toward an exchange of views on "two basic problems connected with the establishment of a sound foundation for a lasting world peace; namely, the establishment of the bases of a sound international economic system, and the limitation and reduction of armaments." We specified that our conversations would not involve present problems arising from the war.

Our purpose in proposing this exchange was to obtain, before the advent of a peace conference, as definite commitments and understandings as possible with other nations on the basic principles of a stable international relationship after the war.

More than two-thirds of the replies we received promised full cooperation. The others were reserved, particularly as to disarmament. Many asked that we set forth our ideas as a basis for discussion.

The economic and disarmament subcommittees accordingly worked hard to prepare a comprehensive memorandum stating the views of this Government on postwar economic relations and disarmament, to be presented at a conference of neutrals. Since the field of their inquiry extended to questions of interest to other Government Departments, especially Treasury, Commerce, and Agriculture, and to the Tariff Commission and the Export-Import Bank, those Departments and agencies were duly consulted. But when Hitler invaded Scandinavia in April and the Low Countries and France in May, further action along these lines became impracticable.

After Welles returned from his trip to Europe in 1940, he informed the President and me that, important as were the territorial, political, and economic problems, security was the basic problem. He thought there might be a slight chance to restore peace if the United States and other neutrals prepared a practical plan of security and disarmament upon which the major powers of Europe would agree. I myself placed not the slightest faith in this recommendation, believing that Hitler was already determined to test the might of his war machine against his ancient enemy, France.

Hitler's overwhelming victories in western Europe forced the Advisory Committee to consider the effects of a peace imposed by the Nazis, with the German system of economic autarchy extended to most of Europe and possibly to other continents as well. Such a peace would confront the United States with postwar economic problems of a totally different nature from those that had been discussed up to that time. To debate this and other issues, the economic subcommittee was thereupon constituted into what became known as the Inter-Departmental Group to Consider Post-war Economic Problems and Policies, under the chairmanship of Leo Pasvolsky, composed initially of representatives of the State, Treasury, Commerce, and Agriculture Departments.

The political subcommittee on May 31, 1940, began to consider what we might have to do if Germany were victorious. It emphasized the possibility that one or more Latin American Republics might find themselves becoming politically dependent upon Germany because of economic necessity as Hitler organized Europe into an economic bloc. To prevent this the subcommittee believed the United States would have to grant export subsidies to the Republics thus threatened.

The subcommittee also considered the possibility that Germany would demand the transfer to her of the Western Hemisphere possessions of the European countries she had conquered. The President and I had already approved the draft of a proposed joint resolution for immediate submission to Congress dealing with this point, and Congress passed such a resolution on June 18, 1940.

The subcommittee finally dealt with the possibility that Japan might move into the Dutch East Indies as a result of the German victory, and recommended that all possible preparations should be made for adequate defense beyond the Western Hemisphere. It also recommended that existing legislation should be changed to enable the Allies to obtain credits in this country and to purchase the needed military supplies.

The work of the political subcommittee regarding the Western Hemisphere was now merged with the work of the American delegation to the Havana Conference (July, 1940) which I headed. At Havana, formal inter-American arrangements (described in Chapter 59) were made for the eventuality of an Axis claim for the transfer of European possessions in the Western Hemisphere to Germany. The Inter-Departmental Group on Economic Problems and Policies, the principal members of which accompanied me to Havana, had meantime prepared the economic proposals that we put forward at the conference, embraced in a resolution on current and postwar economic policies and in a plan for economic assistance to the Latin American countries to enable them to meet the difficulties caused by the war. This resolution, unanimously adopted by the twenty-one American Republics, was in fact the earliest official declaration by any group of nations with regard to postwar commercial policy. It reaffirmed the adherence of the Republics to liberal principles of international trade and stressed the desirability of conducting trade "with the entire world in accordance with these principles as soon as the non-American nations are prepared to do likewise."

Upon our return from Havana, the Inter-Departmental Group resumed its work on a broad scale.

Early in 1941 our consideration of postwar problems intensified. To forward our work in this field I created a Division of Special Research in the State Department, on February 3, 1941, with Leo Pasvolsky as its chief, and Harley Notter and Julian Wadleigh as his principal assistants. When the President dramatically stated the Four Freedoms in his annual message to Congress on January 6, 1941, the promotion of these human freedoms became the basis for our consideration of a future world order.

I was able to state publicly, in an address on April 24, 1941, that the Department was working "at the task of creating ultimate conditions of peace and justice." And again, in a radio address on May 18, I said: "It is none too early to lay down at least some of the principles by which policies must be guided at the conclusion of the war, to press for a broad program of world economic reconstruction, and to consider tentative plans for the application of those policies." I added that: "In the final reckoning, the problem becomes one of establishing the foundations of an international order in which independent nations cooperate freely with each other for their mutual gain—of a world order, not new but renewed, which liberates rather than enslaves."

Congress was likewise displaying interest in postwar organization. Senator Elbert D. Thomas (Democrat of Utah) introduced a resolution to authorize the Committee on Foreign Relations to make a full study of all matters pertaining to the establishment of a lasting peace throughout the world. I wrote Senator Walter F. George, acting chairman of the committee, on June 7, 1941, telling him of the State Department's work in that direction.

The Atlantic Charter agreed to by President Roosevelt and Prime

Minister Churchill in August provided us a further basis on which to build our structure for a postwar world.

Meantime the Department's Division of Special Research was making headway in its exploratory and preparatory work, although by the end of 1941 there was only a handful of officers in the Division. I recognized that this was too small a number for the vast array of problems to be explored, but the demands of war upon the personnel of the Department made a larger organization still impossible. The Division undertook, among many other tasks, the compilation and analysis of all official views and policy commitments with regard to postwar questions, as expressed by the Allied and neutral Governments. Studies made by outside organizations were now beginning to come to the State Department and were carefully analyzed and considered.

Other governments now began to approach us to learn something of our postwar planning. Australia informed us of the efforts she was making. The British Government in October, 1941, asked whether we desired to take part with the Allied Governments in a joint study concerning a future international juridical organization. At that time we could only reply that we were interested in receiving further information, but that, in our work, we were considering the creation of an international court of justice in connection with a world organization rather than as a problem by itself.

Early in 1941, in connection with the establishment of the Division of Special Research, we had begun to consider the possibility of creating a broad-gauge committee on postwar problems consisting of State Department officials, officials of other Departments, Members of Congress, and distinguished private citizens. While this project was under discussion, we began to note numerous indications that other agencies of the Government were reaching out to assume responsibility for postwar planning, which we considered should be the function of the State Department working with other Departments and agencies of the Government. This was particularly true of the Board of Economic Defense, established on July 30, 1941. One of its functions was stated to be the rendering of advice to the President on the relationship of defense measures to postwar economic reconstruction and on steps to expedite the establishment of sound, peacetime international economic relationships.

In October, 1941, Welles and I talked over with the President the whole problem of arrangements for postwar planning, and obtained his oral approval for the creation by his authority of an advisory committee on postwar foreign policy, with the Secretary of State as chairman and the Under Secretary of State as vice chairman, along the lines of our plan considered earlier in the year. Under our proposal, the Division of Special Research, other appropriate divisions of the Department, other Departments and agencies and cooperating nongovernment agencies would prepare research studies and draft memoranda on postwar planning under the aegis of this Advisory Committee, and the committee's recommendations to the President would be made through its chairman. Basically, this was a proposal to draw together the resources of the whole Government and of interested outside organizations toward one end. The mounting crisis in the Far East, however, forced us to suspend action on the plan for the time being. The Japanese attack was approaching.

Within a few days after Pearl Harbor, I initiated the preparation of the Declaration by United Nations. Dated January 1, 1942, and adhered to at once by twenty-six nations, it bound the United Nations together in a common determination to win the fight against the Axis, and support the principles of the Atlantic Charter, thereby providing a foundation for the union we hoped would come to pass after the war was over. At the time we were preparing this Declaration in the State Department I wrote a letter to the President on December 22, 1941, recalling to him the conversation Welles and I had had with him in October. I enclosed a list of proposed members of the committee, which would be known as the Advisory Committee on Postwar Foreign Policy, consisting of several officials of the Government and of several prominent persons from outside the Government with special qualifications for contributing to this work.

The new committee, I said, would maintain close contact with all appropriate Departments and agencies of the Government and with such nongovernmental agencies as might be in position to contribute to an all-around consideration of the problems involved. I then stated that, since it was his further desire that all recommendations regarding postwar problems of international relations from all Departments and agencies of the Government be submitted to him through the Secretary of State, and that all conversations or negotiations with foreign Governments bearing on postwar problems be conducted, under his authority, by or through the Department of State, I should appreciate it if he would cause the heads of the various Departments and agencies concerned to be apprised of his views.

The list of proposed members I transmitted to the President consisted of: myself as chairman; Welles as vice chairman; Norman H.

Davis, president of the Council on Foreign Relations and chairman of the American Red Cross; Myron C. Taylor, the President's personal representative to the Pope; Dean Acheson, Assistant Secretary of State; Hamilton Fish Armstrong, editor of the quarterly *Foreign Affairs;* Adolf A. Berle, Jr., Assistant Secretary of State; Isaiah Bowman, president of Johns Hopkins University; Benjamin V. Cohen, general counsel, National Power Policy Committee; Herbert Feis, State Department Adviser on International Economic Relations; Green H. Hackworth, Legal Adviser; Harry C. Hawkins, Chief of the Division of Commercial Policy; Mrs. Anne O'Hare McCormick, editorial staff, the New York *Times;* and Leo Pasvolsky, Special Assistant to the Secretary of State and Chief of the Division of Special Research.

Within a week the President sent this letter back to me after having written on it: "I heartily approve.—F. D. R."

We were now launched on our postwar work with a definite and prominent committee organized under Presidential authority. Our jurisdiction was clear, and the field was open for truly constructive achievement.

117: Roosevelt-Churchill Ideas

WHEN THE Advisory Committee on Postwar Foreign Policy began its work in 1942, the United States was at war, the entire population was intensely concerned with the outcome, and virtually every American had already begun to think in terms of avoiding a recurrence of such bankruptcy in international relations.

Even as a neutral we had been convinced that we would have an important role to play in the eventual peace conference. But as one of the mightiest of the belligerents, we now knew that we could strongly influence the creation of any international organization to maintain the peace. And because of this increased influence we recognized that our responsibilities for adequate, wise, and careful planning for the postwar world were correspondingly greater. Moreover, the war had by now become so destructive and so vast in its extent, embracing almost the whole world, that we realized that the work of building anew after it was over would be immeasurably augmented.

The Advisory Committee first met in the office of Under Secretary Welles on February 12. It decided that it should not merely provide the President with information on postwar problems, but also submit definite recommendations to him, since his time was so taken up with grave war problems. Because the first months after Pearl Harbor were black with defeat and retreat in the Far East, the committee decided to keep its existence secret for the time being lest publicity on our postwar studies tend to impair the public's realization that a long, hard fight would be necessary before victory could be won. The committee discussed whether its work should be confined to the postwar field or should also cover problems connected with the war. I later decided that the committee should devote itself entirely to postwar problems, leaving current questions to the State and other Departments.

The committee agreed to set up six regular and three special subcommittees, in political, security, and economic fields, and one to coordinate the work and maintain contact with private organizations engaged in postwar studies. The Advisory Committee itself would deliberate on the recommendations prepared by the subcommittees and then would submit its views to me. Usually I would transmit views to the President. The work of the subcommittees would be coordinated through Leo Pasvolsky, who was made Executive Officer of the Advisory Committee and its Director of Research.

There was a subcommittee on political problems, under Welles first and later myself; one on security presided over by Norman Davis; one on territorial problems under Isaiah Bowman; and two economic subcommittees under Dean Acheson and Adolf Berle, which later were combined into a single committee on postwar foreign economic policy headed by Myron C. Taylor. There was also a special subcommittee on international organization under Welles; one on legal problems under Green Hackworth, and one, under Hamilton Fish Armstrong, to consider problems of possible European federation.

Shortly after the establishment of the Advisory Committee we began to increase the number of its members to obtain the benefit of additional ability and to give representation to major points of view, particularly political points of view. Eventually the Advisory Committee itself included forty-five members enlisted from the public, the Senate and the House of Representatives, the State, War, Navy, and other Departments, the White House staff, the Library of Congress, and other Government agencies.

My first concern was to make the membership of the committee absolutely nonpartisan, and to give Republicans as well as Democrats adequate representation. Right from the beginning I was determined that the mistakes made in 1919–1920, which led to the United States' holding aloof from the League of Nations, should not recur. I resolved to do all that I could to get the Republican Party as well as the Democratic Party 100 per cent behind the creation of an international organization to maintain the peace, in which the United States would be a full-fledged member.

The first of the invitations I sent out to new members, after consultation with the President, were addressed on May 27, 1942, to Senator Tom Connally, Democrat of Texas, and Senator Warren R. Austin, Republican of Vermont, respectively the chairman and a minority member of the Senate Committee on Foreign Relations. Austin later became the United States Representative to the United Nations organization.

Later I invited Senators Walter F. George, Democrat of Georgia, Elbert D. Thomas, Democrat of Utah, and Wallace H. White, Republican of Maine, to join. I sent invitations likewise to a number of Representatives of both parties: Sol Bloom, Democrat of New York; Charles A. Eaton, Republican of New Jersey; and Luther A. Johnson, Democrat of Texas. Still later, Senators Scott W. Lucas and Claude Pepper, and Representatives Schuyler Otis Bland, J. Hardin Peterson, Richard J. Welch, Alfred Bulwinkle, and Charles A. Wolverton were invited to take part in the work of special committees set up under the Advisory Committee.

By agreement with the President, I invited many other eminent Americans to join the Advisory Committee. Among them were James T. Shotwell of the Carnegie Endowment for International Peace; Brooks Emeny, director of the Foreign Affairs Council, Cleveland, Ohio; William Green, president of the American Federation of Labor; Philip Murray, president of the Congress of Industrial Organizations; Walter Reuther, United Automobile Workers; and Eric Johnston, president of the United States Chamber of Commerce.

Harry White of the Treasury, Major General George V. Strong, and Admiral Arthur J. Hepburn, representing respectively Secretaries Morgenthau, Stimson, and Knox, shortly became members. Two members of the President's staff, David K. Niles and Lauchlin Currie, were included, along with Archibald MacLeish, Librarian of Congress.

I rigidly kept down the number of State Department officials who were members of the committee, since this was designed to be a national committee advisory to the President through the Secretary of State. Various officers of the Department, however, were constantly assisting the committee and its subcommittees in their work. Many other officials of various Departments and agencies of the Government also took part in specialized discussions. In general, the whole resources of the Government were at our disposal, and we made full use of them.

An enormous amount of extremely valuable work was done by the various subcommittees. The one on territorial problems explored meticulously and comprehensively every aspect we could imagine of postwar territorial problems and adjustments, as well as problems of regionalism and dependent areas. The economic committee formulated far-reaching plans for postwar economic policies and for the creation of international agencies in the field of economic and social problems. The security committee canvassed thoroughly the various phases of postwar security arrangements such as the regulation of armaments. The political committee, in addition to much other work, was the principal one devoting attention to plans for the establishment of a postwar world organization for the maintenance of peace and security and for the promotion of general cooperation among nations.

Since the only phase of our postwar planning that actually came to full fruition before I retired from the Department was that which related to an international organization, I shall devote most of my attention to that problem, which in my thinking was always the central and decisive problem of the postwar future.

Within two months after the Advisory Committee, with Welles presiding, began to meet, it had considered the creation of an interim international political organization during the war, without waiting for the peace, so that, in contrast with what occurred in the First World War, we should have machinery ready before hostilities ceased. This body, to be known as the United Nations Authority, would consist of representatives not only of the four major powers—the United States, Great Britain, Russia, and China—but, in some manner, of all the other United Nations, so that all nations would feel they had a voice in the organization.

The committee likewise considered the creation of an International Relief Council, composed of representatives of the United Nations, the head of which would be an American. The committee believed that, while it was true that the United States would have to bear the main burden of relief, it should do so on an international basis, in cooperation with other nations. It was thought that early action toward the creation of this Council would contribute to the war effort by giving greater substance to the concept of the United Nations and might serve as an experiment with regard to the organization of a United Nations Authority.

The committee disapproved the idea of using relief for political purposes. It agreed that for reasons of morale the peoples of the occupied countries should be informed as soon as possible that the United Nations were conferring on how to extend them relief. It was accordingly agreed that the United States should take the initiative toward the formation of the International Relief Council as soon as possible.

When I met with the Advisory Committee on May 21, 1942, I expressed anxiety over the influences that inevitably would bring their forces to bear against the constructive views for the peace settlement and world improvement contemplated by the committee.

"Such special interest groups and influences," I said, "constitute perhaps the greatest threat that the committee faces, and undoubtedly the best program the committee can devise will be attacked. We need to make better preparation for world peace than was made at the close of the First World War. Even then the chances are only about one to two or three that a sound peace can be carried to fruition. It is of the utmost importance to have the informed support of the American public behind us."

Two months later I publicly stated the gist of our postwar thinking when, in my radio address of July 23, 1942, I said: "It is plain that some international agency must be created which can—by force, if necessary—keep the peace among nations in the future. There must be international cooperative action to set up the mechanisms which can thus insure peace. This must include eventual adjustment of national armaments in such a manner that the rule of law cannot be successfully challenged, and that the burden of armaments may be reduced to a minimum."

Having laid out the general framework for its studies, the Advisory Committee ceased to meet as a whole. Its work of reviewing the findings of the subcommittees then largely devolved upon the Subcommittee on Political Problems, of which Welles was chairman. He continued as its chairman until January 30, 1943, when I took it over. Though I had not been participating in this subcommittee's meetings, I had kept in close touch with its work from the beginning and had had numerous conferences with its individual members. The whole war and possible postwar situation apeared to me such that a stage had been reached where we should begin to arrive at definite decisions, and that I should therefore take charge.

In the same month, we decided to expand the research staff and reorganize the Division of Special Research into a Division of Political Studies, with Harley Notter as Chief, and a Division of Economic Studies, with Leroy Steinbower as Chief, both functioning under the direction of Leo Pasvolsky.

The Political Subcommittee and the special subcommittees continued intensive studies throughout the spring of 1943. Their considerations ranged from the preparation of an international bill of rights and the creation of a war crimes commission, to the future organization of the Southwest Pacific, a plan of international trusteeship for dependent peoples, and the creation of a general international organization.

On the question of trusteeship, the Political Subcommittee first suggested that a trusteeship plan should be drawn up to include all colonial territories. Subsequently, for obvious reasons of political feasibility, it concluded that a trusteeship system should be set up under the international organization to include only the Axis dependencies and the territories mandated by the League of Nations. The subcommittee recommended that regional councils for dependent areas be created, under the general international organization. The dependent areas would be administered, under the supervision of a regional council, either by international agencies or by individual trustee states. It agreed that the United States should restrict her trusteeship responsibilities mainly to the Western Hemisphere and the Pacific.

The Political Subcommittee believed that the United States should not fix a minimum postwar program but should rather set forth a maximum program of sound international relations. We sought to plan an ideal settlement which we should try to attain with other nations as fully as possible. Our discussions were based upon our belief in absolute victory by the United Nations and in cooperation by the United Nations after the war. Although we considered international security our supreme objective, we also maintained that its attainment must dovetail with principles of justice so that it would last. We believed that the American people would support whatever American participation was needed to maintain international peace and security. We further believed that Russian cooperation on the principal international problems was essential and could be obtained.

Our discussions were marked by informality, and I made it clear that the members were not required to make commitments, nor were they bound by any views they might express. This particularly was the case with members of the Senate and House of Representatives from both political parties who were members of the committee.

We kept the President informed of the progress of our discussions at all times. Welles or I frequently saw him in this connection, and we sent him many drafts, particularly those in the fields of an international organization, trusteeship, and the treatment of Germany. In turn we passed on to the committee the President's views expressed to us.

In the spring and summer of 1943 the Political Subcommittee resolved a number of basic questions that still remained. As to whether to revive the League of Nations or set up a new international organization, we decided in favor of the latter. The Political Subcommittee had appointed a Special Subcommittee on International Organization, with Welles as chairman, which concentrated on working out the prospective bases for such an organization. This work began on October 23, 1942, and resulted in the preparation by March 26, 1943, of a draft of a proposed charter for an international organization.

While this draft contained many good features it leaned rather strongly in the direction of regionalism by providing that the Executive

Council of the proposed organization would consist of eleven members, of whom only the four major powers, as permanent members, would be represented as individual nations. The other seven members would each represent a region of the world rather than any individual nation. In this respect the draft reflected Welles's influence, since he was a convinced advocate of regional organization.

When these plans were brought to my attention in the Political Subcommittee, I could not go along with the regional feature; hence I started the subcommittee upon a detailed consideration of international organization in the spring of 1943 on the basis of fundamental issues rather than on the special subcommittee's draft. The subcommittee, after thorough discussion, expressed itself as being overwhelmingly in favor of a universal rather than a regional basis for an international organization.

With respect to regionalism, Welles echoed the ideas of President Roosevelt and Prime Minister Churchill. In the spring of 1943 both the President and the Prime Minister were convinced that after the war the world should be organized on a regional basis. The nations in certain geographical regions would band together to maintain the peace in those areas. There might be an international organization, but it would do little more than coordinate the work of the regional organizations. I, along with most of my associates in and out of the State Department, except Welles, argued on the other side; namely, that we should have a strong world organization which would be supreme over any regional associations, and that the latter should not be constituted in such a way as to interfere with the authority or work of the general organization.

Mr. Churchill stated his ideas to the President in a long message dated February 2, 1943, which he entitled "Morning Thoughts: Note on Post-War Security." Mr. Roosevelt gave me a copy.

After commenting that it was the intention of the chiefs of the United Nations to create a world organization for the preservation of peace based upon the concepts of freedom and justice and the revival of prosperity, the Prime Minister came at once to his own idea. As part of this organization, he said, an instrument of European Government would be established embodying the spirit of the League of Nations but not subject to its weaknesses. The units forming this body would be not only the great nations of Europe and Asia Minor; there was obvious need also for a Scandinavian bloc, a Danubian bloc, and a Balkan bloc.

A similar instrument, Mr. Churchill went on, would be formed in the Far East with different membership, and the whole would be held together by the fact that the victorious Powers continued fully armed, especially in the air, while imposing complete disarmament upon the guilty.

No one, he said, could predict with certainty that the victors would never quarrel amongst themselves, or that the United States might not again retire from Europe; but after the experiences which all had gone through, and their sufferings and the certainty that a third struggle would destroy all that was left of the culture, wealth, and civilization of mankind and reduce us to the level almost of wild beasts, the most intense effort would be made by the leading powers to prolong their honorable association and win for themselves a glorious name in human annals by their sacrifice and self-restraint.

Great Britain, he concluded, would certainly do her utmost to organize a coalition of resistance to any act of aggression committed by any power. He believed that the United States would cooperate with Britain and even possibly take the lead of the world, on account of her numbers and strength, in the good work of preventing such tendencies to aggression before they broke out in open war.

During Foreign Secretary Eden's visit to Washington in the latter half of March, 1943, Mr. Churchill made a radio address in which he came out publicly for regional organizations in Europe and the Far East, while assigning only a vague and secondary role to an over-all world organization.

When Mr. Churchill came to the United States in May, 1943, he presented these ideas earnestly to the President and to other members of the Government. Saying that the first preoccupation in discussions of a postwar structure should be to prevent future aggression by Germany and Japan, he contemplated an association of the United States, Great Britain, and Russia. If the United States wanted to include China he was perfectly willing, although China was not comparable to the other three.

Subordinate to this world council, he believed, there should be three regional councils, one each for Europe, the Orient, and the American hemisphere. The European council, he thought, might consist of some twelve states or confederations. He wanted a strong France re-created because the prospect of having no strong country on the map of Europe between England and Russia was not attractive. The European council would have its own high court and armed forces.

In the regional council for the Americas, Mr. Churchill thought Canada would naturally be a member and would represent the British Commonwealth.

In the regional council for the Pacific he supposed Russia would participate. He thought it possible that Russia, when the pressure on her western frontiers had been relieved, would turn her attention to the Far East.

Mr. Churchill's view was that the regional councils would be subordinate to the world council, and that members of the world council would sit on the regional councils in which they were directly interested. He hoped that the United States, in addition to being represented on the American and Pacific regional councils, would also be represented on the European council.

He added that to the four Powers on the world council there should be added other members by election in rotation from the regional councils. His central idea of the international structure was that of a three-legged stool—the world council resting on three regional councils.

He concluded that he attached great importance to the regional principle, because it was only the countries whose interests were directly affected by a dispute that could be expected to apply themselves with sufficient vigor to secure a settlement. Only vapid and academic discussion would result from calling in countries remote from a dispute.

In July, 1943, the British Government proposed to us and to the Soviet Government the creation of a European commission to coordinate the execution of surrender or armistice terms imposed on the enemy and also to assume far-reaching functions with regard to long-range European arrangements in the fields of security and economic integration. After giving this considerable study in the State Department and after conferring with the President, I replied that we could agree to the creation of such a body for dealing with the terms to be imposed on the enemy, but we opposed entrusting to such a body long-range peacetime functions. We took this up at the Moscow Conference in October and agreed to create the European Advisory Commission with functions limited to the formulation of terms of surrender and plans for their execution.

President Roosevelt agreed in general with the Prime Minister's regional ideas. During the spring of 1943 I found there was a basic cleavage between him and me on the very nature of the postwar organization.

The President favored a four-power establishment that would police the world with the forces of the United States, Britain, Russia, and China. All other nations, including France, were to be disarmed. He felt that the four nations had functioned well together during the war, and he wanted this relationship to continue. He believed in the efficacy of direct personal contact between Churchill, Stalin, Chiang Kai-shek, and himself, and he thought that this direct relationship among the chiefs of the four nations would result in efficient future management of the world.

At that time he did not want an over-all world organization. He did favor the creation of regional organizations, but it was the four big powers that would handle all security questions.

On the economic side he favored the creation of entirely separate functional agencies. It was on this basis that, at his insistence, a plan was developed early in 1943 for the convocation of the Hot Springs, Virginia, conference on food and agriculture, and for the holding of similar conferences on other economic matters with a view to creating a series of uncoordinated functional agencies. While I favored the creation of such specialized agencies, I differed with the President in that I thought it was also necessary to have some sort of over-all agency of coordination in the whole field of economic and social cooperation, such as the United Nations Economic and Social Council which later came into being.

When I called on the President to discuss questions concerning the international organization, I frequently took to the White House some of the men who were working with me on these matters, particularly Myron C. Taylor, Isaiah Bowman, Norman Davis, James C. Dunn, Green Hackworth, and Leo Pasvolsky. We argued with the President to induce him to change his ideas, but for some time without avail.

On one occasion we asked: "Aren't you at least in favor of a world secretariat? We'll need some such organization to handle international conferences."

He laughed as he said: "I'll give you the Pentagon or the Empire State Building. You can put the world secretariat there."

As this trend toward regionalism seemed to me to be assuming a strength that might imperil the future postwar organization, I asked our postwar political subcommittee to give it special study. In the conversations that ensued among us we fully agreed on the necessity of a universal international organization, as opposed to regional organizations, although regional associations of the Pan American type should of course continue and be brought into a proper relationship with the world organization.

We admitted that regional organizations had certain advantages. They could facilitate peaceful adjustments locally. If their members accepted certain principles, the regional organization might be in advantageous position to apply them. Such an organization would provide political, economic, and legal buffers between the nations and the universal organization to absorb the shock of various local controversies. It would give the universal organization greater freedom to carry out its wider functions. And, if a great power crippled the universal organization by leaving it, the regional organizations would offer something to fall back upon.

But it seemed to us that their disadvantages far outweighed their advantages. We argued that regional organizations such as Mr. Churchill proposed would profoundly change the functions of the universal organization. The latter might then have to deal with groups of nations rather than with individual nations.

As regional organizations became solidified, we thought, it might be possible that conflicts would spring up, not between nations but between regions. And the universal organization might find itself incapable of dealing with such conflicts. It would be easier for the proposed United Nations organization to deal with a nation alone than with a nation tied into and supported by a region.

We felt that a regional organization by its very nature set up a special relationship between the one or two great powers and the small states in that region. In the United States' relationship with the American Republics in the Pan American system we, at least under the Roosevelt Administration, had exercised economic and other self-restraint; we had not sought to set up preferential arrangements in the Western Hemisphere or to dominate the economies of the other Republics. But such self-restraint might not be exercised by a great power in another region, and there might develop, in consequence, closed trade areas or discriminatory systems. These would defy the universal organization, induce the creation of similar systems in other regions, and produce serious interregional economic conflicts, with dangerous political repercussions.

From the particular point of view of the United States we could see many objections to international organization on a regional basis. If we participated in the European and Pacific councils we might have thrust upon us the undesirable role of mediating between the other dominating powers in those regions, or we might be used by one against another.

If we were represented on the European council, the Latin American Republics might feel that we were representing them in Europe without having been so chosen.

Further, would we, who had not looked with favor on the participation of European nations in the Pan American Conferences even as observers, be content to see European or Asiatic powers participating in a Western Hemisphere council?

We questioned, too, whether the Latin American Republics would want to see the creation of a council of the Americas, in which the United States might officially have to act as the dominant member.

We did not think that the people of the United States would support this country's participation in a European council and a Pacific council, in addition to a Western Hemisphere council, and also in a universal organization. We felt that the American people were more ready to take responsibilities in a world organization than in any regional plan except perhaps one embracing this hemisphere. Moreover, the latter alternative would be a haven for the isolationists, who could advocate all-out United States cooperation in a Western Hemisphere council on condition that we did not participate in a European or Pacific council.

In general, however, we did not oppose regional and other special arrangements supplementary to the general international organization so long as these did not infringe on the powers we thought should reside in the world-wide association of nations. We recognized the freedom of action of small nations to make such regional arrangements among themselves as might be to their mutual advantage. As an example, we viewed with sympathy the plans for an Arab union, particularly in the economic and social field. We had made clear our desire to see the Pan American system of cooperation continued and strengthened in the postwar period as part of the general plan for international cooperation.

It was my view that, subordinate to the world organization and within its framework, groups of nations located in a given area might with entire consistency carry forward the policies we had adopted in our structure of Pan American cooperation, provided they did not go further than the Pan American system. The American Republics had agreed to consider any danger or threatened danger to any American nation from outside the hemisphere as a danger to all of them, and to cooperate in meeting it. Under a continuance of this policy after the creation of a world organization, the American Republics would proceed to deal with such danger locally, while simultaneously bringing the matter before the council of the universal organization, and cooperating within the framework of that body. When a house catches fire, the nearest neighbors hasten there with the common objective of putting out or preventing the spread of the fire until the Fire Department, which has been instantly notified, can arrive on the scene.

I could see no reason for a clash between the council of the world organization and a regional system of the Pan American type in these circumstances. Both the council and the local organization would have common purposes, the maintenance of peace. The world organization would in the end be supreme.

I recalled the simultaneous efforts made by the League of Nations and the Pan American Conference at Montevideo and also by groups of American Republics to stop the Chaco War. The American Republics nearest the Chaco conflict, and also the United States, made earnest efforts to halt the fighting. Meantime the world organization at Geneva had sent a commission posthaste to the site of the war to exercise its influence and cooperative efforts toward the same end. The Montevideo Conference and the League Commission cooperated fully, understandingly, and in the most effective way possible to find means of ending the conflict. There was complete harmony of purpose and effort on the part of the world organization at Geneva and the American nations, and there was no interference and no need for interference with the supremacy of the world organization.

The more advanced regional ideas of President Roosevelt and Prime Minister Churchill, however, might lead to questions of balance of power, and regional organizations of the type they envisaged might deal arbitrarily with one another and in the internal affairs of their members, whether by military force or economic pressure or their equivalent. This would open the door to abuses and the exercise of undue privileges by greedy, grasping nations possessing great military and economic strength.

In various meetings at the White House, my associates and I presented these arguments to the President with all the force we could. As summer arrived he began to turn toward our point of view.

He thereupon agreed with our draft of the Four-Nation Declaration which I handed Eden at the first Quebec Conference and then presented and had adopted at the Moscow Conference in October, 1943. Despite his earlier views, Mr. Churchill did not object to the Four-Nation Declaration. This expressed the agreement of the four major nations on the necessity of establishing at the earliest practicable date "a general international organization, based on the principle of the sovereign equality of all peace-loving states, and open to membership by all such states, large and small, for the maintenance of international peace and security."

We had originally couched this declaration in the form of a treaty, but changed over to the declaration form for obvious reasons. A treaty would require ratification by the signatory governments. A declaration required no ratification, would come into effect at once, and would have the immediate result of convincing the peace-loving nations that the governments of the four major powers were in agreement among themselves that a general international security organization should be created.

The emphasis was now on a general international organization. Nothing was said of regional security organizations in the declaration, and in the discussions at Moscow I argued strongly against them.

In July, 1943, I approved the setting up within the Department of a drafting group for the United Nations Charter under the direction of Leo Pasvolsky, to work out a new draft charter based on the views of the Political Subcommittee that there should be a universal rather than a regional basis for the world organization. The group, composed of a dozen staff experts, made extensive studies of the experience of the League of Nations and of other international agencies. During the first part of August this group completed a "tentative Draft Text of the Charter of the United Nations" and seven fundamental policy analyses, each dealing with a basic function of an international organization. At their heart lay the same broad basic ideas that were contained in the Four-Nation Declaration I presented at Moscow. This draft and the seven analyses formed the foundation for our proposals presented at Dumbarton Oaks.

In a radio address on September 12, 1943, I gave public indication of the extent of our postwar studies. "The form and functions of the international agencies of the future," I said, "the extent to which the existing court of international justice may or may not need to be remodeled, the scope and character of the means for making international action effective in the maintenance of peace, the nature of international economic institutions and arrangements that may be desirable and feasible—all these are among the problems which are receiving attention and which will need to be determined by agreement among governments, subject, of course, to approval by their respective peoples. They are being studied intensively by this Government and by other governments. They are gradually being made subjects of consultation between and among governments. They are being studied and discussed by the people of this country and the peoples of other countries. In the final analysis, it is the will of the people of the world that decides the all-embracing issues of peace and of human welfare."

It was on the basis of acceptance by the four signatories of the Four-Nation Declaration that, in my address to the joint session of Congress on November 18, 1943, following my return from Moscow, I declared that when the provisions of the Declaration were carried into effect there would no longer be any need "for spheres of influence, for alliances, for balance of power or any other of the special arrangements through which, in the unhappy past, the nations strove to safeguard their security or to promote their interests."

We were now free to work wholeheartedly toward the single goal of establishing the United Nations organization.

118: Planning Intensifies

FOLLOWING THE MOSCOW CONFERENCE, and after President Roosevelt's return from the Tehran Conference, our preparatory work on the United Nations organization intensified. The passage of the Connally Resolution in the Senate during my trip back from Moscow, following the previous passage of the Fulbright Resolution in the House, had cleared the path at home, while the Four-Nation Declaration of Moscow had cleared the path abroad.

I had luncheon with the President on December 21, 1943, directly after his return from Tehran, to discuss with him the steps that should next be taken. Three days previously the British Embassy had handed us a paper from the Foreign Office which suddenly raised the old question of regional organizations. It argued in favor of regional security police arrangements. The nations in a given region would supply armed forces, naval ports, and air bases which would function under a regional supreme commander. Not long afterwards, however, several of my associates were informed that the thinking in London had shifted from regional to worldwide security police arrangements.

The President and I agreed that our postwar planning experts should draw up our latest ideas on the international organization for Mr. Roosevelt's consideration. During the next two days we worked late at the State Department composing this paper. It was completed and dated December 23, and took into account all of the work that had been done up to that time.

On the following day the President stated in a radio broadcast that the four nations "are agreed that if force is necessary to keep international peace, international force will be applied—for as long as it may be necessary."

I sent Mr. Roosevelt on December 29 our memorandum containing the basic ideas that might be embodied in the constitution of an international organization. On February 3 he gave me formal clearance to go ahead with our planning for the United Nations organization on the basis of the draft I had sent him on December 29. Practically all the points contained in this draft were later embodied in the proposals we submitted to the Dumbarton Oaks Conference.

In the State Department we undertook, early in 1944, a general reorganization of our work. The war had brought to the Department a vast increase not only in the number but also in the kind of activities it was called upon to perform. This was particularly true in the economic and social fields. Moreover, the progress of the war itself was making the problems of the peace settlement and of the organization of the postwar world of much greater urgency. We gave these developments formal recognition in the administrative structure of the Department through the reorganization announced on January 15, which was planned primarily by Under Secretary Stettinius.

This reorganization brought together all the Department's functions in the economic and social fields, both of a current and of a postwar character, under two Assistant Secretaries of State. It placed the work on postwar political problems on a par with, though organized separately from, the Department's other operations, and provided for the integration of these activities with the other work of the Department in the formulation of policy. As part of this reorganization we created the Committee on Postwar Programs, of which I was chairman, Under Secretary Stettinius vice chairman, and Leo Pasvolsky executive director.

At the Moscow Conference, Eden, Molotov, and I had agreed that exchanges of views should take place among our Governments, in Washington in the first instance, with regard to the establishment of the international organization which we had envisaged in the Four-Nation Declaration. Not long after the conference, Eden began pressing me to start this exchange of views. On February 8 I requested James C. Dunn and Leo Pasvolsky to inform the British and Soviet Embassies that we should like to proceed with an exchange of documents setting forth the tentative views of each Government as to the nature and functions of the projected organization.

We stated to the British and Russians that we would keep the Chinese Government informed, but that we did not ask at that time that that Government be brought into the discussions, although we might raise the question later. We took this position at the request of the President, who thought we should wait until our discussions with the British and the Russians had proceeded further, at which point he might send someone from the State Department to China to take the matter up directly with Chiang Kai-shek, thus obviating the possibility that our proposals would be discussed by too many persons and become publicly known.

On February 17 we handed the British and Soviet Embassies a list of topics on which we were preparing studies in connection with the proposed organization. We had received a similar list from the British the day before. The Russians were not yet ready, but on April 5 they agreed to use the American and British lists as a basis for discussion.

I devoted considerable attention in my address of April 9, 1944, to an international organization to maintain peace and prevent aggression. "Such an organization," I said, "must be based upon firm and binding obligations that the member nations will not use force against each other and against any other nation except in accordance with the arrangements made. It must provide for the maintenance of adequate forces to preserve peace and it must provide the institutions and procedures for calling this force into action to preserve peace. . . . It must provide for an international court for the development and application of law to the settlement of international controversies which fall within the realm of law, for the development of machinery for adjusting controversies to which the field of law has not yet been extended, and for other institutions for the development of new rules to keep abreast of a changing world with new problems and new interests."

I emphasized that there was no hope of turning victory into enduring peace unless the United States, the British Commonwealth, the Soviet Union, and China agreed to act together. "This," I said, "is the solid framework upon which all future policy and international organization must be built. It offers the fullest opportunity for the development of institutions in which all free nations may participate democratically, through which a reign of law and morality may arise, and through which the material interests of all may be advanced. But without an enduring understanding between these four nations upon their fundamental purposes, interests, and obligations to one another, all organizations to preserve peace are creations on paper and the path is wide open again for the rise of a new aggressor."

There was no suggestion, however, I pointed out, that the conclusions of these four nations could or should be arrived at without the participation of the other United Nations.

Our experts in postwar problems were now discussing with me the method of initiating the establishment of the international security organization. On April 12, 1944, they submitted to me a series of recommendations toward this end. They suggested that the four major nations take immediate steps to reach a consensus in principle on the fundamental features of a plan for the organization. When this consensus had been reached, the four nations would further agree upon the draft of a charter. This would then be transmitted jointly by the four Governments to the Governments of the United Nations, the nations associated with them, and such other nations as the United Nations might determine.

When a general consensus had been reached on essential features of the charter, the four nations would jointly convene a general conference for final consideration, approval, and signature of a general agreement embodying the charter. This conference would establish a provisional United Nations Council consisting of the four major nations and four others elected by the conference. The Council would act on behalf of all the signatories of the general agreement until the first meeting of the General Assembly following the ratification of the charter by fifteen nations including the four major ones.

In April, Under Secretary Stettinius was in London discussing the postwar organization, among other topics, with Prime Minister Churchill and Foreign Secretary Eden. Eden proposed that Moscow be the site of the meeting that would have to be held to reach an agreement on the tentative charter for the international organization. He thought that holding the conference in the Russian capital would overcome Russian suspicions of Britain and the United States. He also proposed that he, Molotov and I meet at a place to be designated by me.

I replied on April 17 that I would give consideration to Moscow as the meeting place for the exchange of views on the international organization. Molotov had, however, agreed along with Eden and me at Moscow that exchanges of views should take place in Washington in the first instance, and it was but natural that Washington became the eventual choice for the conference.

We now drew up an outline of the provisions to be contained in a proposed charter, which, dated April 24, 1944, embodied the conclusions upon which we had been able to agree up to that point. We suggested an Executive Council consisting of the four major nations and four others elected by the General Assembly for annual terms, to have primary responsibility for the maintenance of international security and peace.

This draft recommended that the Council should make decisions by a majority vote—including the concurring votes of all permanent members—on four categories of questions. These were: the final terms of settlement of disputes; the regulation of armaments and armed forces; the determination of threats to the peace, of breaches of the peace, and of acts obstructing measures for the maintenance of security and peace; and the institution and application of measures of enforcement.

Other decisions would be taken by a simple majority vote. In this respect we were resolved to avoid the unhappy experience of the League of Nations, whose decisions required a unanimous vote of all members. Any member of the Council had the right in our plan to abstain from voting, but that nation would still be bound by the decision.

In previous drafts we had provided that the vote of a member of the Council directly involved in a dispute would not be counted, but this we dropped in our draft of April 24, leaving the whole question open. Our experts differed on this point, some maintaining that the veto power should not be impaired and others that the ends of justice would not be served by permitting a nation to vote in a case to which it was a party. We decided to leave the question for future consideration.

To maintain security, our draft stipulated that the members of the international organization should undertake to supply forces and facilities when needed, at the call of the Executive Council. An agreement governing the number and kind of forces and facilities to be supplied would be concluded among the member states at the earliest possible moment after the organization came into existence.

Our draft assigned a wide range of important duties to the General Assembly. Among other functions, this body would, on its own initiative or on request of a member state, make reports on and recommendations for the peaceful adjustment of any situation or controversy which it deemed likely to impair the general welfare. It would assist the Executive Council, upon the latter's request, in enlisting the cooperation of all states in questions of peace and security. It would elect the nonpermanent members of the Executive Council and judges of the International Court of Justice.

We made provision in the draft for economic and social activities by the organization and for a possible system of trusteeship.

A president of the general international organization was also provided for by this draft, although the drafters had reservations as to the advisability of the provision. The president of the organization—"a person of widely recognized eminence"—would be elected by the General Assembly, on the nomination of the Executive Council. He would serve for two years, would act as chairman of the Executive Council, and would be free to take part in the deliberations as representing the general interests and purposes of the organization, though without the right to vote. He would open each new session of the General Assembly and preside until the election of its president.

We likewise provided for a director general of the organization, who would be its chief administrative officer. He would be elected by the General Assembly with the concurrence of the Executive Council.

I now submitted this draft in great confidence to three of the ablest men in America, and probably among the best qualified to pass on the questions involved. They were Charles Evans Hughes, former Chief Justice of the United States, who had been the Republican candidate for the Presidency in 1916 and later served as Secretary of State; John W. Davis, Democratic candidate for the Presidency in 1924, and Nathan L. Miller, formerly Republican Governor of New York State. They were all eminent broad-gauge lawyers. Myron C. Taylor acted as intermediary between us.

After they had studied the document, I had two long conferences with Mr. Hughes, and had luncheon with Mr. Davis and Mr. Miller together. All three signified their approval of the draft while making some useful suggestions.

By this time we had held three international conferences on collateral problems and another was in course of preparation. These were the Food and Agriculture Conference at Hot Springs, Virginia, in May and June, 1943; the Relief and Rehabilitation Conference at Atlantic City in November and December, 1943; the International Labor Conference at Philadelphia in April, 1944; and the Monetary and Financial Conference at Bretton Woods scheduled for July, 1944.

The State Department was not the leading department in these conferences, but we of necessity had to negotiate with other nations for their organization and operation, and many officials of the Department took part in them. The conducting of these conferences was in the hands of the chiefs of other departments, along with their associates and the delegates of other governments. Miss Frances Perkins, Secretary of Labor, conferred with me at length before the Philadelphia Labor Conference, and we agreed on policy and procedure.

These conferences arrived at valuable decisions on food supply, on relief, on the improvement of labor standards, and on the creation of an international monetary fund and an international bank. To us at the State Department they had the additional value of serving as a barometer of the degree of cooperation we could expect from the other United Nations in the establishment of the postwar security organization. They were a rehearsal for the later, much more important conference on the United Nations organization itself.

It seemed to us wise to hold these conferences in advance of the conferences that would determine the structure of the United Nations organization. In general, they embraced concrete problems such as food, relief, and money on which the United States individually was in position to be of great material assistance. These propositions were less controversial than some of those involved in the establishment of an international security organization. I realized that we had to prove to the people of the occupied areas that the major nations were taking steps regarding the postwar world and the handling of the immediate problems of relief, reconstruction, and credits. I felt that we had to convince them that we meant to implement the Four-Nation Declaration, that we were advance proponents for an orderly postwar world to the degree that programs could be developed during the war itself, and that cooperation among the United Nations did not rest solely on winning the war but also on planning for the postwar.

These preliminary conferences served to bring the United Nations together in detailed discussion, to show them the possibilities of working out problems through mutual debate and concession, and to get them accustomed to working with one another.

The discussions concerning the formation of a United Nations security organization, however, embraced security problems which involved special responsibilities on the part of the four major powers that would have to provide the force to keep the peace. It was not therefore possible to envisage a general conference of the United Nations on this objective until a basis of agreement had been reached among the four major nations.

The time had now come for us to approach the three others, Russia, Britain, and China, so that concrete steps could be taken toward the creation of the new·organization. But before going to the houses of others we had to make sure that our own house was in order. We first had to be certain that Congress was with us, lest the tragedy of the League of Nations occur again.

119: Nonpartisan Policy

JUST AT THE TIME when our formative work in preparing for a United Nations organization was forging ahead in 1944, this nation was thrown again into a presidential campaign. After years of striving to maintain our foreign policy on a nonpartisan basis, it seemed to me imperative to concentrate during this presidential year on an effort to keep the discussions concerning the postwar organization out of politics. If that organization became a political issue it might well suffer the fate of the League of Nations in the Senate in 1919.

As a member of the Executive Committee of the Democratic National Committee during the years prior to 1928, I had made a special effort to observe the efficacy of various peace arrangements. This underlined to me the crucifying consequences of injecting partisan politics into any peace movement.

As a result, ever since my entry into the State Department in 1933, I had taken numerous steps to prevent politics from coming into the Department and our foreign policies. My endeavors to achieve nonpartisanship in foreign affairs went along two lines. The first was to keep foreign relations from becoming a battleground of politics. The second was to keep related domestic issues that dovetailed with foreign affairs from being dragged onto the same battleground. This was particularly true of the trade agreements program, where I sought the support of both parties, and where both assistance and opposition to the program frequently departed from party lines.

I had also gone out of my way to maintain friendly relations with the Legislative Branch of the Government, to consult with Senators, Representatives, and other leading members of both major parties, as well as with editors and writers, and to keep them as fully informed as possible. Following the outbreak of war in Europe on September 1, 1939, I intensified this practice, and I heightened it still more following Pearl Harbor. I made Assistant Secretary of State Breckinridge Long the liaison officer between the State Department and Congress, with the task of keeping in touch with Republican as well as Democratic Senators and Representatives. His broad political experience of several decades was of great value to us. Then in 1944 I determined to bring our nonpartisan practice to a head.

The President was fully behind me in my efforts to maintain cordial relations with the House and Senate, particularly their committees dealing with foreign affairs, but he was skeptical that I could achieve a nonpartisan agreement with the Republicans which they would keep. He had expressed this skepticism to me when I began calling in Republican Congressional leaders and going over our foreign policy with them in detail. When I made the agreement of August, 1944, with the Republican leaders that the world organization and the necessity for United States participation in it should not form a battleground of the 1944 campaign, as I shall narrate later, he again said he was skeptical. I asked why. He said in effect: "You'll see. They won't keep the agreement. They'll make a campaign out of foreign affairs."

Nevertheless, he was not opposed to my making the nonpartisan approach, and I accordingly went ahead.

I was trying strongly to keep Congress, and the country as well, fully in the picture in international agreements. I had spoken to a joint session of Congress following my return from the Moscow Conference. In the autumn of 1943, after the United Nations Relief and Rehabilitation Agreement was reached with forty-three other nations, members of the Senate objected to the accord being promulgated as an executive agreement rather than as a treaty. My associates thereupon met with a subcommittee of the Senate Committee on Foreign Relations to rewrite the agreement so that it could be submitted to both branches of Congress as part of a joint resolution of authority for appropriations.

On January 30, 1944, I appeared on a radio program with Senators Connally and Vandenberg, Speaker Sam Rayburn and Long, with Richard Harkness representing the public. I was then able to say that Rayburn, Connally, Vandenberg, and I were in complete agreement that effective cooperation in foreign affairs between the Executive and Legislative branches of the government was indispensable.

Two months later our close contact with the Senate acquired a more specific character. On March 22 I made a two-hour appearance before the Senate Committee on Foreign Relations in executive session. Senator Tom Connally, chairman of the committee, and fourteen other Senators were present. With them I went very frankly through the whole gamut of our foreign relations, from Russia to Argentina.

I concluded by saying that the State Department had been working on postwar plans for more than two years, and it was now ready to confer further with the committee on a number of these topics, especially an international organization to maintain peace and security. I suggested that the committee name two or three Democrats and two or three Republicans to discuss these matters informally at the State Department. I emphasized the need for cooperation between the Legislative and Executive Branches in dealing with important problems relating to the war and the peace to come, and I remarked that in some respects I had had to work harder toward maintaining harmony within our nation than toward maintaining harmony between nations.

The committee accepted my invitation and named four Democratic and four Republican members as a special committee to confer with me from time to time. They were Senators Connally, Barkley, George, Gillette, Vandenberg, La Follette, White, and Austin. Connally and Vandenberg both gave powerful support to an international movement to preserve peace, and each was to render immense service toward the future United Nations organization. Generally it was a notable group of Senators and Congressional leaders with whom I conferred from time to time during this period. Outstanding in ability, they backed the creation of a security organization in the most enthusiastic spirit.

We held our first meeting, in my office, on April 25. I made it clear at the outset that this was an entirely informal meeting, and each one present could feel entirely free and easy, and no one would be requested to express an opinion, much less assume obligations, unless he wished. I then set forth the main points in our draft of the proposed postwar security organization. I emphasized that for nearly two years the work of study and preparation, and finally of drawing up first drafts, had been carried forward by the State Department under the leadership of the President, and that outstanding persons and officials in the Government, in the two Houses of Congress, and in the country, had been fully consulted on each important question under examination. I mentioned the names of Senators White, Austin, Connally, George, and Thomas, and Congressmen Bloom and Eaton, among other Members of Congress, who had sat in on meetings with us for nearly a year and had contributed their impressions and slants of opinion.

"The United States," I added, "has a tremendous responsibility both of leadership and of preparing a plan that will be workable. Therefore we are obliged to proceed in a spirit of mutual concession and avoid long drawn-out consideration especially of details and controversies. Otherwise Russia, Great Britain, and other countries will soon decide that we are not able to function any more than we did in 1920."

I thereupon handed each Senator, in strict confidence, a copy of our draft for a United Nations organization, along with related documents. I suggested that we meet soon again to exchange views so that, if we could get sufficient agreement, we might then in confidence give copies to the British, Russians, and Chinese, and thus our proposal, along with our proffered leadership, would be safeguarded, and delay avoided. The Senators agreed to meet with me the following Tuesday.

I informed them that I had given this document to three men whom I described as being among the ablest and best qualified in America to pass on the plan advanced. I did not give their names, but they were the three I mentioned in the preceding chapter. Two of them were Republicans.

During our discussion, I said that unless the large nations such as Russia, Great Britain, China, and the United States promptly assumed broad responsibilities as we came to them, it would be easy to delay until it was too late to organize peoples and governments behind a suitable postwar program. This was especially true if we waited until chaotic conditions arose among peoples at the conclusion of the fighting.

I stressed the necessity for unity especially among the United States, Russia, and Great Britain, if this postwar international undertaking were to succeed. Malcontents in this country, I pointed out, were doing their best to drive Russia out of the international movement by constant attacks and criticisms largely about minor incidents or acts. Unless it was possible to prevail upon newspapers, commentators, and columnists to refrain from this line of activity which during the past two months had greatly confused the mind of the public with regard to the more essential phases of the postwar situation, it would be difficult for any international undertaking, such as that offered by us, to succeed. I was also appealing to all Russian officials with whom I came into contact to refrain from similar activities against us from their side.

We faced three pivotal questions, I said. The first was to keep Russia solidly in the international movement. The second was to develop an alert and informed public opinion in support of the program proposed. And the third was to keep the entire undertaking out of domestic politics.

That evening I telegraphed the President, who was resting in South Carolina, and summarized the meeting for him. I said that the Senators seemed intensely interested, and that at the end of the meeting the atmosphere was good.

When the eight Senators met with me again, on May 2, they had read and digested the draft for the United Nations organization. I said I had done most of the talking at the previous meeting, and now wondered if they had any comments to make.

A major point was quickly raised, as one of the Senators said he desired to know whether we should have a good or a bad peace agreement before he could commit himself finally to an agency to keep the peace.

Knowing that this was an important question probably on the minds of others as well, I commented that the Senate would of course pass on the peace treaties and therefore would itself have much to do with the adoption of a good or a bad peace. I then asked what we should do if the peace agreement were not quite to our notion. Would we abandon all idea of an organization to keep the peace, or would we proceed with determination—as the statesmen did in bringing about the adoption of the Constitution amidst every difficulty—to perfect the peace and, if necessary, to develop further and perfect further the proposed organization to keep the peace? What would have happened, I inquired, if our Revolutionary statesmen had become discouraged because the outlook ahead for the preservation of freedom was not just what they desired, and if, in consequence, they had failed to establish the Government—which effort had, in fact, almost failed?

Later in the discussion I asked the Senator if he were opposed to perfecting the present postwar organization proposal until he first ascertained whether we were to have a good or a bad peace. He instantly said that not for a moment would he fail to cooperate to perfect the document.

Another Senator wondered about the necessity for some organization to keep the peace before the final peace agreement. I replied that originally we had discussed the creation of a temporary peace organization not very different from the proposed postwar organization, but that for numerous reasons this had not been practical. Moreover, under the Four-Nation Declaration of Moscow, the four major nations—Russia, Great Britain, China, and the United States—were already committed to consult with one another and, as occasion required, with any other nations that might be necessary, with a view to joint action for the maintenance of peace and security until the permanent peace organization was finally established and became a going concern, irrespective of when the peace treaties might be concluded.

When we met again, on May 12, the view was again expressed that it would be unjust to the American people to commit them to supporting a peace that to them might be odious, and that it therefore would be well to see more fully the nature of the peace before any final commitments were made on the proposed postwar organization.

I argued that, if we should halt our forward movement in support of the postwar organization proposal, the remainder of the world would promptly conclude that we had surrendered our leadership in the situation. The small nations, which were looking mainly to us for leadership and for the championship of the basic principles involved, would at once become utterly discouraged. We should also run the grave risk in this country of bringing about a schism between the two great political parties on the question whether we should halt our forward movement to develop and secure tentative approval first from Members of Congress, next from the three other large nations, and finally from the smaller nations.

"A good peace," I continued, "will be much facilitated by keeping alive the beneficial and softening doctrines and policies contained in the Atlantic Charter, the Moscow Four-Nation Declaration, and the Connally Resolution. Otherwise, when the fighting is over, there will be no program halfway perfected even tentatively; our leadership will be gone; and each country will already be preparing to hoe its own row in the future. This Government, however, acting through the Senate, can probably prevent a bad peace, and, failing that, will have nothing to do with it. We will not fail for the reason that we shall be supported by the small nations and probably by most of the large nations."

One of the Senators, strongly supporting my position, emphasized that we were concerned about furnishing leadership and basic programs that would include the preservation of peace and world order under law, and would be most helpful in avoiding what some of the other Senators called a possible bad peace. He added that, if the peace should prove bad, we would not stand for it for a moment, and that naturally and inevitably both the peace treaty and the organization now proposed to keep the peace would all go down in a crash together. I added, "And automatically."

But another Senator argued on the other side, saying that at this time it would be impossible to get ratification by the Senate of our document without some definite assurance that it would not be used to protect and perpetuate a bad peace.

I replied that, by going forward and advocating our proposal, along with the Atlantic Charter, the Four-Nation Declaration, and the Connally Resolution—this Government furnishing the leadership—we should greatly facilitate the working out of a good peace rather than a bad peace.

This question of obtaining a good peace before founding the international organization seemed rivaled in importance to the Senators by the question of the veto power of the major nations on the Council. The question rose when a Senator said he thought it would be a serious defect to let any one of the major nations kill a righteous proposal by interposing its veto.

"The veto power," I replied, "is in the document primarily on account of the United States. It is a necessary safeguard in dealing with a new and untried world arrangement. Without it the United States would not have anywhere near the popular support for the postwar organization as with it in, any more so perhaps than in 1920. We might as well recognize that this is about the best that can be done as a beginning, and that it would be inadvisable to throw out this veto power for each of the four large nations, and especially the United States. We should not forget that this veto power is chiefly for the benefit of the United States in the light of the world situation and of our own public opinion. We cannot move any faster than an alert public opinion in perfecting a permanent peace organization, but we should not be deterred for an instant from pursuing the sole course that is open, the alternative being international chaos such as we have had heretofore."

I said that from the very outset of our work to develop a basic plan for permanent world peace and order we had faced at every turn the realization that it would be unavoidably necessary at the beginning to rely chiefly on the three or four major nations. This meant, in the light of our disastrous experience with the peace movement following the First World War, that we had to adopt provisions of a world organization acceptable to these nations.

As for our own country, we recalled the insistent demand made in Woodrow Wilson's period for veto privileges in the League of Nations. Bitter opposition had been raised to the United States' entry into the League on the basis of erroneous assumptions that, if we became a member of the League, the Covenant allowed an agency of the League to give orders to our military forces in preserving peace. The biggest stumbling block that sent the Wilson movement in support of the League to utter destruction in 1920 was the argument over this point, and no other political controversy during our time had been accompanied by more deep-seated antagonism. The hint in 1919—however false it was—that we were in any sense surrendering or impairing Congress's prerogative to declare war or the President's prerogative to direct the movements of our armed forces proved fatal. I had not forgotten this fact.

My associates and I had carefully sounded out opinion on this question as it related to our own world organization proposal. We readily discovered that on this particular point there was not a chance for us to make any advance with a large number of leading members of both Houses of Congress and with many influential groups and persons in the country. We felt that real time would be necessary to improve and perfect a completed world peace structure that would function effectively and satisfactorily to all. The veto, which had been held up by some as a kind of scarecrow, could unquestionably in our opinion be later placed on a milder basis, becoming less and less an impediment as time went on. We considered time and patience to be absolutely necessary.

In all the discussions with my associates in postwar planning, two important conditions had been understood and repeatedly stated in connection with the veto. The first was that none of the permanent members of the Council would exercise its right of veto capriciously or arbitrarily. It would call this power forth only on a matter of the gravest concern to itself, never on secondary matters and never in a way to prevent thorough discussion of any issue. The veto would be exercised in the same broad, cooperative spirit that pervaded the preparatory efforts of the major nations leading toward the creation of the United Nations. It is obvious that the provision was universally intended to aid and facilitate the maintenance of permanent peace by the security organization. Naturally the entire spirit of any such qualification, intended to be liberalized as rapidly as public opinion would permit, in no sense contemplated the exercise of the privilege except in instances of first importance.

The second condition was that we were thinking largely of the application of the veto power to military or other means of compulsion. We recalled that this had been the chief bone of contention in connection with the League Covenant. In conferring upon the proposed Council the authority to control and direct at least some of the military forces of member nations to any point where the Council believed the exercise of force was required, we also had to give the major nations that would furnish such force the right of veto. It was our thought, therefore, that the main focus of the veto would be military and other means of exercising force, such as economic sanctions, and not the numerous other issues that were certain to come before the Council.

What we were proposing was a substantial advance over the League system, in which every nation had veto powers both in the Assembly and in the Council. Under our proposal the veto requirement would be completely eliminated from the work of the Assembly and would be retained in the Council for the major nations in connection with the discharge of their special responsibility to keep the peace.

A Senator expressed his deep concern over the veto power in the hands of the four major nations on the Council. This, he said, constituted a weakness and also a discrimination against the small nations.

I commented that these four nations would not take on all the responsibilities of keeping the peace if the smaller nations which made but small contributions were given practical control over the administration of policy in connection with the use of force. There was no possible way, I said, to initiate this organization except by each of the large nations on the Council retaining the veto power in connection with the use of force or sanctions. I added that France, too, might be given a seat on the Council with the veto power. But, no matter how many additions might be made to the Council, both with and without the veto power, our Government would not remain there for a day without retaining its veto power. The beginning had to be made on this rather narrow basis, with the hope and expectation that, as time went on and the merits and benefits of this organization revealed themselves, the base of the organization could be broadened in many desirable ways and by unanimous consent.

In our discussions both on the question of a good and a bad peace and on the veto power, it was obvious that some of the Senators were worried over the position Russia would occupy after the war.

"Inevitably," I said, "we all have to recognize that no great world movement sufficient to preserve law and order in international affairs can be set on foot fully developed at the outset. Nations will make mistakes, and we have to reason and plead with each other to refrain from such mistakes and undertake to educate each other toward that end. It would be unspeakably disastrous if we became discouraged at the outset over every little error, or even a single large mistake of some one country, and abandoned the whole peace and welfare of the world. This is a problem that will test the ability, patience, unity, and determination of the peaceful nations and their peoples, both jointly and severally."

One Senator inquired pointedly whether Russia really desired to go forward with us and the other United Nations in the proposed movement of international cooperation. I replied that not only while I was in Moscow, but at all times up to this day, Marshal Stalin and Molotov and their associates had quickly made clear to any inquirer their unqualified desire to become full-fledged associates in the international cooperation movement.

"Our customs and manners," I said, "are about as mysterious to Russia as hers are to us. Time and patience are indispensable if our peoples are to become acquainted and learn to understand each other. Such understanding is absolutely necessary if we are to avoid acts and utterances on the part of both Governments which in themselves constitute errors. We simply must not quarrel with each other, but we must patiently point out the full facts and circumstances and their significance and plead with each other to abandon any acts or utterances not entirely in harmony with the basic principles of the international cooperation movement. All these principles and policies are so beneficial and appealing to the sense of justice, of right, and of the well-being of free peoples everywhere that in the course of a few years the entire international machinery should be working fairly satisfactorily. Of course, some years will be necessary to perfect and broaden and otherwise develop such a political, economic, and peace structure."

The Senators were of course keenly interested in the respective jurisdictions and authorities of Congress and the Executive in relation to the proposed United Nations organization. My view was asked on Congressional and Executive authority in relation to a major use of force. I replied that I felt that the President alone should have the authority to deal with minor breaches of the peace or threatened breaches, keeping Congress fully informed at every stage. No other course, I thought, was practical, because there were threatened breaches of the peace almost every week of the year in some part of the world or other. My position was that major breaches of the peace meant war rather than police action, in which event the prerogative of Congress to declare war would be completely safeguarded.

A question was then asked whether the proposed treaty, whereby each member of the organization would allocate armed forces to keep the peace, would be submitted to the Senate for its advice and consent. I replied in the affirmative, which seemed to satisfy the group.

A Senator remarked that he was under the impression that our proposal was to complete a document as quickly as possible, and then secure unconditional and unqualified ratification by the Senate before the war ended.

I recalled to him that it required more than a year to negotiate the supposedly simple UNRRA agreement with some thirty-five nations, although that was a mere proposal to distribute money for nothing and most of it was to come from this Government. Judging from this, I went on, we need not assume that we could go forward with these tentative plans for informal discussions, first with Congress, then with the three other major nations, and finally with the more than thirty smaller nations, and get the document ready for a final draft without much delay. Our main purpose, I added, had not been so much to complete and ratify the proposal within a given time, as to carry forward the whole undertaking with the idea that, as time went on, there might occur a gradual evolution in its terms that would prove suitable for final approval by all the nations.

I also remarked that, from time to time, persons came to my office to suggest the vital importance of postponing consideration of the postwar organization document until after the November election, since it was so essential that it be kept out of domestic politics. To this I was replying that, much as we all desired to keep it out of politics, I considered it impossible to postpone consideration until after election. One reason was that such a step would itself be calculated to get the whole matter into politics, thereby causing demands to go up all over this country and in other countries to know what we were fighting for, and especially what plans and agencies we had in mind, if any, to preserve peace and world order under law in the postwar world. And such demands could not be resisted.

A Senator, recalling that our Revolutionary statesmen provided that the Constitution should take effect when nine States had ratified it, asked how the peace organization proposal would go into effect.

I replied that there was literally no way to institute this international movement of cooperation to keep the peace except under the leadership and on the initiative of the four large nations which were of necessity virtually fighting the war alone and would furnish almost all the force to keep the peace. Therefore, this movement depended on the ability and willingness of the four chief nations to work together. No two of the three great powers—Russia, Great Britain, and the United States—I concluded, would undertake another world peace organization with one of them omitted, after the failure of the League of Nations when one of the great countries was missing.

An inquiry was then made whether it would not be wise to have regional organizations each select a member of the Council of the United Nations organization, along with the five other members to be selected by the Assembly. I replied that we were not quite in harmony with Mr. Churchill's suggested regional federation idea, which would build a world structure in the form of regional organizations, with a common head at the top.

We felt, I said, that it would be more practical for the nations resident in given areas to agree in advance to join with their sister nations in the same region just as soon as they discovered a breach or threatened breach of the peace, at the same time keeping in close touch with the Executive Council and notifying it of their efforts to ward off breaches of or threats to the peace. This would be their function, I pointed out, rather than the erection of regional structures clothed with jurisdiction and authority that would extend into the very head office of the organization; namely, the Executive Council. The Assembly would no doubt select its nominees for the Council on a geographical basis.

I informed the Senators at our meeting on May 12 that the three eminent jurists to whom I had submitted the document for their opinion had all three approved it in its essentials as practical and workable and as representing a good approach to the conditions to be dealt with.

The Senators all agreed at this meeting that we should go forward with our postwar proposal. Generally they said they looked with favor on our postwar organization draft as a document calculated to meet the views of the American public, and were strongly in favor of carrying it forward. They said they were willing for me to bring it now to the attention of the other large nations.

As the meeting ended, they said they would confer among themselves with regard to their issuing a statement that our document was suitable from their viewpoint and to my taking early steps to get it before the three other governments. But when we met again, on May 29, they were forced to say that, although they had tried to agree on a statement that might be addressed to me and given to the press, it had been impossible to reach an agreement on the wording.

Knowing that the prime difficulty in arriving at that agreement was the continued anxiety of a couple of them over the possibility that a bad peace treaty would be signed which the international organization would have to uphold and administer, I reopened the question. I said I felt that no rational person in any civilized country would for a moment favor preserving a peace that was not worth preserving. There were numerous advantages, however, I added, in not fixing at this time an inflexible date, tied in with the peace treaty, for the going into effect of the postwar security organization. That organization, if perfected in advance, would be of great help in bringing about a better peace than might otherwise be the case, and hence in avoiding a bad peace.

The fighting, I went on, might continue in some parts of the world for one, two, or four years, during which time it might be desirable to put the security organization into operation. Repeating that there was a tremendous demand on the part of peoples to know what their respective governments were planning to do to preserve peace after the war, I said that to announce a broad condition dependent upon the conclusion of a peace treaty would seriously handicap the whole movement.

I therefore suggested that we might state in an announcement that we were all unanimously against establishing and preserving a bad peace. We could state further that the present draft plan would be presented to other governments and that, when an informal plan had been completed and tentatively and informally agreed upon, the Senators, the President, and I and others would confer as to when and in what circumstances the postwar security plans would be put into effect.

A Senator thereupon restated a belief he had expressed before, which he said had been accentuated by reading several articles in a national magazine; namely, that secret agreements existed between the President and the heads of other large nations. The peace organization, he said, was so tied in with the peace treaty itself that it could not be considered separately. Any further consideration of the security organization should be accompanied by a reservation on the part of the Senators to the effect that they should await the full development of the peace terms to see whether they were good or bad.

Another Senator asked me whether reports were true that regional federations had been secretly agreed to for Europe by the President, Stalin, and Churchill.

I replied that I knew of no such agreements.

I then informed the Senators that I must forthwith issue a statement telling of our intention to proceed with discussions with foreign Governments. The President and I had agreed that my conversations with the Senators had brought us enough agreement and support to permit us to take the next step—to set in motion a direct exchange of views among the United States, Russia, Britain, and China. I accordingly read to the Senators the statement, which I released later in the day. This said:

"The first phase of the informal conversations with the eight Senators has been concluded. We had frank and fruitful discussions on the general principles, questions, and plans relating to the establishment of an international peace and security organization in accordance with the principles contained in the Moscow Four-Nation Declaration, the Connally Resolution, and other similar declarations made in this country. I am definitely encouraged and am ready to proceed, with the approval of the President, with informal discussions on this subject with Great Britain, Russia, and China, and then with governments of other United Nations."

The statement added that meanwhile I would also have discussions with leaders of both parties in Congress, and with others. The door of nonpartisanship, I said, would continue to be wide open at the State Department, especially when any phase of the planning for a postwar security organization was under consideration.

Thus ended the first chapter of my conversation with the Senators. I did not accomplish all I had hoped for, but we had achieved much. The Senators were in agreement on the necessity for an international organization to keep the peace, on the importance of the United States' becoming a member thereof, on the general lines of the draft of the organization which we had prepared, and on the advisability of going ahead to perfect the draft and of placing it before the other major nations. Furthermore, the Senators were convinced of my sincerity in wishing to keep the United Nations organization out of domestic politics, and generally they appeared willing to adopt the same position. They also seemed impressed by our willingness to give them all the information in our possession on the full breadth of our foreign policy and on our thoughts with regard to the postwar organization. Only one difficulty, which could still become serious, remained—the insistence of two Senators on a reservation concerning a good peace treaty. The other points that seemed principally to interest the Senators were the questions of sovereignty, involving the veto; of the Executive's authority in connection with the international organization; of avoiding the creation of a superstate; and of the role of small nations in the organization.

I held a meeting of leading Representatives of both parties in my office on June 2. Attending were Speaker Sam Rayburn, John W. McCormack, Majority Leader; Joseph W. Martin, Jr., Minority Leader; Sol Bloom, chairman of the House Committee on Foreign Affairs; Charles A. Eaton, ranking Republican member of the committee; Robert Ramspeck, and Leslie C. Arends. I handed each one a copy of our draft of the proposed United Nations organization, and I covered with them virtually the same ground as during my first conference with the eight Senators. With the Representatives the discussion did not become as involved as with the Senators.

Senators Ball, Burton, Hatch, and Hill having asked for a meeting with me to obtain information concerning the proposed postwar organization, I met with them in my office on June 22. Although I did not give them copies of our draft of the organization, I went over with them generally the points that had been discussed during my meetings with the eight Senators from the Committee on Foreign Relations.

Meantime Assistant Secretary of State Breckinridge Long, working on my behalf, was conducting a quiet campaign to induce the Democratic and Republican national conventions to adopt planks favoring the international organization. He was materially assisted by Secretaries Stimson and Knox, by Myron Taylor, Will Hays, and the Senators with whom I had been conferring. When the platforms of both major parties came out with planks supporting the creation of an international organization to maintain the peace, of which the United States would be a member, I felt greatly encouraged.

As a result of all my discussions with Senators and Representatives, and of the action taken at the conventions, I now had more than a reasonable assurance that the presidential campaign of 1944, however bitterly it might be fought on domestic issues, would not make the postwar organization a gage of battle.

120: Dumbarton Oaks

MY EXCHANGES OF VIEWS with the Senators having achieved sufficiently satisfactory results, I was ready to proceed with an approach to Britain, Russia, and China. Accordingly I asked British Ambassador Halifax and Russian Ambassador Gromyko to come to my office on Memorial Day, May 30, 1944. It was a fitting occasion on which to begin a further stage of the movement to prevent another war.

I informed them in detail of the conversations I had been having with the Senators and outlined our attitude toward the postwar security problem. I said I was now ready to proceed with informal talks with the British and the Russians. I asked them to request their Governments to fix a date, as early as convenient, for these conferences to begin. I said we would be ready as soon as they were.

I then made, through them, a very earnest appeal to their Governments to let China take part in the conferences. I used very much the same arguments I had employed at the Moscow Conference when I struggled to have China become a signatory to the Four-Nation Declaration. They promised to present this matter fully to their respective Governments.

I did not give the Ambassadors our tentative draft for the proposed security organization. Instead I suggested that each of the Governments should prepare its respective draft for consideration at the opening of the informal conference.

That same day I also saw Chinese Ambassador Dr. Wei Tao-ming and made similar statements to him. Seemingly depressed over the general situation, the Ambassador said Russia was undertaking to secure more power and control of the Far East than anyone imagined, and mentioned recent diplomatic exchanges that had taken place between Russia and Japan. I sought in a general way to disabuse his mind as to the significance of this latter development. I was convinced that Russia would go to war against Japan when the time came, and Stalin's words to that effect were still to the forefront of my memory. In any event, I said we would handle the discussions on the international organization so as to take care of China's prestige in every way possible, and I knew this was the President's feeling as well as mine.

I foresaw that Russia, still not at war with Japan, might object to having China present at a conference, just as she had objected with regard to the Four-Nation Declaration. Accordingly, on the following day I telephoned British Minister Sir Ronald Campbell, in the absence of Ambassador Halifax, to make a new suggestion. I said that, if the Soviet Government should not agree to China's sitting in on the conference, I most earnestly hoped that the British Government would be willing to sit in with the United States and China, and, at another time, with Russia and the United States—the procedure followed in the successive Cairo and Tehran Conferences in 1943. I made the same suggestion to Soviet Ambassador Gromyko and to Chinese Ambassador Wei Tao-ming.

Generalissimo Chiang Kai-shek cabled the President on June 2 expressing his gratification that we had proposed that China be included in the discussions.

British Ambassador Halifax informed me on June 12 that the British would participate in the Washington discussions and that the permanent Under Secretary for Foreign Affairs, Sir Alexander Cadogan, would represent Britain. After thanking him, I remarked that we had heard nothing from his Government about China sitting in with us, and that it would be calamitous if the project of bringing in the Chinese should fail. He agreed to take this up with his Government again.

Halifax informed me on June 15 of the contents of a telegram from Eden in which the latter, repeating that he was sending Under Secretary Cadogan to head the United Kingdom delegation, said he hoped I would be on hand, and Halifax for Britain, to follow the discussions generally and take up any necessary points.

As weeks went by without an answer from the Soviet Government to the invitation I extended on May 30, we instructed our Embassy in Moscow to urge Molotov to reply as soon as possible.

The Soviet Chargé, Alexander N. Kapustin, brought me on July 9 an *aide-mémoire* from his Government stating its readiness to take part in negotiations in Washington on the basis of my suggestion of Anglo-American-Soviet negotiations and Anglo-American-Chinese negotiations separately. The Soviet Government was ready to start the negotiations without preliminary exchanges of documents between the Soviet, American, and British Governments; it suggested the beginning of August for the conference, and said Ambassador Gromyko would be the Soviet representative.

In this note, however, the Soviet Government sought to limit the scope of the negotiations. Referring to an exchange of letters it had had with the British Government, the Russians wanted to postpone discussion on two subject headings suggested by the British. One concerned the relations to be established between the economic organs and the main organization. The other concerned the processes of peaceful settlement of disputes. The Soviets were willing to begin discussions on the other points, including the scope and character of the international organization and the procedure for establishing it; safety measures through which threats to peace and violations of peace could be prevented; and plans of combined actions.

We replied to the Soviet *aide-mémoire* on July 12, expressing our pleasure at the Soviet Government's readiness to take part in the discussions in Washington, and suggesting the date of August 2 for the opening meeting. We opposed, however, any idea of limiting the scope of the discussions. We said that procedures for a peaceful adjustment of disputes must necessarily constitute an integral part of any effective scheme for an international organization, and we expected to state fully our own views during the forthcoming discussions. We also said we expected fully to express our views on possible arrangements for territorial trusteeship and on the relationship of specialized economic and social agencies to the general organization.

As a result of further exchanges of cables with London, Moscow, and Chungking, we secured British agreement to a two-phase arrangement for the conversations, and Russian agreement not to limit the scope of the discussion. Accordingly, on July 17 I publicly announced that conversations among the four Governments signatory to the Declaration of Moscow would begin in Washington probably early in August on the subject of an international security organization. I stated that the first phase of the conversations would be among the United Kingdom, the United States, and the Soviet Union, and that conversations among the United States, the United Kingdom, and China would be carried on either at the same time or shortly thereafter.

Two days later I announced that the conversations would be held at Dumbarton Oaks, the former home of Robert Woods Bliss, one of my Special Assistants who had once been our Ambassador to Argentina. He had conveyed Dumbarton Oaks to Harvard University, which, by arrangement with Under Secretary Stettinius, had made it available to us.

By July 18 we had drawn up a new tentative draft for a proposed general international organization. On that day I asked British Chargé Campbell and Russian Chargé Kapustin to come to my office and handed them each a copy. I informed them that we were also sending a copy for each of their Governments to our Ambassadors in their respective capitals. Our thought, I said, was that each of the three Governments might have some weeks in which to consider these suggestions before the meeting opened in Washington. I added that we would be glad to have copies in return of any similar draft proposals that they might offer. Since our own communications with Chungking were better than those enjoyed by the Chinese Ambassador, we wirelessed a further copy direct to the Chinese capital, in addition to handing one to the envoy here.

The draft I handed the envoys was essentially that which I had discussed with the Senators, with one or two noteworthy changes. We now provided that the Executive Council should consist of eleven members instead of eight. We stated that to the four permanent members already mentioned France should be added when the Council found that a Government freely chosen by the French people had been established and was in effective control of the territory of the French Republic.

Another change was the dropping of the office of President of the United Nations. We had had numerous reservations ourselves on this provision in the April draft, and additional objections had been raised during our discussions following its circulation. Our chief thought was that an undesirable competition might ensue among leaders of nations for the position, and that the post might become the goal of overly ambitious men.

The draft specifically left open the question of voting procedure in the case of parties to a dispute by suggesting that provisions would need to be worked out to take care of cases where one or more of the permanent members of the council were directly involved.

Soviet Chargé Kapustin brought me on July 20 an *aide-mémoire* from his Government in reply to mine of July 12. The Russians said they did not consider it necessary to start an exchange of views with the presentation of written drafts. (This note was written before the Russians received our draft of July 18.) The Soviet Government thought it desirable in the beginning to have a more flexible basis for discussion. It felt that oral exchanges of views might better conduce to working out drafts of an international organization which in turn would serve as the basis for a joint draft by the three Governments.

The Russians proposed that the Anglo-American-Russian discussions and the Anglo-American-Chinese discussions should be conducted not simultaneously but at different times, and said they would agree to any sequence of these cycles.

The date of August 14 was agreed upon for the opening session with the Russians. Later, however, they informed us that they had not had available for study a translation of our proposals until August 4; they had not intended to make an advance exchange of documents and, now that they had received ours, they wished to have more time to study it. We accordingly consented to postponement to August 21.

The President and I agreed that Under Secretary Stettinius should head the American delegation and be assisted by those men in and out of the Government who had taken a principal share in the work of postwar planning. These were: Isaiah Bowman, Benjamin V. Cohen, James C. Dunn, Henry P. Fletcher, Joseph C. Grew, Green H. Hackworth, Stanley K. Hornbeck, Breckinridge Long, Leo Pasvolsky, Edwin C. Wilson, Lieutenant General Stanley D. Embick, Major General George V. Strong, Major General Muir S. Fairchild, Admiral Arthur J. Hepburn, Vice Admiral Russell Willson, and Rear Admiral Harold C. Train. Myron C. Taylor was not included, being then at the Vatican. The delegates were aided by the outstanding staff of experts who had been working on every phase of the postwar planning in the State Department under Pasvolsky's direction, including Alger Hiss, Harley Notter, Benjamin Gerig, and Durward Sandifer. This staff functioned as the international secretariat at the conference, serving not only the American delegation but the British, Russian, and Chinese delegations as well.

When the British Delegation, headed by Under Secretary Cadogan, paid a courtesy call on me on August 14, Cadogan and Ambassador Halifax remained behind for a conversation. I brought up with them the suggestion Eden had made that the Foreign Ministers of the United States, Britain, and Russia should meet to discuss international matters. I remarked that before we met, and especially before any formal agreement were reached on the postwar organization, it would be very important first to discuss steps toward conferring with the small nations. I said that if the four major nations should go on until they turned out to the world a completed document and then sent copies to the small nations in a "take it or leave it" manner, as this would be construed, it would be difficult to avoid serious attacks by demagogues, politicians, and uninformed persons.

Cadogan and Halifax said they could see the importance of this suggestion, and they would take it up with Eden.

Both the British and the Soviet Governments handed us their draft proposals for an international organization, the former dated July 22 and

the latter August 12. Fortunately so many exchanges of ideas had occurred among us that we were already thinking along the same basic
lines. As we studied the British and Russian drafts we felt that their
ideas paralleled ours in many respects.

On August 15 I telephoned Senators Connally and Vandenberg and
informed them that the British had in general accepted the principles
contained in the document which I had gone over with the eight Senators. I explained that the conversations at Dumbarton Oaks would be
on a technical or expert level. Neither Connally nor Vandenberg expressed
any desire to be present at the conference, but I told them I would get in
touch with them in case any new fundamental principles arose, and in
any event I or one of my associates would keep them abreast of day-to-
day developments. I telephoned the same information to Speaker of the
House Sam Rayburn, with the request that he pass it on to the Representatives who had met with me on June 2.

Secretary of the Treasury Morgenthau insisted that the Treasury
should have an observer at the conference. I took this up with the President who sent word to Morgenthau that this would not be possible.

I opened the Dumbarton Oaks Conference on August 21 with an
address in which I said it was the sacred duty of the governments of all
peace-loving nations to make sure that international machinery be fash-
ioned through which the peoples could build the peace they so deeply
desired.

"It is generally agreed," I said, "that any peace and security organization would surely fail unless backed by force to be used ultimately
in case of failure of all other means for the maintenance of peace. That
force must be available promptly, in adequate measure, and with certainty. The nations of the world should maintain, according to their
capacities, sufficient forces available for joint action when necessary to
prevent breaches of the peace."

I said it was the intention of the United States Government, following the Dumbarton Oaks Conference, that the conclusions reached should
be communicated to the Governments of all the United Nations and of
other peace-loving nations and made available to the peoples of all countries for public study and debate.

"The people of this country," I said, "are now united as never before
in their determination that the tragedy which today is sweeping the earth
shall not recur."

The first several days of discussion at Dumbarton Oaks revealed that there was a very large area of agreement among the three countries on the basic principles involved and also on a number of matters of important detail.

The most important difference that developed at this time was whether the scope of the projected organization should include international cooperation in the economic and social fields. The British and we favored the lodging of these important functions in the General Assembly and in an economic and social council under its authority. We argued that economic and social cooperation was essential to the creation of conditions necessary to maintain security and peace. The Russians, while fully recognizing the need for economic and social cooperation, believed that these functions should be assigned to a separate organization rather than to a security organization.

The tentative drafts which the British and Russians had given us in advance of the conference seemed to assign a relatively unimportant role to the Assembly, in contrast to our position that the Assembly, comprising all member states, should be given real functions. This was especially true of the Soviet proposals. In the first few days of discussion the British and the Russians substantially accepted our viewpoint.

As the conference got under way I arranged that Under Secretary Stettinius should take up with the President directly, as well as with myself, questions that required decisions on high levels. Two days after the conference opened, the President gave his approval to several important decisions I had made at a meeting with my associates in my office on August 19, two days before the Dumbarton Oaks Conference opened. One was that at this stage the Executive Council should not be given the right to impose the terms of settlement of a dispute. This provision had seemed unacceptable to the British and the Russians. The Council's functions, we agreed, should be to promote peaceful settlement, to make recommendations to the parties to a dispute, and to settle disputes only on the request of those parties.

The President also gave his approval to our new position that the votes of the nations involved in cases before the Council, including the great powers, should not be counted in the Council's decisions on such cases. I had decided this point on the basis of five possible methods of procedure which my associates had submitted to me. In the April 24 draft handed to the Senators and in the July 18 draft submitted to Britain, Russia, and China, this point had been left open. The British, however, had consistently argued that the votes of parties to a dispute should not be counted.

We believed that all the rules of civil justice provided that a person involved in a dispute should not be able to cast a vote in the decision relating to the dispute. He should not be one of the judges or a member of the jury. There was still some difference of opinion among us, however, as to whether this abstention from voting should apply only to the pacific settlement of disputes in which one or more of the major nations were involved, or should apply also to enforcement action.

The President further agreed that we should accept a general provision for a two-thirds, rather than a simple majority, vote in the Council, except for procedural decisions. This was very strongly urged by the British.

The President likewise agreed that France should be given a permanent seat on the Council when she had a Government that was recognized (he said he would like to see another word than this) by the four major powers, and meantime have provisional representation without the prerogatives of a permanent member.

We felt we should also raise at this time the question of giving Brazil a permanent seat. I myself felt strongly on this point, believing that Brazil's size, population, and resources, along with her prospect of a great future and the outstanding assistance she had rendered her sister United Nations, would warrant her receiving permanent membership. The President was fully of the same opinion. During the following days, however, both the British and the Russians emphatically opposed our view.

Yet another point in which Mr. Roosevelt concurred was that we should oppose the inclusion of provisions for the withdrawal or suspension of members of the organization.

An entirely new and startling proposal was injected into the discussions by the Soviet representative, Ambassador Gromyko, as the second week of the conference opened on August 28. The discussion in the steering committee of the conference was revolving around the question of what nations should be initial members of the organization. Both the Russians and ourselves said that the members should be the United Nations and the associated nations. However, there emerged a basic difference of interpretation. We meant that the members should be all the signatories to the United Nations Declaration, together with eight other nations that had not declared war against the Axis but had been materially helping the Allies in the prosecution of the war—helping more, in fact, than some of the Allies themselves. These were six Latin American Republics, Iceland, and Egypt. The Russians said the members should be the twenty-six original signatories to the United Nations Declaration, and they defined "associated nations" as being those that had signed the Declaration subsequently. They did not wish to include the eight nations we mentioned. Our discussion on this latter point was proving inconclusive, and, in fact, the conference ended with it still unsolved.

Suddenly, in the midst of this discussion, Ambassador Gromyko said to the steering committee that all sixteen Republics composing the Union of Soviet Socialist Republics should be made initial members of the United Nations organization. Russia would therefore have sixteen votes. He left Stettinius and Cadogan breathless, but they lost no time in telling him that his proposal would raise great difficulties.

When Stettinius reported this to the President, Mr. Roosevelt said emphatically that the United States could under no conditions accept such a proposal. He instructed Stettinius to explain to Gromyko that it would present untold complications, and that it was just as logical for us to ask for the admission of the forty-eight states of the Union as it was to agree to admit the sixteen Soviet Republics.

When Stettinius reported it to me, I said I was amazed that such a proposal had been made. I added that no such question had ever entered the minds of any of us in the American group who had been working on postwar planning. I concluded by saying I would oppose it with all my strength.

On August 29 Stettinius reported to Gromyko the substance of his conversations with the President and me and stated that it was our opinion that the suggestion was out of order, and that to press it at this time might jeopardize the success of the conference. He appealed to Gromyko to withdraw his suggestion and said that, if the Soviet Government had such a thing in mind, it should more properly present it to the Council of the United Nations organization after the latter's creation.

Gromyko proved most cooperative. He said he had raised the point merely to advise us and the British that his Government had the matter in mind. He agreed that there should be no further reference to it during the conference. Nevertheless, he indicated that on some other occasion his Government would probably raise the question again.

The fact that the Soviet Government had such a question of multiple membership in mind was disturbing. I accordingly asked Ambassador Gromyko to come to see me on August 31, at which time I stated to him as plainly as possible the manifold objections I saw to the suggestion he had raised on behalf of his Government.

I said to him, in effect, that this proposal would "blow off the roof." The large nations, I commented, that would have to furnish leadership and the military force for the organization would have no difficulty in getting their views listened to, whether they had one vote or many votes. The United States, I added, did not think to have more than one vote, and we nevertheless felt that our influence would enable us at all times to assert ourselves.

We prepared at the State Department that same day a message on the subject to be sent by the President to Stalin. The President approved it, with the addition of a sentence saying that our position did not prejudice later discussion of the question after the organization had been formed, at which time it would have full authority to deal with the matter.

This question of plural Russian membership was mentioned once more by Gromyko toward the end of the conference, and thereafter was not again raised prior to my resignation in November, 1944. At no time did the Soviets take up with me their later request for the admission of the White Russian and Ukrainian Republics, to which President Roosevelt agreed at the Yalta Conference. Had they done so, I would have opposed it.

In all our discussions we strove to keep this proposal absolutely secret. Even in our own memoranda we referred to it as the "X matter." It seemed to me so explosive an issue that, if it got out, it would inevitably be dramatized by forces of opposition everywhere and do injury to Russia's situation as well as to that of the conference.

In my conversation with Ambassador Gromyko on August 31 I took up another question that was disturbing us—the Russian attitude toward the provision we were advocating that a member of the Council should not vote in a case in which it was involved. The British held this same view, but in the Dumbarton Oaks discussions the Russians took exactly the opposite position and held to it strongly.

I presented to Gromyko all the arguments I possibly could to support our contention, and he promised to transmit them to his Government.

During the same conversation I strongly emphasized the great importance of an elaborate discussion of economic problems. The Russians were contending that economic and social problems should be handled by a separate organization apart from the international security organization, which should be concerned with peace and security questions only. I argued to Gromyko that peace and security were inextricably linked with economics, because a world in economic chaos would be forever a breeding ground for trouble and war.

I concluded the conversation by complimenting Gromyko very highly on his excellent showing as head of his delegation. I expressed this compliment in all sincerity, for the Russians had in general shown an admirable cooperation from the first day of the conference.

Stettinius and I met with the President at the White House on September 6 to discuss the principal outstanding points at issue at Dumbarton Oaks. Mr. Roosevelt first brought up the question of the location of the new organization. His view was that the various organs of the organization should meet at various spots around the globe.

He thought that the Secretariat of the organization might be established at Geneva, but that neither the Council nor the Assembly meetings should be held there. He believed that the Assembly should meet in a different city each year, and that the Council should have perhaps two regular meeting places, one being in the Azores in the middle of the Atlantic and the other on an island in the Hawaiian group in the middle of the Pacific. He felt that the International Court of Justice should return to The Hague.

The President was serious in stating these ideas, and he said he was planning to discuss them with Prime Minister Churchill, whom he was to meet at Quebec for the Second Quebec Conference later in the month. The State Department prepared maps and memoranda on the suggested locations in the Azores and on the island of Niihau, Hawaii, and the President expected to take them to Quebec with him.

Mr. Roosevelt had given much thought to the location of the United Nations, and this was not the first time he had mentioned his ideas to me. He felt that locating the Council in the Azores or the Hawaiian Islands would bring the benefit of detachment from the world. Being at heart a naval man, he liked the perspective obtained from surveying the world from an island out at sea. He had been eager, in the later thirties, to promote a meeting of the heads of nations on a battleship or on such an island as Niihau. He felt that, far out at sea, the Council would not be subject to the pressure of any country. He recalled the Paris Peace Conference and the pressures to which it had been subjected in that great capital. He felt that the League of Nations had been subjected to pressure in London before being moved to Geneva.

In essence, he said, he wanted to establish something in the nature of an international District of Columbia. (I often found the President stating his views on foreign events in terms of situations in the United States. The most striking example was contained in his speeches in 1940 and 1941 when he compared Axis planes, in the ease with which they could fly from Dakar to Brazil, with planes flying from city to city in the United States.)

It was illogical, however, thus to scatter the international organization throughout the world, and we never seriously pressed these ideas at the Dumbarton Oaks Conference. In any event, it was a question to be decided not by the four major nations but by the full membership of the future organization.

We also discussed with the President a Russian proposal that an international air force be constituted under the United Nations organization and commanded by the Council. Stettinius and I explained the position of the American delegation that we should oppose an international air force, and advanced our proposal of having air-force contingents of the different nations available for service on a combined basis at a moment's notice. This was in line with a statement the President had made on June 15 (Chapter 121) that an international police force would not be set up. The President agreed that we should adhere to our position. Stettinius indicated to Mr. Roosevelt that this question might be raised with him at Quebec by Prime Minister Churchill, because we had heard that Mr. Churchill had been somewhat impressed by the Soviet proposal.

We likewise discussed a Soviet proposal that small countries which were unable to contribute armed forces to the security organizations should be required to contribute territory for bases. Both the President and I strongly objected to this provision as being an infringement on the sovereign rights of smaller countries. We felt that all action of this type should be voluntary, and that smaller nations should not be compelled to provide bases. Russia's idea, however, was given some recognition in the provision in the Dumbarton Oaks proposals calling for special agreements to place at the disposal of the Security Council "facilities" as well as armed forces and other assistance.

In view of the fact that the conference was unable to agree on the question whether voting in the Council should be by a simple majority rather than by a two-thirds vote, we agreed that our position should be that we were prepared to accept either the British position that the majority should be two-thirds or the Russian position that it should be a simple majority. We ourselves had originally proposed a simple majority, but at one time expressed our willingness to go along with the British proposal if the Russians agreed. This point could not be resolved at Dumbarton Oaks, and was left open.

The question whether a member of the Council involved in a dispute should vote on that dispute hung heavily over us. The President and I authorized Stettinius to maintain our position, which the British also maintained, that such a vote should not be counted.

Aside from this, there was no question in our minds, however, that the vote of the permanent members of the Council should be unanimous on questions involving security. This was the so-called veto power. We were no less resolute than the Russians in adhering to this principle, with the exception of our view that the vote of a Security Council member involved in a dispute should not be counted. We felt that only if the United States retained the right to veto a proposal that force or other sanctions be applied, which would naturally include American action, could we hope to obtain Congressional approval of United States membership in the international organization. We had debated various substitutes but agreed on none.

Although the President and I had previously felt that the Charter of the new organization should not contain any reference to the suspension or expulsion of members (Britain had proposed the former, Russia the latter), we now agreed that the American delegation might act at its own discretion on this question, giving in, if necessary, in compensation for a concession on some other point made by the others.

By this time we were frequently referring to the new organization as "the United Nations." We had long since used this title in some of our drafts. The President felt this should be its name, and we agreed that the name under which twoscore nations were fighting the war to a successful conclusion was a happy title under which to work together following their victory. When Stettinius proposed this to the conference, however, we met with unexpected opposition from both the Russians and the British. Gromyko tentatively suggested the name "World Union." Cadogan said he believed his Government did not particularly like the title "United Nations" and had thought at one time of proposing a title including the word "Union."

On September 8 Ambassador Gromyko withdrew the Soviet objection to the inclusion of an economic and social council under the Assembly as part of the international organization.

By September 10, after three weeks of discussion, the British, Russian, and American delegations had achieved a gratifying amount of agreement—enough for the conference to settle upon a proposed final draft of proposals for a United Nations Charter. All the essential points in the tentative draft I had handed to the British and Soviet Chargés and cabled to Chungking on July 18 were incorporated in the draft now accepted by the conference, with the addition of a few new points. Since the basic ideas of the three Governments were remarkably similar right from the beginning of the conference, the new draft was not dissimilar from the original views of the British and Russians either.

This new draft gave the General Assembly greater powers. The Assembly had the right, on its own initiative, to consider the general principles of cooperation in the maintenance of peace and security, including regulation of armaments, and to make recommendations, although action on such questions was still the function of the Council. The latter now carried the name "Security Council," in preference to our former name of "Executive Council" to emphasize its principal role.

The new draft proposed that the agreement or agreements governing the provision of armed forces and facilities should be subject to the approval of the Council as well as to ratification by the signatories through their constitutional processes. This addition was designed to make more certain that all countries would contribute forces and facilities to maintain peace and security. The Security and Armaments Commission originally proposed by us was renamed Military Staff Committee, and the draft proposed that it should consist of military representatives of the permanent members of the Council and that similar representatives of other members of the organization should be brought in when necessary.

The British and Soviet delegations cabled the text of the new draft to their Governments for comment. During the next two days Soviet Ambassador Gromyko informed us of a series of decisions by his Government which enabled the conference to reach a still further degree of agreement. He withdrew the Soviet proposal that countries having insufficient armed forces should make territory available for the establishment of bases. He also withdrew his proposal to establish an international air force. Finally he withdrew his previous opposition to our proposal that the Military Staff Committee should be responsible under the Security Council for the strategic direction of armed forces placed at the disposal of the Council. He also accepted United Nations as the title of the new organization. The British had already accepted it.

Ambassador Gromyko gave us concern, however, when he stated that his Government did not agree to our suggestion that the four major powers should join in communicating to the other United Nations the recommendations agreed upon at Dumbarton Oaks. The Soviet Government preferred a three-nation communication, leaving out China.

On September 13, Ambassador Gromyko gave us still greater concern when he informed the conference that he had received instructions on the question of voting in the Council, and that his Government maintained its position that the principle of the unanimity of the four great powers was inviolable. Russia could not agree that the vote of a permanent member of the Council, even if that country were involved in the dispute being voted upon, should not be counted. He said he had made a number of other concessions, but it was impossible for him to give in on this point.

The conference now resolved itself into a strenuous discussion to break this deadlock with a compromise formula. I leave the conference temporarily at this point to go back a little and deal with our effort to insert the keystone in the arch of our nonpartisan policy to keep the United Nations organization out of politics.

121: Hands Off United Nations

THE REASONABLE ASSURANCE I had that the presidential campaign of 1944 would not make the proposed postwar security organization a puck of politics was suddenly shattered on August 16. Late on that sultry day Governor Thomas E. Dewey, the Republican candidate for the Presidency, issued a statement in which he said he was deeply disturbed by some of the recent reports concerning the forthcoming Dumbarton Oaks Conference. "These indicate," he said, "that it is planned to subject the nations of the world, great and small, permanently to the coercive power of the four nations holding this conference."

When this statement, part of a much longer press release, was issued, I had already left the State Department for home. After I was informed of it I asked some of my principal associates—Stettinius, Long, Hackworth, Dunn, Pasvolsky, McDermott, and Savage—to come to my apartment.

There I expressed to them my concern that Governor Dewey's statement might throw the postwar organization into the political campaign, with disastrous consequences.

Actually, I had already taken several steps to emphasize that the small nations would be given adequate consideration in the postwar organization. I believed that the preliminary plans for the organization should be made, at least tentatively, by the four great nations, Russia, Britain, China, and the United States, because they were the ones primarily conducting the war, and because it would be difficult for a huge conference consisting of representatives of twoscore nations to sit down and begin from scratch to formulate the constitution of a postwar organization. But I had made it clear, I thought, that the smaller nations would be duly consulted and their opinions given full consideration, before any constitution was finally decided upon.

In my address to the joint session of Congress on November 18, 1943, following my return from the Moscow Conference, I had stated: "The principle of sovereign equality of all peace-loving states, irrespective of size and strength, as partners in a future system of general security will be the foundation stone upon which the future international organization will be constructed."

On the same day I had sent telegrams to London, Moscow, and

Chungking, asking the concurrence of those Governments in a formula that we quoted whereby other nations could adhere to Paragraph 4 of the Four-Nation Declaration of Moscow which expressed the agreement that a postwar security organization should be established. This initiative failed through an objection by the British Government. The Foreign Office informed us on December 2 that, while fully understanding the importance of associating other governments with the establishment of the international organization, they thought preliminary conversations should first take place among the United States, the United Kingdom, and the Soviet Union. Otherwise a number of questions might be presented relative to the nature of the organization which it would be awkward to dispose of.

In the spring of 1944 some objections were raised here and abroad that the small nations were not being given sufficient voice in postwar planning discussions. To try to combat this impression I made a public statement on June 1 in which I said: "As far as this Government is concerned, whenever I have said anything on this subject, it has always emphasized the all-inclusive nature of the world situation and our disposition and purpose to see that all nations, especially the small nations, are kept on a position of equality with all others and that, in every practicable way, there will be cooperation."

During the night of June 13 I awakened and, unable to return to sleep, sat up and thought over this situation. Some Republican orators, probably in preparation for the forthcoming campaign, had been continuing their attacks to the effect that we were neglecting the small nations and working toward a rule of the world by the four large nations. Others had been attacking us with the charge that we were attempting to create a superstate. And still others asserted their right to discuss any phase of foreign policy during the campaign, including the proposed postwar organization, in the hope of making political capital. With the exception of my statement of June 1, the Administration had not come out with any statement on postwar plans. I now felt that the President, who had remained quiet on this subject for a long time, should himself say something, and say it emphatically.

As soon as I reached my office in the morning I called in Leo Pasvolsky and asked him to begin preparation of a statement on this point which the President might issue. The following morning I called him again to my office, along with several others of my associates. I handed them the draft of a statement I had dictated, which could be worked into the one they were preparing. They forthwith began to get together a final draft.

Meantime I had communicated with the President, who asked me to see him that morning. Taking Stettinius, Norman Davis, Isaiah Bowman, and Pasvolsky, I had to leave for the appointment before the draft could be typed in final form. Fortunately, we had to wait for the President, and meantime an official arrived from the Department with the text.

The President, as frequently happened, spent the first few minutes talking generally and telling an amusing story. When he paused to light a cigarette, I placed the statement before him and said that the need for such a statement was dictated by the increasing confusion in public discussion of the proposed organization, the possibility of leaks concerning our proposals, the fact that statements had recently been made by Churchill and Eden concerning an international organization, and the approach of the Democratic and Republican National Conventions, at which the organization, and United States participation in it, would undoubtedly be discussed. Bowman suggested, as an additional reason, the increasing number of rumors that the President and I were not in accord with regard to the future organization.

Mr. Roosevelt immediately agreed that a statement should be issued. He read our text aloud and then exclaimed that it was "awfully good." He wanted one or two minor changes made in the text, which we wrote in. The statement was issued at the White House that afternoon, June 15.

It first emphasized the nonpartisan nature of the discussions we had been having on the postwar organization, and then said:

"The maintenance of peace and security must be the joint task of all peace-loving nations. We have, therefore, sought to develop plans for an international organization comprising all such nations. . . . It is our thought that the organization would be a fully representative body with broad responsibilities for promoting and facilitating international cooperation. . . . It is our further thought that the organization would provide for a council, elected annually by the fully representative body of all nations, which would include the four major nations and a suitable number of other nations."

The statement made clear: "We are not thinking of a superstate with its own police forces and other paraphernalia of coercive power. We are seeking effective agreement and arrangements through which the nations would maintain, according to their capacities, adequate forces to meet the needs of preventing war and of making impossible deliberate preparation for war and to have such forces available for joint action when necessary. . . . The hope of a peaceful and advancing world will rest upon the willingness and ability of the peace-loving nations, large and small, bearing responsibility commensurate with their individual capacities, to work together for the maintenance of peace and security."

The President's statement calmed the clamor over the small nations for a time, but Governor Dewey's statement showed that it was still an issue that could easily be magnified into a major campaign conflict. When my associates met with me at my apartment on the evening of August 16, I said I felt I should immediately answer Governor Dewey's charge. I accordingly requested several of them to return to the State Department and begin to prepare a response. They brought it to me later that evening. After approving it, I read it over the telephone to Senator Connally, who concurred in it. It was issued the following morning.

"Governor Dewey," I said, "can rest assured that the fears which he expressed in his statement are utterly and completely unfounded. No arrangement such as described by him, which would involve a military alliance of the four major nations permanently to coerce the rest of the world, is contemplated or has ever been contemplated by this Government or, as far as we know, by any of the other governments. . . . The meeting at Dumbarton Oaks is for the purpose of a discussion among the signatories of the Moscow declaration as to the most feasible and desirable methods of establishing the kind of organization envisaged in that declaration and in the Senate [Connally] resolution, preliminary to similar discussion and early conference among all the United Nations and other peace-loving nations, large and small."

This controversy had aroused considerable excitement, and my press conference later that morning was crowded. In response to questions, I said I should welcome a conference with Governor Dewey to straighten out any points connected with the postwar organization and a nonpartisan approach to it.

On the afternoon of August 18 I received a telegram from Governor Dewey accepting the proposal I made at the press conference and designating John Foster Dulles, a well known lawyer who was his adviser on foreign affairs, to confer with me for him. Dewey said he was convinced that every effort to organize both temporarily and permanently for the establishment of lasting peace should be accelerated and he was happy to extend his fullest cooperation to the end that the result should be wholly bipartisan and have the united support of the American people.

This message arrived while I was attending a Cabinet meeting at the White House and was sent me there. The President agreed that I should send a reply agreeing to confer with Dulles, although he continued skeptical of any nonpartisan agreement with the leading Republicans. My telegram, in which I said I was immensely gratified to receive Governor Dewey's assurance of bipartisan cooperation in the effort to establish lasting peace, went off that afternoon.

Dulles came to Washington the following week, after putting out several statements giving his views on foreign affairs. When he arrived he consulted with Wendell Willkie and with Republican Senators, among others. The Senators, especially those on the Foreign Relations Committee, told him they had agreed with me on keeping the postwar organization on a nonpartisan basis, and advised him that Governor Dewey should follow the same course.

Our conversations began in my office on August 23. At the outset I handed Dulles a copy of our latest draft on the postwar security organization, dated July 18, and a copy of a four-page summary of its major provisions. One page of this summary dealt with the position of small countries in the United Nations organization, and contained six references to the draft of the United Nations Charter showing that the participation of the small nations was fully provided for.

I said to Dulles that the word "nonpartisan" rather than "bipartisan" should be used to describe the correct approach to the problem of keeping the United Nations organization out of domestic politics. "Bipartisan," I explained, meant that both parties would be involved on a political basis in policy toward the United Nations organization. "Nonpartisan" meant that neither party would be involved in that policy on a political basis.

Dulles argued warmly for "bipartisan." His thought apparently was that his party would thereby be recognized as being equally involved in the formulation of the United Nations agreement and could obtain some political advantage thereby.

I maintained, however, that, under our constitutional structure, we could not have both parties sharing the responsibility. The party in power had the responsibility for the execution of foreign policy. This responsibility could not be delegated. The opposition party, in my opinion, had the moral responsibility not to base its opposition, if any, to our proposals for the United Nations organization on partisan grounds.

I went to a dictionary and studied the definitions of the two words. "Nonpartisan" seemed to me ever more right. I called Dulles's attention to the fact that "bipartisan" referred to two parties, and there might come a time in American history, as there had come in the past, when three parties would have to be considered.

I did not believe it possible to have a nonpartisan approach to foreign policy on all current issues. All I insisted on was that both parties should approach postwar problems, especially the United Nations organization, on a nonpartisan basis, and that they should be agreed on this point.

I emphasized to Dulles that Governor Dewey was in a position where he might destroy the movement under way to get a postwar security organization, if he wanted to do so. I added that Dulles had a real opportunity to help put over this project which meant so much to mankind.

After a discussion literally of some hours over the words "nonpartisan" and "bipartisan" and all the potentialities of their meanings, Dulles agreed with me to adopt "nonpartisan."

When he came back for our second discussion, on August 24, Dulles said he had studied the draft of the proposed United Nations Charter and the four-page memorandum I had given him, and he considered the draft excellent. He appeared to think that it amply took care of the small nations. In this connection I emphasized the interdependence of nations, large and small, saying that they were all interconnected, and we could not consider large nations in one compartment and small nations in another.

The memorandum I had handed Dulles explained the position the small nations would occupy in the United Nations organization, citing chapter and verse of the draft Charter. The organization was open to membership of all peace-loving nations, large and small, on the basis of their sovereign equality. All members were equally represented in the Assembly and voted as equals except that on budgetary questions they would vote proportionately to their contributions (this last clause was later dropped). All small nations were equally eligible to membership on the Executive Council and would participate in the election of Council members. There were more small nations than large nations on the Council. No decisions of the Council on security matters could be made without the concurrence of at least some of the small-nation members of the Council; thus the large nations, although having the veto power in the use of force, could not by themselves undertake any coercive action. Finally, all members of the organization, large and small, would share in the application of measures not involving the use of armed force and also would contribute armed forces and facilities for joint action in accordance with their respective capacities and on the basis of agreements entered into by them. Dulles appeared satisfied with this exposition.

I went over with Dulles virtually every aspect of our foreign policy and our relations with any nations in which there was any particular interest. I doubt that any real point of our foreign affairs was left untouched.

During our discussions of the proposed United Nations Charter, it developed that there was an omission relating to the ratification of agreements for the use of armed force to assure peace and security. I immediately had a sentence inserted providing that the agreement would be subject to ratification by each country in accordance with its constitutional processes.

During the second meeting and during our third and final meeting on August 25, I went over with Dulles successive drafts of a statement we might issue. On the morning of the third day Dulles came to my office and said, in a tone of much satisfaction, that Dewey and he—meaning all the Republicans for whom Dewey was speaking, therefore the Republicans generally—were prepared to go the entire distance with me. We had been talking out differences very earnestly for two days, and we were both immensely pleased at this outcome. I was particularly gratified because at about the time of our conferences some leading Republicans close to Dewey had asserted their right to discuss during the campaign any foreign policy, including the postwar organization.

In the midst of our final meeting, Dulles telephoned Governor Dewey to talk over our proposed statement with him. I left my office so that he might have complete privacy, and, when I returned, found that Dewey had approved it with the insertion of one word—"full"—before the phrase "public nonpartisan discussion."

The statement, which was issued on August 25, read that Dulles and I had had an exchange of views on the various problems connected with the establishment of an international peace and security organization, and "there was agreement of views on numerous aspects of this subject." It went on:

"Secretary Hull and Mr. Dulles expect to continue to confer about developments as they arise.

"The Secretary maintained the position that the American people consider the subject of future peace as a nonpartisan subject which must be kept entirely out of politics.

"Mr. Dulles, on behalf of Governor Dewey, stated that the Governor shared this view on the understanding, however, that it did not preclude full public nonpartisan discussion of the means of attaining a lasting peace.

"The question of whether there will be complete agreement on these two respective views and their carrying out will depend on future developments."

I felt that our agreement was of much aid in uniting the Republican leaders in support of the policy I was both practicing and urging others to practice. Be it said to the credit of Governor Dewey that from the date of this agreement he uniformly rendered excellent service to the nonpartisan approach toward the United Nations.

A number of Democratic leaders and advisers of the President had communicated with me just before and during my conversations with Dulles, and had criticized the nonpartisan policy I was undertaking to follow. Their theory, like that of the President, was that the Republicans would not observe the obligation they had undertaken to give nonpartisan treatment to the postwar organization problems, and they continued to retain their doubts until the last. Some other Democratic leaders had felt that the international organization could not be kept out of politics. Nevertheless, once the agreement with Dewey was reached, they too were scrupulous to observe it.

I have seldom worked harder on any project than on the preparation for and conduct of the conversations with John Foster Dulles. I was convinced that, if I did not reach a satisfactory agreement with him, successful American participation in an international security organization might be seriously jeopardized. During the three days of our conversations I held repeated conferences with my associates to get their views and to communicate to them the observations being made by Dulles.

Governor Dewey wrote me on August 25 expressing his deep gratification at the result of the discussions. They constituted, he said, a new attitude toward the problem of peace. I replied on September 4, after submitting my letter to the President for his approval, that these conversations and his letter constituted a heartening manifestation of national unity on the problem of establishing an international peace and security organization.

I also wrote Governor Dewey suggesting that our exchange of letters be made public so that there might be fuller public understanding of our common ground on this important subject. He telephoned me on September 6 and said he would be delighted to have our letters given to the press.

He volunteered to send me shortly two or three suggestions in connection with the Dumbarton Oaks meeting, and added that he hoped he and I could carry on as we had done, regardless of the result of the election.

Two days later I received from Governor Dewey a memorandum suggesting several changes in the proposed Charter of the United Nations. One was that the right to bring a question to the attention of the General Assembly or the Executive Council ought to be extended to any state, and not limited to member states. Another was that the subject matter that might be brought to the attention of the Assembly or the Council should include treaty conditions.

We felt that the powers given to the Security Council and the Assembly to consider and make recommendations on any situation likely to endanger international security or peace took ample care of any need for recommendations by the United Nations relating to existing treaties. Nevertheless, I immediately sent Dewey's suggestions to Under Secretary Stettinius at Dumbarton Oaks, with the request that, if possible, they should be incorporated in the joint document then being formulated. The American delegation agreed that the suggestions should be inserted if there were no objection from the other two Governments concerned. The Russian and British delegations offered no objection, and the suggestions were written into the joint draft.

The Republican leaders wholeheartedly maintained their agreement to keep the postwar security organization out of the presidential campaign. In only one or two minor instances did I find any cause for complaint. As one example, Governor Dewey had begun to make references to the nonpartisan agreement and to infer that his party had taken the initiative in reaching it, and thus should have the credit for it. I finally drew up a statement that the President made public, calling attention to the origin of the agreement and the role I had played in it.

As another example, Governor Dewey made a strong attack on what he regarded as the secrecy being maintained at the Dumbarton Oaks Conference. I asked Hugh Wilson, our former Ambassador to Berlin, who was now seeing me on behalf of Dewey and Dulles, to convey to them my regret that the Governor should have made a remark that was destructive in effect, instead of one that might have been constructive.

I continued, however, to remain in contact with Dewey and Dulles through Wilson, and to keep them informed in detail of developments at Dumbarton Oaks. On September 11 I handed Wilson a five-page memorandum stating the principal changes, additions, and omissions that had been made by the conference to date in the original draft of July 18 which I had handed to Dulles.

At the same time I asked Wilson to inform Dewey and Dulles of the movement under way to call for Congressional approval of all specific applications of force under the security organization. I said that this movement might endanger the whole peace program if it were not nipped in the bud, and that it was up to the Republican leaders to do something about it before it was too late.

Dulles telephoned me the following day, September 12, to express his pleasure over the progress being made at Dumbarton Oaks. I told him the suggestions Governor Dewey had made for changes in the original document had gone through all right. I said that I was talking with Republicans and Democrats alike to get the question of Congressional approval disposed of. The difficulty, I said, was that if we got into a lively controversy over it, the Russians and the British would be scared off, believing that we would not be in position to implement an agreement on an international organization. I commented that we had enough ticklish questions with the Russians already.

Meantime I had continued my conversations with the special committee of eight Senators. On the morning of my last conference with Dulles, August 25, I met in my office with Senators Connally, Austin, George, La Follette, Vandenberg, White, and Thomas. The last-mentioned, Elbert D. Thomas of Utah, was added to the group because he had participated during the previous two years in the work of postwar committees in the State Department and had been out of town when the Senators conferred with me during the spring. Senators Barkley and Gillette were away from Washington.

Two days before our meeting I had sent these Senators a copy of our latest outline of the United Nations organization. During the meeting I called to their attention a number of changes that had been made since I first gave them a copy of the draft in April. These were based on my discussions with Congressional leaders and others.

Among them was a new paragraph providing for the encouragement of the use of local or regional procedures to settle local disputes through peaceful means. Another was a provision for the eventual addition of France to the permanent members of the Council. A third called attention to the fact that in the event of a dispute in which one of the nations on the Council was involved, the vote of that nation would not be counted in the Council's decision. Another was the dropping of the provision for an office of President of the organization, while retaining an office of Director General.

During our conversation the question was asked whether the Executive or Legislative Branch of the Government, or both, should decide upon the application of force under the postwar organization. Two Senators took the position that there must be Congressional sanction of the use of force in some instances.

I replied that the only practicable way to make the security organization work would be to leave to the Executive the decision as to the use of force. I added, however, that I presumed that the President would consult Congressional leaders in important instances before taking action. I urged that we go forward with our plans for the organization and that, when the Senate received the agreement for the application of force under the organization, it would have an opportunity to deal with the subject, which was really domestic.

I had a similar conference with Senators Ball, Burton, Hatch, and Hill on August 28. I then met in my office on the following day with Representatives Arends, Bloom, Martin, McCormack, Ramspeck, and Rayburn. Representative Eaton was absent from Washington. From neither of these two meetings came any objection to our plan and procedure for establishing the security organization.

Senator Vandenberg, however, wrote me a long letter on August 29, in which he stated that, if the American delegate to the security organization voted in favor of the use of force, this was tantamount to a declaration of war and therefore conflicted with the exclusive power to declare war lodged in Congress by the Constitution. He said he might be willing to see the President and his delegate to the international organization act in the Western Hemisphere without Congressional reference, but if an aggressor arose who could not be curbed except through another world-wide war, he did not see how we could escape the necessity for Congressional consent.

Two days later, however, Green H. Hackworth, Legal Adviser of the State Department, gave me a memorandum in which he held that, when the Senate approved the treaty stipulating the American military forces to be made available, in conjunction with other members of the United Nations, for use in maintaining peace and security, the President would have the right to use those armed forces for this purpose without further recourse to Congress. I had this circulated among the Senate Foreign Relations group and in due course, Senator Vandenberg's objections on this score ceased.

I met with the Senatorial committee again on September 12, present being Senators Barkley, Connally, George, Gillette, Vandenberg, and White. I brought them up to date on the progress of the Dumbarton Oaks meetings, and they indicated their satisfaction.

Several Senators raised objections to the proposal on which we had been working for many months calling for economic and social cooperation with regard to dependent peoples. They were greatly afraid of extreme views being advanced which they said were very unpopular in the United States.

I replied that I sympathized 100 per cent with their apprehension, and that no one was more opposed than I to the drastic views that had been expressed on some phases of this question by Henry Wallace and Wendell Willkie. I explained the more practical view we maintained, as exemplified by our course toward the Philippines, politically and economically. With one-half of the world's population lying on its back and living on the lowest levels of existence, I contended, if we should pass up an opportunity to exert our best efforts for an awakening throughout the world with respect to dependent peoples and their welfare and progress and instead leave them to be exhausted by their parent, reactionary governments, it would be a world calamity that would greatly impair the prestige of our peace organization. No special issue was taken with my views, although various Senators held out against extreme attitudes.

We spent some time discussing the question previously raised by Senator Vandenberg about the right of Congress to participate in directing the forces of this Government allotted to the keeping of the peace in conjunction with those of other members of the security organization.

I said to the Senators that we were approaching the most critical stage of our peace undertaking, and that there was, as they had indicated, a serious situation in the United States because of the question posed by Senator Vandenberg. Russia, I pointed out, was watching closely to see whether the American people were strongly behind our document or whether they were showing prime interest in this question and forgetting the whole question of future peace. Russia would want to know with reasonable assurance that this Government would not adopt a plan which, by allowing Congress to direct our military forces under the security organization, might not function as promptly as a threat to the peace called for.

Bringing up again the proposition that a good peace should be assured before the security organization entered into effect, I said there should be no issue betwen us on this point. I informed the Senators that we hoped soon to see our conferences with the three other large nations concluded, and then our work, with tentative reservations, would go straight to the other United Nations. I hoped to see a full-dress conference called to meet, probably in this country, in the fore part of November. When that conference concluded its work and the agreement on an international organization was ratified and put into effect, the appropriate nations would then proceed to investigate and analyze carefully the whole situation of the world with a view to synchronizing the steps to be taken in reference to the coming peace treaties. I should then hope to see the existence of the security organization made a powerful lever to promote the most satisfactory peace settlement in all respects, thereby insuring the best possible treaty to accompany the operation of the peace organization agreement.

As the meeting ended, the Senators seemed fully conscious of the extreme danger ahead for the peace movement if the United States became greatly aroused over this question, with the probable result of running Russia out of the picture.

The following day, September 13, I met with the leaders of both parties in the House of Representatives, Rayburn, McCormack, Bloom, Eaton, Ramspeck, and Arends, and went over the same ground with them. The next day I covered the same ground with Senators Ball, Hatch, and Hill.

As a result of all these penetrating discussions of the constitutional problem involved, in the course of which it had become so clear that immediate American participation, if necessary, in enforcing peace had to be assured, the American delegation at the Dumbarton Oaks Conference proposed a specific method which happily proved acceptable to all concerned. This took the form of the provision that all members of the international organization should undertake to make armed forces, facilities, and assistance available to the Security Council in accordance with "a special agreement or agreements," and that these special agreements should in each case be subject to ratification by the signatory states in accordance with their constitutional processes.

As I have already remarked, I had scarcely ever devoted so much concentrated effort and attention to any one project as to the nonpartisan policy toward the United Nations organization. I made detailed preparations for each meeting with the leaders of the two major parties. When we met, I had before me memoranda of the latest developments in our postwar planning, so that I could keep the party leaders accurately and minutely informed. Previously I held meetings with my associates in the State Department so that I might have the benefit of their advice. I have never argued more strenuously for any objective than I argued, not only with Republicans but also with Democrats, for keeping the United Nations organization planning completely out of politics.

The result of nearly twelve years' striving to lift foreign policies out of partisan politics was all that I could have hoped for. The United Nations did not become a campaign issue in 1944. The nation was not split over this question so vital to its future, as it had been over the League of Nations in 1919 and 1920. When the elections of 1944 were over, the nation was as resolved as before, and both major political parties were as resolved as before, that a United Nations organization should be founded to keep the peace, by force if necessary, and that the United States should not only be part of it, but also take her share of the leadership in creating and maintaining it, with all the responsibilities such leadership entailed.

122: Cornerstone of United Nations

THE MID-SEPTEMBER DEADLOCK at Dumbarton Oaks over voting procedure in the Council would not resolve itself. I kept in close touch with the President and with Under Secretary Stettinius and the American delegation as we labored night and day to compose the difference and bring the first phase of the conference to an end.

In accordance with our suggestion, the President had sent a message direct to Stalin appealing to him to authorize Ambassador Gromyko to agree to the British and American position that the vote of a member of the Council involved in a dispute should not be counted. Mr. Roosevelt sent this telegram after Stettinius, by agreement with the President and myself, had taken Gromyko to the White House at seven-thirty in the morning—a most impressive time—for a bedside conference.

The President and Gromyko talked for more than an hour. Mr. Roosevelt pointed out that when husband and wife fell out with each other they stated their case to a judge and abided by his ruling; they did not vote in the case. This principle, that any party to a dispute could be heard but could not vote, he said, had been imbedded by our forefathers in American law. He added that the idea of a member of the Council voting in a dispute involving itself would be unacceptable to the small nations, most of whom would not be members of the Council.

He sought and obtained Gromyko's consent to his sending a telegram direct to Stalin to put the case up to the Marshal. The President said this had to be settled at Dumbarton Oaks because if it were not it would be necessary for the British and American Governments to state publicly— five minutes after debate opened—that they were in agreement on this point, in contrast to Russia.

To the President's cable Stalin replied in the negative on September 15. He emphasized the importance which his Government attached to the preservation of the principle of unanimity among the four great powers in the organization on all questions, even those involving one or several of these powers. Returning to the suggestion we had made in our July 18 draft that a special procedure for voting in the Council be worked out for disputes in which one or more of the major nations were involved, he said that in his opinion this was the correct approach. But he pointed out that any departure from the principle of unanimity of the leading powers in establishing the international organization would be a deviation from the understanding reached on this point at Tehran.

The Marshal, saying that unanimity among the great powers pre-supposed the absence of mutual suspicion between them, remarked that the Soviet Union had to take account of the existence of what he called certain ridiculous prejudices which frequently hampered an objective view toward the Soviet Union. He said that other nations of the world should consider the consequences that would ensue if the leading powers failed to preserve their unanimity.

He hoped that the President would appreciate the importance which he, Stalin, attached to the question of unanimity, and that a satisfactory solution would be found.

The experts of the British, Russian, and American delegations now worked out a compromise formula as a basis for discussion and without any commitment on the delegations' part, for submission to their respective Governments. Under this formula the Security Council would act on a dispute, without the vote of the parties to the dispute being counted, even if those parties were permanent members of the Council, so long as en-forcement action was not involved. On the other hand, consideration of and decisions as to enforcement action of any kind would require the unanimous consent of all the permanent members of the Council, whether or not one of them were involved. I regarded this formula as a substantial concession to the Soviet point of view and the absolute minimum of what we could accept.

When Stettinius, after consulting with me, telegraphed this solution to the President, who was now at Quebec for his conference with Prime Minister Churchill, Mr. Roosevelt replied that neither he nor the Prime Minister was inclined to approve it. He thought that the compromise pro-posal should merely be mentioned in the final Dumbarton Oaks draft as having been discussed but without a decision having been reached, so that it could be left up to a meeting of the full United Nations. He said that Mr. Churchill, however, was afraid that this last suggestion would be unacceptable to the Russians, since they would know that they would be overwhelmingly defeated in a United Nations meeting and might "get sore" and try to take it out on the other major nations on some other issue. I had the impression that the President and the Prime Minister were so busy with their discussions at Quebec that they simply did not take the time to give the question the serious consideration it deserved.

I thereupon suggested to Stettinius that he go to Hyde Park, New

York, where the President had gone from the Quebec Conference, and discuss the question with him personally. When Stettinius telephoned the President at Hyde Park on September 17 to make the appointment, Mr. Roosevelt said that Mr. Churchill was arriving the following morning, he himself was tired, he did not see how he could work in a discussion with Stettinius, and he asked Stettinius to tell me he hoped to be in Washington the following Wednesday, at which time he would be delighted to talk over the whole problem with me. He added that he had tried to get Mr. Churchill interested in the subject, but that the Prime Minister took the position that he had not studied the papers and did not have the time to get into it.

The British and we informed the Russians that the compromise formula was not acceptable to either of us, and Ambassador Gromyko stated that, although he had not heard from Moscow, his Government probably would not accept it either.

I asked Stettinius to see Gromyko and emphasize to him, on my behalf, the very serious consequences, both for the creation of an international organization and for the Soviet Union, which might result from ending the Dumbarton Oaks Conference without an agreement on voting procedure in the Council. Stettinius did so and asked Gromyko whether his Government would be willing to reconsider our position or discuss some new formula. Gromyko replied that his Government's position was final, and that continuing the conversations for a week or for a year would not change it. He said emphatically that the Soviet Government would never consider joining an organization in which a major power involved in a dispute did not vote. He added that he did not think his Government would agree to the holding of a conference of the United Nations before agreement had been reached among the four powers on this vital question.

Sir Alexander Cadogan likewise stated that his Government could not accept a plan to bring the draft proposals before a United Nations conference prior to agreement by the four major nations on all basic issues.

A difference of opinion now developed in the American delegation. One group favored proposing additional compromises to the Russians and, if the Russians did not accept, agreeing to the Russian position. It felt that continuance of the disagreement would prejudice the holding of a successful United Nations Conference, would impair the military cooperation among the three large Western powers in bringing the war to a victorious conclusion, and would adversely affect the prospect of Russia's entering the war against Japan. Some of them also felt that the Russian position was essentially sound.

The other group insisted that the effect of a lack of agreement on the voting arrangements was being overemphasized. A quick compromise on the Russian terms, they thought, might conceivably imperil the creation of the United Nations organization because it might be rejected by the British Dominions, the Latin American Republics, and other countries. They thought that most of what we could expect to achieve at Dumbarton Oaks had been agreed upon, and that the vital issue of voting might be referred for discussion at a higher level; namely, the chiefs of state. They therefore suggested that the Russian phase of the discussions be brought to a close and Ambassador Gromyko informed that the voting question had been referred to the heads of state.

Meantime both groups proposed that the President send a further personal appeal to Stalin, although each suggested different phraseology.

At that point I called the entire delegation to my office on September 19 to canvass the whole situation. I remarked that all who had seen the recent motion picture, *Wilson,* were probably impressed, as I had been, by the remarkable similarity between the conditions that confronted American leaders at that time and those that now confronted us. It was instructive to see, I said, that American statesmen then had done their best, often in the face of difficulties and obstacles, to arrive at agreement on ways to preserve the peace.

With regard to the present conversations, I suggested the need of patience and of taking a friendly attitude in dealing with our friends from the Soviet Union.

"In my judgment," I said, "which I formed at Moscow and have had confirmed in the months of the remarkably substantial progress since then, the Soviet Union has made up its mind to follow the course of international cooperation. All Russia's interests caused her to take this course. It is only through international cooperation that she can advance her general economic interests, her industrial development, her social welfare—all of her permanent interests. Like some other nations at various times and under various circumstances, the Soviet Union might get off the line, but if this happens she would have to come back into line in time because she would discover that any course other than cooperation was against her own interests."

I remarked that we had made so much progress already, and everything seemed to have gone off so well, that sometimes we who were in the midst of this effort were likely to forget that in any great endeavor such as this to establish an international organization, there would be hitches now and then. I said we could not expect to attain rapidly all our objectives, including this big objective.

It had been my thought for some time, I said, that the international organization might not actually be established as soon as some people thought desirable. As one of our problems I mentioned the view presented to me that we should wait to establish the organization until it could be seen whether we were to have a good peace or a bad peace. Another problem was our effort to bring into the organization the nations associated with the United Nations which had broken off relations with but had not declared war against the Axis. I had particularly in mind the six Latin American Republics in this category, not including Argentina.

"I have thought for some time," I added, "that it might be desirable to take all the necessary steps to perfect the lines on which the United Nations organization should be established and then to halt, in order to survey the political and economic conditions and settlements before deciding when we should actually establish the organization and set it in motion."

I again emphasized that it would be unwise to let ourselves think of rushing through with our task. The movement for an international organization to maintain peace and security had already taken four hundred years, I commented, going back in our country as far as William Penn. Moreover, the public might require time to get a clear understanding, particularly of new proposals. And the very process of getting agreement on points demanded patience. For example, it was necessary to explain certain things to the Russians that they did not understand; then there had to be time for discussion among the Russians themselves at Dumbarton Oaks; and finally there had to be time for the Soviet Government to discuss the issues. I concluded by saying we would discuss the points in suspense with the President in the next day or two.

When the meeting was over, I felt that my talk with the delegation had stimulated them to return to the conference with the determination to bring it to as successful a conclusion as possible. The two segments of the delegation—one urging in effect an agreement on Russia's terms and the other urging adjournment of the conference followed by a discussion among the chiefs of state—withdrew the separate memoranda they had presented, and redoubled their efforts to agree on a common program.

When Stettinius and I talked over the conference situation with the President on September 21, being later joined by James C. Dunn and Leo Pasvolsky of the State Department and Vice Admiral Willson and Lieutenant General Embick, the President said he felt that the only course to pursue was to recess the Dumbarton Oaks Conference with the Russians as quickly as possible. He thought that the voting question should be left for the future.

General Embick stated the view of the Joint Chiefs of Staff that, whatever course was followed, it should be worked out in a harmonious way so as not to endanger our relations with the Soviet Union. He and Admiral Willson agreed with the plan of postponing a settlement of the pending questions.

The proposed further message from the President to Stalin was left in abeyance. The President was then looking forward to another personal meeting with Stalin and Churchill in a matter of weeks, at which he could take up the voting question with Stalin personally. This meeting, however, was delayed from week to week because of Stalin's refusal to go to any city far removed from his general headquarters—the same situation that had arisen prior to the Tehran Conference. The President and the Prime Minister finally had to give in, and the meeting was held at Yalta, on the Black Sea, in February, 1945.

There the three statesmen, although each had previously rejected it, agreed to a voting formula almost identical with the compromise formula worked out at Dumbarton Oaks, to the effect that in the pacific settlement of a dispute the vote of a party to the dispute, even if a permanent member of the Council, would not be counted, whereas it would be counted in balloting on enforcement action. The voting formula actually adopted at Yalta had been worked out by State Department experts in the interval between the Dumbarton Oaks and the Yalta Conferences, and accepted by the President. He proposed it at Yalta.

To return to the Dumbarton Oaks Conference, Ambassador Gromyko on September 27, after receiving final instructions from his Government concerning the latest draft of the proposed United Nations Charter, communicated to the conference a series of concessions. His Government accepted the chapter on amendments. It agreed to the insertion of a provision that the American delegation had proposed relating to the promotion of human rights and fundamental freedoms. It consented to the paragraph proposed by the British to the effect that the section on pacific settlement of disputes should not apply to matters of domestic jurisdiction.

The conference agreed to insert in the text of the proposed Charter a statement that the question of voting procedure in the Council was still under consideration.

Gromyko took the edge off his concessions by stating that he wanted to make it plain that his Government's agreement to a general conference of the United Nations depended upon two conditions. The first was that the British and American Governments should meet the Soviet proposals as to voting in the Council. Gromyko reemphasized his Government's contention that the principle of the unanimity of the four great powers had to be applied unconditionally. The second was that those Governments should agree that the sixteen Soviet Republics would be initial members of the United Nations organization.

The President and I both felt that some agreement could be reached on Russia's first condition, but we thought Stalin's desire to include the sixteen Soviet Republics as members of the United Nations an insurmountable obstacle, and resolutely opposed it.

There were now five questions concerning the United Nations organization left unsettled, for future decision. These were: voting in the Council; statute of the International Court of Justice (the creation of the Court as a part of the United Nations organization had been agreed to); initial membership; trusteeships; and liquidation of the League of Nations.

To my great disappointment, the project of trusteeships under the United Nations, to replace and liberalize the old system of mandates under the League of Nations, had not been brought up at the conference. This had been a project conceived and elaborated in the State Department by my associates and me and enthusiastically concurred in by the President. We had not brought it up at the Dumbarton Oaks Conference, however, because of the specific and insistent request of the United States Joint Chiefs of Staff.

The Joint Chiefs felt that a discussion of the trusteeship system would inevitably embrace concrete questions of who should be trustee over what territories, and that dissension might therefore arise among the major Allies.

Furthermore, they were anxious to keep the whole matter open pending a determination within our own Government of a definite policy with regard to the subsequent disposal of some of the Japanese islands in the Pacific, including those held by Japan under mandate. It was their view that complete control of these islands by the United States for military purposes was necessary to our national security, and they felt that this could perhaps best be achieved through outright annexation rather than through a trusteeship system.

My associates and I, on the other hand, were convinced that the security interests of the United States in the Pacific, including the attainment of the specific objective of United States control of the islands for military purposes, could be fully secured through a system of trusteeship. Such a system was eventually worked out at San Francisco. While we agreed to the omission of this subject from the Dumbarton Oaks discussions, we did not intend to let the project die and hoped to bring it up again at the general meeting of the United Nations.

The Russian phase of the Dumbarton Oaks Conference ended on September 28, and the Chinese phase began at once. In opening this second stage, I said to the delegates that I was fully convinced that the excellent work already done, and that which we were about to undertake, would carry us a long way toward complete understanding among our Governments and toward the wider understanding which the peace-loving peoples of the world so ardently desired.

I added that the joint recommendations to be made by the representatives of our Governments would, upon the conclusion of the second phase of the conversations, be made available to the peoples of all peace-loving nations for full public discussion. "The strength of the organization which we propose to establish," I remarked, "can be no greater than the support given to it by an informed public opinion throughout the world."

It was also our hope, I said, that a full United Nations conference might be convened at an early date to bring to fruition the work already done.

The conversations with the Chinese delegation, headed by the eminent and very able statesman, Dr. Wellington Koo, offered no particular difficulties. The Chinese delegation had been currently informed of the developments in the first phase. Moreover, in general, they were already of our way of thinking. They offered a number of cogent observations, but they were willing to go along on the basis of the draft already agreed to and to bring up their further views at the general conference.

At the end of the Chinese phase of the conference the British, Chinese, and Americans agreed in two documents on changes in wording of the proposed Charter, for submission to the full conference of all the United Nations. In the first document we agreed that the Charter should

provide specifically for settlement of disputes "with due regard for principles of justice and international law." In the second, relating to the
economic and social council, we agreed that the council should provide
for the promotion of educational and other forms of cultural cooperation.

The three delegations felt that all three of these concepts—justice,
international law, and cultural cooperation—were already imbedded in
the text of the proposed Charter as agreed upon during the first phase of
the Dumbarton Oaks conversations. They were perfectly willing, however, in order to avoid any misunderstanding, to see them introduced
textually into the draft. It seemed too late at that point to discuss the
matter with the Russians, particularly since to open up this issue might
entail long delays because of the need to exchange communications with
Moscow, and might therefore retard the publication of the text already
agreed upon. The British, the Chinese, and ourselves therefore decided
that the understanding reached would be brought to the attention of the
Soviet Government after the publication of the Dumbarton Oaks text
with a view to securing their approval to having it presented to the full
conference in the name of the four Governments. In the meantime these
supplementary documents were not to be made public. The Soviet approval of this understanding was obtained shortly after the opening of
the San Francisco Conference, and the points contained in the understanding were then presented to the San Francisco Conference as a proposed amendment by the four major nations.

As the Anglo-American-Chinese conversations neared their close, British Foreign Secretary Eden suggested to me through Ambassador Winant
on October 4 that a follow-up meeting should be held by the foreign
ministers of the four nations to accept the conclusions of the Dumbarton
Oaks Conference and to sign documents. He suggested a meeting place
in Africa. The illness that was now overtaking me did not permit my
accepting his proposal.

Prior to the release of the Dumbarton Oaks draft to the press I sent
copies to John Foster Dulles for Governor Dewey. I had previously telephoned him on September 23 to inform him that the first phase of the
Dumbarton Oaks Conference had resulted in practical agreement, and
that we and the British would shortly go into conference with the Chinese. Dulles wrote me on October 13 that Governer Dewey and he highly
appreciated the proposals agreed to at Dumbarton Oaks. Although there
were many imperfections and inadequacies, he added, the main thing was

to get started, and the proposals brought that within the realm of early possibility. "For this," he continued, "the world owes you much."

Also prior to the release of the proposals we sent copies to our diplomatic missions in Latin America to be handed to the Governments of the American Republics. Throughout the conference we had kept the representatives of those Republics as fully informed of developments as we possibly could. A few of the statesmen of Latin America nevertheless had felt that they were not being sufficiently consulted on postwar planning.

It was impossible, however, to bring the American Republics into a preliminary conference such as Dumbarton Oaks without bringing in all the other United Nations. It was obvious that the most effective way to prepare the Charter was for the four major nations to reach tentative agreement first among themselves, always with the thought that their conclusions were not fixed and final but were subject to modification after discussion with the other United Nations. A full-scale conference among the United Nations at this point might have led to innumerable difficulties and differences of opinion and to great delay. Meantime the Latin American Republics, as well as all United Nations, had had full representation at the other conferences, such as the United Nations Food Conference, the International Labor Organization Conference, the Monetary and Financial Conference, and the United Nations Relief and Rehabilitation Administration Conference.

Prior to and during the Dumbarton Oaks Conference I had made every effort to keep the Latin American Republics, except Argentina, as fully informed as possible. On June 26 I had called the Ambassadors of the Central American Republics—Costa Rica, El Salvador, Guatemala, Honduras, Nicaragua, and Panama—to my office and had given them in comprehensive background report of our efforts to date.

I had sent a circular telegram to all our diplomatic missions in Latin America, except Argentina, on July 11 instructing them to inform those Governments that we were about to initiate exchanges of views with the United Kingdom, the U.S.S.R., and China on a postwar organization, and that as soon as possible thereafter exchanges of views would be held with other United Nations and associated nations.

In our studies, I said, we had devoted particular attention to the special relationship that existed between the United States and the other American Republics. I invited their attention to the President's statement of June 15 and asked their comments.

I said there was no inconsistency between what I had described in my June 1 statement as "our disposition and purpose to see that all nations, especially the small nations, are kept on a position of equality with all others" and the fact that our first conversations were to be held only with the United Kingdom, the Soviet Union, and China. Since these three nations and the United States, I pointed out, inevitably had to bear the major responsibility for the maintenance of peace in the postwar years, there was no possibility of the successful establishment of a general international organization unless all these nations were prepared to support it.

As the Dumbarton Oaks Conference neared its conclusion, I had two long conferences with Latin American representatives to give them all information possible on the conversations. On September 15 I called in the representatives of Brazil, Chile, Colombia, Mexico, Peru, Uruguay, and Venezuela, and on the following day the representatives of Bolivia, Costa Rica, Cuba, the Dominican Republic, Ecuador, Guatemala, Haiti, Honduras, Nicaragua, Panama, and El Salvador. I pointed out that in the Dumbarton Oaks talks we had insisted on certain principles already established in the inter-American community—for example, nonintervention and nondiscrimination. I added that we had also insisted on the observance of the rights of middle- and small-sized nations, that we recognized that the large and small nations were interdependent, and that we had sought in every way to increase the functions of the United Nations Assembly, in which every nation would be represented.

On October 9 we released to the press the proposals for the establishment of a general international organization agreed upon at Dumbarton Oaks. The President, Stettinius, and I made statements expressing our satisfaction with the work thus far accomplished but emphasizing that the task of planning the United Nations organization still required constant effort along with an unfailing determination that the sacrifices of the war should not be in vain. Mr. Roosevelt, referring to his extreme satisfaction and even surprise that so much could have been accomplished on so difficult a subject in so short a time, stated: "This achievement was largely due to the long and thorough preparations which were made by the Governments represented, and, in our case, was the result of the untiring devotion and care which the Secretary of State has personally given to this work for more than two and a half years—indeed for many years."

Three days later, on Columbus Day, Under Secretary Stettinius represented me at a reception given at Blair House for the chiefs of diplomatic missions from the other American Republics and talked with them further about the achievements of the conference. On my behalf, he assured them that he and I, as well as other officials in the Department, would welcome all opportunities to discuss postwar questions with them. A series of discussions between Latin American diplomats and Department officials followed.

After the Dumbarton Oaks Conference adjourned, a temporary lull came in the series of meetings on postwar planning I had held during six months with Congressional leaders. I took that occasion to send each of them a letter thanking him for his extremely valuable service as we moved forward in a spirit of nonpartisanship toward the creation of machinery for a just and lasting peace.

One of my last acts in office was to request Under Secretary Stettinius to set up a committee within the State Department to give continuing attention to keeping the security organization out of politics. Stettinius sent me a memorandum on October 19, the day before I left my bed at home for the hospital, saying he had instituted such a committee. Political Adviser James C. Dunn would keep in touch with Hugh Wilson so that Governor Dewey would be kept informed of steps taken to carry forward the work begun at Dumbarton Oaks. Stettinius also talked with Benjamin V. Cohen, one of the President's advisers, to ask that he do what he could at the White House to continue scrupulous adherence to the nonpartisan agreement I had reached with Dulles.

I likewise gave my hearty endorsement to a proposal Stettinius took up with me that the Department, because of the enormous stake of our people in a successful general international organization to keep the peace, should undertake off-the-record conversations in all sections of the nation to discuss with the people everywhere the meaning and limitations of the proposed organization and our expectations concerning it. In this way not only was the public informed and taken into our confidence, but also the responsible officials of the Government received the benefit of the thinking and indeed the prayers of the American people as a whole. These talks also revealed that Americans in overwhelming majority, as well as the leaders of the political parties, regarded the question of the future peace and security of the world as above any partisan consideration.

During October, Myron C. Taylor, who had returned to the Vatican as the President's personal representative, had a long audience with Pope Pius XII. Without expressing a final determination as to Vatican policy, the Pope raised the question of possible Vatican membership in the

United Nations, and sought information as to the terms under which a small state such as Vatican City would be admitted.

After studying this question, however, we did not believe it advisable to encourage Vatican membership. While recognizing the world-wide and beneficent influence of the Vatican, we concluded that Vatican City was too small to be able to undertake the responsibilities, such as participation in measures of force to preserve or restore the peace, which every member of the United Nations had to incur. We recalled that the League of Nations had similarly discouraged the admission of very small states.

In the same month Prime Minister Churchill had an exchange of messages with the President prior to his going to Moscow, in which he said in effect that he knew the President's mind so well that he thought he could speak for both countries and take up with Marshal Stalin the questions left unsettled at Dumbarton Oaks. Mr. Roosevelt replied, however, that he preferred to wait until the three of them could meet, and Mr. Churchill agreed.

The Dumbarton Oaks proposals were now before the peoples of the peace-loving nations for discussion. Before I resigned the following month I had the satisfaction of seeing these proposals meet with reasonable approval. Naturally there were criticisms, some of which were well taken. And admittedly the question of voting procedure in the Council still had to be ironed out.

Nevertheless, we had now laid a basis on solid rock for the formation of the United Nations organization, in agreement with the other major nations having the same aspirations as ours.

The San Francisco Conference in April, May, and June, 1945, worked on the basis of the Dumbarton Oaks proposals. These were supplemented and amended by suggestions put forward by the various delegations, including those of the four nations that had participated in the Dumbarton Oaks meeting. The final results were embodied in a formal legal text accepted unanimously, without reservations, and signed by representatives of fifty nations on June 26.

The San Francisco Conference is entitled to great credit for the immense services it rendered. No one would be disposed, however, to question the general opinion of those participating in the Dumbarton Oaks Conference and later the San Francisco Conference that the chief foundations of the world organization, including its basic principles and machinery, grew out of the five years' study and preparation that culminated in the meeting at Dumbarton Oaks, the results of which, in turn, became the chief foundation for the San Francisco Conference. In fact, if out of the Charter of the United Nations that emerged from San Francisco one were to take the Dumbarton Oaks proposals, the remainder would in a large sense resemble a tree without a trunk or roots.

123: Fourth Term and Resignation

SOME TIME BEFORE Franklin D. Roosevelt was nominated at Chicago on July 20, 1944, for a fourth term, he again proposed to me at the White House my nomination as Vice President. He said he knew I could have the nomination if I would take it.

The President knew I would not take it, however, because the war was still on and I was thoroughly involved in foreign affairs. I felt as I had in 1940, when I repeatedly refused an identical suggestion; namely, that I could serve better, in the circumstances, as Secretary of State than as Vice President. I expressed my appreciation to the President, but said I was deeply engaged in foreign policy and did not feel I could leave it.

The fourth term seemed more natural to the general public, including myself, than the third term. The tradition had already been shattered, and in 1944 we were at war, which had not been the case in 1940. The President felt the situation was difficult, we were in so deep, he was at the helm, and therefore he should yield to the widespread demands that he stand for election again.

I took no part in the campaign that followed. I was thoroughly absorbed in working for the creation of the United Nations organization and in solidifying a nonpartisan policy approach to it. I particularly wanted to keep free of politics while engaged in this work, which I believed to be above party.

The President sent me a memorandum dated September 29, 1944, in which he said: "I hope much that, in making your plans, you will arrange to go on the air about twice between now and election day. The country needs some of your clear thinking and needs to have it kept up to date."

He then said it was his thought that he would make one speech between then and election day on foreign policy, and he would be "eternally grateful" if I would have prepared for him a draft of a speech containing six points. These were:

"(1) What we have done in the past to promote peace in the world.

"(2) What we have done to promote international trade.

"(3) How we tried to keep our own peace after Poland was attacked, and before Pearl Harbor.

"(4) Some of the specific steps taken by the Republican leaders to block our efforts in all these things.

"(5) The steps we have taken for the future peace of the world in the past two years.

"(6) The prospects of a permanent international peace in the future."

The President concluded his memorandum by saying: "It is my thought that if you could outline what you would say in your two speeches and what you suggest I should say, the three of them will not conflict. It seems to me that this is a practical way of going about it, and I need not tell you that what you say will have very great weight both in the later peace proceedings and in our own election."

When I received this memorandum I had already planned to call on the President at the White House the following Sunday and inform him of my forthcoming resignation. I made the call as planned and told him, with a feeling of the keenest disappointment, that I had been overexerting myself for some time and now found myself in such physical condition that I should have to resign. I said I was leaving my office within another day or two to go straight to bed, where I must remain for an indefinite period.

The President did not seem to want to believe me. We had a rather casual conversation before I left his office. The question of preparing a speech for him and of my making two campaign speeches was not mentioned by us then or thereafter, although the Department later assisted the President in preparing his major foreign policy address of the campaign.

Three days later, on October 2, my seventy-third birthday, I left the State Department a very ill man. I spent eighteen days at my apartment trying vainly to recover, during which I carried on my work to some degree, and was then taken to the Naval Medical Center at Bethesda, Maryland, where I remained for about seven months, at times in very grave condition. The terrific strain of nearly twelve years in the State Department—half again longer than anyone else in our history—during one of the most crucial periods in the life of our nation, had utterly exhausted me.

Soon after I arrived at the hospital, the President sent the White House physician, Vice Admiral Ross T. McIntire, to reassure me about my condition and to convince me that I would recover sufficiently to resume my duties within a reasonable time. Then the President visited me for an hour and a half during which he urged upon me the wisdom of not resigning. He assured me I could take some leave and, after a reasonable period, return to my office at the State Department.

I did not hesitate but promptly declined to withhold my resignation. I said it was next to taking my life to be compelled to resign, with the tremendous plans to which I had been giving my chief attention not yet adopted. But, I added, I had almost utterly exhausted my strength in undertaking to carry forward these gigantic efforts, and I had swung down to the lowest rung on the physical ladder; I could not possibly retain my office with its terrific responsibilities and at the same time make a recovery.

The President then urged very insistently that I not resign until the end of his present term, January 20, 1945. I replied that personally I should be extremely glad to take this course; but I pointed out that if I did so critics would begin almost in no time to emphasize the tremendous responsibilities resting on me and the State Department and, while expressing sympathy for me in my illness, they would soon begin to insist that the critical nature of conditions required a Secretary of State on close watch at the Department, with the result that they would soon be criticizing the President.

Mr. Roosevelt then asked that I withhold my resignation at least until after the election. To this I agreed.

On October 26, a fortnight before the elections, I issued a personal statement praising President Roosevelt's leadership and characterizing him as a statesman equipped by nature and experience to meet the enormous problems confronting the nation.

A fortnight after the election I dictated a letter to the President, tendering my resignation. Happily, the war was now largely won. Allied forces occupied virtually all of France and Belgium, part of Holland, and the Italian peninsula up to Florence. American forces had landed in the Philippines. The menace of German submarines and raiders in the Atlantic had been largely overcome. Bulgaria, Rumania, and Finland had surrendered.

"It is a matter of special satisfaction to me," I said in my letter of November 21, "that throughout my almost twelve years at the Department of State, our personal relations have been uniformly and invariably agreeable, and that, by our joint efforts, many difficult tasks growing out of the foreign relations of this country before and during this war have been brought to partial or full completion; many great questions have been faced successfully; and many forward movements of surpassing importance to friendly relations among nations have been instituted."

Looking ahead, I continued: "As the war draws to a close there remains a vast area of complex and difficult conditions and problems which must be dealt with in the months and years immediately ahead. It is a supreme tragedy to me personally that I am unable to continue making my full contribution to such great international undertakings as the creation of the postwar peace organization, the solution of the many other problems involved in the promotion of international cooperation, and the final development of a full and complete structure of a world order under law."

I concluded by saying that when I recovered my health I should be always at his service in every possible way.

The President that same day wrote me a splendid letter, which he began by saying that my letter had hit him "between wind and water." "It has been very sad," he went on, "for me even to contemplate the ending of our close relationship during all these twelve years. It is not merely that our personal relations have been so uniformly and invariably agreeable, or that our joint work has borne true success in so many fields, as it is the personal feeling of not being able to lean on you for aid and intimate interchange of thought.

"This is especially true because we have come so far along the road of friendly relations among nations that I have counted so much on your help in carrying this work through the final stage of complex and difficult conditions which still face us.

"Your health is honestly my first thought, and I am really confident that you will be on your feet again in a relatively short time, even though you are limited to special tasks and avoid the daily routine of Department work. As of today, therefore, you must devote all your thought to getting back on your feet and on this all your friends will join in helping."

He then repeated his suggestion that I continue in office until the beginning of the fourth term, saying:

"I will, of course, accept your resignation as Secretary of State if you want me to do so. But I wish you would, as an alternative, allow me to accept it as of January twentieth, which is the end of our Third Term. Perhaps sentiment enters into this suggestion a little bit, but it would give me great satisfaction if we should round out the three terms. That means two months more, and during that time I could see you from time to time and get your advice on some of the things that will come before us."

The President then made a suggestion which would have been dear indeed to my heart had I been able to accept it. "Incidentally," he said, "when the organization of the United Nations is set up, I shall continue to pray that you as the Father of the United Nations may preside over its first session. That has nothing to do with whether you are Secretary of State or not at the time, but should go to you as the one person in all the world who has done the most to make this great plan for peace an effective fact. In so many different ways you have contributed to friendly relations among nations that even though you may not remain in a position of executive administration, you will continue to help the world with your moral guidance."

The President's appeal was so heartfelt and affected me so greatly that I had an earnest talk with the doctors who were treating me. Their answer was that I could not possibly return to my office for a long time to come. I did not think it fair either to the Government or to myself, therefore, to accept the President's suggestion that I remain in office until January 20. I felt it was only just that a new Secretary of State should be named to take over. And I felt that, as titular head of the State Department, I would be held responsible for foreign policies in the formulation of which I had no active part.

I therefore replied to the President on November 23, telling him I was deeply moved by his letter and eternally grateful for his kind solicitude about my health and his generous references to our close personal and official relationship of twelve years. After repeating that it was a personal tragedy to me that my state of health made it impossible to continue in the public service, and after stating that I would always cherish the ties between us of friendship and affection, I said:

"With all my heart I wish that I could meet your desire that my resignation as Secretary of State become effective on January 20 rather than now. I have consulted again with my physicians. The speed of my recovery is definitely connected with the extent to which I can be free from all worry and responsibility. You can well understand that, at a time like this, it is impossible for me to lay aside the heavy responsibilities of the Secretaryship of State so long as I remain in that office. In fairness to the cause for which you and I have worked so long together, to the country, to you, and to myself, I feel that my resignation must become effective now."

I repeated that, as soon as I recovered my health, I would be entirely at his service with whatever contribution I could make individually to the solution of the tremendous and crucial problems that lay ahead.

The President now accepted my resignation, and announced it on November 27. He named the Under Secretary of State, Edward R. Stettinius, Jr., to succeed me. My tenure ended officially on November 30, 1944.

In the days that followed I received messages of regret from foreign ministers and leading statesmen and citizens throughout the world, including Churchill, Molotov, and Eden. Mr. Churchill assured me of his "admiration for your long service in such exacting times" and hoped I should "soon be restored to health and able once more to bring to our counsels the great weight of your experience and wisdom in international affairs." Molotov, sending me Marshal Stalin's regards and wishes for good health, said he hoped that "your knowledge and experience will continue to serve the cause of collaboration between the United States and the Soviet Union as well as between other United Nations for the achievement and cementing of our common victory." I regarded all these messages as tributes to the principles I had long been advocating rather than to myself.

The President came to see me at the hospital several times. On one occasion, looking tired and worn—he was then only a few weeks from death—he said to me as I lay in bed, "I ought to be there where you are."

During the seven long months in the hospital I was frequently heartened by signs that, though I was out of office, my work was not forgotten. On November 24, 1944, the Variety Clubs of America conferred upon me their Humanitarian Award for 1943. On December 29 the personnel of the Department of State and the Foreign Service presented a bust of me to the Department. The United States Senate, on January 3, 1945, established a precedent when it accepted a bust of me for placement in the Capitol. The bust, sculptured at the initiative of the *Evening Times* and *Sunday Times* of Cumberland, Maryland, was presented by Senator Millard Tydings and accepted by Vice President Wallace, presiding over the Senate. A motion permitting its acceptance had been· made by Senator Kenneth D. McKellar of Tennessee and passed by the Senate and the House.

The Tennessee State Legislature also unveiled a bust of me in the State Capitol at Nashville on January 9, 1945. The State Senate passed a joint resolution, the House concurring, paying me many compliments and also, to my delight, specifically praising Mrs. Hull. The resolution resolved "that Tennessee, through this means, voices the State's grateful acknowledgments to Mrs. Hull, not only for her devoted and unremitting attentions to her illustrious husband during his illness, but for the intelligent support she has uniformly given him in his efforts to fulfill his responsibilities to his office, to his Country and to all mankind."

President Roosevelt wrote me on February 10, 1945, from the Yalta Conference that I was his and Secretary Stettinius's first choice as chairman of the American delegation to the United Nations Conference. He added that Admiral McIntire, his physician, felt, however, that in my own best interests I should not be asked to assume this arduous task. The President therefore requested me to be a member of the American delegation and senior adviser to it.

Also from the Yalta Conference I received a cable signed by Roosevelt, Stalin, Churchill, Molotov, Eden, and Stettinius, saying: "We have missed you at this conference and send to you our affectionate greetings. We wish for you a speedy recovery in order that all of us may have the benefit of association with you again."

I should state at this point that I was not consulted by the President or anyone else on policy issues prior to or during the Yalta Conference. The President visited me at the hospital just before departing for Yalta, but he did not take up any of the topics he expected to discuss with Stalin and Churchill or the decisions he might make. Nor was I informed beforehand of the purposes of this Government at any other important conference subsequently, except that at San Francisco.

I should say, in fairness to others, that since my resignation I have not taken part in the conduct of our foreign policy. I have followed in a general way from the sidelines the course of world affairs, commenting in public statements now and then on basic questions and talking informally with both private citizens and officials, but referring mainly to our policies in operation while I was at the State Department. On account of my health I have been obliged to refrain from any role of consultant or adviser to officials of the Government on foreign affairs, with the exception that, as a delegate, I offered some long-distance advice during the San Francisco Conference, and that I made one suggestion to Secretary of State Byrnes with regard to the Emperor institution in Japan, which I have related in the last chapter on the Far East. In conversations with officials who called to see me I sought only to repeat and emphasize the principles to which this Government had adhered up to the time of my resignation. It is not the province of these Memoirs to take up our foreign relations since the date of my resignation.

Two months after the Yalta Conference I was stunned on April 12 by President Roosevelt's sudden death. He had come to see me the day before leaving for Hyde Park and then for Warm Springs, where he died a few days later. On the occasion of his visit I admonished him about his health, saying he should take more rest. He said he was leaving the following day for this purpose. On the day of his death I issued a statement saying: "No greater tragedy could have befallen our country and the world at this time. His inspiring vision, his high statesmanship, and his superb leadership were factors without which the United Nations could not have come to the present phase of the war with victory just in sight. That leadership is gone, but his vision and the spirit of his statesmanship must continue to inspire us for the crucial task which even now is before us, the task of building a world peace. Mankind will be vastly poorer because of his passing."

President Roosevelt, in my opinion, was one of the greatest social reformers in our modern history, even though many persons might disagree with certain of his reforms. As Commander-in-Chief, his achievements were outstanding among those of other commanders-in-chief. In my opinion he had no contemporary rival in political skill. As long as I knew him he was always an earnest follower of individual liberty, freedom, and other basic rights and privileges necessary for the welfare of the private citizen. These included the ideals of justice, law, and order. He was a strong and consistent, and oftentimes an extreme, liberal in his views. The steps he took in the military field which led straight toward victory meant everything to us in the diplomatic field by giving to the force of our diplomacy the indispensable backing of military success.

When the President died I was composing a letter on trade agreements, which had formed one of the cornerstones of the foreign policy of his Administration. This I sent on April 14, 1945, to Representative Doughton, chairman of the House Ways and Means Committee, to urge strongly the passage of a resolution to extend the Trade Agreements Act, which otherwise would expire June 12, 1945. I was later gratified to see the Act extended.

Prior to his death, President Roosevelt had appointed me, as he had suggested from Yalta, a member of the American delegation to the San Francisco Conference and its senior adviser, with Secretary of State Stettinius as chairman. Being still in the Naval Hospital, I was unable to take a large share in the proceedings at San Francisco.

In a letter to Stettinius on April 20 telling him that I should be unable to attend the opening of the conference, although I hoped to attend its later stages, I said: "What happens at San Francisco will be an acid test of whether mankind has suffered enough and has learned enough to have acquired the vision and the resolution to build a structure of organized international relations, through which order under law can be established and maintained.

"I have profound faith that, whatever the difficulties, the labors of the conference will be crowned with success. I shall follow its work from afar with absorbing interest. So far as my strength may permit, I shall endeavor to make whatever contribution I can to its successful outcome."

Stettinius sent a daily telegram on the proceedings at San Francisco to Under Secretary Joseph C. Grew, addressed to the President and me, and I followed developments with close attention. Several times Stettinius telephoned me directly. I gave advice when I thought it would be helpful. Carlton Savage, who had been one of my associates at the State Department, was designated by Stettinius to keep me informed of the developments at San Francisco and telephoned me almost daily.

To Secretary Stettinius over the telephone I spoke as strongly as I could against admitting Argentina to the San Francisco Conference. I said that the American delegation had to regain the leadership in the Argentine question that the United States had lost at the Mexico City Conference.

I said it was evident that other delegations had outmaneuvered the United States on the Argentine question, and that consequently irreparable harm had been done. As I have already mentioned in Chapter 101 on Argentina, I would have voted against the admission of Argentina to the United Nations had I been called upon to vote. I was suddenly informed, however, that our delegation had already voted unanimously to admit her.

I also said to Stettinius that if the American delegation were not careful we should get Russia into such a state of mind that she might decide that the United Nations organization was not going to furnish adequate security to her in the future. Thereupon, I added, she might decide that, while giving lip service to the organization and keeping up her membership and paying her dues, she ought at the same time to go back home and establish outposts, bases, and warm-water harbors in many areas and add buffer territory and otherwise prepare her own outward defenses just as fully as if the United Nations were not in existence.

When Stettinius telephoned me to discuss the problem of regional security I commented that, if we could not check the trend of nations to rely on national and regional self-protective measures, the United Nations would gradually fade away.

On another occasion I warned against the great danger of military preparations as an alternative to international organization. I said that such programs were a question that concerned both Russia and the United States, and that if these two countries did not agree soon on the limitation of military preparations Russia might enlarge her activities for building up a federation of nations close to her. I added that if we were not careful the United States would create enough precedents to estop us from protesting against Russia's activities taken in the name of self-defense.

When Secretary Stettinius explained over the telephone Russia's attitude on the veto by permanent members of the Security Council, I said I felt that the Russian position would definitely narrow the base of the United Nations organization and that we must continue, with great patience—I emphasized this last phrase—to press the Russians to modify their attitude.

In general, aside from my disappointment over the admission of Argentina, I felt that the results achieved at San Francisco were highly satisfactory. I sent Secretary Stettinius on June 26 my warmest congratulations on the successful conclusion of the conference and the adoption of the United Nations Charter.

In a public statement on the same day I said: "We now have, at long last, a Charter of a world organization capable of fulfilling the hopes of mankind. It is a human rather than a perfect instrument. It has within it ample flexibility for growth and development, for dynamic adaptation to changing conditions.

"The Charter will work, and grow, and improve, if our nation and all nations devoted to peace maintain the spirit in which they have created it and remain eternally vigilant in support and defense of the great ideals on which it is founded."

Secretary Stettinius was good enough to write me on June 23 a letter from San Francisco in which he said: "Your many years of leadership in the preparation for this conference, including your historic achievement at Moscow in 1943, have paid rich dividends during our work here. The evidences of your wise statesmanship have ever been apparent. Your outstanding contributions to this great cause merit more than ever Franklin Delano Roosevelt's designation of you as the 'Father of the United Nations.' "

It was with keen pleasure that I personally signed the Charter. As

I affixed my signature, I felt that the many years I had devoted, ever since the First World War, to the study and then to the preparation of an international security organization had reached fruition. The task was now in other hands, but I was confident that with reasonable understanding among the nations, particularly the major ones, the organization could move forward with the grace of God to the task of keeping the peace.

By now I had been able to return from the Naval Hospital to my apartment to complete my recovery there. I issued a statement on the occasion of VJ day to mark our victory over Japan, and went to the White House at the invitation of President Truman to observe this historic event. At about this time I began to work on a long exposition of our policy toward Japan up to the time of Pearl Harbor, to be made to the Joint Committee of Congress on the Investigation of the Pearl Harbor Attack. I was assisted by Joseph W. Ballantine and Maxwell M. Hamilton, who had aided me in the negotiations with the Japanese. I personally presented this statement, about 25,000 words long, to the committee on November 23. That afternoon and again on November 26 and 27 I answered questions addressed to me by the committee.

At the end of 1945 I received the Nobel Peace Prize, awarded me by the Nobel Committee of the Storting (Parliament) of Norway, on December 10, 1945. I had been recommended for this award a number of times in my twelve years as Secretary of State. The first time was in 1934. I had then been occupying the office of Secretary of State only a year and a half, but some persons and organizations, whose identity I do not know, thought fit to suggest my candidacy for the prize to the Nobel Committee. The basis for their friendly suggestion was my work for trade agreements as a means toward obtaining peace.

In 1936 I championed the candidacy of Dr. Saavedra Lamas, the Argentina Foreign Minister. This was successful.

The following year, he proposed my candidacy, and other kind persons made similar recommendations. The Governments of Argentina, Uruguay, Peru, Nicaragua, Panama, Chile, Honduras, Bolivia, Belgium, and Greece formally nominated me. I then became aware that President Roosevelt had also been proposed. In April I made a full appraisal of the claims of the President in contrast with any claims I might have. My conclusion was that he was really more entitled to this recognition than I might be.

Accordingly I wrote strongly to the Nobel Prize Committee at Oslo, emphasizing the claims of the President and earnestly supporting his nomination. Simultaneously I requested and insisted that my name be withdrawn from consideration. I also notified Dr. Saavedra Lamas to this effect, along with others who I knew had transmitted to Oslo their recommendations in my behalf.

At the same time, however—and unknown to me—the President endorsed my candidacy. Later I was informed that the Nobel Committee had been distressed at my withdrawal and had decided to continue their deliberations as if they had not received it.

In 1938 President Roosevelt again proposed me. Dr. Saavedra Lamas did likewise. On December 27, 1939, the President wrote me: "I have been careful for a number of years not to let you know that I have been recommending and re-recommending you for the Nobel Peace Prize. Just for your own family records I think you may care to have copies of my previous letters and of this year's letter to the Nobel Committee. I do not need to tell you that I hope, before I am through, this very just and well earned award will be made to you."

In his letter of January 13, 1938, to the Nobel Committee the President wrote: "Since the spring of 1933, Mr. Hull has been largely instrumental in establishing on a firm footing among the twenty-one American Republics the so-called principle of 'The Good Neighbor.'" Also: "In the world field, largely through Mr. Hull's efforts, trade barriers have at least been lowered on the principle of the most favored nations' clause, thus making it possible for nations voluntarily to join in the reduction of economic barriers which have been so greatly responsible for isolation and, therefore, for hostile actions."

In 1939 Mr. Roosevelt based his proposal of my candidacy on my work on behalf of the Good Neighbor Policy. "It is my belief," he wrote, "that what has been accomplished in the American Hemisphere has been of great moral influence in other parts of the world, for it has furnished an example of what can be accomplished by such leadership."

In 1940 I again proposed Mr. Roosevelt as a candidate for the prize. But in April of 1940 Nazi troops invaded Norway, and six years were to pass before another Nobel Prize was awarded.

When I was informed in December, 1945, that I had been awarded the Nobel Prize for 1945 I was unfortunately in too poor health to make the trip to Oslo to receive the award in person. In response to a kind address by Gunnar Jahn, chairman of the Nobel Committee, outlining and evaluating my work, our Ambassador to Norway, Lithgow Osborne, read a message from me. Stating that "peace has become as essential to civilized existence as the air we breathe is to life itself," I noted that the first

General Assembly of the United Nations would meet the following month in London.

"I fully realize," I said, "that the new organization is a human rather than a perfect instrumentality for the attainment of its great objective. As time goes on it will, I am sure, be improved. The Charter is sufficiently flexible to provide for growth and development, in the light of experience and performance, but I am firmly convinced that with all its imperfections the United Nations organization offers the peace-loving nations of the world, now, a fully workable mechanism which will give them peace, if they want peace. To be sure, no piece of social machinery, however well constructed, can be effective unless there is back of it a will and a determination to make it work."

When I was notified I was to receive the Nobel Peace Prize, I promptly said to my wife that she had been so helpful to me in innumerable ways indispensable to the success of my work that she was richly entitled to one-half of the award. I meant that she was entitled to equal credit for whatever achievements I was able to bring to pass during the nearly three decades of my public service that followed our marriage. When the award arrived, I divided it between us.

I began the new year, 1946, by starting in January to work on my Memoirs. I had long had these in mind, but there had been no time during my arduous twelve years in the State Department to do more than think about them, and during the thirteen months since my resignation I had not had the strength to undertake them. I decided to begin them after I obtained the assistance of Lieutenant Colonel Andrew Berding, an old friend, a veteran newspaper correspondent and writer, with an education, including Oxford University, in modern history, who was then about to leave the United States Army after a long period of overseas service.

Our work on the Memoirs was somewhat hindered in the spring of 1946 by my receipt of 169 interrogatories submitted by Senator Homer Ferguson, Republican member of the Congressional Joint Committee on the Investigation of the Pearl Harbor Attack. Although my health was still precarious and I wanted to concentrate on these Memoirs, I spent some weeks, with the help of Joseph Ballantine, in preparing complete responses, and sent these to Senator Alben W. Barkley, chairman of the committee, on May 16, 1946.

I wrote a long letter on July 12, 1946, for publication, to Speaker Sam Rayburn of the House of Representatives, advocating passage of the resolution under discussion to extend a $3,750,000,000 credit to Great Britain.

On July 30 I went to the Canadian Embassy to receive the Canadian Club of New York Award Medal in recognition of efforts toward furthering friendship and understanding between the United States and Canada, and delivered a short address to point to the admirable relations between the two countries as an example to the rest of the world.

At the end of July, 1946, I was gratified by the issuance of the report of the Congressional Joint Committee on the Investigation of the Pearl Harbor Attack. The majority report, in which two Republicans joined, found: "The diplomatic policies and actions of the United States provided no justifiable provocation whatever for the attack by Japan on this Nation. The Secretary of State fully informed both the War and Navy Departments of diplomatic developments and, in a timely and forceful manner, clearly pointed out to these Departments that relations between the United States and Japan had passed beyond the stage of diplomacy and were in the hands of the military."

In September my doctor, sensing a coming relapse in my health, had me return to the Naval Hospital at Bethesda. There I prepared a statement to be issued on my seventy-fifth birthday, in which I pleaded for more cooperation among the large nations, without which the United Nations could not function effectively. But before my birthday arrived I had a collapse, and throughout that day I was unconscious.

Since then my return to health has been slow, but, with the assistance of Colonel Berding, I have gone on working on these Memoirs, convinced that the principles of sound international relations for which I fought deserve a full exposition.

In April, 1947, I was delighted to receive a visit at the hospital from President Harry S. Truman, who conferred upon me the Medal for Merit, with oak leaf cluster in lieu of a second medal. He read from one citation: "With a high order of statesmanship based on deep loyalty to his country, Mr. Hull served with great distinction and selfless devotion during the years of crises and difficulties. . . . He endeavored to prepare the United States to meet the rising dangers from abroad. He contributed immensely to the Good Neighbor Policy, which was to bear rich fruit in a tragic hour for the United States and the entire Western Hemisphere."

Then the President read from the second citation: "He made diplomacy a powerful weapon in support of our armed strength. He made diplomacy also a potent instrument in laying the foundations of a stable and peaceful world order in the postwar era. As a tribute to his effective work in bringing about the establishment of an international organization, he is now known as the 'Father of the United Nations.' "

124: What of the Future?

MY STORY BEGAN among the hills of Tennessee in the troubled aftermath of the greatest war the United States had fought up to that time; it comes to an end in the difficult epilogue of the greatest war the United States has ever fought. In the three-quarters century of my life I have seen this nation grow from a continental to a world power, with interests in every corner of the globe. As a boy I felt the effects of the war that solidified the nation so that it could forge ahead as a unit. I took part in the war that projected us into the Orient. I was in Congress during the war that taught us the interrelationship of the continents, though the lesson went unheeded. I conducted our foreign relations, under the President, in the war that proved to us all the need for a world organization to prevent further wars.

We are today powerful in arms and powerful in the cause of peace and humanity. But with our great strength have come great responsibilities. The heaviest of these, which we have accepted in the light of our power and duties, is that of providing our full share of leadership toward cooperation among nations for peace, justice, freedom, and progress.

It has been a popular view in the past, supported by tradition, that the United States has nothing to fear, that the future is assured, that our great resources and organizing ability guarantee our destiny, and that our institutions will endure forever. No belief could be more dangerous.

We have, in fact, reached the time when we should stop, look, and listen. We should analyze ourselves and our position in the world with sharp introspection.

Are the people of this generation better off than their predecessors of former generations? Science and invention have given us many more of the desirable items of enjoyment, and in this respect we are undoubtedly much better off. We have all sorts of new things to eat and wear, and amusements to follow, compared with the limited possessions and means to enjoy life in the past. But in certain other respects we are worse off. We suffer from a striking lack of a broad education and of devotion to the spirit of liberty and law, and we fail to maintain the deep interest and keen alertness necessary for the proper conduct of public affairs.

Organized society during the past generation has, in my opinion, deteriorated. Behind the broad world policy I have outlined lies a first duty of civilized people everywhere to restore and preserve intact the precious ideas and ideals on which organized society must always be based. This goes to the very heart and foundation of world civilization and peace.

We have seen a striking deterioration of the whole political international structure, with threats of destruction of the entire international economic structure. In political and economic affairs the human race has suffered a steady decline, and it will not do to put everyone to sleep by singing of our progress in science and invention. Unless the citizens of our own and other countries keep themselves informed and give something of the same degree of thought and attention to public affairs that they do to their private businesses, we are going to fail signally in dealing with our own internal affairs and the problems of peace, greatly augmented by the invention of the atomic bomb.

Liberty and democracy in the world were more seriously in danger a few years ago than at any time since they were overwhelmed in the last days of the Athenian democracy. Our whole modern democratic civilization twice hung by a thread during the recent war—once during the summer of 1940 after Dunkirk and the fall of France, when Britain even with her Navy might have failed to repulse a full-scale German attack across the Channel, and again during 1942, when German submarines were sinking three Allied merchant vessels for every one constructed, and when almost every sea lane in the Pacific was blocked by the Japanese. I shudder to look back on those hairbreadth escapes. Civilization was brought to the edge of the precipice by the failure of many peoples, including ourselves, to understand and be alert to world conditions.

I cannot overemphasize that, unless there is a greater awakening, more intelligence, and more alertness on the part of the people everywhere, especially with respect to international affairs, and a greater understanding of what Government officials are trying to do, liberty and democracy are destined to a more dangerous and uncertain existence than that which they have recently so painfully experienced.

Democracy is not a static structure, like a cathedral or a skyscraper. Once erected, it cannot be expected to stand by itself from generation to generation. It is a living organism, and therefore must be cared for, guarded, nurtured, and guided.

We cannot rest on past achievements and present possessions. All the liberties we have today came from resistance to tyranny, either domestic or foreign; and most of them were won by blood and iron. Liberty came through the efforts of those men and women who were willing to die for it. We are their heirs, and must be vigilant to guard our heritage.

We Americans should return again and again to the fountainhead of our national greatness, the founding fathers. Their thinking, their struggles to obtain cooperation among the thirteen states, are magnificent prototypes for the thinking and struggles we must undertake today to bring cooperation among the nations. Like Antaeus who gained renewed strength each time he touched the earth, we can renew our faith and fortitude each time we study the writings and actions of the fathers of the Republic.

The founding fathers were familiar with all that human experience had taught about government; but, being mindful of the natural ambitions of man and the danger of too great a centralization of authority, they formed a government of checks and balances. They did know the meaning of human liberty, and hence it was the Bill of Rights and a series of restrictions rather than the powers conferred upon the Government that made the Constitution a charter of liberty. In the widest and deepest sense, however, our American history does not begin with the Constitution and the Declaration of Independence, but centuries ago in England.

The capacity for self-government is something inherent in the people themselves. It can be developed by education, but it cannot be created by arbitrary law. Elihu Root defined it as organized self-control. Men must be trained to self-government over many generations. The generations that founded the American Government derived their training from the Anglo-Saxons. With the growth of the country, other nationalities have been melted in and have fought for these same ideas.

Our form of government has proved itself in the past; it has brought us greatness and prosperity; it has preserved us comparatively untouched by foreign invasion. It has been able to function under the rapidly changing social, political, and economic conditions of the nineteenth and twentieth centuries. It must be preserved; but we shall not preserve it unless we are willing to defend it, support it, and give it every contribution of which we are able.

Our people should know that their own enlightened interest in their Government is the greatest safeguard of their liberties. They should realize that study and attention to public affairs demand real time, sacrifice, and effort on their part—day by day, week by week, year by year, and not just during a Presidential or a Congressional campaign. In the early days of the Republic, when two Americans met on the road they discussed the Government. They felt they were a part of the Government and the Government was a part of them. In these days, when two Americans meet they are more likely to discuss the motion picture they saw the night before. Government, of course, has become more complicated than in the days of Washington, Jefferson, Jackson, and Lincoln, but its interest for the citizen is none the less compelling.

The future of mankind rests upon the ability of statesmen and peoples to recognize that all are living in a brand-new world, and that the salvation of those who love liberty and civilization renders imperative a genuine awakening and a far more consistent and broader performance of their duties to the Government, to world order under law, and to organized society itself. We love liberty more than life; life must mean liberty, or it is death; and, under the modern methods of waging war, peace means both life and liberty.

Public opinion is an instrument the strength of which the public itself often ignores. A Minister of Louis XVI defined public opinion as "an invisible power which, without treasury, guards, or an army, ruled Paris and the Court—yes, the very palace of the King."

There are people throughout the world who make their living by creating confusion. Disaster to the peoples will follow if they are led astray and fail to rededicate themselves to an active, vigilant discharge of the imperative duty of keeping themselves informed and manifesting their considered opinions on events of national and world importance.

We, who are but a few generations removed from those who fought and conquered the wilderness, still have with us today the frontiers of endeavor. We still have to conquer the wilderness of want, oppression, ignorance, and fear. Has civilization finished its task—with poverty, despair, conflict, and even barbarism existing in some parts of the world? Our ancestors were without material comforts and aids to life as they pushed back the frontier. Each helped the other in time of trouble, and out of this mutual aid there developed in our people a growing concern for the welfare of their neighbors which characterizes the modern American in his attitude toward the rest of the world. This American is imbued with a disposition to help his fellow man less fortunate than himself. Hence his altruism, his philanthropy, and his idealistic schemes to help others. Let that spirit not weaken but expand in helpfulness toward other nations less richly endowed. It is one harvest that cannot fail.

Let us choose for our leaders men who know the needs of the people. Some of our leaders, like Jefferson, went into public life to promote democratic doctrines and to give the people their benefits. Jefferson cared not for power, still less for place or patronage for its own sake, and even tried to substitute Madison for himself as a candidate for the Presidency. Surely we have men today imbued with the same exalted spirit.

We have a desperate need for more religion and morality as the background for Government. The religious and moral foundations for thought and conduct require strengthening here, as well as throughout the world. There is no higher civilizing influence than religious and moral concepts. Corruption and tyranny can be driven out of Government only when these concepts give men the faculty to recognize such evils and the strength to eliminate them.

The States should exercise ceaseless vigilance to protect the civil rights of their citizens. The right of all citizens freely to vote should be guarded, and their pathway to the voting booth should not be obstructed.

Congress should deal with national problems from a national viewpoint. If what would bring an immediate benefit to a few States would ultimately redound to the disadvantage of the nation, the welfare of the nation must predominate.

The utmost cooperation must prevail between Congress and the Executive. The separation of powers of the Government ordained by the founding fathers makes such cooperation essential. Unlike the British Cabinet, which grows out of Parliament and is directly responsible to it, the American Executive Branch is an individual entity, responsible directly to the electorate. The Executive Branch must take Congress as fully as possible into its confidence.

I believe it vitally necessary that Congress and the Executive observe strict economy in government, and that the States, counties, and cities do likewise. In this modern world there is little regard for either public or private economy on the part of an increasing number of officials and individuals. There is great need today for more definite and stable rules and policies that will afford the fullest practicable measure of comfort and social satisfaction to the people, along with the fullest measure of wholesome economy in government consistent with efficiency. There is no practice more pernicious or contagious than indiscriminate spending by governments. And the most effective sinking fund for the retirement of national debt is economy of expenditure.

Let us adhere, as closely as developing conditions permit, to our time-honored policy of individual initiative and free enterprise. Government has an essential role of supervision and inspection to fill, to ensure that free enterprise is truly free and fair and that the people as a whole are protected; but it must not kill the spirit that made our nation great.

Congress and the Executive have an inescapable responsibilty to keep our foreign policy on a nonpartisan basis. Partisan considerations have no place in foreign policy, for there the welfare and perhaps the future of the whole nation are at stake. It is always licit to criticize foreign policy, provided the critic honestly bases his argument on his conception of our national interests; but it is inadmissible to inject advantages of party or of person into foreign policy. Attempts to do so weaken the influence of our Government abroad by presenting to foreign and possibly hostile governments a picture of divided councils, confusion, and lack of popular support of this Government's position toward the world.

I continue to believe that the two-thirds requirement for Senate consent to the ratification of treaties should be changed by Constitutional amendment to a simple majority.

The American people, Congress, and the Executive must keep sharp watch lest the United States return again to the dangerous policy of isolation. Two major wars within a generation should have convinced all Americans that we are an important part of the world, that conflict abroad cannot but affect us, and that our welfare, peace, and security are tied to those of other nations. We have a responsibility for leadership and cooperation which we cannot avoid, if we would.

There will inevitably be disputes and quarrels, disappointments and disillusionment in our relations with other nations, just as there are among individuals. But let these not support the argument that, if we mind our own business and have no ties with other nations, we can be safe and prosperous. For we cannot.

Few things are more certain than that during the 1930's peace-loving nations, had they not been hamstrung by isolationist forces in and out of governments, could have armed adequately in time, and by joint representation could have demanded a showdown with the aggressors, Germany, Italy, and Japan, and averted the recent World War. In the same way they could have prevented its predecessor. The age-old experience that free peoples are always slow to arm adequately for self-defense asserted itself disastrously throughout the period from 1930 to 1939.

Isolationism is not merely political. It can also be economic and social. It is an interesting fact that the American people, however much they adhered to political and economic isolationism until recent years, have never hewn to social isolationism. They have cooperated with other nations to the utmost and have had the most fruitful exchanges in the fields of science, medicine, education, philanthropy, and social services. They are the world's most numerous tourists. Had our cooperation in the political and economic fields attained the same high level, the world today would be a better place in which to live.

In the past, until 1934, perhaps our most flagrant violation of our duty to the world was economic isolationism. Ages of civilization have taught us that international commerce promotes material welfare, peace, and advancement. Intellectual and social progress in the Ancient World, the Middle Ages, and the Modern Era was the result in large part of the reciprocal influence of nations on one another. But we Americans have not fully learned this lesson. We showed the world a true example of the right way from 1934 until the end of the war by embracing a policy of liberal commerce, tariff reduction, and nondiscrimination, but since the end of the war there has been evidence of tendencies to return the United States to the disastrous course of the twenties and early thirties. High tariffs do not bring us prosperity. They do bring us unsalable surpluses at home and the resentment of other nations abroad. If each nation could have profitably exchanged its surpluses from 1922 on, there would have been no economic collapse in 1929.

The people of the States in which special interests demand high tariffs of an embargo nature should understand this. They should know that one successful attempt to put a stone on the high-tariff wall in favor of one product inevitably leads to similar attempts to put many more stones on the wall in favor of other products. Let them realize that high tariffs affect them in their daily life through higher prices, and let them, as consumers, keep their Congressmen advised that the interests of the people at large are superior to those of the comparatively few industrial and agricultural interests that clamor for "protection."

And let the Members of Congress appreciate the still higher issue involved—our cooperation with other nations. We cannot erect high-tariff walls around our nation and expect to cooperate, politically or economically, with the rest of the world.

The people, Congress, and the Executive must recognize the imperative need to bury isolationism as an American tradition. It should no longer be a part of American life any more than is the covered wagon. When President Washington said that Europe's primary interests were different from ours, there was then no steamship, no railroad, no wireless, no telephone, no telegraph, no internal combustion engine, no airplane anywhere—and no atomic bomb. The United States was then isolated geographically as well as politically from the world. The geography has not changed, but its significance has altered. Our language and customs may be different from those of the rest of the world, but we have the same interest in public welfare, peace, and international trade. Sarajevo was an unknown town to us until June, 1914; but what happened there was the first step that brought us into the First World War. What happened in the thirties in China, Ethiopia, Austria, Czechoslovakia, and Poland—all far removed from us geographically—was a cumulative series of steps that led unerringly to our involvement in the Second World War.

President Washington spoke against permanent alliances with other nations, although he countenanced temporary alliances. We are now, however, a member of the United Nations, which is in the nature of an alliance against aggression. Let none of us be shocked by this fact of an alliance. It is not an alliance against a combination of other nations but against **any** aggressor. It is an alliance not for war but for peace.

The creation of the United Nations organization, embracing all the peace-loving nations, was in my opinion a turning point in the political development of the world. The United Nations came into being after elaborate, painstaking study over a period of years by experts of many countries. At San Francisco fifty nations formulated and unanimously accepted its Charter as the beginning of a great, solid world structure of peace, able to defy any and all forces or influences calculated to weaken or undermine it. No one before or since has suggested any other mutually acceptable plan that was as good, much less better.

Let us not, however, expect the United Nations to perform a miracle. Its Charter is a human instrument, not a perfect one. The organization requires time, patience, and a spirit of cooperation among nations if it is to function effectively.

Major wars are generally followed by a widespread feeling of uneasiness, impatience, unrest, and suspicion. Our people and leaders and the peoples and leaders of other nations must be willing to overcome this feeling. They must examine with sympathy and patience the views of others. They must try to ascertain the true facts in any situation. They must avoid assuming adamant positions. They must refrain from exaggerating and overemphasizing their own claims and from appealing to prejudice.

The new spirit of understanding can find its most fruitful expression in the United Nations. The success of that organization requires that the frequent conferences of representatives of the nations made possible by the provisions of the Charter should be grounded on the broad patriotism of world peace and human progress.

The United Nations deserves and must have the unwavering support of the American people. Let us not be discouraged over the dissensions voiced in the initial councils of the new organization. Let us not on the one hand insist that the United Nations cannot work and we must therefore return to nationalism and isolation, nor on the other hand urge that the United Nations is inadequate and we must therefore replace it with a world government. Restless persons, agitators, and even well-meaning persons will offer plans and projects for new organizations, the sole effect of which will be to obstruct the peace movement. We can do the cause of peace no greater service than by working at all times possible with and within the United Nations, and neglecting no opportunity to promote its prestige and the prompt acceptance of its conclusions.

It would be impossible to exaggerate the importance to nations and peoples of maintaining at all times a spirit of peace and of cooperation to maintain peace—by force if necessary. This common world undertaking must contemplate the availability of armed forces at all times sufficient to prevent the use of any kind of military force or any kind of weapon capable of undermining, materially injuring, or destroying the world structure of peace based on world order under law.

We should strive, however, to promote the idea of universal reduction of armaments, with complete United Nations inspection in all countries to make sure it is carried out. A wild race of armaments, economic and military, is an indictment of civilization. Proponents of heavy armaments are playing with the lives and property of tens of millions of men, women, and children. But disarmament must be comparative, and we must never again permit the United States to decline to a level of relative military helplessness. Other nations, in looking at us as we explain our foreign policies, must still be able to see over our shoulder the symbols of our power, sufficient at all times to preserve our security.

We Americans need to practice moderation in our expressions of opinion concerning other nations. As a people we are too prone to condemn other nations and rulers, to apply epithets, to caricature, to ridicule. We forget that our sharp words are not buried in newspaper columns or lost on the rostrum or radio. They come to the knowledge of the governments and peoples they anathematize; they are reproduced and commented upon by the press and radio of those countries, which may not understand our freedom of criticism; and they hamper the conduct of our foreign relations. To the old rule that one should count ten before berating another individual I would add a new rule that we should count ten hours or ten days before berating another nation, and meantime we should try to ascertain the true and full facts of the event that seems to call for condemnation.

This rule I would call to the particular attention of the minority groups in the United States, whether racial, national, or religious. The Constitution was designed to protect all the people, but especially minorities. Nevertheless, in recent years some of these groups, aided by the improvement of methods for diffusing information and propaganda, have raised a voice and exerted a pressure in foreign affairs far out of proportion to their numbers. These interfering minorities are generally composed of or influenced by left-wing or reactionary extremists and also by persons who have immigrated in recent years and are chronic agitators and advocates of ideas calculated to undermine both our political and our economic structure. On many critical occasions, when the international relations of our Government require the most delicate and careful handling and the support of a unanimous and aggressive public opinion, some of these groups scatter poison or otherwise play havoc with them. Men and women who have left other countries and chosen the United States as their home should think of foreign policy not in terms of the land they left behind them but in terms of the land that is giving them refuge and sustenance. And at the same time the majority of our citizens, while scrupulously guarding and protecting all the rights of minorities, should be consistently on the alert to prevent the confusion, misunderstanding, and misrepresentation, with steadily increasing bitterness and hatred, that inevitably result from widespread, violent, and troublemaking propaganda on the part of minorities.

Our great nation should stand always for the progressive attainment of self-government and eventual independence by dependent peoples when they are ready for it, in accordance with our example in the Philippines. But let our policy in this respect not be limited to one of exhortation only but also embrace active economic help to raise the level of life of such peoples.

Let us stand, too, for the free play of public opinion in the world. Today there is, generally, no free press or radio around the globe. Perhaps half the nations suppress, filter, or color information. Not until the thoughts of peoples can be fully and freely communicated from one to another can we hope for the attainment of the real understanding that will make wars impossible.

We must recognize and be willing to assume our commitments regarding our former enemies, Germany and Japan. If it is necessary to maintain surveillance, military and otherwise, over them for decades to come, then we should be willing to maintain it. There should be no thought among us of quick withdrawal from Europe or Asia. We cannot withdraw, for where can we go? The world is with us, here and now, and all about us. It is in our front yard, in our back yard, at our side porch. To withdraw from Europe and Asia is to pull Europe and Asia in upon us.

In the Western Hemisphere let us continue to develop and expand the Good Neighbor Policy in all possible ways. The fruit we have gathered from that policy is sufficient warrant for the planting of further seed. In our time of need our friends to the South, with one exception, became our friends indeed. Let the Good Neighbor Policy become a permanent foundation of our foreign policy. In sowing a crop of cooperation in our own garden we can give the world an example of the highest type of political harvest.

We should maintain forever the friendliest relations and the closest cooperation with the United Kingdom and the British Dominions, but with the proviso that this be not exclusive. Let us not be persuaded that a union of the English-speaking peoples is the cure-all for the ills of the world. Let us consult with other interested nations whenever we consult with Britain.

Despite the dangerous conduct of the Soviet Union in the last several years, let us follow in respect to it a policy of patience, combined with firmness, inspired by calm strength, and rooted in an unswerving determination that, so far as lies in our power, mankind shall at long last attain a just and peaceful world order. In dealing with the Soviet Union we must never waver in this determination, or give any evidence of weakness, or cease to insist that, though the Soviet Union is entitled to freedom from intervention in its domestic affairs by any other nation, its government has no right to force Communism on other nations or to intervene in their domestic affairs in any other way.

During my years as Secretary of State we consistently pursued the broad policy of nonintervention, and we lost no opportunity to condemn and oppose all practices in violation of that precious doctrine, whether such practices were conducted by Germany or Japan or the Soviet Union or any other country. We repeatedly emphasized to the Soviet Government that its idea of penetrating into other countries by promoting within them subversive movements designed to supplant their established forms of government with Communist systems like its own, while at the same time claiming for the Soviet Union immunity from such intervention, was a hopelessly unsound and hazardous theory of international relations. No nation that had once dedicated itself to popular forms of government could tolerate indefinitely the enforced substitution for its free institutions of a system of tyranny, destitution, and lowering of all moral standards that are the inevitable concomitants of a police state. We repeatedly stressed our hope that the Soviet leaders would themselves in due course recognize this.

The sovereign equality of all peaceful nations, large and small, and the right of each of them to freedom from intervention in its internal affairs are among the cardinal principles of the United Nations, to which the Soviet Union, together with the United States and more than fifty other nations, has pledged its solemn adherence. The faithful observance of these principles constitutes an indispensable foundation for international cooperation without which no nation can progress or feel secure. Much time, perhaps many years, of unremitting effort may be necessary before the Soviet leaders come to understand fully that the ways of cooperation with other nations are to their country's benefit as well as to ours. However difficult and hopeless the task may on occasion appear to be, let us take this time, employing neither denunciation nor threats, but a friendly, honest, stalwart approach. Every feasible opportunity should be used to converse with the Soviet leaders, within the United Nations or wherever possible.

It may be that our efforts will fail and the leaders of Soviet Russia will fall into the same tragic error that has brought to their doom so many ancient and modern masters of police states. If that utter calamity should come to pass, let it not be said that the United States had neglected any honorable means to avert it. While keeping ourselves strong to face any eventuality, let us work unceasingly toward the end that the leaders of the Russian people and we may ultimately see eye to eye on the values of human freedom and on the preciousness of enduring peace based on justice and fair dealing.

My twelve years as Secretary of State were a difficult period in which to live. It was an epoch filled with conflicts, tragedies, and seeming impossibilities. One could not come through it, however, without feeling its vibrant pulsations. And it has left the nations of the world with an opportunity for advancement such as they have never had before, such as they may never have again.

But our nation and all nations, including especially our major allies in the recent death struggle against the forces of tyranny, would merely deceive themselves if they failed to realize that they are facing the supreme crisis of all ages. If they resolve that the forces of peace, order, and civilization shall proceed unceasingly with the task of restoring their economic health and solidifying their political and moral strength, they will thereby become powerful enough to preserve the peace, freedom, and culture of the world. On the other hand, if some nations or peoples persist in destructive policies and methods calculated seriously to cripple or shatter this great world undertaking, the human race may yet be dragged down to unimaginably low levels of barbarism.

All peace-seeking nations should make every effort without ceasing to prevail on one another to do teamwork, on a basis of fair dealing, equality, mutual respect, and nonintervention in one another's affairs— with understanding and trust but without favoritism or appeasement— toward the attainment of the basic principles of international relations to which they committed themselves in accepting the Charter of the United Nations. The one inescapable duty and responsibility of all nations and peoples is to maintain and develop the United Nations as an international organization capable of establishing real peace and keeping such peace permanently. It is well-nigh axiomatic that all countries will receive equal and incalculable benefits from a faithful performance of their United Nations duties, but a bottomless pit is liable to open in the pathway of nations failing in such performance. It is beyond any doubt to the best interest of each and all to join together in perpetuating the world organization and in making it truly effective.

The experience of the League of Nations proved conclusively that a world security organization could not function effectively toward this all-important end unless all major nations were members and were cooperating. The same is true of the United Nations organization. If any of the major nations should choose the course of noncooperation, the others, willing to support this great world movement, must nevertheless carry it forward with all their strength. They must resolutely resist in every legitimate way any acts calculated to impede or undermine the organization. But the door should always remain open to all nations, including those that are temporarily misled into recalcitrant noncooperation, once they had demonstrated their willingness to follow the principles embodied in the United Nations Charter.

I am firmly convinced that in the world of today all nations will be forced to the conclusion that cooperation for law, justice, and peace is the only alternative to a constant race in armaments—including atomic armaments—and to other disruptive practices that will bring the nations participating in them on either side to a common ruin, the equivalent of universal suicide.

I conclude these Memoirs with the abiding faith that our destiny as a nation is still before us, not behind us. We have reached maturity, but at the same time we are a youthful nation in vigor and resource, and one of the oldest of the nations in the unbroken span of our form of government. The skill, the energy, the strength of purpose, and the natural wealth that made the United States great are still with us, augmented and heightened. If we are willing from time to time to stop and appreciate our past, appraise our present and prepare for our future, I am convinced that the horizons of achievement still stretch before us like the unending Plains. And no achievement can be higher than that of working in harmony with other nations so that the lash of war may be lifted from our backs and a peace of lasting friendship descend upon us.

THE END

Index

[Roosevelt, Churchill, Stalin, De Gaulle, Mussolini, and Hitler are so closely identified with the policies of their respective countries that, in order to avoid repetition, entries under their names have been limited to personal matters, with policies indexed under country and by subject. Entries for the author have been treated in the same manner.]

CPSIA information can be obtained at www.ICGtesting.com
Printed in the USA
BVOW06s0030230615

405647BV00017B/505/P